PERDITA KIRKNESS NORWOOD, stepmother to four now-adult children, is a stepmother advocate who leads support groups, focus groups, and workshops on the subject. She welcomes comments from readers and can be reached via e-mail at PerditaKN@cs.com. She lives in Connecticut.

TERI WINGENDER is a freelance newspaper and magazine writer. She lives in New York.

THE
Enlightened
Stepmother

REVOLUTIONIZING THE ROLE

**PERDITA KIRKNESS NORWOOD
WITH TERI WINGENDER**

Quill

An Imprint of HarperCollinsPublishers

For my husband, Otty, and mother, Kay,
the perfect support team,
with my love and thanks.
—Perdita

To Allan, with whom marriage is simple arithmetic:
count the blessings threefold
and divide the sorrows by half.
—Love always, Teri

HarperCollins books may be purchased for educational, business, or sales promotional use. For information please write: Special Markets Department, HarperCollins Publishers Inc., 10 East 53rd Street, New York, NY 10022.

First Avon edition published 1999.

Reprinted in Quill 2003.

Designed by Kellan Peck

Library of Congress Cataloging-in-Publication Data
Norwood, Perdita Kirkness.
  The enlightened stepmother : revolutionizing the role / Perdita Kirkness Norwood with Teri Wingender.
    p. cm.
  Includes bibliographical references and index.
    1. Stepmothers—United States—Psychology. 2. Stepmothers—United States—Attitudes. 3. Parenting—United States. I. Wingender, Teri. II. Title.
HQ759.92 .N65 1999   98-46447
306.874—dc21   CIP

ISBN 0-380-79604-X

03 04 05 06 07 RRD 10 9 8 7 6 5

Acknowledgments

Almost 200 women in various stages of stepmotherhood gladly offered their time, stories and wisdom in the hope that others might benefit from their experience. But they were promised anonymity and must remain nameless. They know who they are and I am grateful to every one of them for baring their hearts and souls during my research.

The book would more than likely not have become reality without the initial confidence and moral support of Diane Erdos, Sheila Pakula, Khris Hertz, Penny Bowers and Linda Zamelsky, who knew that a book from the stepmother's perspective was necessary and encouraged me through the early stages. Then, with perfect timing, Teri Wingender appeared. Finding we were a good mix, the book came to life and took off.

In addition to people mentioned by name in the book who were extraordinarily generous with their time and expertise, we are grateful, in no particular order, to others who advised in specific areas as work progressed: among them Peter Bloch, Diane Rosenthal, Carole Shaff, Alison Scavone, Susan and Ron Benizio, Ethel Levine, Mary Jacobson, Bernard McKenna, Edward Frick and particularly Michelle Hubbard for her legal help and Kay Pasley whose constructive comments were invaluable.

We would not have become enlightened stepmothers without our stepchildren—Beth, Pam, Rob and Constance / Brett and Ted—and there would never have been a book. *Pax vobiscum!*

Our special thanks to the staff at the Westport Library in Connecticut, the halfway point where we met and worked (through the renovations!) and to Sakura Japanese Restaurant in Westport, our favorite place for lunch and endless pots of green tea in their "tatami room." Also to the staff at the Blackstone Memorial Library in Branford, Connecticut, for their invaluable research assistance.

We'd like to thank our original editor at Avon Books, Charlotte Abbott, who first showed faith in us; Jennifer Brehl, who continued her good work; and our agent, Victoria Pryor, for her encouragement and support.

Contents

PART 2
Relationships: Spheres of Influence
Overview • 83

PART 3
Lifestyle and Practical Matters
Overview • 245

Contents

PART 4
Is This What I Want?
Overview • 373

Introduction
Stepmothers: As American as Mom and Apple Pie

When you were a little girl, the question adults asked most often, just after, "Did you wash those hands, young lady?" was "What do you want to be when you grow up?" Our answers might have changed from day to day, like the outfits on our favorite dolls. We might have had some notions of glamorous careers as doctors in sparkling white lab coats, even spies in black leather jackets, and maybe having babies (however that happened) along the way, but one role we never considered was "stepmother."

We knew about the stepmothers in our books of fairy tales. They were the reason we begged our mothers to leave a night-light on. We knew they were ugly and evil and without feeling for other living things. We knew they had no fashion sense. Few of us probably knew any in real life, and we hoped there would never be any in our own lives.

Real Stepmoms, Real Lives

Now that you're all grown up, you know that a stepmother can look a lot like you. She is a daughter, a sister, a grandmother, aunt, mother, granddaughter, niece, or cousin. She can be your best friend or your favorite coworker. Her current status may be a not-yet-married single, living with a partner,

1

married, widowed, or divorced; she could be a biological, adoptive or foster mother, or child-free.

She might even be you. Maybe you're getting serious with a father of two active toddlers and wondering what stepmotherhood would be like. Perhaps you're already married to the man of your dreams, newly awakened from the bliss of denial and trying to nurture a nice relationship with his adult daughter, whose behavior, from your perspective, is nothing short of a nightmare.

It's important to know you're not alone. Stepmotherhood is an easy job to get, and there are many of us out there. In the United States, about seventy-five percent of divorced men and women remarry. Of these, sixty-five percent bring biological children to their new marriages. As we enter the twenty-first century, the U.S. Census Bureau predicts that the stepfamily (a combination of full-time and part-time stepfamilies) will be the family configuration of the majority.

Given the current statistics for divorce and remarriage, no female in the United States is exempt from the possibility of becoming a stepmother at some time in her life. She is as American as Mom and apple pie.

Why This Book Is Revolutionary

Whatever your situation—a potential, new, or veteran stepmother—chances are you have found very little information or support in taking on this role. Like many women, we've never found a book about stepmotherhood that just said: "Look—here are the real, messy issues of marriage to a man with children. Privacy. Money. Legal and off-the-record promises. The ex-wife, a.k.a. "Mommy." Step-pets. So, if you still want to do (or already did) this crazy thing, here's what you must find out about your unique situation in order to stay sane, and solvent and give yourself the best chance of making your new life work."

That's what we've needed all along, but the books we thought would help us are, like most of our friends and relatives, concerned with how the kids are doing. Jean, now a veteran stepmother, was amazed that "even my own mother was more concerned about how my stepchildren were handling the changes in their lives than how I, her own daughter, was coping with mine."

The basic approach of most stepparenting guides is *How can you (the new stepparent) fit into the existing family's lives?* These are often about "surviving" or "coping"—a traditional mind-set that leaves readers (perhaps inadvertently) with the impression that stepmotherhood is an unpleasant role that you wouldn't choose if you had more control over your life. They suggest that it's not a position you can plan for, though with a cheerful outlook you can overcome problems and be a "good" stepmother.

On the other hand, the premise of this book is that the challenge for the contemporary stepmother (especially working, career-oriented women) is *How do all these new people fit into my life? I need to look at my circumstances realistically. I need to have control of and take responsibility for my life. I need to determine how and if I can make this work. I need to be sure before I make a commitment that I can help my husband and stepchildren recover from the emotional experience of divorce (or death) and remarriage so we can all move on together. . . . It's* an attitude that has taken women up the career ladder, helps them plan their families, and ultimately benefits the people closest to them.

Rather than tell you how to be a "good" stepmother, we're assuming that you already are a terrific person for even considering the monumental task of playing an integral role in the lives of someone else's children.

Stepmotherhood, like other life choices, entails making thoughtful decisions and coming to reasonable conclusions about your life and the real people in it. You can plan ahead; in fact, you can prevent problems before they happen. With practical information (not psychological advice, because we're not therapists), we'll help you, the well-intentioned stepmom, take a proactive approach to the challenges ahead—to avoid the common misunderstandings and conflicts that plague stepfamily life.

Why We Wrote This Book

The inspiration for this book grew out of our personal experience as stepmothers. Each time we met another stepmom who agreed to share her experience with us, we became more convinced that women needed a resource written with stepmothers' well-being and point of view firmly in mind. Perdita is passionate in her determination to ensure, via this book, that "no other woman be as ill-prepared and uninformed as I was." Married for the first time in her mid-forties to a widower with three daughters and one son, all in their late teens/early twenties, she explains: "I underestimated how long the grieving process takes and did not recognize that stepchildren, whatever their ages, will always remain children to their dads."

Hoping one day to have a baby of her own, Teri, who is twenty years younger than Perdita, met her husband-to-be at the age of twenty-six and lived with him, a forty-seven-year old divorced dad with two teenage sons, for five years before making a legal commitment. "During the early years, there were many difficulties simmering under the surface, a minefield of unpredictable feelings and problems I had no context for," she notes. "The issues were impossible, certainly counterproductive, to sort out using the mind-set of a member of a biological, nuclear family. We all had to come to terms with the past and develop fresh ways of thinking about one another. Ten years later, our relationships are still evolving."

Apart from what we learned on our own about living in a stepfamily, we realized that there was very little out there—neither self-help books nor academic research nor other media—that accurately described what being a stepmother is like from a stepmother's perspective.

Our research for this book began with a five-page questionnaire, which we thought would cover most of the information we were seeking. But time and time again, the stepmothers we interviewed would simply not stop talking! For many, it was the first time someone had shown more than a passing interest in their thoughts and feelings. Moreover, our interview marked the first time *any* of them had received unconditional support for their role as a stepmother.

The stepmoms we met ranged from Jill, an upbeat, recently married twenty-five-year-old, who worked full-time by day and cleaned houses at night to help support her husband's ex-wife and six-year-old son, to Sophie, a seventy-five-year-old widow whose husband had died, leaving her with total responsibility for a severely retarded forty-two-year-old stepdaughter. While it was impossible to compare the different situations, we realized—as voice after voice resonated with the common struggle to make it work, often with no understanding and little help—that when stepmothers meet, there is an instant bond of recognition.

The length of the interviews could not be limited, either. The longest took place in a hotel, starting at 6:30 P.M. after an early dinner. At 1:30 the next morning, we were creeping through the hotel kitchen, trying to find something to eat, as Pat had talked herself into virtual starvation. And still she wanted to tell more.

What we heard was the other side of the story of stepmotherhood, a side that has simply never been presented. This book was written to support and encourage the many well-intentioned stepmothers who need honest information about the role they are considering or have accepted.

In addition to the stepmoms we interviewed, we talked to counselors who work with them; attorneys who represent them in divorce, custody, and peripheral legal matters; and their financial advisors. We have changed names to guarantee stepmothers' privacy, but all the stories are factual.

The New Pioneers

Stepmotherhood is an issue our society has been reluctant to talk about, which is strange, considering our garrulous response to nearly everything else. Stepmothers—one of the last social groups still in the closet—often arrive in the wake of familial transition: divorce, death, abandonment. Our culture, which has deified motherhood, has not yet acknowledged the contributions of the stepmother. She makes us uncomfortable, we don't understand her, she's in our way, with no specific role to play—and the stepmom herself is ill at ease because of this. Ultimately this has meant that the window on the stepmother's experience has remained closed.

First and foremost, the death or divorce of the mother provokes concerns about the effect of this upheaval in the lives of the children. As a society, we tend to be consumed with the "good of the children" and to strive to "put children first." (Perhaps that's why books on stepmotherhood focus on children, not on the woman trying to make the role work for herself as well as the family.) The arrival of the stepmom is a signal that it is time for the family to rebuild, yet she is often perceived as someone with the potential for further disruption. Rather than deal with the stepmother's needs and capabilities, many would rather ignore her and hope she'll go away.

Stepmothers are still pioneering this sociological frontier. It's time to dismantle, not simply "overcome," the myths and fairy tales about wicked stepmothers. This book is a healthy attempt to give stepmoms the support they deserve and shake society out of its denial. Our numbers are huge. We can no longer be content to allow so many women to struggle on in isolation.

The reality is that the new American "blended" family depends on the ability of the stepmother not only to function as the pivotal person in the stepfamily but to take on that role starting from a position of strength, self-esteem, and respect. Without those ingredients, the fledgling family either will not survive or will hobble sadly along with clipped wings, joining the statistics of failed second marriages.

Stepmotherhood is not a choice that should be "winged" no matter how smart, sensible, and sensitive you are (although those qualities certainly help). What it takes to succeed and thrive in this role (sooner, rather that later) is preparation, realistic information, and customized research about yourself and the family you will be joining or are already living with. Few stepmothers do this, believing it is enough to start out with the best of intentions. Says Judy, a new stepmother, thought all I had to do was smile and be nice to everyone, and they would like me"—a fairly typical approach to the task.

Control of the Role

The accomplishments of women in this century—from gaining suffrage to CEO titles—have changed America's perception of what women are capable of. We're smashing stereotypes as we go, along with a forceful assault on the glass ceiling. Women are deciding what their roles will be and how they want to fill them. The approach to stepmotherhood should be no exception. Along with the many other responsibilities she already holds—perhaps including raising her own children, working full-time on top of running the home, and looking after elderly parents—a stepmother starts her new marriage with the additional responsibility of helping to care for her husband's child or children.

She gets new titles, too—"stepmother" and "second wife"—neither of which has a very prestigious connotation in contemporary times. According to *Merriam Webster's Collegiate Dictionary* tenth edition (1997), the term "stepmother" dates from before the twelfth century, though the occasion of its first use is unknown. The Middle English word "step," from the Old English "staepe," also circa 1200, has multiple meanings: an "advance or movement"; "to go through"; "to construct or arrange"; "a stage in a process"; "a support."

We might guess, judging by these positive, affirmative definitions, that the stepmom of medieval times was viewed differently than contemporary stepmothers. The role was clear: she was to fill the place of the mother who was often dead by thirty from childbirth or disease. The stepmother raised her predecessor's children, had a few of her own to work in the fields, and ruled her mud-thatched household with authority. Her husband's place was behind an ox, eighteen hours a day. The issues were life and death—everyone pulled together for survival.

A New Attitude

We can't go back to those "good" old days (and who'd really want to?), but women of the twenty-first century, with a raised awareness of the collective good stepmothers do, have the opportunity to change the way future stepmoms, our families, our communities, and our society view the role of stepmother.

In the wake of family-oriented legislation, our continuing dialogue about "family values" and how to provide the best parenting possible must include comprehensive recognition of the crucial contributions stepmothers make. Stepmothers, for example, would be greatly helped by "maternity leave" provisions for the arrival of a child, just as biological or adoptive mothers are. Julie, a young corporate secretary who had to make the instant transition from single career woman to married full-time stepmom of two children, aged three and five, said, "After all, most women get nine months to prepare for having just one baby. I had to take responsibility for two little kids immediately."

While many *parenting* classes are widely available, women like Julie could be helped by step-parenting classes, which can raise awareness of how these roles differ. It's of little help for Julie to be told what not to do, because she isn't her stepkids' biological mother. Whether they become full- or part-time stepmoms, warm, loving and talented women such as Julie can, with encouragement, make enormous contributions to the lives of their stepkids, if they only know what to do.

At the most practical level, the stepmother is a role model and a nurturing influence for the new generations of strong marriages and stable families in the next millennium. Most important, this generation of well-intentioned stepmothers has the right and the opportunity to be happy and have support now.

We wish you the best of luck—we're behind you all the way!

How to Use This Book

The Enlightened Stepmother was designed to be user-friendly as well as a friend—after all, it comes from the minds and hearts of women who offer information they needed to know, but didn't, in the early stages of their own stepfamily life. Included in this book are the insights, seasoned advice, and stories of real stepmothers to help you consider issues from an experience-based standpoint.

How to Do Your Research

The book is divided into four parts: "Getting to Know *You*"; "Relationships"; "Lifestyle and Practical Matters"; and "Is This What I Want?"

Within each part you'll find chapters with questionnaires that emphasize customized research—of your own life, the people in it, and specific challenges. As you gather this information, your task is to observe, not analyze or act precipitously. Attempting to change things too fast is usually not the best course.

Your personal research will prepare you for many of the issues and situations common to stepmothers so you can build a foundation for success, not simply react when problems are on top of you. For example, if the questionnaire we've given you in our chapter on finances shows you that your main concern is long-term expenses, and you still don't know if your stepchildren's mother plans to help with her children's college education, the rest of that section will guide you toward resolving that issue. To this end, we've inserted "action boxes" at the end of each chapter. These are our recommendations for action you can take right away, while relevant issues are fresh in your mind.

We strongly recommend that you set aside a special notebook—we call it a "stepmom's idea book"—to record your answers to questions in writing. It's easier to refer to them when the time comes to act on what you've learned. Think of your idea book as your place for brainstorming (a productive, often exhilarating, creative tool.) Take your time with each question. You don't need to answer them all at once, and some will be of more concern to you than others. Let your ideas flow, and respond in as much detail as you can or want to. As you compile your lists, insights, and ideas, try not to be overly influenced by the opinions and wishes of others.

Please note that we refer to your mate throughout the book in various terms: husband, husband-to-be, fiancé, partner, lover, etc. We anticipate that women reading this book are in a range of situations, from just thinking about marriage to a man with children to veteran stepmotherhood. The spirit of the advice, however, remains the same for all.

Stepmom's Quick Primer

We suggest you read all of *The Enlightened Stepmother*, which is designed to help you focus on your specific concerns, but here's a quick primer on the big picture. Listed below are the twelve essential gems of wisdom culled from our own personal experience with stepmotherhood, and conversations with almost two hundred other stepmoms, which the veteran stepmothers promise will save years of confusion or distress.

These points are experience-based: all are commonsense fundamentals. Some are in contradiction to what therapists or "family experts" have said in the past.

1. Preparation for stepmotherhood is essential. Without exception, the most common comment by new and veteran stepmoms who initially believed they could wing their role with charm and grace is "I didn't think it would be like this." Gathering information about yourself and your new stepfamily will help you pinpoint relationship, practical, and lifestyle concerns and circumvent needless problems.

2. Start as you mean to go on. From day one, whatever the situation, insist upon courtesy and respect among all stepfamily members. This is the basis of any relationship. It is hard to make a comeback once you've taken the line of least resistance and allowed a breach of this basic requirement.

11

3. Understand and accept that you are not and, with only rare exceptions, can never be your stepchildren's mother. Whether she is alive or deceased, your stepchildren have or had a biological or adoptive mother who can never be replaced. A stepmother is an entirely different role, although it may include nurturing or "mothering" responsibilities. (See discussion of exceptions in chapters 3 and 15.)

4. Recognize you are a pioneer. You have no "ideal" role model or "official" job description. Any preconceived ideas you may have about being a stepmother are likely to be inaccurate. Ignore all the myths and fairy tales you may have heard; discount the negative statistics. Every stepmother is unique, and the way you play your role should be based on what's comfortable for you. Above all, nobody knows what "normal" is in the context of stepfamilies.

5. Recognize and accept that you will be sharing your husband with his children for the rest of your married life. Your husband had a family prior to your arrival, and his love and loyalty to his children are a strong bond, which they now share with you—and which all of you deserve. You can avoid jealousy by understanding this early on.

6. Make your marriage your priority. Without the unconditional support, encouragement, and understanding of your husband or partner, nothing you do as a stepmother will work. Care and attention to your marital relationship, the presentation of a united front that provides security and clear guidelines for appropriate behavior, must come first, before you can work on other relationships in your new family. When you are secure in your new role, with your mate's unconditional support, you will perform at optimal level to the benefit of all stepfamily members. Only when you are performing at optimum will you receive the recognition your role requires and the status it deserves.

7. Immediately accept your responsibility as the female head of your new household. Yours is the pivotal role in the stepfamily; you set the tone and emotional pulse of the home. This responsibility requires that you seriously and actively become involved, as an equal partner with your husband, in the detail of your life together, the smooth running of your household, and the guidelines for behavior of all members of your stepfamily, both residential and visiting.

8. Explain and be willing to discuss the reasons for any requests you make or action you take, including, if appropriate, the feelings that motivate you. Stepfamily issues are complex and new to everyone. Err on the side of over-discussion, particularly in the early days: with your husband, with your stepchildren, with your own children, with your family of origin, with extended family members, and/or any combination of these family members. This will affirm your standard of mutual respect and fairness and will help you avoid the "wicked stepmother" tag.

9. Recognize that in the minds of others, you are occupying a place and space that rightfully belongs to your predecessor, now deceased or divorced. The challenges you encounter—and there will be many—are usually a result of these circumstances. Any negativism toward you on the part of your new family is directed at the intruder, Dad's new wife, not at you personally.

10. Don't forget: this is your life too. Your needs, wishes, and well-being are as important as everyone else's. Make them known. Take care of yourself in whatever way is necessary. Don't be self-sacrificing: you will end up feeling resentful and be of no help to anybody.

11. It is not reasonable for you to expect, or to be expected, to love your stepchildren immediately, or vice versa. Do not feel guilty if you find yourself disliking, or in extreme cases even hating, your stepchildren at first. These are not your own offspring with whom you have an intimate bond, unlike your biological or adopted children (if you have any). If you have several stepchildren, you may like one more than another. As time goes by, as you design and grow into your role, your feelings will change. Aim only to be fair and even-handed in your relationships with your stepchildren. Be interested in their lives, health, and happiness. Relate to them with courtesy; treat them with respect. In stepfamilies, as in any other sphere, intimacy and love take time to develop—often years.

12. Develop a working relationship with your stepchildren's mother—it's one of the best favors you can do for yourself. It's time to revolutionize this relationship and trash the myth that women are natural adversaries. You both have at least one thing in common: the well-being of your stepchildren, her children. You don't have to like her, but you may come to respect her, and that's enough.

PART I

Getting to Know You

*Hmmm...I don't
have such a place!
Need to create this is
our bedroom, a haven for me*

OVERVIEW

Just for a moment, picture yourself in a place you
love. Maybe it's your bedroom, where all your favorite things are gathered—family photos, colorful
handmade pillows, and your collection of favorite
novels. Or the special quiet corner where your current project is in the throes of creation. Wherever
it is, it's a place that's special to *you*, where you
experience security, self-nurturing, pleasure, and
confidence, where the focus is on your desires,
dreams, or comfort. As with the special place you
love, this part of *The Enlightened Stepmother* is just
about *you*.

You may think, as many other women do, that
the challenge ahead is simply about your ability to

get along with people who feel like strangers to you, who've suddenly become, on some level, your intimates. If you have children, you may not yet recognize the complexities involved for them in the radical changes that lie ahead as they learn to adjust and accept your husband as their stepdad.

Of course, other people, including your children and step-children, are of major concern, and you'll be considering the issues and feelings of all the members of your stepfamily in detail, but it's not the first task at hand. You need to be sure you are making the right decision for yourself first. Is marrying a man with children, becoming a stepmother, the right thing to do for *you*? The decision about whether or not to marry or to move in with this wonderful man you have met is entirely yours. Children can't make this decision for you, although obviously you will take their feelings into account.

If you have already joined a stepfamily, consider whether or not you are recognizing your own needs in your quest to build a successful stepfamily.

We've learned that before you can discover and consider in an open-minded way what the members of your stepfamily are experiencing—the beginning of building relationships—you need to consider your own goals, preferences, and requirements as you take on the role of stepmother. Unfortunately, very few women do this, staking their happiness solely on the good graces (or good moods) of others.

Affirming who you are and how you want to play your role as stepmother, among the many other roles you may play, engenders confidence and a positive outlook—you'll know what you're striving for. Acknowledging and respecting the importance of your own well-being as you join your life to a ready-made family means you won't depend on others to define stepmotherhood, including the practical and emotional consequences of that choice for you.

You are a woman with a lifetime of experiences, someone with likes and dislikes, strengths and weaknesses, values and beliefs. All these attributes are going to affect what kind of stepmother you want to be—sisterly or maternal, friendly or formal. These approaches and many more are open to you.

Our questionnaires and the stories of other stepmothers will help you think about this new role in your life in a broader way. As we discussed in "How to Use This Book," we strongly suggest you set aside a special notebook to record your thoughts as you read and write out answers to the questionnaires since it will be helpful to refer to them later.

Ultimately, your choices about stepmotherhood should grow out of a considered exploration of your own capabilities and goals—quite frankly, what you're willing to do and what you're not. You owe that to yourself and to the family you're joining.

In the following chapters, you'll review your short-term and long-term goals, considering the stage of life you're in; your emotional and physical health; your family and marital background, including your beliefs and expectations about blended families and the role of stepmother; how to create the role for yourself; where to find support resources; and finally, what "success" as a stepmother means to you.

CHAPTER 1

The Enlightened Stepmother's Self-Portrait

Your Goals: Now and Later

There's something wonderful about the future, no matter how much we're encouraged to "live in the present." Our goals and dreams are pristine, made perfect by hope and determination. Best of all, they're possible. (Writing this book for you was one of ours.)

How does joining a stepfamily work with your life's plans?

It's a key question, usually asked in reverse, as in "How can you fit into your stepfamily's lives?" Stepmothers need to be wary of falling into that mind-set. You're not a piece of furniture for which a corner must be found. (If others stubbornly persist in viewing you as furniture, make sure they see a sturdy, steady, solid piece in prime condition that rightfully claims a central position!)

This is the time to get to know yourself as thoroughly as possible so you can decide if you are ready, willing, and, most important, *able* to handle what lies ahead. In "Stepmom's Quick Primer," number 10 is especially relevant: This is your life too. Your hopes and dreams are as important as those of every member of your prospective stepfamily.

Some of your personal goals will require an investment in time, some in money, others, just plain grit. A trek in Nepal?

Founding a new charity? Maybe you want to start trying to conceive a child as soon as you're married. When you know where you wish to head and what you need to get there, you can take the proactive route. If you're just considering stepmotherhood, this will be the first stage in deciding if that choice will work for you. If you're already a stepmom and want to take better control of your life, we will show you the way.

Don't "Second Best" Yourself

If you compromise on an issue you consider non-negotiable, you will live to become resentful. If you join your stepfamily accepting second best for your life, you will be expected to continue to do so. Follow-up interviews with new stepmothers indicated that in less than a year, some had "learned" to "put up" with what in any other social situation they would have considered intolerable. Why? As one stepmom put it: "For the sake of peace." What was intolerable—the stress of putting their feelings, opinions, and desires on the back burner while trying to forge new relationships—had become routine.

Sacrificing your goals to fulfill the wishes of your new family does not work. This is not being selfish; this is being realistic.

In your list of priorities, there will probably be some issues about which you feel more flexible. Moving to a bigger home to accommodate visiting stepchildren might not be financially feasible, but building a modest addition in a year might be. A honeymoon in Tahiti may blow six months' mortgage payments, so you may be willing to settle for a delayed, or different, wedding trip. But if you want to continue to volunteer with your community theater after the wedding excitement is over, you need to make sure that your avocation and time are respected.

Yes, there are emergencies and plans that go awry, but the importance of knowing your goals is to see if your life and a commitment to a stepfamily are going to make a good match.

- have our baby
- live in P.V. w/ horses   - invest in
- work P.T. for our co. from home
- design again eventually

You need to feel that the power to fulfill your dreams remains in your hands in spite of the unexpected.

A Stepmother for Every Season

During the course of our interviews, we discovered issues that were important to stepmothers in similar age groups. Depending on the stage of life you're in, you can use the following sketches as a guide to your own reflections:

The Tender Twenties

If you are in your twenties now, stepchildren are probably the last thing on your mind—until you meet that special man who happens to have a child or two from a previous marriage or relationship. If you are truly serious, perhaps even considering giving up your carefully made plans and marrying right now, consider how these young children will impact your life. They will become partly your responsibility. Are you ready for this? You may be a college graduate with a fledgling career, or partway through your studies. Perhaps you didn't complete your degree but are planning to return to college later. If you become a full-time or part-time stepmother, will you be able to spare the time and energy from your career or schooling to help support a ready-made family?

Maybe you're working as a saleswoman in the top boutique in your town, with an eye toward becoming a partner in the business someday. If your mate has part-time care of two little daughters, are there adequate child-care provisions to allow for the hours you need to put in at the shop? Consider the effect on your carefree life not only of a husband but of two young people as well who will become integral to your everyday planning and thinking.

If your husband pays child support and alimony (sometimes called "maintenance") these expenses may stretch many years in front of you—when money's tight, will you be able to further your education in pursuit of a better job or be able to afford your first home (or first child) together? Do you want to see the world before you take on responsibilities for other people besides yourself? Think about whether you feel you've had a chance to experience life with a capital L before you commit to stepfamily domesticity. Are you ready to help raise his children, when you don't even think you want one of your own yet?

It's sometimes difficult to think long-term when you're just starting out, but your talent and potential should have all the room in the world to grow. Consider whether you will be able to integrate the possibilities you see for yourself with marriage to a man with children.

When Jill, a radiant twenty-five-year-old with an infectious laugh, first came to one of our support groups, we all fell in love with her. Jill was a bright and compassionate young woman but, like so many stepmothers at any age, had completely misjudged how stepmotherhood would affect her life. Married for two years to a father—of a six-year-old son by a former girlfriend—who also had an ex-wife claiming alimony (fortunately there were no children from that marriage), Jill had underestimated the pressures she would be under.

Prior to her wedding, Jill gave up the opportunity to attend her state college when she discovered she was pregnant. Instead, she married Dan, gave birth to her son, Josh, and also took in little Dan, her husband's son. She began working eight to four as a gofer at the local radio station and cleaned houses at night. Her extended family included Dan's mother, married three times, her father, twice married, and her husband's brother, a substance abuser who drifted into Jill and Dan's home occasionally.

"What a mess I got myself into!" Jill exclaimed at one of our meetings. "I'm trying to make a stable home for Josh and little Dan, who has a lot of problems—I see more of him than either of his parents does. I wouldn't be without Josh for anything, but I sometimes think I'd have been better off as a single mom. Before I got married, my mother insisted she would help me take care of him. I could have gone to college and would now be making a decent wage. Instead, I'm barely making ends meet. Dan is out of work right now. He's trying to find a job, but he gets so depressed with all his responsibilities."

Jill is managing her difficulties through sheer guts, determination, and hard work. But her regrets and anxieties have taken a huge toll on this young woman, and at the time of this writing, she wasn't sure her marriage was going to last.

Abby, on the other hand, was adamant about completing college. "I've knocked myself out for three years; I have one more year to go. Although I would love to marry Brad right now, I'm going to wait until I've got my forestry degree and a running start on a well-paying career. And I want to have lots of children, which will take two incomes to support." (We hope Abby will discuss her wish for several children with Brad before they marry. Brad, like many single dads, might have different feelings about having more children.)

Experienced stepmoms stress the importance of making every effort to maintain your existing friendships, both male and female; don't cut yourself off from those who know you well and can offer support, should you need it. Though your lives may seem worlds apart once you have someone else's children in your life, your single and child-free friends can still provide a valuable sounding board for you.

The Thoughtful Thirties

If you're in your thirties, perhaps your profession is starting to take you into the big leagues. As a bonus, you've found the man of your dreams too. When it rains, it pours. Will more obligations and success at your job allow room for the additional responsibilities of stepmotherhood?

Or perhaps your career isn't going in the direction you had hoped; becoming a stay-at-home stepmom seems an attractive idea and is something your husband is encouraging. Be sure this is what you want in the long term and not just a temporary escape from a career slump. Remember point number 3 from "Stepmom's Quick Primer": "Understand that you are not and . . . can never be your stepchildren's mother." This will be an especially crucial point to reflect on—can you commit many years of your life to the trials and tribulations of helping to nurture and shelter to adulthood someone else's children, without the inherent advantages of motherhood?

Of course, you'll want to establish a healthy, happy home for your new husband and his children, but consider what plans you'd like to fulfill for yourself as the children grow and your husband's career flourishes. To "help out with expenses," you may be able to take a part-time job at the local bakery while your stepchildren are in school, but in your heart you might really want to own the bakery someday. Will you be satisfied with devising a realistic time line to pursue your dream later?

When Maryann married for the second time at the age of thirty-four, she resigned her physical education teaching post at a small suburban school to care for her son, aged six, and her husband's children, aged seven and eleven. Encouraged to become a stay-at-home mom by her parents as well as her husband-to-be, she decided this challenge was a more important job than spending her day with other people's children. Eight years later, as a frustrated Maryann was filing for divorce, she came to the conclusion that her husband had married her "only to provide a home and take care of his sons."

Maryann told us that if she had it to do over again, she would not have allowed herself to be pressured into giving up a career she loved. Worried that she had lost her edge in the job market, Maryann was not relishing the search for another teaching position at the age of forty-two and was beginning to think she had better acquire some computer skills.

Don't allow other people, even people you love, to pressure you into making major changes in the life you've chosen for yourself. Bear in mind that the thirties are often the make-or-break time for careers.

Many women in their thirties can and do make the decision to balance career, children, and stepchildren. In your career's fledgling years, a family of your own might have seemed a distant prospect, but now the reality of reproductive shutdown as you enter young middle age presents you with a now-or-never choice. If you want to have a baby before you get much older, you probably will want to aggressively pursue pregnancy; it's hard to nurture another woman's children while longing for your own. For several thirty-something stepmothers we interviewed, a major concern was the affordability of having another child.

The Fabulous Forties

In your forties, you might be fully established in your profession and starting to consider life after children. Money may become increasingly important as your children, biological and step, prepare for college. If you're married to or are seriously dating a divorced man who maintains two households, consider very carefully your financial position—your retirement plan, will, and assets—now that you're approaching what is likely the last half of your working life. (See chapters 17 and 18 for a discussion of financial and legal issues.) Many stepmothers approaching middle age have found, unexpectedly, that they are helping to finance education and wedding expenses for their stepchildren when they would have preferred to invest the money elsewhere—in a cabin in the mountains, a convertible to help cool off those pesky hot flashes, or their retirement fund.

Pearl, forty-eight, is a stepmother from San Francisco whose husband, Mark, promised his only daughter from the day she was born that she would be a princess on her wedding day. The daughter's idea of princesshood was worth more than a hundred thousand dollars at a time when Pearl and Mark were struggling to put his son through technical school.

Mark was devastated to realize he would lose his credibility with his daughter when she could not be talked out of her extravagant wedding. He even offered her twenty-five thousand dollars to elope. Pearl reluctantly decided her 401(k) was less important than Mark's losing face with his daughter, and her savings melted like marzipan.

Mark was grateful, and Pearl's stepdaughter to this day does not know that her stepmother's savings went to pay for her wedding. Pearl didn't think about whether or not her 401(k) was a non-negotiable item until it was too late. Long after the lavish bouquets have faded, Pearl is resentful, and her relationship with Mark has been seriously damaged. "The light went out," she confided. Not for his lack of money—he was, after all, maintaining two households, four children, three cars, medical bills, etc.—but for his inability to explain their financial circumstances to his daughter and the fact that he put four hours of gratification and a few photos ahead of their retirement lifestyle.

The Spirited Fifties

In your fifties, if you are still working, you and your husband will likely be at the height of your professions and, we hope, reaping the rewards. Your children and stepchildren may now be full-fledged adults, on their own, and you and your husband will probably have more time alone together than women who become stepmothers in their twenties or thirties.

The women we interviewed who became stepmothers in their fifties—either by marrying for the first time in their lives, having been consumed with other priorities until now, or by marrying for the second or even third time—are unquestionably some of the most successful stepmothers we found. (We discuss how to form your own definition of success in chapter 21.)

The high success rate of the fifty-something woman seemed commensurate with her increased self-confidence and her accumulation of life experience. Nothing really surprises women in their fifties anymore—they've seen it all. A number of fifty-plus women have also told us they feel a renewed sense of "spirituality" born of maturity, wisdom, and greater compassion, which they say they were able to bring to bear on their relationships with their new families.

Fiona, a fifty-two-year old divorced woman who has no children of her own, drew on her experience as a school principal to make the transition to stepmother of five ranging in age from late teens to late twenties. "I've done most other things by now," she said of her decision to become a stepmom. "I knew I couldn't be a biological mother, but I wanted to experience 'parenting,' even though these kids were adults, or almost, when I married their dad. Of course, it helped that I was head over heels in love with their father."

Physically, the fifty-plus years may be a difficult time for you, depending on how much self-esteem you have tied up in maintaining a "youthful" appearance. Stepmothers at this age report concerns about menopause and related issues—hormone-replacement therapies, sexuality, and energy. For those stepmoms who have relied on their notorious good looks as a morale booster throughout their lives, dealing with sags and wrinkles *and* a rebellious teenage stepdaughter can be a lot to cope with. So can bursting into hormone-induced tears or suffering through a paralyzing hot flash just as your stepson, who arrives home three hours later than his curfew, has told you to butt out of his life.

Energetic women in their fifties often express a desire to pursue passions they haven't felt secure enough or free enough to act on in the past. Women interested in the arts might decide to change careers, becoming professional painters, sculptors, or photographers—avocations they wouldn't have seriously considered when time and money (and confidence) were scarcer. Another woman's story underscores how important inheritance issues become at this stage of life. When we first met Mary, she was engaged to Lawrence, a respected oncologist with four adult sons, all in the medical profession. Mary had found true love for the first time at age fifty. "It's almost too good to be true!" she exclaimed.

Unfortunately, it was. Mary dismissed the importance of getting to know Lawrence's sons before the wedding, reasoning, "There'll be plenty of time after we're married." But the wedding never took place. Soon after the date was set, Lawrence's sons collectively took their father aside and pressured him to call it off. They didn't want to see their inheritance spent in the ensuing years on a new wife. Regrettably, Lawrence did not stand up to his sons, even though he had spent a great deal of money educating them, and each son was making a substantial living. Ideally, Mary and Lawrence together would have announced their wedding plans to his sons and addressed their concerns about money, with Lawrence making it clear that Mary was to be included in these discussions.

As a further complication in their lives, stepmothers in their fifties often have aging parents to care for, giving them full membership in what's been called the "sandwich generation." Possibly offsetting these new responsibilities, grandchildren and stepgrandchildren can be a source of great joy, presenting an opportunity to start over, perhaps to erase mistakes made previously with children and stepchildren.

Later Love

Women in their sixties, seventies, eighties, and beyond are younger, more active, more interesting, and, yes, sexier than ever before. Finding love and a mate in our later years is a wonderful bonus to retirement.

Many of your responsibilities to others will have ended by this age. Your parents will likely have passed on, your children are probably grown, perhaps even grandparents themselves. You're at an age when you have that great blessing: leisure time.

If you marry a man with children, however, you still become a stepmother, regardless of the "kids'" ages. A forty-year-old stepdaughter is still a child to her dad. Wills, which are always an important issue, become especially critical now. Some stepmothers in the senior age bracket, while relishing their newfound love, claim that their stepchildren see no further than an unwelcome addition of another heir.

We interviewed Meg in her trailer home in Florida. She and Fred had married just after he'd retired. Unfortunately, two years after the wedding, he'd died of a sudden heart attack. "We had such a wonderful, exciting time, even though it was so short," Meg said.

Fred had provided for Meg while still leaving most of his assets to his children. Explained Meg, "We knew Fred had a 'dicky heart,' as he called it. He wanted me to be financially secure if he died suddenly, so he adjusted his will when we married."

Fred's children challenged the will when he died. Meg, of

a generation when many women did not handle even the most basic money matters, was completely flummoxed by this turn of events. "His children said I was 'only after his money.' It was their word against mine, and there are three of them— one son is a lawyer. I ended up with nothing whatsoever. I live here on my social security with my memories."

Unfortunately, it is sometimes possible for children to challenge a will. Chapter 18 explains what stepmothers like Meg, and in fact women of any age, should know and do to protect their legal rights.

The Instant Stepmother: Just Add Kids and Mix

Joining a ready-made family comes with the often jarring realization that stepmotherhood is a lot like those little envelopes of soup mix you take along on family camping trips—instant! Unlike the months or years that biological and adoptive mothers enjoy after their weddings to plan for children, there is no such transition period for a stepmother. Ideally, before you marry you should understand what your duties are going to include and how you're going to integrate them with your other commitments and interests.

If you are going to be a full-time stepmother of young children, for example, you will immediately begin facing your responsibilities. Before your honeymoon, you and your husband might need to make arrangements for ten-year-old Becky to stay with Grandma and six-year-old Tommy to be cared for by your husband's sister. Or perhaps you'll decide against a honeymoon, preferring to wait until you've all "settled in."

Maybe you had visions of being the "perfect" stepmother: you brought Becky and Tommy with you to Aruba so they wouldn't feel left out. Now you spend your honeymoon lining up babysitters so you and your husband can get in a few romantic dinners for two, with a phone close at hand to check on the children. You keep a watchful eye on the kiddie pool and remind yourself to have the children's laundry returned by tomorrow afternoon, or both of them will have to sleep

naked, which they'll think is wonderful but may be an indication to you that *already* you may not be the perfect stepmother.
You return from your honeymoon feeling you need a vacation
and wonder how, with a hundred things to take care of for
Becky and Tommy, will you find time to prepare for your
company's monthly meeting?!?

How Are YOU?: Caring for Your Physical and Emotional Health

As a stepmother, you will not be able to help anyone else
make adjustments to stepfamily life unless you are functioning
well, a point that's been virtually overlooked in most discussions of stepmotherhood. As one eight-year-old remarked to
her mother, who was struggling in her new marriage with two
adolescent stepsons, "When you're down, Mom, we're all
down." As the pivotal person in the stepfamily, Mom/stepmom
needs to be well and truly "up."

It's logical that a stepmother who's relaxed and prepared
for her business presentation can perform better as Becky and
Tommy's stepmom. Your first task in building a strong stepfamily—emotionally, practically, and financially—is to take an
honest look at what you need to feel good about yourself and
stay healthy. The greatest gift you can give your children and
stepchildren is the role model of a healthy mom/stepmom, a
good marriage, and a secure family life.

When we asked women what surprised them the most as
they took on the role of stepmother, many mentioned that
relatives and friends alike seemed concerned solely about how
the children in the stepfamily were feeling or coping with the
new marriage of their dad. This can be disconcerting, to say
the least, especially when you've come to expect caring, solicitous support from those closest to you. You can also expect
that other members of your new family will be concerned with
their own adjustments, not yours. Everyone is trying to regroup and restablilize his or her own life, with varying degrees
of success.

Bottom line: you need to take care of yourself, because you will be the only one doing so. If you're tired, stressed, overworked, physically unfit, or depressed and you're thinking about becoming a stepmother, we can tell you right now it's not a great state to be in as a stepmother. (If you're a stepmom now, you know exactly what we mean.) You cannot afford to sacrifice your good physical and emotional health to meet the demands of your stepfamily—it's too high a price to pay. And not only for the toll it takes on you; you can't give unless you've got.

Perhaps, like a lot of us these days, you feel you could be more fit, use more energy? This might be a good time to start an exercise program and get a complete checkup. And if you're going to be scrutinized by new family members, they might as well see someone glowing with good health and self-confident beauty. Good grooming doesn't have to cost a lot, and it says a great deal about what you think of yourself.

Perhaps Joy, who was about to become a stepmom, had the right approach.

Joy and Rick's wedding date was set for Valentine's Day. Most of the arrangements were made, invitations printed and ready to mail out on the first of January, after the Christmas rush. Everything was in good shape except the bride-to-be! She had been running on fumes for several weeks, planning the wedding, holding down a busy job, and striving to make a good impression on Rick's relatives, including his three sons, aged seven, nine and fourteen. Fortunately, Rick and his ex-wife shared custody in what Joy described as "an amazingly civilized way."

Joy realized she needed a breather. "I simply cannot handle Christmas on top of everything else," she remarked. "Rick and I have decided to have separate Christmas vacations this year. It will be his last one alone with his kids—their mom is going skiing with a boyfriend. I'm going to a health spa for a week."

With this little break, Rick and his children were able to share a special, quiet Christmas, giving Rick the opportunity to talk to them about their new life as a stepfamily and to

walk 8-9 every day

ease their concerns about having a stepmom. Joy had some downtime to recharge her batteries.

Remember, you are setting your standards now. The way you treat yourself is the way your new family will expect to treat you. Let them know you are top-of-the-line and expect top-of-the-line treatment.

Trying to fit these feel-good, look-good rituals into your schedule when you are living with your new family isn't always easy. But you must find the time and space to nurture your body, mind, and soul. That's nonnegotiable.

meditate again

Personality Peccadillos

If you think you have a couple of personality traits, habits, or even (heaven forbid) defects in your character that you wish to change or overcome, this is the time. It's a sticky issue, but your flaws can and will be used against you, say stepmoms.

Angela used to wind up almost everything she said with the conclusion "So be it." Her siblings had implored her to stop the annoying verbal tic, to no avail. When she married into a stepfamily, her stepchildren initially thought it was funny. Angela would pronounce; "OK, you guys, dinner is ready. Wash your hands and come to the table. So be it," or, "Time to get up. Hurry, the school bus will be here before you know it. So be it."

After a while, the "so be it" flourish began to drive Angela's stepkids crazy, too, and they retaliated by using the phrase themselves: "Angela phone for you. So be it!" someone would yell. Gradually the joke turned sour, and the kids started calling her their "so-be-it stepmother." This changed into the "so-so" stepmother, and then to the "not-so-good" stepmother. At that point Angela dreaded letting the words slip out and became withdrawn and anxious.

A very sensible suggestion from her husband helped. He suggested she write down some replacement phrases she could use and deliberately work down the list. This task forced her to be conscious of what she was saying. Now instead of "So be it," Angela has a repertoire of phrases, ranging from a simple "Thanks, guys" to "Let's go." Failing any homegrown solutions to your own unwanted habits (some obsessive-compulsive habits, for example, can be debilitating), you may want to consider getting professional help.

Nipping potential criticisms in the bud is sensible anyway, especially if these characteristics are making *you* unhappy about yourself. What are some of last year's New Year resolutions? Now is the time to actually fulfill them, whether it's January the first or the middle of August. If all your life you have burst into tears when someone says no to you, maybe it's time to talk it over with a friendly therapist. It will be more difficult to become an effective stepmother if you carry unwanted baggage into your new life. Hang on to the eccentricities and traits that you like about yourself, however, regardless of how others view them. They make you the interesting person you are and are probably among the reasons your husband-to-be loves you so much.

Not a Hair out of Place, or Ruffled Feathers?

Think, too, about the way you handle new and unfamiliar circumstances. Are you normally the "wing it" type, just plunging in on a wave of confidence, assuming that everything will turn out OK? We know this doesn't work for stepmothers—preparation and information are the better half of success. Or are you the meticulous planner who tries to organize down to the nth degree but is thrown out of whack when life doesn't conform to your way of doing things? We know this doesn't work either—you can only organize yourself, not the members of your new stepfamily.

Claudia was a "wing it" type. She knew she wanted to marry Adam, the staid and solid stockbroker father of two daughters, aged thirteen and fifteen, even though his carefully organized lifestyle was a far cry from hers. Claudia considered herself a free spirit. As a freelance landscaper, she took only assignments that appealed to her when she needed money—

and she didn't think she needed much. She happily muddled through, living in a tiny studio over a gatehouse on a huge estate.

Claudia began to see, however, that life with a man with children required a bit more structure and preparation. When Adam suggested "dinner at eight," he actually meant dinner at eight. To Claudia, dinner at eight had always meant eight o'clock—give or take a few hours!

Claudia's early solution to this apparent incompatibility was as creative as she is—she prepared herself for life with this family by bringing together the best of both worlds. Knowing the family's need for structure, Claudia purchased two calendars, a large one for her apartment and a small one to carry with her. On the dates of "custody days," Claudia filled the boxes of her calendars with ideas for unusual activities together. The girls loved her offbeat (to them) suggestions—walking in the woods to find wildflowers, trips to the local university observatory to look at constellations. On days when Adam didn't have the girls, she agreed to adhere to Adam's habit of "dinner at eight" but, when it was her turn to cook, presented exotic entrees that neither of them had ever tried.

Gradually Claudia eased her stepfamily in her own carefree, imaginative world while integrating her new family's need for plans. Married in her cottage garden with her stepdaughters as bridesmaids, Claudia has created a sunny, lighthearted new household that the girls love, the lack of formality providing a wonderful escape from their mother's somewhat rigid rules and regulations.

Consider your own attitude toward obstacles during your life. If you are a person who falls apart in the face of difficulty—even the garden-variety conundrums life is famous for—you may need to work on this. If your former spouse coped with the fix-it list, whereas your fiancé usually manages to destroy a wall when hanging a picture, do something about it now. Putting together a list of emergency telephone numbers or arranging to trade services with a handy neighbor could be on your agenda.

Other Stepmoms: Your Precious Support Resource

Many stepmothers we spoke to agreed that the greatest lifter of spirits and sounding board for plans and problems is lunch or a night out with their girlfriends, particularly if they are also stepmothers.

When Janey, a woman who married in her early twenties, became a stepmother to four small children, she found herself facing crisis after crisis, with very little experience to draw upon. She was unprepared for full-time care of little kids who were virtual strangers; her salvation was not only having an older, understanding, supportive husband but the fact that she had a friend living nearby in a very similar situation.

The two young women frequently met for a quick coffee break or grabbed a sandwich together and supported each other through self-doubt and frustration. Janey is convinced she would not have been able to mature through those early years as a stepmother quite so well without this friend.

Other stepmothers can even help you break the ice with your new family members. Pam, a shy woman who married for the first time in her late thirties, felt outnumbered and overwhelmed by her stepchildren, who were always telling her, "We don't do it like that." Two of Pam's friends, also stepmoms, thought it might help if they came around a lot to show support. "We'll come over, sit in your kitchen, and chat with you," they offered. Gradually Pam's pals befriended her stepchildren, which helped lay common ground between them.

If you don't have a friend who's a stepmother and you really want to be able to talk with other women with similar issues, we highly recommend a stepmothers' support group. Later in this book we'll discuss the fundamentals of forming one of these groups and their importance to the stepmother.

Questionnaire

When you can find some quiet time to spend alone, take out
the idea book you've set aside for answering the questionnaires
in *The Enlightened Stepmother*. In this one we're asking you to
consider your personality and goals—what makes you tick and
what you want out of life. The more you acknowledge what
you are comfortable with, how you react to various situations,
and what fulfills your particular needs, the better prepared you
will be for your new life.

1. List all the qualities you like about yourself, including per-
    sonality characteristics and skills (e.g., cheerful early riser,
    good cook). *creative, courageous, intelligent, nurturing*

2. List what you consider to be your greatest accomplish-
    ments, personal and career-related. *Bunny, partnership w/ Paul, design 512, travel, MBA 4.0, and career*

3. Right now, are you happy with yourself, the woman who is
    80% considering becoming a stepmother or who is in the early
    stages of stepmotherhood? If not, why? What actions do you
    want to take to improve your satisfaction with yourself? What
    do you need from others to enhance your happiness?

4. List everything, major and minor, currently happening in
    your life that is contributing to your happiness. *Bunny, Tati, Paul, feeling healthier (BP)*

5. Is there anything that is troubling you right now? What is
    it? What do you believe you could do or should do (even
    if you're not sure if it's right) to improve the situation or
    alleviate the problem? *when getting married? starting business this year*

6. What are some of your characteristics you are not so happy
    alot, self centered about, the traits you believe you need to work on, e.g. a
    bad temper, procrastination? *impatient*

7. What activities make you feel good? Given two free hours
    manage my own, not bathing around before a dental appointment, how would you choose to
    spend them? A walk in the park? Shopping? Having your
    hair restyled? Weeding the garden? Make a list of all the
    wonderful treats you cherish—don't forget to include *tea, yummy, clutter-free home, riding!*

the cheap thrills as well as more extravagant ones. Make
the list as long as you want.

8. List the things that make you sad. Include actual experiences and temperamental leanings (e.g. the time your boss
   screamed at you; the thought of anyone going hungry).

Baby care in Daycare
orphans
.

9. When was the last time you had a complete physical?
   When are you due for your next Pap test and mammo-
   gram? Do you have any symptoms that concern you?

10. Are you easily pleased? Can a child at play make you
    smile? Do you feel joy the morning the first forsythia
    blooms? Or does it take a major "dinner and a show" to
    make you happy? List the everyday, ordinary things that
    please you (e.g. A perfectly quiet, clean house; a full, busy
    schedule; someone cooking dinner for you).

Yes

11. What does it take to make you feel put out or annoyed?
    An earthquake, burning the breakfast toast, or something
    in between? List the kinds of experiences that trigger an-
    noyance for you. *Sudden changes*

Being tired
Time pressure

12. Do you bear grudges? Do you have any right now? What
    are they? How long does it take for you to get over an
    angry exchange? *No but I don't forget — people repeatedly transgress*

13. How do you react to emotional stress? Do you cope well
    on your own, or do you look to others for help? Think
    about specific stressful times and detail your reactions. In
    retrospect, were these reactions reasonable or would you
    rather have handled things differently?

I get crispy, lash out

14. Do you enjoy your own company, happily spending hours
    or days with your own thoughts and projects? Do you
    need constant company? If neither, where do you fall be-
    tween these two extremes? What are some of the things
    you like to do alone?

yes

15. Can you usually take care of everyday predicaments and
    problems yourself, or do you need reinforcement from oth-
    ers? Can you handle the plumber, the head waiter, the post
    office clerk who is rude to you? Are you in awe of the
    doctor, nervous about asking questions? If you would like to
    be more assertive, describe how and in what situations.

history of getting into conflict

in intimate relationships

❧❧❧
Action Box

❧ Make doctors' appointments if you're overdue for checkups.

❧ Browse the lifestyle and health books in the library or at your local bookstore. They have inexpensive but effective tips for health and beauty that you may want to try, especially if you can't afford professional services.

❧ Decide if there are changes you wish to make in your health or exercise routine, and begin. A twenty-minute brisk walk burns calories and gets those feel-good endorphins going. (Talk about cheap thrills!) *Start running*

❧ Make a list of your goals, short-term and long-term. How do you plan to achieve them? Include financial goals, educational and career plans, and that personal "secret" wish you've never told anyone about.

❧ Consider your personal support system. Make your mate your best friend (we show how in chapter 6), but schedule get-togethers with your friends, preferably other stepmoms, for moral support when you need a good listener.

❧ If you've never been in therapy but feel overwhelmed in a specific area—communicating your needs or organizing your time—take the plunge! But first read chapter 20: "The Stepmom's Resource Guide." Selecting the wrong therapist can multiply your difficulties.

CHAPTER 2

Your Family and Marital History

Thinking about your family background is a lot like taking a trip into the attic—it's dark in some corners, but there's treasure buried in others. Consider this chapter a virtual trip to the "family attic"—where many of your attitudes and beliefs about blended families and the role of stepmotherhood are stored.

By taking note of your personality and goals in the first chapter, you began to develop a picture of how the life you want and the life you're getting into might match up. The purpose of reviewing your family and marital history, as you will do as you read this chapter, is to make you aware of the prejudices as well as positive influences you bring to stepmotherhood.

Our quest is practical. Awareness of your "only child" status, for example, and the characteristics and feelings generally found to accompany it, will help you realize that you don't have a personal context for sibling rivalry. So if your husband's children are constantly arguing, you won't think it's because you're an inept stepmom. Instead, you might just feel motivated to learn more about this particular phenomenon.

Conversely, if you grew up in a large, boisterous family, the second youngest of eight children, you might not understand how your stepdaughter, an only child, can stay alone in her room all day with a book. But just because you were unable to find a peaceful spot in your home to read doesn't mean your stepdaughter is sickly or antisocial. Her behavior might simply mean she is accustomed to being alone, enjoys her own company, and loves to read.

The First Family

The home your parents provided offers the most revealing clues about how you have come to think men, women, and children should behave, either because of or in spite of the way your parents ruled their roost. You might remember a loving marital relationship, many happy occasions, and family traditions, memories of siblings that always bring a smile to your face. Perhaps you'll want to re-create those good times in your stepfamily.

One of Sue's dearest recollections of growing up in Canada was her mother's insistence on family Sunday dinner at six. Sue and her three brothers used to call this "the royal command," but even as they grew up and married, all four siblings made superhuman efforts to keep the hallowed tradition. Dinner was in the dining room, with the best china and all the trimmings. Sue's mom felt this important "date" served a couple of sterling purposes: in spite of hectic lifestyles, the family was able to share meaningful company on a regular basis, and the children learned how to comfortably handle a relatively formal occasion.

When Sue married, she carried on the tradition for her two stepsons and the new baby. She was thrilled when she overheard her older stepson on the phone with a friend, explaining why he couldn't go ice skating on Sunday night. "He was actually boasting about our royal command!" Sue exclaimed. "It's one of the things I'm proudest of."

You might remember less happy times with your family of origin too. Perhaps there were many children vying for the attention of a single parent, and now that you're stepmom to three young girls, you are determined not only to work hard at your marriage but to ensure that everyone feels cared for and special. If your parents argued all the time, loud shouting matches might frighten you even now. Bad memories can help you take positive steps in your new family too.

Regan, thirty-three, a full-time stepmother to two girls, aged ten and twelve, realized that the inappropriate responsibilities she had had as a child of an overworked, inaccessible single mother were a burden she did not want to pass on to her stepdaughters. "I hardly saw my mom. I made meals for my brother and me, cleaned the house, worried when money was short. I do not have memories of playing or even just being taken care of. At first I saw my stepdaughters' natural interests as a total lack of responsibility—I was always on them to shape up."

One day Regan saw a TV commercial that caused an epiphany: "The ad showed a little girl asleep in bed, her mother calling her to breakfast. It actually brought tears to my eyes— I could feel the luxury of waking up slowly, knowing that someone who loved me was downstairs, waiting to feed me," Regan said. "This hit me very hard, and I started loosening up on my stepdaughters. I may be leaning too far in the other direction now, but I'm determined that they have a free and easy childhood."

Big Sister or Baby of the Family?

There are some fascinating theories about birth order (still disputed by some, however, as not scientifically supported) and how it influences our approach to life. *Living in a Stepfamily without Getting Stepped On: Helping Your Children Survive the Birth Order Blender* (Thomas Nelson, 1994), by Kevin Leman, an internationally known psychologist, is particularly helpful to stepmothers who have children and stepchildren living under one roof; it's a good source of information about birth order–related behavior, including your own. It turns out your place in the family can also affect your approach to stepmotherhood!

Eileen is a classic "independent" first born with three

Relate like big sister to chris

younger siblings. Married for the first time at age thirty-two to a man with two young adult sons, this usually confident professional woman was initially at a loss about how to behave.

"I thought I was supposed to be motherly or at least sort of formal with Steve's kids. After all, I was sleeping with their dad," she explained. But Eileen was uncomfortable with the maternal approach—her husband's sons were just ten and seven years younger than she.

Then she realized that her "big sister" status was one of her most confident and cherished roles; "I understood that I really saw my stepsons as younger brothers. It was entirely natural to me."

For Eileen the "big sister" experience was the key to successful stepmotherhood. "Everything just fell into place—communication, relationship building, problem solving—everything. Now it's as if I've always known them. My husband jokes that he married me so his kids could have someone to hang out with."

On the other hand, even the experience of the youngest child who may later grow up to be a stepmother can come in handy.

The youngest of three daughters, Chris had grown up in a farming community in Iowa. Money was tight. "Mom made everything she could," explained Chris, "and then remade it. My sisters and I shared everything, including our underthings." Adds Chris, "Today I make sure my stepdaughters have new, pretty panties all the time, because I still remember how it felt having second-hand and even third-hand, worn-out ugly old stuff! Ugh!"

From Stepchild to Stepmom

If your parents split up and you subsequently became a stepchild, you'll want to emulate the good things your stepmother did. What you found hard to handle—perhaps her passion for punctuality or her insistence you eat every scrap on your plate—may be indelibly etched in your mind as a horror to be avoided at all costs. In fact, your prior experience in a step family offers you the unique advantage of being able to relate to your stepchildren's perspective.

Patti is a lab technician in her forties with no children of her own. When she met Luke, he was a widower with two young daughters.

Patti is also a stepdaughter. After her parents divorced, Patti lived a reasonably happy, quiet life with her mother. Then her mom met Arthur, Patti's stepfather. "To give him his due," Patti explained, "he included me and treated both of us to nice things. But I felt Arthur was taking my mom from me. When they married, I cried hysterically through the wedding."

When Patti met Luke, she knew what his children were feeling. "Luke's girls reacted to me in virtually the same way I had treated my stepfather," Patti says. "And while I understood where they were coming from, they said and did many really hateful things, some of which are hard to forget."

But Patti made it clear to the girls that she loved their dad, cared about them, and was there to stay. Patti, who considers herself an unusually good listener, has gradually begun to engage Luke's daughters in conversations about stepdaughterhood and other kinds of "just-us-girls talk" marathons, which sometimes last hours at a time. "I'm determined to hang in there, because I eventually came to accept Arthur as a wonderful husband for my mom and a good friend to me. Luke's girls recognize that I share their experience, and they know I'll listen. It's a very good beginning."

Attitude Check: Ready and Willing or Against It From the Start?

Along with the preparation you're doing now, we urge you to recognize that the more positive you can be about becoming a stepmother, the better your chance of success. Your positive attitude should be founded on a sound knowledge of what lies ahead and the security of knowing you have done everything in your power to prepare yourself, rather than the "I'm so nice everyone will love me" approach, which is unrealistic. —

Of all the stepmoms we met, only Joan began life as a stepmother without good intentions toward her stepchild. The manager of a doctors' office, Joan married Jerry when she was thirty. Jerry had one daughter, Felicity, age eight, whose mother had died in childbirth. The youngster had been living with her maternal grandparents until Jerry felt able, financially and emotionally, to get back on his feet.

Because she was so in love, her head in the clouds, Joan had been unable to focus on anything but her new relationship with Jerry. She had simply assumed (a verb every stepmother should erase from her vocabulary) that Felicity would continue living with her grandparents and that her stepdaughter would visit on the occasional weekend—she was not prepared or willing to be the full-time stepmother Jerry expected. Joan's complaints about Felicity were endless: "Her grandparents spoil her rotten"; "She won't get out of bed before noon on weekends." Finally, after they had been married for less than a year, Joan issued an ultimatum: "Either Felicity goes back to live with her grandparents, or I'm leaving."

Clearly Joan mishandled her situation, but, even more important, she had had different plans for her life. As the second oldest of eleven children from a noisy, disruptive first family, Joan's main requirement for her adult life was peace) and tranquillity.

The problem was, she had fallen deeply in love with a man with a child. Having decided to marry Jerry, however, Joan might have reasoned that she could make a welcoming home for Felicity based on mutually agreeable ground rules for their household and a gradually increasing schedule for Felicity's visits. She could have considered how much responsibility she could handle, what she needed in terms of time and space for herself—down time, vacations, etc—and how much of their domestic life Jerry would need to take care of, without forcing Jerry to choose between his daughter and his wife.

With planning, the couple might have had a chance of

success. As the situation devolved, however, we weren't surprised when Joan and Jerry later divorced.

Alternately, a positive attitude can take you through the roughest times. Not long after Alexandra and Frank returned from their honeymoon and picked up her daughter and his two sons from their respective grandparents, Frank started complaining of a pain in his side. Over a period of three months, he was diagnosed with cancer, and his right lung was removed. Since Frank's first wife had died of lung cancer just four years before, his sons, aged twelve and fourteen, were terrified they would lose their dad too.

Alex, in her mid-twenties at the time of her marriage, displayed compassion and maturity beyond her years. She nursed Frank at home, set a shining example of the powers of positive thinking for their children, and kept the whole family involved with upbeat projects, cooking special meals for Dad, and even planning trips for when he was better. Through the shared goal of nursing Frank back to health, the boys grew to love Alex as a special friend and confidant.

Recently the family celebrated Frank's fifth anniversary as cancer-free and have taken two of the trips planned by his sons in darker days. All five stepfamily members feel very fortunate. Said Alex, "Our mutual love for Frank gave us the strength we needed to pull together as a family."

The Divorcée's Spring Cleaning

Divorce expert Judith Wallerstein, in her book *The Good Marriage: How and Why Love Lasts* (Houghton Mifflin, 1995), reports that "second marriages fail earlier and even more frequently than first marriages, and the most important factor in these failures is children."

This might not come as any surprise to stepmothers already grappling with the difficulties of blending children in a stepfamily. But our focus here is on whether you have resolved all the issues from your previous marriage, if there was one. You might have been so happy to escape wedded discord and feel so lucky to have found a potential new partner that you might not be aware of what a complex task this is. Explains Wallerstein in her book: "The first step in separating from the earlier marriage involves mourning the loss of what that marriage represented emotionally and symbolically. Even if it ended miserably, there were bright dreams and hopes at its beginning, which must be lamented before being consigned to the past."

Your marriage has ended, but you will always be mother to the children you and your former spouse had together, and you will probably need to remain in touch and involved with your ex-husband on issues that concern the children.

You can fully recover from a divorce, however painful it may have been. But you have both internal and external adjustments to make prior to taking on your role of stepmother; trying to resolve the past and build the future at the same time is stressful, and not fair to your new family.

Specifically, your divorce should be finalized, and your kids' custody and/or visitation arrangements organized, with all financial details agreed upon. You need to start your new life knowing how much money you will have, knowing when your kids will be living with you and/or staying with their dad. Possessions should have been divided—are you still holding your ex's expensive button-down shirts hostage until he surrenders the cappuccino machine?

Widow's "Weeds"

If you are a widow, it may be even more difficult for you to mourn and heal, but your new role demands full attention from a well-functioning, not grieving, woman.

Some wonderful books on this issue are listed in our recommended reading list, one or two written by women whose husbands have died, and who have detailed their personal experiences. These books contain practical advice on surviving and moving on following the death of a spouse. Talking with a therapist can be helpful if you are in doubt; it may be necessary to have only a few sessions to clarify your feelings. Your task includes contemplating whether or not you are ready to accept and embrace a new husband, especially one with children.

For years—too many to count—Thelma had kept, in a side pocket of her purse, a photo of her first husband, taken when he was barely twenty. The picture of Jock, her smiling young sweetheart, was dog-eared and yellow with age. When Jock died after thirty-four years of marriage, Thelma couldn't bring herself to remove it.

Once, when she was rummaging through her bag for her lipstick, the picture fell out. Henry, Thelma's new husband, silently picked it up and handed it back to her.

Said Thelma, "Henry understood my attachment to it but couldn't bear knowing I carried it around like a religious card." Henry, a reasonable man, gave her time, and eventually Thelma placed Jock's photo in an album along with other memories of "life before Henry."

Dr. Joyce Brothers, America's best-known psychologist, lost her husband, Milton, after more than thirty years of marriage. In her book *Widowed* (Ballantine, 1992), which details how she dealt with her despair, she says, "If there should ever be another good man with whom I share my life, there will still be that empty corner of my soul. I know what I had and what I lost. I hope I will not spend the rest of my life alone. But if I do, I will not be sorry for myself. Life goes on, and I am ready to join the parade again."

Like Dr. Brothers, you will never forget your husband— he will remain part of you forever. Please don't think we are unsympathetic or less than understanding by insisting upon the need for moving on with your life. What we do understand fully is stepmotherhood, and we have to repeat that unless you are in first-class shape, you cannot entertain this role.

On the practical side, consult with your attorney to finalize your husband's will, and arrange to disperse or dispose of his possessions, however hard you find this task. If you do not feel equipped to do this yourself, seek out a trustworthy friend or relation to help you handle financial matters, especially if

you have dependent children and will have to con
education.

Finally, both divorced and widowed women have been
through an emotionally (and physically) wrenching time. Studies indicate that the death of a spouse and divorce are the first
two on the list of the most common stressful situations a
human being can encounter. You may be nutritionally depleted
or depressed or both, which you must address right away.
Consider the suggestions to boost your health and well-being
detailed in chapter 1. Some worthwhile books are listed in the
recommended reading list (page 438).

Questioning Beliefs

There aren't any fairy tales depicting the "wonderful" stepmother, although a very few modern-day childrens' stories of
"good" stepmothers are creeping into the bookstores. (Consider this a wake-up call to all children's literature writers out
there.) So the reason that you, as stepmother, have not been
regarded in our culture in a positive way is not hard to see.

But what about what *you* believe? It can be startling to
realize that you're not much different from anyone else when
it comes to holding stereotypes of stepmothers.

During the course of our research we found that the majority of stepmothers felt they . . .

> should grin and bear it.
> should make life pleasant for everyone else.
> should put up with what others dish out to them.
> should not complain.
> should fit in with the existing family lifestyle.
> should keep their stepfamily's traditions inviolate.
> should place stepfamily wishes and expectations before
> their own.

We believe that a stepmom's tendency to retreat, illustrated
by the *shoulds* listed above, is a direct result of cultural prejudices and stereotypes. Persuaded by a pervasive negativity

about her role, a stepmother begins to question her own worth. After all, she is not the "real" mother. She is the "second" wife—the "first" wife is the mother of her husband's children. No one, including the stepmom herself, is sure where she fits in. Perceived by some as intruding upon a formed family, she is expected to defer to others and hold existing family traditions and procedures sacred at the expense of her own.

During our interviews stepmothers tried, often obsessively, to find the cause of problems in themselves and focused on putting aside their own needs in order to please. Like the old Avis advertisement, being number two might mean to a stepmother that she must try harder. Feeling inadequate, overburdened, and unappreciated, she begins to think the reason she has no say is that she doesn't deserve any. Her self-esteem plummets.

And to complete the vicious cycle, her depressed feelings of being a nonperson may be reinforced by others, including therapists. Jenny, a stepmom of four young adult stepdaughters who tried to get help from a psychologist specializing in stepfamilies was offered this solution: "You have an impossible situation. I suggest you smile, keep your mouth shut, and fit in where you can." According to Kay Pasley, EdD, associate professor, Department of Human Development and Family Studies at the University of North Carolina at Greensboro and chair of the Research Committee of the Stepfamily Association of America, "It's this kind of comment from 'experts' that is so harmful."

Mirror, Mirror: Reinventing Stepmotherhood

We think it's vital that you look clearly at your own attitudes and beliefs about stepmothers, the starting point for shaping your role in a positive way that works for you—our task for the next chapter. Were you raised on fairy tales, to the extent that you really believe, even if only at the back of your mind, that there is a tendency for stepmothers to be mean, or that second wives really are second best? It is *essential* that you rid yourself of these notions if they exist. You cannot start out, or continue if you're already a stepmother, with these ideas in your mind. (If this a real problem for you, refer to chapter 20, "The Stepmom's Resource Guide.")

Maybe negative connotations are virtually all you've ever heard. Speaking of the "natural" mother can suggest that the stepmother is "unnatural." The word "stepmother" conjures up other horrific images and adjectives: "wicked," "jealous," "ugly," "cruel," "manipulative," "greedy."

The effect of the brothers "grim" was made abundantly clear to Jane, mother of four-year-old Emily. When Jane explained to her little girl that she was going to marry John, whom Emily knew and liked, Emily's eyes opened wide when she understood that her loving, affectionate mother would also be a stepmother to Jim's child. "Will you be wicked, then?" her young daughter asked.

When "Sisterhood" Comes Up Short

Women often turn to other women for encouragement and support in difficult times. But unless they are stepmothers themselves, other women, especially those with children, are rarely sympathetic to issues common to stepmoms. This surprised us at first, but it was a frequent complaint. Many stepmoms had been disappointed at the reactions of friends who they felt were letting them down at one of the most crucial points in their lives.

Perhaps unwittingly, women who are married with children harbor a nagging feeling that "but for the grace of God," their own children could someday have a stepmother. In all fairness, we have to admit there is something alarming about the thought of another woman's raising your children and sleeping with your husband! Whatever the reason, it means that at the time of her greatest need, a stepmother can rarely turn to those who normally would be a source of great support.

We found an eye-opening example of this sometimes built-in prejudice against stepmothers when we interviewed Debbie, a thirty-five-year-old mom and stepmom who was trying to cope with a troubled six-year-old stepson and a husband who was being manipulated by a combative ex-wife. The bright spot in Debbie's life was her newborn son, a happy, chubby baby who was obviously the center of her world.

Partway through our interview, Debbie grabbed Johnny from his crib. "God, I love him so much," she said, hugging him close. Then, quite spontaneously, she said, "I hope he never has a stepmother." She was so embarrassed—before Johnny's birth, Debbie had been almost militant in her quest to raise awareness of the good that stepmothers do. When we spoke to Debbie again a year later, she was still trying to balance her feelings between her dual roles of mother and stepmother.

Changing Minds, Changing Lives

Five years into her marriage to Carl—and becoming the stepmother of his three children, a girl of twelve and two boys, aged fourteen and fifteen—Beth felt she was at the end of the line. The couple had lived together for two years before marrying, and Beth had started out with great confidence. An intelligent, introspective woman, Beth had read about stepfamilies and was prepared for some initial difficulties. She loved Carl with a passion and was determined to rescue this sorry bunch of souls, to bring happiness, light, and laughter into their lives.

Her husband, Carl, had lost his own mother at the age of four, had been raised by a stepmother he hated, and was a very troubled man following his divorce from his previous wife. Beth learned only deep into her marriage that Carl was convinced that all stepmothers were as bad as he believed his own had been and fully expected his children would hate Beth.

Which is exactly what happened. Her three stepkids made

Beth's life "a living hell," and their father defended them with the mistaken idea that all problems began with Beth

Within five years Beth's confidence had eroded completely. Carl's belief that no stepmother could possibly have a redeeming feature had rubbed off on Beth, who felt she must be a bad person for having failed to save everyone. She had absorbed the idea that stepmothers were second rate and could hardly expect to be liked or respected. She blamed herself for conflicts with her stepchildren and was afraid to open her mouth in her own home. Still, she wanted to make the marriage work.

When supportive friends offered some positive thoughts about her contributions to the family, Beth began to see that nobody could change the situation but her. "I realized I was being a willing victim, that I needed to do something about it."

Beth began making requests for help and saying no when she didn't want to do something or if one of the kids behaved in a way she found unacceptable. "I also knew we'd have to get some professional help," Beth admitted, "so we sought out a therapist. We discussed Carl's stepmother in one of our sessions recently, and I'm hoping his attitude toward me as a stepmom is going to change."

Stepmothers need to unearth where negative beliefs about stepmothers and stepmotherhood come from. Some women have unpleasant memories of a stepparent or might have heard horror stories from friends, from a mate, from relatives, or simply from fiction. If there is a person in your circle who is down on stepmoms, you should correct them pronto or, if that doesn't work, avoid them—you need to surround yourself with as many positive people as you can.

More than a few stepmothers said that people they meet—at parties, in business, in the supermarket—seem disconcerted when they mention they are stepmothers. Said Emma, stepmom of eight-year-old twins, "I feel ill at ease sometimes when I describe the twins as my stepkids. People either stare at me blankly or change the subject. I've never heard 'how nice' from anyone!"

Stepmothers interpret this kind of reaction as rejection, or feel devalued by it. Several said they found it easier to hide the fact of their stepchildren or even to let people think their stepchildren were their own, than to explain their personal situation to relative strangers.

Sometimes stepchildren would rather avoid the name "step" as well—in one case, for a surprising and deeply affecting reason. When Sheena was out and about with her two daughters and stepdaughter, people often assumed she was the mother of all three girls. Valerie, Sheena's stepdaughter, was always quick to deny this to strangers, explaining that Sheena was her "aunt."

Because of Valerie's assertion, Sheena was careful never to describe Valerie as her stepdaughter in her presence, as she didn't want to upset the sensitive and troubled young girl. But in time Sheena wearied of the subterfuge and decided to have a talk with Valerie, who was more than willing to explain. The youngster thought the prefix "step" had something to do with "stepping away from," so if Sheena was her "stepmother," it meant she could "step away" and leave Valerie and her dad. Three years earlier, Valerie's biological mother had walked out on them, and the child was fearful of another abandonment. In Valerie's mind, an "aunt" was not likely to disappear. Said Sheena, "It just broke my heart. But I was so relieved, especially since it was so simple to assure Valerie that I had no intention of going anywhere, ever, that I loved her and her dad very much."

The discussion between stepmother and stepdaughter restored Valerie's confidence in herself and in Sheena's commitment to her as another parent. "I'm just beginning now to talk with her about why her mother left, because it's something her dad hasn't been able to do," Sheena explained. "She's starting to deal with it. Now Valerie proudly tells people that I'm her stepmom."

A Fair-er Tale

Likely as not, most people have heard only one side of the story when it comes to stepmothers. Because it is so easy to sympathize with a stepchild and the stories he/she tells, most people don't take the trouble to hear the stepmother's point of view or even realize she has one. If you've absorbed this stance, it's helpful to recognize it.

As an illuminating exercise, we've conducted an imaginary interview with Cinderella's stepmother. Bet you don't even know her name. That's because she doesn't have one. Apparently, the authors of this tale (there are different versions in a number of cultures) thought she didn't deserve a name, never mind a hearing of her experience with her famous stepdaughter. We'll call her Gertrude.

Author's Note: *At the hour of my appointed visit to interview Gertrude at her home, I was pleasantly surprised that, despite her terrible reputation, she was a gracious, intelligent and attractive hostess, resembling none of the visual or verbal renditions of Cinderella's stepmother.*

PKN (PERDITA KIRKNESS NORWOOD): Gertrude, we're trying to help women make an easier transition into stepmotherhood by sharing what others have learned. . . .

TRUDI: Oh, please, Perdita, call me Trudi. All my friends know me by that name. I'm so happy to be asked for my input. Normally all people want to hear about is how Cinderella is feeling.

PKN: I know you have two daughters by a previous marriage. How did your first marriage end?

TRUDI: My first husband, Frederick, died just after my second daughter, Drucilla, was born. I was a single mother for eighteen years before I met Charles, Cinderella's father. It was wonderful, finding him after all that time. And I was looking forward to meeting his adorable daughter, Cinderella, who was just fifteen.

PKN: How did you feel when you married Charles and became a stepmother to Cinderella?

TRUDI: I thought we'd all be so happy. I couldn't wait to make a nice home for Charles and all our girls, to bring stability and happiness into their lives. Charles and Cinderella had lived such an odd life since her mother died. They didn't relate well to each other, and he seemed to have very little time for her, being so busy with his job. But together, there seemed no limit to what we could achieve.

PKN: Did you or Charles or the girls have any preparation for life in a stepfamily?

TRUDI: Preparation? It never entered our minds! I believed everything would be perfect. I wanted to treat Cinderella to some new, pretty clothes—she's such a beautiful girl, but for some reason she was wearing raggedy dresses that were too small. And I was determined to get some good food into her— she was so thin and drawn. It seemed to me she needed feeding and lot of loving. I knew the marriage was going to be hardest for Cinderella, but I thought once we got past the initial settling in, she'd want to get to know us.

PKN: It didn't work out that way?

TRUDI: Cinderella hated the three of us from the beginning. I can understand how difficult it was, suddenly having two older stepsisters and a stepmother around. She felt outnumbered, I think, because her father was away so much. Cinderella was used to keeping house and seemed to want to continue that way. She had no interest in the pretty dresses I bought her—wouldn't even try them on. She shuts herself up in the kitchen and sits and cries in a corner about how unhappy she is. Sometimes she visits her mother's grave three times a day— it's such an unhealthy existence for a child.

PKN: How do your daughters feel about what's happening in your home?

TRUDI: I explained to the girls how difficult it was for Cinderella to accept all these changes in her life so soon after her mother's death. I think they have been incredibly good, considering how hostile she is toward them. She taunts them and calls them "ugly." It's true—my girls aren't great beauties like their stepsister—but I wish Cinderella wouldn't hurt their feelings.

PKN: Have you tried talking to her?

TRUDI: Of course, but she just screams, "You're not my mother!" and slams her door in my face. But that's not all.

She tells everyone that we mistreat her. And people believe her—they see this unhappy and, I suspect, bulimic waif dressed in ash-covered rags, going back and forth to the cemetery. No wonder they think we're mistreating her—I would probably think so, too, without knowing what's really going on—but it's all over town that I'm abusing my stepdaughter. I wouldn't be surprised if it appeared in *print* one of these days—that's how bad the gossip is! Oh, Perdita, I never thought it would be like this!

PKN: Have you asked Charles to speak with his daughter?

TRUDI: Oh, my, yes. But he's never around, so he feels we must not be trying hard enough with her. He says an adult woman should be able to handle a fifteen-year-old child. I'm beginning to think he's right. I'm a terrible failure, not being able to help her. And worst of all, I'm starting to dislike her, and I feel so guilty about that. It's having a bad effect on my marriage—our sex life is nonexistent because of the tension in the house, and my girls are becoming depressed too. I just . . . I just don't see a resolution. . . . I wish Charles and Cinderella could see that I'm trying my best. I'm . . . I'm ready to give up. . . .

Author's Note: *At this point Trudi burst into tears. I passed the box of tissues I always carry and gave up asking any more questions. As she talked through the evening, I gently reminded her to care for her own health and well-being before tackling relationships, which take a long time to develop in a stepfamily.*

Questionnaire

1. Do you believe your parents' relationship was a love match? Did they snatch romantic evenings together, leaving you and your siblings with a baby sitter? Can you look back happily at the life they had together? What are some of the qualities of your parents marriage you would like to repeat in your own?

2. What are some of the qualities in your parents' relationship you'd like to avoid? *dads violence* *on/off*
moms depression & distance

3. How did you get along with your siblings? Consider your birth order and how that has influenced your approach to life. Were you an independent firstborn or an only child? A flexible <u>middle</u> child or the attention-grabbing baby of the family? What traits do you recognize that flow from your place in the family? How are these traits helpful or unhelpful to you? *accommodating middle* *— rebelled vs overbearing sister*

* — very successful older sis to Chris

4. How would you characterize your relationship with your parents (e.g., easygoing, closeknit, strict)? Were you able to discuss anything on your mind with them?

5. Was your childhood a stable, secure one, or did your parents argue or fight? What effect did this atmosphere have on you? *cant bear fighting*

6. If your parents divorced, what effect did the breakup have on you? If either parent remarried, what was your reaction to this? If you were part of a stepfamily, what are the overriding emotions and memories that come to mind? *horror, discomfort, loss*

7. Describe your stepparent. If you had a stepmother, did you like her? Why or why not? Were you and your brothers and sisters mean to her?

8. Write down any points you consider important about the relationships within and behavior of members of your childhood stepfamily. Did you have stepbrothers or stepsisters? How did you relate to them? Are they still in your life? Do you think of them as friends? What were the turning points in your relationship?

9. Have there been other divorces/remarriages in your family? Note the effect your <u>siblings'</u> marriages have had on you, what you've learned, for better or worse.

10. Think about and list the major events in your childhood, going as far back as you can remember. Are these mostly good memories of a happy childhood? Or was it an ordeal you are relieved to have left behind? If so, why?

11. Did your mother work outside the home? By choice or out of necessity? Do you know her feelings about balancing work and family? Was she there for you when you returned from school? Did this influence how you feel about women with children working?

12. What is your relationship now with your parents, if they are still alive? With your siblings and their in-laws, if they have married?

13. If you have already been married, at what age did you marry? Was it happy in the early days? What went wrong? Was it your husband's first or second marriage? If his second, were there stepchildren? (In this case you're an experienced stepmother!) What did you learn from this experience?

14. If not part of one, did you know any stepfamilies? What were your feelings about the children in this family? Did you envy them all the adult attention they were receiving, with the two sets of parents and "extra" grandparents, aunts, and uncles? Were you sorry that either one of their parents, who had not remarried, seemed lonely? *mom*

15. What have been your beliefs and attitudes about stepmotherhood? Are they the same now? If not, how have your views changed? *I could be a better one!*

ↄⱨↄ
Action Box

- Decide upon a way to present yourself to the world with pride so you will never be caught off-guard and made to feel inferior by an inquiring neighbor or a nosy co-worker. Practice introducing yourself (to the mirror, if necessary): "I'm John's wife, and stepmother to his two daughters" or "I met John a couple of years after his wife died [after his divorce], and we married last year. I'm becoming very fond of his daughters." Say whatever you are comfortable with, positively and with confidence.

- Consider your previous marriage in terms of unresolved issues. Try to list these. What steps can you take toward resolution before you take on your new role? If you have children, help them do the same.

- If you know a stepmother or have heard of one among your acquaintances, try to seek her out. Ask her if she would be willing to discuss stepmotherhood with you, since you are considering becoming one, or are already one, and would appreciate any thoughts or suggestions. We can say with virtual certainty that she would welcome this overture.

CHAPTER 3

Great Expectations: Being Realistic without Becoming Disillusioned

One of the most irritating and ironic rejoinders stepmothers hear, after expressing amazement at how complicated life has suddenly become, is "Well, you knew what you were getting into when you married him, *didn't* you?"

Of course you didn't, unless you're psychic or are one of the extremely rare stepmothers who researched what their new life would entail or were able to get straightforward, comprehensive advice from another stepmother.

Innocence prevails. Stepmothers aren't prepared for marriage to a man with children because they don't know they *need* to be prepared. Before her wedding and in the early stages of stepmotherhood, a woman is unaware that her life will bear little resemblance to that of her sister or her friend who is marrying a child-free man.

The differences seem obvious, but in the hazy glow of love, unless problems have already emerged, a stepmom's expectations are legion: "I thought we would all pull together;" "I thought the children would be so happy for us;" "I thought we'd be a big, happy family."

Only in retrospect do women realize that many of their ideas about stepmotherhood are unfounded, ill-advised, or downright wrong. Virtually every woman we interviewed agreed she had been naive about what stepmotherhood would entail. Many talked about the fun they expected to have with their husband's children. Several thought it would be easy being a stepmother. Not one had any doubts prior to her marriage about her ability to handle what she *expected* her circumstances would be. Conversely, most were able to acknowledge the things they did that were helpful and worthwhile—the insights and advice they wished to pass on to the next generation of stepmothers.

In this chapter we'll evaluate some common misconceptions women have about stepmotherhood, offer more realistic perspectives from veteran stepmoms, and discuss how to shape a role that works for you in your stepfamily.

The Things We Accept . . .

Throughout this book we are trying to be upbeat and very positive. Stepmotherhood is a difficult role, and you need a positive outlook. But a solid grounding in reality is vital. This knowledge is a constructive building block for your future and the future of your successful stepfamily. Make up your mind that you're going to *demolish* the dire statistics for second and third marriages. We must look at some negative issues, but we'll do so quickly and move on. The good news is that knowing the bad news means you can take positive action to prevent years of confusion, distress, and trouble and, ultimately, another broken marriage:

- You are battling statistics that, according to the Stepfamily Association of America, show that at least sixty percent of second and subsequent marriages end in divorce. Bottom line: you, personally, have at best a forty percent chance that your marriage will last.

- As a stepmother, you face a new family life where you will be occupying a position lost by your predecessor through death, divorce, or abandonment. All three states of loss have repercussions for a stepmother stepping into the breach.

- You have no time to enjoy a honeymoon period like other

brides, because your husband's children become an essential part of your life starting on the day of your marriage.

• You have to accept the fact of your husband's children, whether or not your would have preferred otherwise, and develop a workable relationship with them (discussed in Part 2.)

• There will always be another woman in your marriage— your husband's ex-wife, your stepchildren's mother. You will have to come to terms with her, whether she is alive or deceased.

• You must actively spurn ingrained, negative images of step-mother myths, fairy tales, and cultural prejudices.

All Dressed in White

Though both are newlyweds, the experience of a child-free bride and a stepmother bride are worlds apart.

If she selects a child-free man, on her wedding day a woman becomes a wife, a marital partner—a thoroughly positive role. Her wedding, whatever its size, is a joyful occasion. She usually has time to savor this exciting new period in her life, to have a relaxed, intimate honeymoon, to experiment with her new identity and grow into it. In normal circumstances she experiences the goodwill of her family and friends. Her parents are excited about the potential for grandchildren, and when she becomes pregnant, there is more celebration. Attention, gifts, praise, help, support, guidance, and love are showered upon her.

The newlywed stepmother's marriage often begins quite differently. The wedding is usually less grand—her husband might still be paying support to a first family. Her family and friends may feel she could have "done better" than saddle herself with someone else's children, and her stepchildren might be sad or resentful that Dad is getting married to a woman who is not their mother: the celebration is not entirely joyous.

A bride who instantly becomes a stepmother to young children is denied that precious, romantic time during which she has her new husband all to herself. In fact, the honeymoon may be a rushed one-nighter at a local hotel, with her new responsibilities starting the next day. His kids might even accompany the new couple. The stepmother is assured that when there is more time, she'll get the wedding trip she deserves, or when there's more money, maybe she'll be able to have a baby of her own. In the meantime, she's a stepmom!

For a bride on her second time around, all the "trimmings" of a first wedding might not be important. But for the woman whose first marriage takes her into a stepfamily, it can be a discouraging start. Not allowing her disappointment to show, however, she will start out smiling, hoping everyone will like and accept her. Her childhood dream of a big white wedding has assumed far less importance than the immediate needs of her stepfamily. "Caution" becomes her prevailing guideline, lest she upset someone.

Sound familiar?

Why Are You Doing It?

Given this daunting scenario and the above list of "things we must accept," why would any woman in her right mind consider joining the ranks of stepmother? Besides the fact that she's fallen in love, which blinds her to the potential challenges she might face, we found two other common reasons:

- To compensate for a lack of biological children, stepmotherhood seems like a good alternative.

- To save a group of hurting, disappointed people and restore happiness to their lives.

At thirty-eight years old, Suzy felt more than ready to settle down, though she worried that she might have waited too

> To have a partner who I know is already a great dad.

long to have a child. When she met Doug, the man of her dreams and father of three, the prospect of an instant family thrilled her. Doug had an adorable ten-year-old son, Jason, who lived with him, and two daughters, Daisy, twelve and Lara, fourteen who visited their dad on weekends under a joint-custody arrangement. Suzy thought it was perfect—all she needed was a baby of her own to complete her ideal family. Doug agreed they should try to conceive as soon as possible.

Suzy considered Doug's love sufficient reward for any problems that might come up. What did it matter that Doug's first wife was a little "uncooperative," as he put it, or that he hadn't been able to afford a vacation for six years, due to substantial support payments? She believed love would resolve everything. Anyway, she had a well-paying job herself.

That was the extent of Suzy's preparation prior to marriage. She concentrated on her wedding plans, paid for by her parents with a loan taken out to cover the cost.

Three years later, while her parents are still paying off the loan, Suzy is divorced. Shortly after she had decided to leave Doug, she said, "I just didn't realize it would be like this. The girls hated me. Whatever I did wasn't good enough. Doug always took their side, and it was just an impossible situation." Suzy recalled, "Whenever I mentioned some of the problems I was having, I can't tell you how many times people said to me, 'Oh, well, you knew what you were getting into.' But I didn't. I had absolutely no idea."

Julie was in the "I'm going to save them" category of prospective stepmoms. A self-sufficient twenty-eight-year-old corporate secretary, Julie realized she would need time to adjust when she learned that Philip, her husband-to-be, expected her to be an instant caretaker of his two children, aged ten and eight. Philip had lost his wife to cancer three years earlier; father and kids were still traumatized. Julie was quite serious when she asked her boss for "maternity" leave to make the transition from single go-getter to married go-getter/stepmom. When her request for maternity leave was refused she decided to wing it and hope for the best.

Julie attributes the fast failure of her marriage to lack of preparation. Julie was little more than an acquaintance to Philip's children and had no clue what being a stepmom would mean, while Philip assumed Julie would automatically know what to do. "I was married on a Saturday, and we took a perfect week together in the Caribbean while Philip's mom took the kids," Julie told us. "I moved in the following Sunday and went back to my office on Monday. No time was spent bringing order to a house overwhelmed with our combined possessions, organizing routines—or even stocking the refrigerator!

"We had no plan whatsoever—I think we just let ourselves get 'dumbed out' by the romance of the wedding and our honeymoon. By the middle of my second week as a married woman, I was wondering what in hell had hit me. I realized we should have discussed in detail what raising kids was about before the wedding. We disagreed about everything and muddled through the year with sulking, difficult children who I barely had time to talk with, much less 'save.' At the end of an awful year, I couldn't wait to get out."

From Fiction to Real Life

You certainly knew your lover had kids. You might even have known a few facts about the family before you married. But before you can fulfill your personal definition of who and what a stepmother is—your role—you have to start out understanding what is achievable. Let's look at some common expectations stepmothers have and then consider them in a more realistic way:

Expectation: "All our children, biological and step, will be as pleased and excited about our new marriage as my husband and I are."

Real Life: This is usually not the case, stepmothers report. The children have no choice about the marriage or who will become their stepparent. Depending on how happy and secure they are about their own lives, and whether they're children, teens, or adults, they may feel anger, resentment, anxiety, or sadness about this enormous change. Now it's final—Dad really *isn't* going to get back together with Mom. You are in love, your husband is in love, but it is unrealistic to expect your children or his children to feel the same way.

Expectation: "Everyone in my new stepfamily will welcome me, because I'm a nice, good person who wants the best for them and will do all I can to make this new life work for everyone."
Real Life: Quite frankly, some stepfamily members might not even like you for quite some time, if at all. You might not like them to start with, either. This is normal. (See number 9 of "Stepmom's Quick Primer.") Understand these negative feelings, and accept them as reasonable human reactions. Strive simply to establish an environment of respect and consideration that forms a basis for stronger feelings to develop later. Don't waste time and energy being disappointed when you discover there is no red carpet to welcome you—just don't expect it to be there.

Expectation: We'll be one big, happy family."
Real Life: Moving from negative to positive feelings within a stepfamily takes time, usually a long time. (More about this in part 2.) Recognize that everyone needs a period of peace to make their own adjustments at their own pace. Keep the lines of communication open, and be willing to discuss feelings, opinions, and fears—even those you may not want to hear about—with your children and stepchildren.

Expectation: Everyone will soon forget their previous lives and be eager to start fresh."
Real Life: People are shaped by their past. Members of the stepfamily have different backgrounds, and they need to be gradually incorporated into the new family, each person sharing and benefiting from the diversity of experience, beliefs, and ideas. You can enjoy your new life while preserving what's positive and familiar to each family member. You won't forget your previous life, so don't expect that anyone else will.

Expectation: "I won't make the mistakes I made in my previous marriage(s)."
Real Life: It is human to make mistakes. This new marriage and family will be neither better nor worse than your previous family or families; it will simply be different. Accept your inevitable mistakes as part of growing, be sure to learn from them, and move on.

Expectation: "I will be a mother to my stepchildren."
Real Life: A mother is a very special person; nobody, however well-intentioned, can replace her. It is unrealistic for you to attempt this. You need to learn to function under another title, or without one at all. Why not "freelance," using your own name?

Expectation: "I will be the perfect stepmother" or "I will be a better 'mother' to my stepkids than their biological [or adoptive] mother."
Real Life: Both these thoughts, variations on the previous one, are quite common among stepmothers. Neither is realistic. Nobody is perfect, certainly not a stepmother faced with a multitude of challenges. Anyway, nobody really knows what a perfect stepmother is. Remember, this is not a competition—*especially* not against your stepchildren's mother. Your aim is to be yourself, comfortable in your role.

Expectation: "Because I'll be a part-time stepmother—my husband shares custody of his kids with his ex-wife—it will be easier for me than if I were a full-time stepmother."
Real Life: The issues a part-time stepmother faces are not necessarily easier, just different. One advantage is that you will have some down time when the kids are with their mom, which you can use to regroup and catch up with your husband. You get the opportunity to review how you're doing, what you can do differently. But you lose continuity in your relationships with your stepkids, and everyone has to learn how to handle the sometimes painful transition time when the kids are leaving or returning to your home.

Expectation: "Becoming a stepmother after the death of my stepchildren's mother will be less stressful than having their biological mother around after a divorce."

Real Life: Again, not necessarily. Handling the aftermath of death and grieving or working with an ex-wife and the ramifications of divorce each presents its own stresses for the stepmother.

Expectation: "Showing our kids how much we love each other will help resolve any problems."
Real Life: Your love for each other may do nothing more than make the kids uncomfortable, particularly if you display it too often by kissing and hugging when they are around. You cannot count on a display of affection to have a positive influence on the children.

What Do They Expect from Me?

Erica De'Ath, former chief executive of the National Stepfamily Association in London, England sums up the ambivalence people have about the stepmother's role: "She's seen as brave for attempting the job but as an intruder by people who don't like her style. And she isn't given time to settle into her position—a position which nobody understands anyway."

While there's no official job description for a stepmother, most of the members of your new family, both close and extended relatives, will have some ideas, perhaps at odds with your own, about how you should behave, what your responsibilities are (and are not), and even what's off-limits to you. Some may interpret your actions as competing for love and attention, at cross purposes with the rights of the biological mother, or even as interference by someone who doesn't belong.

Many stepmothers initially believe that with charm and grace they can win everyone over in the space of a month or two. (We tried that too!) Much has been written that reinforces that belief—that by understanding adolescent angst or humoring the moods of her stepchildren and working to be a "good" stepmother (a variation of the "good girl" tag), we will eventually be loved.

But veteran stepmothers have learned it's illogical to spend their time attempting to fulfill the expectations of others in the hope of matching some imagined ideal. Remember what the important older woman in your life used to say when you were a teenager grappling with new, adult relationships? Be yourself. It's still good advice, but with a grown-up twist: You don't have to try to buy your stepchildren's love or respect. They'll know (and you'll know) you're just faking it.

It simply makes more sense for you to be comfortable living your life the way you believe it should be lived. As we discussed in chapter 1, you do not need to change your personality, likes and dislikes, or goals for other people. You are perfectly fine the way you are, unless *you* have decided you need self-improvement to suit yourself. Start out behaving in a way that is most natural to you, and accept that sometimes others will approve, sometimes not. This is truly all you can realistically expect of yourself, and all others can reasonably anticipate.

Yours Is the Pivotal Role

You, as a stepmother, have the central role in building the new stepfamily relationships. This sounds obvious, but time and again stepmothers have made themselves bystanders in their own lives. How? By believing they need to stay out of what happens between stepchildren and Dad and, generally, avoid stepping on toes. That, however, is the do-it-yourself plan to becoming a doormat!

At the most basic level, you will be the female head of your household. Depending on the age of your stepchildren, the number of people in your household, and whether or not you also have children of your own, your role may involve many of the practical duties of motherhood—anything from carpooling and helping with homework to setting up standards of behavior in your home. Within this framework, theoretically you're free to develop the details as you think best.

Assume your role as female head of your household right away, in conjunction with your mate. On a purely practical

level, you are and should think of yourself as a full-
member of your stepfamily immediately. Do not grin an~ ~~...~
it if you don't like what's going on in your home—it isn't fair
to you and will do nothing to build genuine relationships,
which take a great deal of time. Stepmothers who are "old
hands" emphasize that unless you project yourself as a player,
and pretty quickly, someone else is going to decide how much
influence you have.

No woman should be expected to have no say in running
her own home, along with all the new and demanding situations she faces. If you allow others to determine your function
in the early stages of stepmotherhood, later on it can be difficult to claim your position, to collect the acknowledgment and
respect you and your role deserve. It's demoralizing to let life
in your household go on around you, over you, under you,
through you, determined by other family members, with little
or no reference to you.

If you already find yourself in this very common situation,
however, one woman's story may inspire you:

Janis, who lives in a tiny village in upstate New York, told
how she was relegated very quickly to the post of unpaid maid
when she became part-time stepmother to her husband's brood
of five children, all under the age of seven at the time of her
marriage: "I wanted to be the perfect stepmother. The children
were so small that I had to do everything for them when they
were with us. But it continued as they grew older—it was just
assumed that I would do all the housework, shopping, cooking, and cleaning up after meals. I just allowed it to happen,
instead of taking control and organizing some sort of
delegation.

"One day I just went on strike and didn't do anything.
There was no dinner, the beds were unmade, no cleaning up—
nothing. Everyone was stunned as I sat in the living room,
reading *Cosmo*. When my husband asked what was going on,
I calmly explained that I was tired and that I could not and
would not do all the work all the time anymore!

"After their initial shock, we sat down together and worked
out a schedule for everyone to do their bit. Now they all pitch

in. And I ask for help. There's a completely new atmosphere. Even their mother is excited about it. They're helping her out too."

You deserve respect and support from the start. Make sure you insist on that. Remember, a strong role model is a source of strength to your stepfamily. By your example, you can provide a sense of direction, continuity, security, and, most of all, pride in overcoming adversity. Love and affirmation hopefully will blossom in time.

The "Perfect" Stepmother

Many stepmothers are determined to be "perfect," believing that there are people waiting for them to fail. While there's no doubt you will be observed fairly closely, you need to realize that people's agendas aren't always so bleak.

Tara, who married when she was a "young and naive" twenty-five, found the scrutiny of her new family unbearable. Her husband, Ben, had two older sisters, who were very much involved in their "little" brother's life. When Ben was married, for the second time, to Tara, the woman who would be stepmother to their adored six-year-old nephew, the sisters lost no time in asking a torrent of questions.

Tara felt her sisters-in-law meant no harm, but she believed they watched everything she did, what she ate (and fed their nephew), how she dressed, what she said, where she shopped, what she paid for everything, and on top of that *why* she did what she did. His parents and friends seemed equally rapacious for information.

"I felt turned inside out," Tara recalled. "I felt I had to do everything perfectly, or someone would notice. It was like living in a fishbowl."

One day Tara just broke down and cried. "I was so tired. I had come in from the supermarket in the pouring rain, and I found Ben's older sister, who was babysitting for me, staring at the hem of my dripping raincoat. Sure enough, about a two-inch section had come unstitched, and she had spotted it. I burst into tears and told her I couldn't take this scrutiny anymore. She was so kind, she hadn't realized what she and her sister were doing. They were just curious about how I was going to run things, which in their view was far better than Ben's ex. They apologized, and we are very good friends now."

A Soccer Stepmom—Who, Me?

From our discussions in previous chapters, you will already be forming some ideas about what you're willing to do and what you feel you cannot possibly handle, regardless of other people's expectations of you. Perhaps your ten-year-old stepson is on the local soccer team and plays every Saturday afternoon. You might have an abiding dislike for the great outdoors, particularly the cold and muddy great outdoors, and while you want to show support, you know quite well that sitting for endless hours on hard, creaky bleachers is beyond your comfort zone.

Address situations like this in a light, positive way. "I can't do this, but I will do that" is generally a good tradeoff. Simply explain, "Dad and Aunt Felicia will watch you play on Saturdays, and when you get home, we'll all have hot chocolate, and you can tell me about the game." Your Saturday-afternoon hot chocolate session might even become a cherished stepfamily tradition.

Likewise, if, like Vivian, you like to spend Sunday morning in your robe, reading the paper with a cup of hot coffee and a fresh bagel, it might be hard to join in your stepfamily's routine of early-morning church and a huge breakfast at the diner afterward. Vivian decided to explain to her stepfamily that while her spiritual beliefs did not include a formal service in church, she would love to drive over to the diner and meet everyone for breakfast afterward.

Remarked Vivian, "I felt pretty good about the whole thing, because I took the initiative, expressed my position, and encouraged a good, positive experience for my husband and his kids in the same breath."

You'll probably be deciding how involved you want to be in various activities and plans on a gradual basis, but be proactive as early as possible. It would be pointless for you to go reluctantly to the soccer match, become cold and resentful, and make everyone miserable by complaining that you feel lousy. Or, if you're a soccer lover and would resent being left at home when everyone else is going to the game, make that clear too: "I really want to see how well you play."

Preserving Memories; Ultrasensitive Expectations

Irene knew of the car accident in which her husband's first wife had died, four years before. She realized the date of the woman's death, July 2, couldn't be allowed to pass unnoticed, but neither did it have to obliterate the July 4 holiday for her stepfamily for the rest of their lives.

"The first year I was with my stepfamily, after marrying Bobby in March, I suggested a 'Remember Mom Day' on the Sunday of the July Fourth weekend," Irene explained. "I knew everyone would remember the anniversary of her death forever, but I thought it would be good if we openly recognized it in a special way."

Bobby agreed. Said Irene, "Our 'Remember Mom Day' starts with all of us going to church together. Then Bobby takes the children to visit their mother's grave, and they go to lunch afterward. That way they can reminisce about the good times they had with Mom and talk about her without feeling inhibited by me. While they're doing this, I usually go to see my own mother—quite frankly, the day really makes me appreciate how lucky I am to have her."

In the evening, Irene helps her stepchildren prepare one of their mom's favorite dinners, the way she used to make it. "Bobby appreciates my sensitivity to the family's memories, and I think the kids do, too, though they haven't actually told me so," she remarked. "Maybe someday they will. In any case, I believe this is part of what I need to do as their stepmother."

Playing Your Role: Open to Interpretation

Even as your revise your expectations of stepmotherhood, it's best to recognize that the role is one of the few in our culture for which there are no clear-cut guidelines. Having no role models means no one can be quite certain what's right or wrong, so you have plenty of leeway to perform as you see fit.

Stepmothers are dismayed to discover how generally poorly they are viewed and how resistant stepdaughters are to turn to them for support. In her book *Motherless Daughters* (Addison-Wesley, 1994), Hope Edelman discusses where daughters who have lost their mother to death turn to find female support and comfort. (No time frame is provided.) "Of the ninety-seven women who said they found one or more mother substitutes, thirty-three percent named an aunt; thirty percent, a grandmother; thirteen percent, a sister; thirteen percent, a teacher; twelve percent, friends; ten percent, a coworker; and the rest cited, in descending order, neighbors, friends' mothers, mothers-in-law, *stepmothers,* husbands, lovers, and cousins. Some women named more than one mother substitute. The largest group, thirty-seven percent, said they hadn't found anyone."

That kind of statistical data is disappointing to stepmoms, but we believe the preparation and time you're committing to now will help you build this traditionally unrecognized role into one that is visible and positive for you and to others. Because you're in the early stages of forming your ideas about your role, keep in the back of your mind the fact that you still have much to learn about your stepfamily, our focus in part 2.

The Things We Can't Control . . .

In spite of what we know and what statistics tell us, women who marry men with children persist in underestimating the limitations stepmotherhood places on their lives. Be aware of the outside influences you can't control—it is essential to defining your role realistically. Whether you're a corporate executive handling a multimillion-dollar budget or a stay-at-home mom with primary responsibilities for children, as a stepmother you will find that others can claim the right to make decisions that affect your life with little or no input from you.

This can be awfully disconcerting if it is unanticipated. If your husband is divorced, for example, your life may be regulated by a mandate from the courts that determines how often and for how long your stepchildren will live with you, and where you may travel with them. Your stepchildren's biological mother, grandparents, and other family members may also claim rights, both practical and emotional, that will impact your schedule, your plans, and your developing relationship with your stepchildren.

Suppose, for example, that for the past eight years you have spent your birthday at a romantic getaway cabin with the man you love, pretending to be Adam and Eve. This, to you, is the *only* way to turn a year older—communing with nature. But if you're a stepmom, and your birthday happens to fall on your husband's custody day, you're going to be getting the kids the day you turn forty—it won't be the Garden of Eden this year.

. . . And the Things We Can Change

You may be living with a court-ordered visitation schedule— something you have to accept—but you don't have to go along with trading days, the all-too-common practice that goes on to suit other people's convenience. Stepmothers, for example, report that ex-wives often try to change a set-in-concrete visitation schedule, especially if they have a new lover who isn't particularly interested in children. If your stepchildren's mother has a full-time job and you don't, there might also be the assumption that her time is more valuable than yours. Your best bet, as you develop your role, is to determine which factors are out of your hands and which are under your discretion and act accordingly.

We can change other, more global things too. It's a fact as a stepmother, you are facing some of the most negative connotations the world has ever dumped on a particular social identity. Reject these out of hand starting now. Your task is to dismantle the myths, not just overcome them as if they were once true. You do not deserve to be viewed so poorly. *There should be no doubt in your mind that accepting the task of helping to nurture another woman's children is something to be proud of.* Let the magic of that truth begin with you—and share it with others. *extremely noble undertaking*

. . . By Any Other Name?

Virtually any other prefix for mother—biological, adoptive, or foster—inspires feelings of support, approval, or praise from others and is usually not a lonely venture. Acquiring a child through the foster-care system or adopting a child is normally a joint decision of husband and wife. Having a biological child is usually welcomed as an expression of a couple's union. In all three cases, both husband and wife spend their waiting time together, in happy anticipation and preparation.

You are considering or have already made a different choice—to marry your lover who happened to have children. This decision, and the accompanying title, presents different challenges from those of adoptive, biological, or foster mothers. Your husband already knows his children well—they share thousands of memories and intimate moments. You are the lone unknown factor, as well as the one who has the least information about the family. You may feel unable to express concerns or doubts or raise questions for fear of seeming negative. Empathy and support are reserved for your husband's children because of the trauma (divorce, death, or abandonment of their mother) that has befallen them. Even more difficult, friends and family members think, the poor kids are "getting" a stepmother through no choice or fault of their own. Everybody, including the extended family and friends, feels sorry for them.

Many stepmothers feel that if they had been able to escape the tag "stepmother," their task would have been easier, that the negative implications of the title might be avoided by using another term. The French word for stepmother, which replaced the previous, pejorative term *maratre,* is *belle-mere,* meaning "fine mother" or "beautiful mother." The word is also used to refer to a mother-in-law.

Several of our focus groups, at which stepmoms met to discuss one specific issue, such as a revised title for their role, have tried to come up with alternative descriptions—we had a lot of fun trying, but not much success. "Dad's wife" was considered by some too dismissive. "Friend" was a possibility, but friends usually select one another's company on a voluntary basis, whereas a stepmother and stepchildren are brought together by a third person, their dad, your husband. "Advisor," "mentor," and "confidante" were acceptable but uninspiring.

In one group someone suggested "fairy godmother." We laughed at first—it sounded corny—but then we started to think about the effect that term could have on a group of children presented with the proposition of their dad marrying a magical, kind wisewoman able to grant wishes and bring all sorts of good luck to her stepchildren. As fairy godmother, a woman would enter her role with everyone, including her, in a very different frame of mind. Children would be considered lucky and would be envied by their friends. Perhaps a little farfetched . . . and yet?

Beyond Mother

A very small percentage of the stepmothers we interviewed made it clear prior to their marriage that they were not interested in children and wanted as little to do with them as possible. One or two of these arrangements turned out to be very successful, but the overwhelming majority of women initially liked the idea of being a mother to their husband's children in some fashion.

The word *mother* has very definite associations for each of us, based on mothers we have known, perhaps as a mother to our own children, and of course in our relationship with our own mother. Abandoning the idea of being a mother to stepchildren has proved to be the most difficult issue for some women to accept. Yet you must accept from the start that besides one or two rare exceptions, detailed on page 00, the role of their mother is already filled, whether she is alive, missing, or dead.

We cannot say this too emphatically: You are not your stepchildren's mother; you cannot be their mother; you should not expect to be their mother; you cannot replace their mother; you should not be encouraged to think you're supposed to be their mother. Unless you can acknowledge that the role of mother is off-limits, you will be setting yourself up for failure and much personal pain.

To help you understand why, consider some facts. The role of mother is idealized, even sacred. She gives birth to her children, can often conveniently time their births and holds complete jurisdiction over the way she raises them. She has the protection of her extended family, society in general, our legal system, and the school system. Woe to anyone who attempts to intrude on this powerful prerogative. She can treat her child well, or, if she is an abuser, the child can be removed from her care for protection but may be returned at her request solely on the basis of shared biology. However unfit she may be, the child belongs to her, and she has a legal right to custody. Social services will bend over backward to help rehabilitate an unfit mother so she can keep her child. Biology, rather than common sense or the well-being of the child, usually prevails.

The stepmother, on the other hand, especially if she marries a man with small children, will have many of the same nurturing and logistical responsibilities, but with little authority. As stepmother to teens, she will have to experience the normal turbulence of adolescence without having shared the more tender years with the children. With adult stepchildren, she must form a relationship whether or not there is anything in common and regardless of whether or not she likes them.

You can have a huge impact on the futures of your step-children, nurturing them, guiding their emotional lives, receiving love and devotion from them, but not under the title "mother." Some stepmothers who have found themselves filling in or covering up for a neglectful mother complain about not being able to claim the title of "mother." That's correct—the children already have, or had, one. Your role is as important, sometimes even more important in the case of a neglectful mother, but at the same time it's different, which is the reason you need to formulate your own, comfortable way of fulfilling it.

Having said that, we need to point out those exceptions to this emphatic advice. The first is the case when a woman marries a widower with a baby or small child who does not remember his/her biological mother, as discussed in chapter 8. The second exception is the case of a very needy stepchild whose biological mother may not be fulfilling her role or has egregiously deprived the child of nurturing. The third when your husband's ex-wife dies.

When Sarna married Gabriel, who was divorced from his alcoholic ex-wife, the mother of his daughter, Mikki, she was dismayed to find that Mikki wouldn't let her out of her sight. The little girl clung to Sarna and called her "Mommy" from day one. "She begged me to meet her at the school bus to show her friends she had a mom," said Sarna. "She referred to me as her mother to her teachers, to our neighbors, to anyone who would listen."

If you become a stepmother to a child who desperately wants you to be a mother to him or her and you are willing, then enjoy this role. But remember, this can only happen when the *child*, at whatever age, chooses it. Be aware also that the child can change his/her mind if the mother reappears to claim him/her—a possibly hurtful situation for you.

These exceptions are unusual. Our general advice stands: Don't consider yourself a mother; you are a stepmom. Nor should you be misled when, as your stepfamily evolves, you find that your stepkids refer to you and their dad as "my parents" when talking with their friends. You may even overhear a reference to "my mom" (meaning you)—and once in a while a stepchild may even call you "Mom." Frequently this means nothing more than that your stepchild is avoiding the necessity of explaining family relationships. It would be foolish for a stepmom to assume (that word again) her stepchild finally has come to consider her his mom.

Stepmothers who are unable or unwilling to differentiate themselves from "mother" prior to or early in their marriage report an extremely difficult period of adjustment. One young stepmother we met was truly distressed when her husband—who had endured a bitter divorce from his ex-wife, whom he thought was a bad mother—told her upon their engagement, "Now you'll be the mother they never had." In her heart she knew this was unrealistic, but she wasn't sure there was any alternative—what was a stepmother, after all, but another kind of mother?

The fact is a stepmother can be exactly who and what you want her to be. Free yourself from the implications of the word "mother." (Remember Eileen in our last chapter, who realized "stepmother" for her meant "big sister.")

Dawn had no intention of being "maternal" when she married Ted, a widower with two daughters, Elizabeth, ten and Paula, seven. A VIP in advertising, Dawn saw herself destined for even greater heights and viewed motherhood as an underachiever's alternative to a high-powered career.

Since she made a huge salary (almost twice Ted's), Dawn decided to play "Auntie Mame," the glamorous, world-at-her-fingertips role made famous by actress Rosalind Russell. Dawn was more than willing to indulge her stepdaughters financially—on her terms, at her convenience.

On a Saturday when she wasn't wining and dining a client, Dawn would take the girls on a whirlwind spending spree in New York City, at some of the most expensive addresses in town—she would buy them fabulous clothing at Bergdorf's, a pair of giant stuffed pandas at F. A. O. Schwarz, then rush via taxi to the Plaza Hotel for an outrageously extravagant lunch.

The girls adored her. They rarely saw their stepmom during the week, but on weekends when Dawn felt inclined, she

gave them her undivided attention. Soon, under Dawn's tute-
lage, the girls could easily relate to French waiters, uniformed
doormen, unpredictable taxi drivers, and polished salesladies.
It wasn't the kind of lifestyle Ted originally had planned for
his daughters, but he recognized that they and Dawn were
quite happy with this limited arrangement. Ted vowed that
his daughters would be given the best opportunities possible
for careers of their own that would pay as well as Dawn's—
they'd need them! Dawn was thrilled at her success with the
girls. She thoroughly enjoyed their company (and adoration)
and found herself wanting to increase the frequency of their
days out.

There are many ways to be a stepmother and many kinds
of stepmothers. Trust yourself—when you feel you are doing
a good job, contributing in your own way to the lives of your
stepchildren, you can consider yourself successful. Make a decision to do everything in your power to become part of the
success statistic.

∽∾∾

Questionnaire

1. Do you know any stepmothers? If so, have you discussed
   their experience with them? Was there a great difference
   between your perception of her experience and her actual
   experience? Detail.

2. Make a list of the characteristics and responsibilities you
   think a stepmother should have. *whatever she aspires to*

3. Make a list of what you expect from life with this stepfamily. In another column list what you think they expect of
   you. Are the lists complementary?

4. You've learned that you can't replace/be your stepchildren's
   mother. What are your feelings about that?

5. Are you aware of any constraints—time, legal, emotional,
   financial—affecting the role you wish to play as stepmom?
   What are they?

I feel I give them many things their mother doesn't

❦

Action Box

🍂 Review your own expectations of stepmotherhood, which may be similar to those we've listed earlier in this chapter. Do you have any other preconceived ideas about stepmotherhood? Are they realistic? If you don't know, challenge them with what you learned from this chapter, or find out by asking another stepmom questions. Begin a dialogue with your husband, children and stepchildren, and, if appropriate, your extended family members about the ways they would like you to become involved in their lives.

🍂 Open a discussion with biological and adoptive mothers you know about their view of stepmothers.

🍂 Discuss openly, and very soon after you decide to marry, the fact that you have no intention of replacing your stepkids' mother. Encourage stepchildren to question you about your role. Depending on their age and what they can understand, your explanation should be straightforward and simple: "You already have [or had] a mother. I am marrying your father, and together we will run this home we all live in." Or "You have a dad and a mom. I'm your stepmother and can be 'another parent' if you wish [and of course if you as the stepmother wish it too], but I know I cannot be your mother. I would really like it if we can become good friends."

provide — a reliable home, partnership w/ their dad, presence. I know I am having an effect but that they won't appreciate it for years.

    ❧ Review, for your own benefit, the positive qual-
       ities you bring to your stepfamily. (Don't forget
       to count your new ability to be objective!)
       Awareness of these contributions will boost
       your morale and confidence.

    ❧ Start a list of issues you believe you and your
       mate need to discuss concerning your role, and
       bring them up when you have a quiet mo-
       ment together.

When we first got together I heard so many negatives re Marcy as a mom from Paul, & the boys realizing she didn't keep her promises or pay attention to them at home. I am a maternal person & a rescuer, so I got into giving them what their mom didn't, for their sake & Paul's. I think she has improved & if Neil & Katie I don't really have time, And after all the rejection I lost my taste for it, I'd rather be their "fairy godmother" giving them slam-ups that I want to give, not the day to day thankless grind. I need my home to be clean & organized w/o working like a slave on it. I don't want to be their mother, I demand respect & politeness, &

PART 2

Relationships: Spheres of Influence

OVERVIEW

So much has been written about the effects of divorce and remarriage that the subject should probably have its own code in the Dewey decimal system. Even so, the only truly unanimous conclusion of researchers is that trying to regroup after a family breakup is difficult for everyone involved. Unless you have a particular interest in the studies of divorce and remarriage, the best means of understanding the new stepfamily you've joined is to conduct your own research about the people in it. That's where the real insights are.

Paul's support on this 100%.

How to Do Your Research

In Part 1, you had to challenge your own beliefs about what or who a stepmother is or should be. Was it a surprise? Now we'll use a similar approach to relationships. Thanks to TV talk shows, we're all amateur pop psychologists these days, but we're asking you to put all that aside.

Learn about the real people in your life. Make observations; with a fresh, objective eye, take note of what you like and what concerns you. Using this approach, it's easier to avoid the stereotypical tags that dictate how everyone is supposed to be interrelating. This research will also keep you from prematurely casting people in roles—the way people may wrongly, automatically cast you in a "wicked" stepmother role (tagging people unfairly is how a lot of trouble starts.) Don't depend on stereotypes of ex-wives, caricatures of mothers-in-law, or assumptions about your stepchildren for your information.

Simply make an effort to spend one-on-one time with each member of your stepfamily. Find out the facts; pay attention. Everyone is going to have a different perspective on this fragile step situation, and you should hear them out. You might not like some of it, either. But this is your chance to initiate your role as female head of the household by being available and open to all these points of view.

In the early stages of building relationships, you need a good supply of salt—a grain for every unthinking comment or unkind act perpetrated by anyone making his or her own adjustments to your arrival. Often children and other relations are reacting to your marriage to their father/son/brother/ex-husband/nephew/uncle and their personal feelings about the event, not to you personally.

Similarly, you are not expected to like everyone you're meeting now. Initially you may dislike one of your step-children, your mother-in-law, or your husband's sister. This is normal, and time will alter many feelings. Keep an open mind. Someone you think is going to be a great ally might turn out to be a source of friction in the future. The stepdaughter who is wary of you now may turn out to be one of your greatest friends.

Who's on First?

Initially, not having a standard for who's who and what's what in the stepfamily can cause vertigo in even the most level-headed among us. But having no "standard" means you and your husband have a wonderful opportunity to build a new family—in corporate parlance, a "zero-based" family. Good relationships develop among strangers (like those in your stepfamily) when we share information about ourselves, our memories and milestones, our interests and opinions—living day-to-day together through the mundane and the momentous.

In other families, where you have biological ties, you tend to have a clearer idea of what your position is, how to play your role, and how to relate to other members. In your new family, the kind of stepmother you want to be is up to you, a concept we've now discussed in depth. But remember, the other members of your stepfamily are facing the same task—no one is really sure in the early stages where he or she fits in. Once you're all living together, your oldest son, with his budding leadership qualities, might be stunned to find himself treated like a baby by his three older stepsisters, challenging his very identity as a person. Everyone's feeling a bit disoriented—yet another experience you all have in common. Use that point to open a sympathetic discussion and explore the rich possibilities.

Give-and-Take

Common sense and experience tell us relationships are based on give-and-take, although many family therapists suggest that the stepmother should remain the mature adult at all times, regardless of what other people do or say. Unrealistic expectations like those keep us from really getting to know one another. Better to relax, be yourself, and hopefully come to care about one another naturally—warts and all—even if it takes years. It usually does. But they can be very interesting years. Building relationships bit by bit, you may be pleasantly surprised to find that your twenty-one-year-old stepdaughter shares your passion for weekend antique hunting in the station wagon or that your ten-year-old stepson loves animals the way you do.

Common ground can get you through the bad patches you don't have control over too. For several years, while Eileen's husband was having leftover financial battles with his ex-wife, and the tension between the two families was most intense, Eileen and her adolescent stepson found an oasis of relief in their shared interest in books. Their ongoing literary finds were virtually their sole topic of conversation, lifting them above the animosity between the boy's parents and providing a foundation for a friendship that outlasted the tough times.

In Part 2 you'll be reviewing specific relationships and people—ex-spouses, children, extended relatives, and other people important to the stepfamily, including friends and neighbors. You'll learn about the stages of development all stepfamilies go through and why stepfamilies are not like biological families. This information will provide a context for the situations you and your stepfamily experience as you try to form your step relationships. Finally, we'll offer some tips about dealing with people you might find difficult to relate to.

CHAPTER 4

Your Stepfamily: A Family like No Other

The word *family* evokes immediate and intimate associations for us. Family is the faces and voices of parents, siblings, grandparents, cousins; celebrations and sorrows; the aromas of familiar recipes handed down; the photo albums you've seen a million times; the famous family stories told over and over again that never fail to provoke laughter among your own.

Family is bigger than you. When you marry, the circle widens—your husband's family becomes yours too. Marrying into a family encourages similar associations of commitment, loyalty, a sense of place and belonging with your in-laws, strengthened by the addition of blood ties—the children you and your spouse have together.

By the time we join our stepfamily, virtually all of us will already have been part of at least one family, a birth or adoptive family, sometimes called the family of origin. Prior to your marriage to a man with children, you might also have been a member of a second family as a wife and mother.

What Does a "Stepfamily" Look Like? Yours!

The stepfamily comprises adult heads of household, each of whom may bring to the union biological, adopted, foster, or even other stepchildren from a previous marriage or marriages. Add to this assortment of people the extended relatives of stepfamily members, and you have a veritable United Nations.

The step household can be a continually moving conveyor belt as children move in and out under custody arrangements. Sometimes it's hard for a parent to know who's at home (or who's supposed to be) at any given moment. On occasion the two parents might be alone, with the kids all at their second homes. Another time it might seem like summer camp, with a bevy of kids all vying for the bathroom. Since there's simply no standard for the life you're living as a stepmom, whatever you find acceptable and are comfortable with is fine.

The New American Family Album

Our culture tends to view the conventional biological family—the two-parent, 2.1 children configuration—as the model family lifestyle, though it is now less common than ever. According to the Stepfamily Association of America (SAA), more than half of Americans today have been, are now, or will eventually be in one or more step situations during their lives and that currently one out of three Americans is now a stepparent, a stepchild, a stepsibling, or some other member of a stepfamily. But Kay Pasley, chair of SAA's research committee, when discussing the stepfamily, admits: "Empirically, there are more unanswered questions than answered ones. We know so little in this area—it is such an open field of research and study."

Here's a sample of more startling facts about stepfamilies:

- About forty percent of all marriages are remarriages for one of the adults.

- One out of six children under the age of eighteen is a stepchild.

- If remarriage rates continue as they are now, thirty-five per-

cent of all children born now will live in a stepfamily household by the time they reach the age of eighteen

- There are 20.64 million stepparents in the nation. Of those,
  31.6 percent have stepchildren living in the household,
  while 68.4 percent have stepchildren living elsewhere.

Try to leave behind your old notions about stepfamilies—
much of the information about life in a stepfamily, quite
frankly, has come from sources who've never lived in one.
Many people believe that as long as there is love and nurturing, and the needs of all members are being met, no type of
family is necessarily better than another, and they live their
lives accordingly.

Don't Try to Mimic a Biological Family

It's especially important that you, as a new or potential stepmom, understand that your stepfamily doesn't (and can't) re-
semble the traditional biological family idealized in the fifties.
Yours is not a dysfunctional family trying valiantly to mimic
the way a healthy biological one functions.

A traditional family evolves gradually, with the heads of
household enjoying time alone together in the early days of
marriage. A mother and father have nine months to adjust
their priorities and lifestyle to accommodate their child and
form a intimate bond with their children even before their
births.

A stepfamily, you may already have found, doesn't automatically feel like "family," in the traditional sense. Beyond the
fact that a stepfamily is instant, without the benefit of a shared
family history, everyone in this group, including you, has different personal histories, memories, and old loyalties. Emotionally, it's a fragmented family. Some members may have strong
feelings about who their "real" family members are and take a
long time to adjust. There is a lack of bonding; each person
has a separate agenda or is involved in his own world, details
of which you, as a stepmom, may know little about.

Affection between steprelations, if present at all initially, is not unconditional, and there are widely varying degrees of love, even separate alliances, within the home. Some or all of the stepfamily members may be complete strangers living in the same house, members of two different households bound by various custody imperatives and visitation schedules. This is not a family pulling in the same direction, as a biological family usually does.

The stepfamily is like a biological family in one way, at least: the heads of household bear the responsibility of providing material necessities, care, emotional support, and guidance to the younger members—of creating a life together that benefits everyone in the family. The responsible adults also devise the standards that will guide how their home is run. If they are wise, they will encourage each member to feel a sense of belonging to the new family.

Stepfamily Complexity: Family Ties or Tied in Knots?

Take a look at the charts on the following pages. They're an interesting visual expression of how complex the stepfamily can be and of the number of personalities who can impact a stepmother's life.

Chart 1 shows the simplest stepfamily possible, where a woman marries a man with one child whose wife has died. There are three adults: a stepmother, her husband, and the husband's ex-wife, the mother of his single child. (We include the deceased previous wife because, as you'll see later, she has an enormous influence on those still living.) All three adults have two parents each, making three sets of grandparents for the child. Not included are the peripheral players in the new stepmon's life: her husband's siblings, friends, and more-distant relatives.

Chart 2 is a little more complicated. In this family tree, the stepmother has been married before and brings three children to her new marriage. There are now two ex-spouses: the stepmother's ex-husband, and the new husband's ex-wife, by

Chart 1

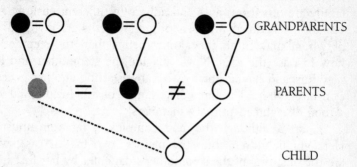

GRANDPARENTS

PARENTS

CHILD

● Male
○ Female
◐ Stepmother
= Married
≠ Divorce/death
— Biological relationship
---- Step relationship

Chart 2

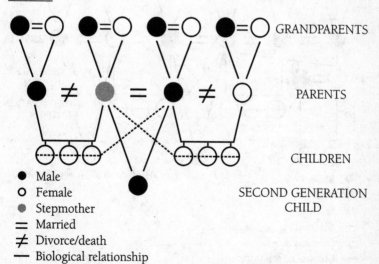

GRANDPARENTS

PARENTS

CHILDREN

SECOND GENERATION
CHILD

● Male
○ Female
◐ Stepmother
= Married
≠ Divorce/death
— Biological relationship
---- Step relationship

whom he had three children. These six children in the stepfamily are of various ages and adhere to different custody and
visitation schedules; four sets of grandparents are involved, all
of whom may think they know better than the stepmother
how to raise the kids. Now, imagine the stepmother and her
new husband having their own baby, starting another generation of children. The immediate family of this lucky child has
a total of eighteen primary members!

Chart 3, although the most complex, is far from unusual.
Here grandchildren enter the picture, two in this case, who
are the offspring of the stepmother's daughter by her first husband and are coincidentally about the same age as the new
baby just born to the stepmother and her third husband. Her
husband's ex-wife and her new husband have just presented
the world with a brand-new baby as well, thanks to the miracle
of in vitro fertilization.

Chart 3

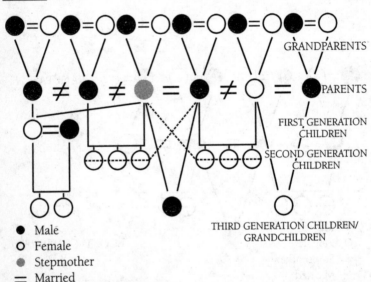

- ● Male
- ○ Female
- ◐ Stepmother
- = Married
- ≠ Divorce/death
- — Biological relationship
- ---- Step relationship

Get the picture? It can seem like a Brady Bunch nightmare just on paper, never mind real life, which is why personal research of your "stepfamily tree" is essential. Although all may interact, the stepmother, while attempting to claim her role as mistress of her new household, will be on the receiving end of many comments, suggestions, moods, and difficulties. It's a lot for one person to handle. Being prepared for this crowd of new people will keep you from feeling totally overwhelmed.

The Language of Step

New areas of expertise and knowledge always give rise to new terminology or language. (Just think of how computer technology has impacted our lexicon.) The stepfamily is at the forefront of a new era of societal development, and we, as its pioneers, have the opportunity to coin language to describe it.

The terms currently used to describe the stepfamily and its relationships have been adapted from the biological family. But as we discussed, step and biological families are very different, and attempting to describe them with the same language is an exercise in futility—like trying to translate the dozens of words Eskimos have for snow into Swahili. This adapted, biological-family language also tends to reinforce the prejudice that the stepfamily is a less than satisfactory form of the biological family, a status that is unacceptable.

Here's our summary of "Terms We'd Like to Change" to open the discussion on terminology and encourage a productive dialogue among stepfamilies.

Get Rid of "Re"

Calling the stepfamily "reconstructed," "reformulated," "regrouped," or "reorganized" implies that we are trying to reassemble and repair a broken or inadequate biological family or that we are doing something over again because it wasn't quite right in the first place. A "reconstituted" family sounds as though we are unsuccessfully attempting to make orange juice (and not fresh orange juice at that!). Describing a stepfamily as a "remarried" family is reasonably fair, because that is exactly what it is, but it's still not sufficiently upbeat.

The "Opposite" Of?

Some words imply their opposite in relation to the stepfamily. The traditional, biological, nuclear family is still exclusively described as "intact," "normal," "natural," "real." Using the terms in such a narrow (and unenlightened!) way suggests that a stepfamily, or any other kind of family unit for that matter, is "fragmented," "abnormal," "unnatural," "unreal."

Dire Descriptives

Other words allocated to the stepfamily are incredibly bleak, reinforcing the negative image that automatically applies to a stepmother. We come together as the result of a *tragedy;* members are *traumatized, devastated, heartbroken* over the *catastrophe* or *breakup* that has *befallen* them. Perhaps Dad has *abandoned* his family, our new husband being guilty of divorcing his former wife or *deserting* his children. We talk of the "natural" mother, the "real" mother, signifying that the stepmother is *unnatural,* a fake or *imposter.* She is referred to as an *intruder, outsider,* or *stranger* in her own family.

It is up to us as stepfamily members—particularly as stepmothers, since we are the ones taking the brunt of the stereotype—to address and rectify this image. Nobody is going to do it for us. The longer we allow negativity to surround us, the harder it will to operate in a positive way and to be accepted as a vital part of our new families.

We speak of *custody* (connoting ownership) and *visitation,* as though we are running a prison rather than enjoying our children and stepchildren when they live with us. It is easy to see why a *custodial* or *residential* stepmother would scare a stepkid—the terms make her sound like a prison warden.

We prefer the way the British refer to a stepmother married to a husband with total custody of his kids. She's simply a "full-time stepmother," rather than a custodial or residential stepmother. Similarly, one whose husband shares custody with his former wife is referred to as a "part-time stepmother."

Some emotionally loaded words are guaranteed to put people's backs up but are easily replaced by more positive terms. Most stepchildren, for instance, balk at being *disciplined* by a stepmother. Although professionals advise a stepmother against "disciplining" her stepkids, leaving it solely to the father, we advocate devising and enforcing standards of behavior together with your mate from the start, but you can do so under different terms. You can *explain* the rules of the house or *discuss* what you expect stepchildren to do while they are in your home and *follow up* to see that they do so. It might not make keeping order in your household any easier, but at least you've done away with the dreaded D word.

Be sure to refer to your husband's former wife as exactly that—his "ex-wife" or his "former wife." Don't refer to her as your husband's "first wife," because for you the implication of being his "second wife" is second best. You are his *wife*. No descriptive word is necessary. You have little enough acknowledged status as it is—by all means, claim what is rightfully yours.

Many stepmothers have trouble with the only word currently in use to describe what they are: *stepmother*. We still seek a word (perhaps not *fairy godmother,* but just as positive) that will have stepkids lining up to get one!

Similarly, a satisfactory term for how stepchildren come into our lives eludes us. We currently use *getting, inheriting, acquiring,* and even *receiving* stepchildren, but none of these words seems quite right. *The Enlightened Stepmother* welcomes readers' suggestions.

How *Love* and *Assume* Spell Trouble

Two words need to be struck from the vocabularies of the stepmother completely, especially in the early days. Those are *love* and *assume*.

We have discussed that a stepmother should never assume anything. Unless she has had experience in a stepfamily, it is inevitable she will guess incorrectly about what's in store for her. *Assume* nothing; do your research.

The word *love* is highly charged and sensitive under any

circumstances, but particularly so in the stepfamily. During our interviews stepmothers told us, "I really love my stepkids," only to enumerate a list of difficulties that clearly showed they did not love, or even in some cases like, their stepkids. They felt obliged to say they loved them, for fear of being tagged *wicked.*

Being expected to *love* one another is too big a burden for a fledgling stepfamily. To have a stepmother inflicting love where it's not wanted is overbearing. Pretending an emotion you don't feel toward a stranger is an imposition and an embarrassment. Conversely, it's a sad stepmom who wants to be *loved,* but isn't.

Rather than providing an enriching, positive feeling, using the word in the wrong place and making an issue of it turns it into a negative. "You don't *love* us." "Why don't you *love* my kids?" And when you combine the *assumption* "I love him; therefore, I'll love his kids," with the realization that you don't even like them, you have the foundation for feeling like a huge failure as a stepmother.

Let's forget all about love (except between spouses and between biological and adopted children and their parents) until it develops gradually and, more important, voluntarily—then it's what love should be. Right now it's much more important to create a mutually warm, comfortable feeling among stepfamily members without necessarily giving it a name. If you respect and like one another, that's a wonderful bonus.

Not Everything's a Problem

We try to avoid the word *problem* in our classes and focus groups. While some disdain euphemisms, many stepmothers felt that the alternative word *challenge* gave them a psychological wind at their backs. "Being up to the challenge," "enjoying the challenge," or "meeting the challenge" definitely beats out "having a problem." Of course, it's hard to find a stepmother without challenges!

~&~

Action Box

~&~ Have fun brainstorming new step terms you'd like to use yourself. Think of all the benefits a stepfamily provides. What words and phrases come to mind? Cheat a little, and look ahead to chapter 21, where we list some of the many advantages of living in a stepfamily. The way you talk about your stepfamily, both within the family and to others, will impact how positively people view you. Here are some suggestions from other stepmoms to give you a head start:

• We're forming a brand-new family.

• We have all been given opportunities—to grow, to learn, to expand our horizons.

• We're meeting new people, nurturing new relationships, creating new traditions.

• We cherish our existing relationships, those formed in our previous families.

• We're discovering so much about one another, but most of all about ourselves.

• We're pioneers of a new sociological frontier— all-American originals!

• We don't take affection for granted; we're earning it from one another.

• Our differences are our strength and character; our stepfamily is unique and therefore special.

&. Building a stepfamily tree is an interesting way to get to know both sides of the family and to create a sense of unity. Encourage all members of your stepfamily to join in, to contribute their imaginations, memories, and artistic talents:

• Use a large blackboard and chalk (it's easier to erase mistakes, and the final version can be transferred to a more permanent form at a later date when it is completed).

• Use posterboard and self-adhesive stickers or Post-it notes that can easily be unstuck and removed if mistakes are made.

• Make your tree large enough so you can insert names, perhaps ages, and important dates, birthdays, the date your stepfamily was "incorporated," and anything else you'd like to commemorate. You might include just primary members, or the whole extended group. You can also trace it back through earlier generations, if your family is so inclined.

• Stepmoms report having lots of fun telling family stories as each new name is put in place and learning about their new relatives. It also makes an appealing conversation piece for visiting family members who might wish to add some "bloom" to the tree, leading to discussions on the various personalities and relationships among the branches.

CHAPTER 5

The Stages of Stepfamily Development

Stepmothers often want to know if what's happening in their stepfamily is "normal." Muddying the waters, however, is the fact that the word "normal" in our contemporary lexicon has come to mean that which is "right" or "good," an unfair interpretation at best. Webster reminds us that it really means "conforming with or constituting an accepted standard, model, or pattern; esp., corresponding to the median or average or a large group in type, appearance, achievement, function, development, etc."

Comparing one stepfamily with another is like comparing apples and oranges. There are too many variables—combinations of children, previous marriages, legal imperatives, etc. There is, however, a pattern to the way a stepfamily forms into a mature, stable family unit—identifiable stages of stepfamily development.

A Model of Orientation

In the mid-to-late 1970s, when Patricia L. Papernow was doing qualitative research on stepfamilies for her dissertation, she identified developmental shifts that took place within each stepfamily as it evolved.

Those working with stepfamilies have accepted these shifts,

or stages of development, and found them to be of enormous value; they are now widely used as a tool to help stepfamilies integrate, with some adaptation, renaming, and modification. Dr. Papernow, a psychologist in private practice in Cambridge, Massachusetts, applauds this, believing that the changes demonstrate their practical, evergreen usefulness.

In the introduction to her 1993 book *Becoming a Stepfamily: Patterns of Development in Remarried Families* (Jossey-Bass, 1993), Papernow explains: "The power of a developmental model is that it offers workable ideas about what is normal and predictable as opposed to what signals a crisis. It provides a realistic notion of where to start. It offers a guide for where to spend energy that will help move the family forward. It offers reassurance that a difficult stage will not last forever. And it helps to prevent spending energy wastefully and even destructively to make the impossible happen."

Modified for the Stepmom

We have modified these stages again, making them specific to a stepmother and her needs, to enhance her ability to aid her new family's progress. The Five Stages of Stepfamily Development provided in this chapter are based on Papernow's original seven and use the adaptations of others where appropriate, particularly those of Elizabeth Einstein, a well-known writer and lecturer on stepfamily issues, and Linda Albert, Ph.D., a family counselor, columnist, lecturer, and author. We also incorporate the experience gained and passed on by the veteran stepmothers we spoke with.

After we explain the basics behind the five stages, review them carefully. We also recommend rereading the stages occasionally over the next year or so as events and relationships unfold in your new family and even to anticipate what lies ahead. Whatever is happening in your stepfamily (other than criminal, life-threatening, or other harmful actions) can probably be considered understandable within the context of the stepfamily, however strange it may seem at the time.

Other Life Cycles: In Harmony or Conflict?

While the stepfamily passes through its stages as a whole, each member of the family, including you, is working through other life cycles, which may or may not mesh with the group. These include:

• Your individual cycle

• The marital cycle (you and your mate)

• Your stepfamily's cycle (all members of your new family)

• The sub- or mini-family cycles, within the stepfamily. (Your mate and his kids form one such mini-family; you and your biological kids, if you have any, form another. Within these mini-families, there is common history, and the members know one another well.)

Often conflicts in stepfamilies occur because the individual cycles of one or more members are not in harmony, either with each other or with the family cycle. For example as a newlywed, you want and need to experience the initial stages of the couple cycle, to complete the getting-to-know-you phase with your mate. Your husband, however, may be fully occupied with his sub- or mini-family cycle, feeling guilt, and trying to compensate his kids for their upheaval, while his kids, still mourning the disintegration of their family of origin, are unwilling to start forming a new family cycle with you.

The inevitable result, as you all struggle with your own agendas, is conflict. For our purposes, we're going to describe only the stages of stepfamily development.

Keep two facts in mind as you review these stages:

1. Forming a stepfamily is a PROCESS.
2. Forming a stepfamily takes TIME.

How Long Does It Take?

Stepmothers are sometimes asked if they have resolved the problems they have had with their stepkids. It's hard to honestly answer yes. You might be having a calm period at a particular moment, but just as with a biological family or any other group of people who are living and growing, a crisis (of any proportion) can be just around the corner. Your stepfamily is a work in progress, a characteristic all families share.

The length of time it takes for stepfamilies to progress through these stages of development varies enormously—some professionals say four to seven years, while stepmothers who've actually experienced the stages say it can take ten, twelve, even fifteen years. The process can't be rushed and depends on the personalities, individual life cycles, and amount of good will involved.

The time this progression takes also depends on whether you are a full-time or part-time stepmother. Part-time stepmoms may have a less intense process with stepkids visiting periodically, but it may take longer to get to know them well and to move through all five stages. Experienced stepmothers suggest you do not make the mistake of comparing your family with any other.

How to Use the Stages

These are how Einstein and Albert describe each stage of step-family development:

1. Fantasy
2. Confusion
3. Crazy Time
4. Stability
5. Commitment

As you read, try to identify where you and your family are right now. Don't worry if it seems you are in more than one stage at a time—this simply means that in your progression, you might have taken the proverbial two steps forward, one step back. That's quite common.

You might notice, as you read and think each stage through in relation to your own stepfamily, that some of the effects of one or more of the stages could have been diminished had more preparation and planning taken place before the stepfamily got together.

For example, if you and your mate had taken time for some in-depth financial discussions prior to moving in together, you might not be in turmoil over the fact that you are spending several thousand dollars each summer to send his two teenage daughters to a weight-reduction camp. Or if you had learned more about your eight-year-old stepson, you would have known that the highlight of his week is Saturday morning, when he goes to riding school, a seventy-five-mile round trip, when you really need the car for errands.

You might also find your burden lightening a little during a particularly stressful time when you realize the inevitability of moving through each stage. "This, too, shall pass" is a phrase that has sustained many stepmoms during their Crazy Time.

For an in-depth look at these stages in expanded form, take a look at Patricia Papernow's book *Becoming a Stepfamily*.

The Enlightened Stepmother's Five Stages of Stepfamily Development

1. Fantasy

This stage is sometimes called "Illusion." At the outset, you or your husband, or both, are thinking, "We'll all be one big, happy family." Romance is in the air with your new marriage; you assume that love will overcome any problems. All your unrealistic expectations (see chapter 3) are in full swing. You dream that you will form the perfect family, with all members instantly loving one another. His kids will love you, because you're such a nice person and want only the best for this new family. You love your husband, so of course you'll love his kids. You forget that love is blind! You, the stepmother, might also be experiencing the "rescue" fantasy, imagining you will sweep in and solve everyone's problems, rescuing them from anger, bitterness, and sadness. You will be the perfect stepmother, loved by all. You'll be an infinitely better parent than your stepkids' mother, and maybe your stepchildren will even think of you *as* their mother. You bake, buy goodies, supply treats. Denial is rampant. Sneaking suspicions that all is not well are immediately quelled.

2. Confusion

Clearly, something is wrong! All stepfamily members begin to feel that this new family is not working out as they expected. There is a suppression of feelings all around—nobody wants to rock the boat, but everybody's jittery. Members withdraw from one another. Roles are unclear; boundaries are unclear. The needs and expectations of each member are not meshing. You, as stepmother, start to wonder, "What am I doing here? What am I doing with my life—I don't need this!" Stepmothers attempting to form relationships with their stepkids are met with rejection. Romance starts to wear thin. Fear of failure is in the air. There is an increasing realization that insufficient preparation has taken place for this new family situation. The kids are wondering where, or if, they fit in. Financial obligations irritate; unaddressed legal matters surface. Loyalty conflicts between this new family and former families abound. Extended family members watch you struggle, and offer unwanted advice. Since you are the newest member of the family, the outsider, the conclusion is that the person creating this chaos must be you. You actually start to believe this; you question your actions, your values, your very being. You may become depressed, panicked, and feel you are failing.

3. Crazy Time

This very difficult period is inevitable. The stress and inaction of the previous stage forces matters into the open. Family members experience pain, anger, dissatisfaction, guilt—any number of negative emotions. For the stepmother, disappointment that your initial expectations are failing can trigger an avalanche of paralyzing emotions. Your self-esteem is stripped bare. Chaos reigns. Fights and arguments break out; resentments smolder. Relationships are unclear; figuring out what's realistic (now that you know what's unrealistic) seems next to impossible. There may be serious family division: your mate and his kids vs. you and your kids. If you don't have children of your own, you may feel alone, lonely, scared, depressed, isolated. You may feel you have lost control of your life and your personal freedom.

This is decision time. Make-or-break time. During this stage, a stepmother and her mate either give up and separate, perhaps divorce, or turn everything around by renegotiating, rebuilding, seeking help, communicating, expressing a desire for resolution, and continuing to work together. It is a time for action to take place. This stage is unavoidable if any progress is to be made; your response to it will determine whether you as a stepmother will succeed or fail. We suggest you consider this stage your turning point. And we strongly recommend you do not give up. You *can* survive this!

4. Stability

When handled positively by all members, this stage can be a poignant and exhilarating time of coming together. Usually it is the stepmother who initiates this step. You persevere day after day, facing challenges and resolving them, encouraging and strengthening family bonds. It is a time of shared responsibility, of accepting one another's flaws and recognizing one another's value, when the words "us," "we," "our family" begin to be heard. Family members start to connect in ways that are natural to them. Small signs of stabilization emerge. There will still be days when you may wonder what you're doing here, but you and your mate are weathering one challenge after another on the path to success. You feel that after all that's gone before, you can handle any crisis; you feel proud of your marriage and what you're accomplishing. You feel you've made a contribution to this family, and little by little others are recognizing this too. Your role as stepmother is becoming clearer to you and to your stepfamily. You begin to feel more comfortable in your role and take charge in some areas. Your mate welcomes this. Becoming open to change, feeling more secure, you develop new attitudes, and the family can move to yet another level. You start to build traditions and set goals, to plan family activities. Other family members begin to see their roles falling into place.

5. Commitment

This stage probably needs a subheading: "Acceptance." This is the beginning of your final stage, when you can accept change as nonthreatening or when you can feel serene about saying, "this is probably as good as it will get." At least, some calm time for insight and reflection. A time when members choose to deepen their relationships. When difficult relationships can be restored and renewed or simply tolerated. When past difficulties are put aside. There's continued individual growth for all members, who are learning that finding the courage to confront problems can result in rich rewards. A new atmosphere will develop that is cooperative, supportive, and flexible and where needs can be met in an atmosphere of receptiveness, respect, trust, and confidence. Your stepfamily has begun to feel solid and reliable. Positive feelings begin to replace negative ones. The decision to succeed, to be loyal to one another, has been made. Finally, you begin to reap the rewards you have worked so hard to achieve.

Stepmothers Respond!

After a presentation of these stages in support groups or classes, there are usually several different reactions. Some stepmothers sit back, eyes wide open, and exclaim, "Wow!" Some women completely reject them, with the reaction, "We haven't experienced any of this. We're doing fine." (Those were the stepmothers still in stage 1, "Fantasy").

"I wish I had known this earlier; I could have avoided so much worry, and the feeling of failure" is a common response from stepmoms learning about the stages of development for the first time. But it's one thing to know that every stepfamily passes through them and quite another to know what to do about them.

Nobody said it would be easy. We are offering you this

information because we *know,* from the experience of other stepmothers, that recognizing there is some sort of order in this seeming turmoil will help you outlast it.

Here are suggestions from stepmothers who have made it to stage 5:

• It's probably enough to absorb, right now, that there is some order in the universe, after all. If you can, identify which stage you and your family are in. Sometimes this is difficult, but later, upon reflection, your position may become clearer.

• Acknowledge that forming a healthy, stable stepfamily is far from easy and that you will need support, especially from your husband. Recognize that if your marital relationship does not hold together, you won't *have* a stepfamily to worry about. Commit to it, strengthen it, preserve it, and above all enjoy it.

• Now that you know this complex job is a process, resolve to be one of the successes. Make up your mind to stay the course through stage 5.

• Draw strength from the fact that you are not alone. Every other stepmother has felt overwhelmed (and terrified) as she and her family worked through these stages. It's a relief to discover that what you thought was some horrifying, insane episode happening to you alone is actually going on in all stepfamilies. There will come a time, other stepmoms can assure you, that you will laugh about some of these incidents—eventually.

• Do not panic, get depressed, or move to Tahiti. We've suggested before that you find some stepmoms to talk to. If you haven't done so, now's the time. Chat, compare notes, talk about these stages, laugh. It's important to keep your mood light and positive.

• Don't spend too much time on this chapter now; it can be overwhelming on first sight. But come back to it regularly to check your progress. Reviewing the stages will explain why certain things are occurring—they have to in order for the family to work through them and move on.

- Continue to talk about your role of stepmother to those who are interested in hearing about it. You will find that not many people are, as we have discussed before. But if our society is ever to understand how complex a role we are undertaking, it will be only because we tell them.

- Do you think you're stuck in one particular stage? Perhaps you need help to move on. If so, get it. A few sessions with a family counselor might help get you over a sticky issue more easily.

- Check out our Recommended Reading List (page 438)—you are likely to find a worthwhile book that can offer a helpful perspective. Or perhaps a nice, cozy discussion or two with your husband will help you figure out what's holding you back.

- Continue to refrain from making negative comments about members of your stepfamily. You might regret your words, especially if they get passed around as family gossip. If you have stuff you want to get off your chest, depend on other stepmothers or trusted friends or relatives. A support group where confidentiality is valued is ideal. You need to be very careful whom you tell that at this particular moment you can't stand your twelve-year-old stepdaughter. There are very few people who would understand this passing mood, and you can do yourself great damage by not being selective about your confidants. Be careful not to choose your husband for this. She is his daughter, and criticism is tough to hear about your own flesh and blood.

༄

Action Box

- Maintain as much control of your own life—
  your well-being, your personal goals—as you
  can to offset the chaos going on around you.
  Stay on top of what is going on in your home.
  Use your stepmom's idea book to record ideas
  or just to vent. Make suggestions to yourself,
  plan events, etc. It can be easy to lose control
  of these basics while grappling with the major
  issues.

- Take regular breaks from the turmoil and confusion in your home to be alone with your husband and *not* talk about the trouble. If there
  are matters you cannot agree on, you can at
  least agree not to discuss them for specific peri-
  ods of time while you just enjoy each other.

See Paul on the cute for a few hours w/ NO KIDS!

CHAPTER 6

Your Husband: Together Forever, in Step

Your husband is your partner, father to his children, possibly stepfather to yours. Like you, he needs to feel confident about his ability to fulfill his new roles and to feel that he can count on the people closest to him for support.

A strong marital relationship is the foundation for a strong stepfamily. Unlike men in "traditional" families, however, your husband faces special challenges specific to stepfamily life. Understanding his perspective about these issues will help you foster the kind of communication and commitment your new life together requires.

Sharing Your Husband

On your wedding day, you become the wife of the man you love. Marriage usually means major changes in lifestyle: sharing a home, pooling resources, including someone else in your plans small and large.

When you marry a man with children, the commitment is an even deeper one. At the moment of your vows, your husband's children also become an integral part of your life. They might be young children who will live with you, visiting teenagers who need their father's vigilant guidance, or adults spread out across the country who love to see their dad as often as their frequent-flier miles permit.

Whatever your situation, as a stepmom you will be sharing your husband with his children in some way for the rest of your life.

Especially in the early days of courtship and marriage, most women focus on one thing: the fact that they have (at last!) found the right man. One stepmother, knowing true love for the first time in her life, was serious when she said, "I love him so much, I want a hundred percent of his attention a hundred percent of the time." She was soon forced to acknowledge that this was unrealistic.

Getting used to sharing a husband—his time, person, support, and love—is one of the first and most fundamental adjustments a stepmother needs to make. The children, meanwhile, will have to adjust to sharing their dad with *you*. The only disparity among these genuine, understandable, and distressing feelings is that some resentment on the part of your stepchildren, no matter what their age, is to be expected and accepted, while stepmothers haven't been able even to hint at having that sort of negative reaction. (We don't have to tell you the word generally used to describe a stepmother who protests a bit, do we?)

Is it unfair? Sure. So, why not get on top of that negative, energy-consuming emotion before it sets in? You must, from the start, employ an entirely different mind-set than a woman who is looking forward to becoming one half of a permanent couple. So examine your feelings about "sharing your husband" as soon as possible.

Who Is This Man?

Your husband is the wonderful guy you have promised to love "for better or for worse," with whom you wish to spend the rest of your life. He is the one who will know you better than all others. You will know him with equal intensity. Let's take a look at him:

- He has been married at least once before he married you.

- He has at least one child.

- There is another woman out there, either still alive or dead, who will always be a part of his life in some way.

- He is experiencing loss—perhaps of daily access to his children, of his former home and lifestyle, or both.

- He might have been a single parent when he met you, attempting to be both mother and father to his child(ren).

- He might have developed a dependency on other people: his mother or other relative, a neighbor, social worker, etc.

- He is worried about his kids' emotional health and what short- and long-term damage has been done to them as a result of the breakup of their family.

- If there was a divorce, he might worry his kids will stop loving him or will side with their mother.

- He might have financial problems from supporting two residences, or unpaid medical bills if his wife had a long illness before she died.

- He might feel guilty that he has found happiness again with you while his children are still grieving or have not come to terms with the divorce and their new lifestyle.

It's important to know how your husband's previous marriage ended and to discover the effect this had on him. Death, divorce, and abandonment all have repercussions—no one situation is necessarily easier.

Here are some of the most common issues stepmothers say we should be aware of, depending on how your mate's previous relationship ended:

The Widower

When you meet him, a widower may not have completely finished grieving. He may be devastated, brokenhearted, angry, scared, or worried. Being a single parent is a frightening and lonely job—he may feel overwhelmed by the responsibility of being both mother and father to his children, of handling household, school, and medical matters that his wife used to oversee.

Obviously, if the children are minors who are now without a mother, it means that with your agreement, you will become a full-time stepmother and have your stepchildren living with you permanently—a fact you may view as either an advantage or a disadvantage.

Stepmothers say that marrying a widower whose previous marriage was, in his opinion, "made in heaven" can be difficult and requires great sensitivity. If you can, talk to your husband about his previous wife. She must have been a good person if your wonderful new mate could have fallen in love with her and married her all those years ago. After all, his taste in women is impeccable—he chose you, didn't he? (Try to keep your mind off the fact that your mate would not be with you now if she had lived—you can say "what if" about almost any life-changing event.)

Even so, some men can have trouble letting go. Vicky, a stepmother who married Tom after his twenty-year-marriage to Joyce, the mother of his four children, revealed, "My husband felt he was betraying her, being unfaithful, every time we made love. Joyce was his childhood sweetheart, the only woman he had ever seriously dated, let alone slept with. Overcoming the feeling of infidelity was a real problem for him."

It's important for you to know something about this "perfect" marriage, a description you should also take with a grain of salt. Your research should include gently probing his family and friends, because what he is willing to reveal of his marriage might not be what others know of it. Your husband, like your stepchildren, will remember only the good things. Odds are, however, that your mate's previous wife was human, just like you. It's memories that make her perfect.

Most mothers who know they are dying will be concerned about the futures of their children. Promises to "take care of the kids" will weigh heavily on your mate when he considers remarriage. Of the stepmothers we spoke with, virtually all had every intention of becoming involved in their step-children's lives. It's very important to your mate that he *hears* this from you. He needs you to reassure him that you will look out for his kids.

Talking to women who married widowers, we discovered that these men usually have the most unrealistic expectations. Previously happily married, a widower will often expect the instant creation of "one big, happy family" the second time around too. The combination of your children, his grieving children, assorted animals, the memory of his deified wife, and the presence of your ex-spouse each weekend as he picks up your children for his scheduled visit, however, does not have the makings of the happy family of his dreams. It is up to you to calmly point out the reasons for this and to assure him that if you can build a united front together with mutual, unconditional support, the possibility of eventual harmony exists.

Vicky understood that some people, her husband among them, mourn those they love till the day they die. "I wanted to marry Tom, and I knew I had to help him recover and move on," she said. Vicky encouraged Tom to focus on how fortunate he was to have had a wonderful twenty-year marriage to Joyce and the devoted love of their four children, rather than on the sadness of losing her. "It was important for Tom to know I understood how good his first marriage had been and that I wanted a good relationship with his children," said Vicky.

Together the couple talked about Joyce and at times even discussed what Joyce might advise when Vicky was having problems with her stepsons. When her stepchildren were still quite young, Vicky made a point of remembering Joyce's birth-day, and this has become an annual tradition. "I wanted to help the kids feel comfortable talking about her," Vicky explained. "One year we made her a birthday cake—a few of my friends thought that was sick, but it worked for us!"

Discover where your mate is in the grieving process. Of course, he will never forget his previous wife—she has been a huge part of his life—but he needs to have completed his active mourning.

Becky, the biological mother of two-year-old Nell, is now the proud adoptive mother, formerly the proud stepmother, of four-year-old Wendy. Becky took over Wendy's care shortly before the child's first birthday, when she married Aaron, whose former wife had taken her own life. While she loves Wendy as her own, Becky has been surprised by an issue that to her was completely unexpected—the realization that Aaron had not made peace with the fact of his former wife's suicide.

"I really didn't want to talk about this—it's very hard for me," admitted Becky. "I love Wendy so much, but sometimes I wonder if Aaron really loved me when we married or if he just needed someone to take care of his baby so he could grieve in peace. Luckily I don't have much time to think about it, I'm so busy with my girls. But the thought keeps nagging at me, especially when I see Aaron's sad eyes."

Before his new family can begin to function well, a widower needs to have accomplished several things that go along with accepting the death of his former wife. For instance, he should have decided what to do with her personal possessions. Any bequests she made in her will should have been dispersed. If the children are very young, this can mean storing certain items—jewelry, treasured trinkets, etc.—so they can be presented to the children at an appropriate age. As stepmom, you should know what these are, where they are kept, and approximately when Dad wishes his children to receive them. Her will should be probated, or well on the way, and any other financial or legal matters resulting from her death dealt with—again, you do not need to be involved here. You might need to gently encourage your husband to accomplish these difficult tasks. Some widowers find them so distressing that they procrastinate.

Finances should be simpler for you than for the wife of a divorced man, since your husband has only one household to maintain and only one set of everything. If your husband's previous wife suffered through a long illness, though, there might still be some unpaid medical bills, which you will most likely share.

If you move into your husband's home and blend your children with your new stepchildren, you may find that you get very little time alone with your own kids, due to your hectic new schedule. They, too, will have changes to contend with as they adapt to a stepfather, their stepsiblings, the lack of privacy, rivalry for attention, personality conflicts, an absentee father, and an upheaval in their lifestyle or home environment. Unlike the wife of a divorced man, however, you won't have an ex-wife in your life, and there will be none of the custody or visitation battles common to those circumstances.

Some stepmothers we interviewed, who are widowed or divorced themselves, married widowers they had known for years when each was part of another couple. In these cases the resulting stepfamily was quite successful. Both sets of children made adjustments, but since the stepchildren already knew their stepmother as a friend, the transition was easier.

Of particular help was the fact that there was no awkwardness on the part of the new stepmother or her stepchildren in talking about the dead mother, since they all had known and loved her. Rachel, who married a close friend's husband after her own divorce, reported, "I was always in and out of the house, I knew where everything was kept, and I think they looked upon me as a part of their family anyway. So when I moved in permanently after our marriage, nothing was very different, except I didn't go home at night. I was an old friend, and I think for them it eased their mother's passing."

The Divorced Man

Divorced men, like widowers, have experienced the gamut of pain, anger, depression, resentment, fright—emotions your partner might still be feeling or have bottled up. He might have decided never to let himself feel love again or have determined to remain a bachelor.

On the other hand, you might not be able to keep him

quiet on the subject. Some divorced dads are so filled with anger, they rant and rave, detailing the failings of their ex-wives ad nauseam. This anger can be destructive in a new relationship, and if you find it so, you need to encourage him to resolve lingering problems and move forward, accepting the past as over and done with. Find out where he is on the road to recovery, and be available to him to talk about the experience of divorce and his previous marriage.

On the practical side, a divorced husband might have either visitation rights or joint custody of his children. In any event, he will become a part-time parent and lose day-to-day access to his children—a change, stepmothers report, that can be devastating to fathers. He might fear that the children will grow to dislike him, that a bitter ex-wife might try to turn them against him or blame him for the breakup of the family. He will now be facing additional financial responsibilities and might be worried about his ability to handle them.

Depending on custody arrangements, you will probably get some time off when the children return to their mother, which some stepmoms consider an advantage. But while they enjoy the downtime, they report that this can become difficult in the long run, because the children's schedule and the logistics of coordinating the activities of two households (both of which your husband in all likelihood is financing) become the major focus of your married lifestyle. Also, there's a lack of consistency in your developing relationship with your stepkids that you might find disconcerting.

Unless your husband experiences a very civilized mutual-consent divorce, there will probably continue to be battles over the children—over scheduling, lifestyle, financial, and educational issues—you name it. It is understandably hard for divorced couples to agree about anything. Stepmothers often find themselves in the middle, trying to remain calm, soothing troubled waters.

In a few cases, the stepmothers we interviewed met their husbands before their divorce from their previous wives. While they denied that they were the cause of the breakup, and insisted that their husband's marriage had deteriorated anyway, there were predictable consequences.

Debra, a teacher living in a small town in California, met and had an affair with the school's principal. "We wanted to be together and didn't consider what might happen," she explained. "But it caused a scandal, with editorials in our local paper about inappropriate behavior." Debra, also a certified social worker, resigned her position to escape the scrutiny and accepted a job in another town. "The fuss just drew us closer together. All I wanted was Dan. He divorced his wife, and we married. We assumed his grown-up children would be as happy as we were, since their parents had been so miserable together."

The couple weathered the bad publicity, but Dan's ex-wife delivered an ultimatum. "She told her children they couldn't visit her if they maintained ties to their father," Debra said. "It took time and perseverance, but Dan and I were determined not to lose contact with his children because of our marriage." To this day, Debra's twenty-four-year-old stepdaughter won't visit their house, but the other three children now do. Explains Debra, "They realized their parents had not been happy together and gradually came to accept me."

The Abandoned Man

Unexpectedly, we found stepmothers with husbands who had been abandoned by their previous wives. While we read and hear a great deal about deadbeat dads or fathers who simply vanish, stepmothers told us about mothers who have left for reasons of their own—most commonly pressure from a boyfriend who didn't want a relationship with her children or a quest to fulfill some long-held ambition without the burden of kids.

When a wife and mother leaves her family—unless she has made her reasons clear and the family knows whether or not she will return—uncertainty and insecurity are the prevailing feelings. (Some stepmothers in these circumstances say that their husbands had believed the marriage was stable and were shocked when their previous wives left.) In cases where a wife disappears without divorcing her husband, there are practical repercussions for a potential stepmother—she cannot marry her mate and has an indefinite, common-law status.

For stepmothers whose husband managed to divorce the wife who abandoned the family, life isn't much easier—the children bear the extraordinary emotional scars of abandonment and divorce.

Helping Your Husband Put the Past behind Him

As stepmothers, we think so much about what the next day or year will hold for us in our quest to build a thriving stepfamily that we sometimes overlook the past You need to know that your man has dealt with all the major issues from his previous marriage (such as those listed in our discussion of death, divorce, and abandonment) before he is ready to move on with you.

When Jim remarried, he was so consumed with guilt about having left his former wife, Andrea, that he would stop by her house on the way home from the office, "just to see if she's OK," as he explained to his wife, Sara. One night, two hours late coming home for dinner, Jim told Sara he'd been fixing Andrea's leaking hot-water tap. Another night the attic fan had broken down, and the kids were sweltering—again, he stayed for hours to fix it.

Sara got nowhere in trying to convince Jim that this activity was inappropriate now that he was divorced from Andrea. "I can't leave my kids in a house that's too hot, with water leaking, etc." was always Jim's response. It wasn't long before Sara learned, during an emotional confession by Jim, that on one of Jim's visits Andrea had been so upset by her inability to cope without him that they had ended up in bed together, with Jim trying to comfort her.

Sara was horrified, especially when she realized that Jim didn't view this infidelity as serious. "I slept with her for sixteen years. What does one more time matter?" he reasoned, to Sara's utter amazement. Jim did not understand why it was beyond Sara to have compassion for his dependent ex-wife, nor did he understand how betrayed Sara felt. Finally, Sara insisted that she and Jim seek marital counseling.

Ongoing discussions between you and your husband about his previous marriage and lingering anxieties can prevent a serious marital crisis. Ideally, by talking to Jim about his previous marriage and divorce, Sara would have been alerted to Jim's concern for his dependent ex-wife, and *together* they could have found ways to help her become less so—suggesting she enroll in a home-maintenance evening class or locating a handyman and presenting Andrea with a name and telephone number for leaks, electrical shorts, and holes in the wall.

Ask questions, and communicate, communicate, communicate. Often it's hard for men to do this at first, but stepmothers report three key positive circumstances that have helped their husbands open up: a stepmother's comfort in herself and her role (see Part 1: "Getting to Know You"), a stepmother's verbal acknowledgment of her husband's difficulties and burdens, and a mutual commitment to unconditional support in the marital relationship.

And Some Things Not to Ask

Seasoned stepmothers have also given us advice about what to avoid in these ongoing discussions with your husband:

• *Don't ask your husband to make comparisons between you and his previous wife*—whether he loves you more, whether you are better in bed, whether you're a more accomplished cook/breadwinner/housekeeper, etc., or whether he thinks you're prettier. She is history—you're here-and-now.

• *Don't ask him to choose between you and his kids.* If he has promised to take his seven-year-old daughter, Belinda, to a long-awaited party, forgetting you were due at the Browns' for cocktails at 6 P.M. the same day, don't issue an ultimatum. Everyone makes mistakes and a little girl's party date *is* important—you can call the Browns and get there later.

His Fathering Style

The death or divorce of your husband's former wife, or her abandonment of her family, will profoundly affect the relationship your mate has with his children. You'll need to evaluate the interaction between them, including the degree of influence your husband's children have on him and how the father–child relationship affects you and your marriage.

Your mate's fathering style—the concern and involvement he displays with his kids—is important to you, especially if you have children of your own or are planning to. (You need to consider seriously whether you want a husband who can forget about his children for weeks on end, who neglects their birthdays, who breaks promises to them, or who stands them up if he gets a better offer, even if it's one from you!)

If your husband feels guilty about the loss his children have experienced, he might be trying to compensate for it, sometimes in troubling ways for a stepmom. You know his children need time and attention, but consider your own feelings too. If it came to a decision between a spontaneous request, "Can we go out for ice cream, Dad?" and a long-promised quiet evening with you, what would the result be? Could the kids persuade him? Would you be disappointed? Do they play on his anxieties: 'We know you love her, Dad, but it's so hard for us." Can he handle this, or does he cave in repeatedly?

Other fathers might lavish material goodies on their kids or think they need to spend every waking hour either with their kids or worrying about them. If your husband is a willing participant in manipulation by his children—either because he sees less of them than before or because he feels guilty—this might become a strain on your marriage.

Freddy's custody agreement with his ex-wife gave him every other weekend and six weeks in the summer with his daughter, May. Donna, May's stepmom, had expected to develop a friendly relationship with her stepdaughter over time. What happened during May's visits, however, took Donna by surprise. Her usually loving, attentive husband focused exclusively on his daughter, leaving Donna feeling like a fifth wheel. May mostly ignored Donna, leaping into the front seat of the car and leaving Donna to take the back. Freddy and May held hands when they went out, leaving Donna to walk alone.

Donna was expected to indulge May's every whim at mealtimes, serving food that neither she nor Freddy cared for. When May visited, the three went to expensive restaurants and got theater tickets, treats the couple never enjoyed alone together.

Donna felt like a nonperson when May was around. But when she explained her feelings to Freddy, he was unable to understand why his wife couldn't allow him and his daughter to enjoy themselves. Freddy saw May so infrequently that he wanted to spend as much time with her as possible. "I would understand if the situation were reversed," he told Donna. Following up a year later, we learned that Donna had given birth to her own daughter but that Freddy was continuing to cater to May over the needs of his wife and his new baby. Since Freddy would not agree to marital counseling, Donna decided to consult a therapist on her own. (This couple ultimately divorced.)

You'll need to find out what standards of behavior your mate has set for his children in spite of his concern that they have been deprived of their mom or former family lifestyle. Is he more permissive than you would be? Many stepmoms related problems with Dad's blind spot concerning his kids' behavior.

Clare was in her early thirties when she met Bob, the father of three girls, aged twelve, thirteen, and fifteen. Their mother had died four years earlier, and their father was trying to raise them by himself. The girls were sweetness and light when Dad was present but, out of his earshot, treated Clare to a growing repertoire of vile insults. Related Clare, "The middle one, Tina, actually looked me in the eye and for no reason said, 'Fuck you, Clare.' I wasn't sure what to do—she isn't my child, and I didn't want to say anything I'd regret—so I told Bob what happened. He didn't believe me! He just said, 'My children don't swear, Clare.' "

Helping Him Understand Your Dual Role

Almost without exception, fathers and the women who marry them are concerned with the children's adjustments to step-family life, often at their own emotional expense. As a couple, you need to strike a healthy balance between meeting the children's needs and caring for each other. As stepmother to your husband's children, you also have the right to feel and act like a newlywed, especially if this is your first marriage.

If he can give you the emotional security and romantic attention you need as a bride and his life partner, you'll be better equipped to form relationships with his children and adjust to your new, often challenging role. Tell him that. Explain your concerns, uncertainties, vulnerabilities. He is not a mind reader—he needs to know when you're hurt or want his undivided attention or when you find something hard to handle. Together, you'll have to create "honeymoon" moments as you go along—they are necessary to creating a vital, flourishing stepfamily.

Building a United Front: A Commitment to Unconditional Support

Your eight-year-old stepdaughter, Susie, with you for the weekend, comes to the dinner table one night with every item from your cosmetic drawer plastered full-strength on her face.

"Susie, I think you should wash your face before we have dinner," you suggest.

"No, I like it like this," Susie says.

"Please, sweetie, go wash your face. When we have time,

I'll show you how to put the make up on properly—we'll have fun." You believe you are handling this very well.

"But I want to keep it on the way it is, Serena," she complains. "I don't want to wash my face."

Your husband pipes up "Oh, for crying out loud, Serena, just leave her, and let's eat."

Most people would think you have a problem with Susie. But you don't, stepmoms. You have a problem with your husband.

Making Your Marriage the Priority

You will soon learn, as did all stepmothers we've talked to, that almost any problem you have with a member of your stepfamily is actually a problem with your husband and is an indication that there's a lack of unconditional support for you. Together, you're practically invincible. Divided—well, it won't really matter what you do, because it's very unlikely you'll succeed under those conditions.

It's vital that you support each other at all times, even when you don't totally agree with the other's resolution. You can disagree in private and work out a compromise for presentation later, but there cannot be a hint of division when anyone else is present, especially children, either yours or his. The most you can do when anyone else is present is stall for time when you don't agree: "Wait a minute, honey. I need to think about this one. Give me until after dinner" is a good hedge.

If there's one piece of advice you must take from this section, it's this: Make your marriage your priority. Bringing a stepfamily together is a joint partnership. If his children are rude to you, *we* need to resolve it. If they refuse to pick up after themselves when you ask, it's *our* problem. If the stepmother's role in her new family is the pivotal one, the heart around which everyone revolves, the marital relationship is the backbone. Both you and your husband will draw strength and support from standing together, indivisible by family members or outsiders. Forming this united front is your first major job together. Your stepfamily cannot achieve stability until the couple relationship is in balance.

Talking It Out

Studies show that married couples spend only half an hour a week in intimate conversation! A stepfamily marriage needs that much and possibly more every *day*. One of the common mistakes a stepmother makes is to put off discussing problems with her husband because she doesn't want to start an argument, be seen as unable to cope with problems on her own, or be perceived as a nag. Or maybe she simply would rather talk about something more romantic than troubles with the children.

All understandable. But it's vital that you and your husband discuss, in the minutest detail, every issue that comes up to be sure you are both on the same wavelength and agree on possible action. He is the one to talk to when there is just a glimpse of something that may become a problem.

According to Judith S. Wallerstein, a highly regarded authority on the effects of divorce, more marriages fail due to continued small incidences of lack of consideration or respect for a partner than from major acts of infidelity or other betrayals. One stepmother reports that the day her husband threw out her favorite magazine without asking if she had finished reading it was the day she decided to leave him.

Obviously, it wasn't the latest issue of *Vogue* that caused the divorce—it was simply the last straw in a long series of thoughtless acts. Another said she just woke up one morning and decided that this was not what she wanted for the rest of her life. Her days were consumed by a constant round of disagreements, lack of respect from her two teenaged stepsons, and lack of support from her husband. What was left over for her? She decided to bail out.

Pulling Together

The life of the remarried dad, like your life as a stepmother, is complicated. He has a new wife, who might have her own children, who will become his stepchildren. If his ex-wife isn't deceased, she likely has custody of his children, which means he probably has visitation rights or they share custody on a prescribed schedule. This makes him an absentee parent who may spend more family time with his stepchildren than with his own.

In the good old days, before the death or divorce, everybody in the father's home pulled in the same direction. Now he feels as though he's being pulled apart. His kids want his time, energy, attention, money, and love. They want Mom and Dad back together. Instead, their dad has met you. He has found happiness, but his kids are left to eat the dust of the way it was.

Ouch!

But here's the interesting part: he's suffering from feelings similar to your own—confusion, uncertainty, and other strong conflicting emotions. You have a lot in common. You need consolation from each other. Acknowledging this, you realize you're not adversaries (he *doesn't* have to choose between loyalty to you or loyalty to his kids), and the realization helps you begin to pull together.

Here's where your continuing research comes in. At the end of this section, you'll answer some questions about your husband and your relationship. Use the results as a foundation for further inquiry about his opinions on matters that affect you both—everything from what kind of responsibilities he thinks his fifteen year-old-son should have around the house to whether you should throw a bridal shower for his daughter because her mother isn't going to. Assure him that you want to get to know his children as much as you want him to get to know yours but that this will take time—for everyone.

What About Susie?

Back to the dinner table, where Susie still sits with your makeup on. You've decided to bite your tongue after your husband's entreaty, because you don't want to make it worse now that Susie might have an idea her father is taking her side against you. If Susie thinks this is the case, she'll probably look to her father for support another time you ask her to do something, perhaps something more serious than removing makeup.

What should you do about this incident? Later, you need to discuss what happened at the dinner table with your husband and explain why it's important for him to support you in front of Susie. Ideally his reaction to Susie's refusal to obey you will be "Susie, please do as Serena asks. We can't have dinner until you wash your face." Then he'll have to respond accordingly if she refuses, since it is now his responsibility to handle his daughter if she defies *him.* You'll feel wonderfully supported, which you convey to your husband. He'll feel good, because he's fulfilled your agreement to back each other at all times. Susie will be a little put out but will learn what her boundaries are.

Eventually, Susie will become accustomed to doing as you ask in the first place, knowing her father will instruct her the same way. While discussing the makeup incident with your husband, you could also agree on future guidelines for Susie about asking to use other people's belongings, so that if a similar incident occurs, you'll both already know the other's views.

Practice on minor things to prepare for the big issues. Obviously, you don't have to agree on every subject under the sun—he might hate pizza, which is your Friday-night supper of choice. You might hate war movies, the only kind he watches. Of course, it's acceptable for kids to hear this kind of disagreement. But they cannot hear you disagreeing over behavioral situations.

The concept of unconditional support is sometimes hard for dads to understand. It's often perceived as having to make a choice between wife and children. But that's not what it means. Picture this scenario: A teenager comes home four hours after her curfew while her distraught dad and worried stepmom wait up. It's one o'clock in the morning. Stepmom, angry and scared, screams at her stepdaughter, "How dare you walk in at this hour—we have to get up for work soon. You're grounded for two weeks!"

Meanwhile, Dad is just glad his child is alive and thinks Stepmom's response much too severe. He opposes it. Here's where unconditional support comes in: He does not oppose the punishment in front of his daughter but instead suggests, "Let's talk about this in the morning." He discusses his disagreement with Stepmom later, in private. Together, they can lighten the punishment—maybe it turns out that the teen had a flat tire and just forgot to phone. It's still a transgression, maybe worth a week's grounding. Perhaps they will also agree that Stepmom should apologize for screaming. Amendments can come later (also presented together, as a team), but while an incident is happening, you must preserve a united front.

His Assumptions

Many husbands assume that because their new wife—the stepmother of their children—is a woman, she will instinctively know how to handle children and want to nurture them. That may be the case with lots of stepmoms, but it might not be true of you, especially if you do not already have children of your own.

Perhaps you are willing to try, but your husband needs to know you can't do it alone. You will need to encourage him to focus on how you are going to cope with these new responsibilities *together*.

A great amount of attention in other discussions of stepmotherhood has focused on the "duties" of the stepmother. Your husband also has responsibilities to fulfill to you. These might surprise him, especially if he was not fully supportive of his former wife in childrearing. But it's absolutely essential that you clarify your expectations of each other and discuss the issues that will help you run your stepfamily successfully. Here's what stepmothers we've interviewed say you need from your mate, right from the start:

A Husband's Responsibilities

- He should ensure that you are not left out of the family circle, by including you in plans and discussions and making sure your thoughts and opinions are heard.

- He should let his children know that as his wife and as the female head of the new household, you have certain rights and privileges, which they must accept.

- It is his responsibility to insist that his children treat you with courtesy and respect even if they don't yet like you.

- He should help foster friendship between you and his children by telling them positive things about you and by encouraging them to help you in the house, to thank you when you do special things for them, or even to remember your birthday with a card. It is his job to help them understand that relationships go two ways and that giving goes along with taking.

- He needs to understand that you cannot handle the job of stepmotherhood alone. Running a stepfamily is a joint partnership. Together, delegate responsibilities that seem fair to both of you.

- He should encourage his children to see your arrival in their lives as an opportunity. Once they get to know you, they will have access to a wonderful woman with talents and accomplishments you will be willing to share. You have a family of origin who will welcome them and give them time and attention. They gain another set of grandparents, more aunts and uncles, more cousins, and possibly stepsiblings who can become their lifetime friends.

- He must be willing to work with you to foster good communication and a workable method of conflict resolution

between the two of you and with the children in your
household.

- You both must make time to be alone together—your husband needs this too! It's an investment in your marriage, so
  don't feel guilty. Even a short, quiet walk around the block,
  holding hands, can work wonders.

A Reality Check

Many stepmothers tell us that becoming someone's second wife
seems to have the odious connotation of second best or second
place, not only in other people's minds but sometimes even
her own. This is another myth, like the "wicked" stepmother.

No one who agrees to take on the job of being a stepmother can possibly be considered second-rate. Your husband
is a very lucky man to have found you. Through wisdom
gained by experience, past mistakes, or sorrow, he had the
good judgment to have selected a first-class new partner, a
stepmom to his kids, a woman with whom he can build a
new life. So when people tag you with the "second-wife, sec-
ond-best" myth, remind them of the reality.

❦

Questionnaire

1. Do you believe you have a good relationship with your
   mate right now? If yes, list what you value most about it.
   If no, what concerns you?

2. Are you comfortable enough to discuss with him anything
   on your mind, your feelings, opinions, concerns, including
   matters about his previous marriage or his children? If not,
   what's off-limits? Why?

3. Is he able to accept/understand your feelings, both positive
   and negative, on most issues, particularly those concerning
   his children, his ex-wife, his previous life?

4. Is he able to tell you how he feels on most issues? Will he tell you when he is worried or upset?

5. Have you begun to make plans for your future? Is he hesitant about marriage? If so, why? Do you agree on most points concerning your future family life? List areas of disagreement, large and small.

6. Are you familiar with his thoughts on stepmothers in general? His previous knowledge of or experience with stepmothers might affect his ideas about what he expects from you:

   a. Is he a stepchild himself?
   b. Does he have friends who are stepchildren?
   c. Does he know any stepmothers? If so, what does he think of them?
   d. Does he have any built-in ideas of how stepmothers should play their role?
   e. Does he have emphatic ideas about what he wants from you as the stepmother to his children?

7. Do you believe your husband is ready to make another commitment—this time to you? Consider your answer from an emotional and practical standpoint. List what you know are his reasons for wanting to marry you.

8. If you have children who will live with you when you marry, how do you feel about this man becoming their stepfather? Do you have any concerns about his ability to relate to them in a way you can approve? Will he be a willing or reluctant stepfather? How do you feel about his overall potential level of performance in this important area?

9. Is he aware of his responsibilities toward you as his new wife and stepmother to his kids? Have you discussed what you expect of him?

10. Is your mate involved in his children's lives? Does he discuss their schoolwork or other interests with them? Does he know their friends or show up for school functions?

11. Can his kids bring their concerns and problems to him

for his help and advice? Can he discuss with them any subject under the sun, including sex, drugs, violence, moral values, and the death or divorce of their mom?

12. Is he an affectionate dad? Does he regularly tell his kids he loves them, and hug them?

13. Does he have a reciprocal relationship with them? Have they been taught to be considerate of their dad and mom? Do they remember his birthday? Father's Day?

Action Box

- If you haven't already done so, encourage your husband to read this book and discuss it with you. If he doesn't have time for the whole book, at least let him read this chapter.

- Discuss with your mate the husband's responsibilities listed on page 129. Make sure he finds them reasonable and is willing to fulfill them.

- Review with your husband the list you compiled in part 1, describing what you believe your responsibilities will be in your new stepfamily. Agreeing on these points will contribute greatly to your united front.

- Encourage him to seek out other men in his situation to talk to and to read books on other men's experiences. It will help him put his life in perspective and see that his feelings are normal in this context.

- Most couples, especially in the early stages of stepfamily life, are not good at communicating clearly without too much emotion creeping in. If this is your concern, read some books on the subject (see the Recommended Reading List, page 438). Particularly helpful is *Men Are from Mars, Women Are from Venus (Harper Collins, 1992),* by John Gray. This book is fun to read together and can help take the heaviness from your difficulties.

🐜 Review your answers to the questions we asked earlier in this chapter. Discuss any points that concern you with your husband.

🐜 If you think your husband might need professional help dealing with any of the issues raised in this chapter, see chapter 20, "The Stepmom's Resource Guide."

CHAPTER 7

The Children: Basic Issues for Stepmom

In this chapter you'll be observing the children in your new family—your own, if you have any, and your stepchildren. Your combined offspring will share one very important experience: being simultaneously biological children and stepchildren. Some might even be "double" stepchildren, with both stepmother and stepfather, if their other parent has also remarried.

Children who have experienced the death, divorce, or abandonment of a parent have suffered upheaval in their lives. The adults have, too, of course, but children rarely have very much control over what happens next, who their parent remarries, or where they will live. For the first time, your daughter or stepson might feel insecure about love, having a home, the future, even his place in the family.

Our aim in this chapter is to offer insights from experienced stepmothers and family experts, about the basic needs of children in stepfamilies and their issues. These will help you understand how your children and stepchildren are handling the breakup of their former family, what concerns them, how to communicate with them, and, perhaps most important, your role as a mom and stepmom in helping them recover, move on, and adjust to stepfamily life—a daunting, delicate, and above all, necessary task.

This is probably a good time to remind yourself of the

stresses you, too, are experiencing as you prepare yourself, your kids, and his for their new lives. Although much of the responsibility for a smooth transition into the new family will fall on you, be kind to yourself, and remember that this is a difficult time for everyone.

How the Experts See It

In her book *Family Politics: Love and Power on an Intimate Frontier* (McGraw-Hill, 1983), Letty Cottin Pogrebin says of children in the stepfamily: "Beyond the complex interactions is one stunning surprise: The stepfamily configuration seems to increase the power of the child. That is to say, compared to other parents, remarried parents seem more desirous of their child's approval, more alert to the child's emotional state, and more sensitive in their parent–child relations. Perhaps this is the result of heightened empathy for the child's suffering, perhaps it is a guilt reaction; in either case, it gives the child a potent weapon—the power to disrupt the new household and come between the parent and the new spouse."

Judith S. Wallerstein, co-author of *The Good Marriage: How and Why Love Lasts* (Houghton Mifflin Co., 1995), elaborates on this point, "To put it bluntly, children and parents in [remarriage] have many colliding interests. What the couple wants and needs during their early years is not what the children want and need."

Even Benjamin M. Spock, MD, in whom untold millions have placed their trust as parents, was personally overwhelmed by the difficulties of stepfamily relationships. The father of two biological, adult sons, Dr. Spock admitted to frustration in trying to relate to his eleven-year old stepdaughter. In his book *A Better World for Our Children: Rebuilding American Family Values* (National Press, 1994), he said, "I found being a stepfather at age seventy-two the most difficult relationship of my life."

Living with the "Professionals"

Even the most loving parent will probably agree that there are times when a child can be manipulative and that a certain degree of selfishness is part and parcel of growing up. Combine that with the additional power children in stepfamilies wield as a result of parental guilt, and it's no surprise that stepmothers frequently find themselves dealing with some fairly "difficult" children, their own included.

Some stepmothers described their children and stepchildren as "professionals," able to wring every ounce of sympathy from authority figures, teachers, baby-sitters, relatives, and particularly their parents in an effort to get their own way or to excuse misbehavior as an understandable result of their first family's breakup. Stepmothers also relate behavioral "trades" on death or divorce to escape chores, curfews, or other responsibilities: "I can't—I'm too upset, because I haven't seen Dad today" or "I never feel good when I come back from Mom's house." Similarly, the child who loses his or her mother to death can justify bad manners and disobedience with a simple "You can't blame me; I lost my mother" for a long time—sometimes many years—stepmothers report, before anyone has the courage to suggest it is time to get back to normal.

In Brandy's case, her mother died of breast cancer when the little girl was five years old. She was raised by her single father and his parents, who fulfilled Brandy's every wish— toys, clothes, trips and, at the time Lucy was considering becoming her stepmother, a pony. Likewise, Lucy was expected to be an indulgent stepmother, because Brandy, now fifteen, had grown up without her mom.

"It was as if her mother died yesterday," exclaimed Lucy, "instead of ten years ago. It was really eerie. When I met Edward, he seemed a cheerful, active sort of guy—I discovered he had a sad demeanor only at home." Lucy knew she couldn't marry Edward and live in that environment and decided to have a heart-to-heart talk with everyone separately. "I found out that each person was grieving for the other!" Lucy marveled. "Brandy thought her dad needed it; Ed's parents thought

Brandy needed it; Ed thought everyone else needed it! Getting this out in the open was like watching a family awaken from an enchantment. We were left with a relatively well-adjusted girl and four adults relieved beyond measure to let happiness back in."

The Alchemy of Stability

More and more children from divorced families are seeing the parent they live with remarry and divorce again. Family experts tell us that the primary reason these second and subsequent marriages tend to fail is "problems with the children." It's a vicious cycle—the more marital breakups children endure, the more severe the consequences are for them, and the more problems there are "with the children." Stepmothers report difficulties with kids "acting out," adjustment problems, custody/visitation fights, personality conflicts, jealousy, rivalry sabotage—sometimes all of these things at once. Welcome to the modern Tower of Babel.

What's wrong with these families?

We think it's more helpful to rephrase the question and ask, What makes a successful stepfamily? Interviews with stepmoms who believed they had well-functioning stepfamilies revealed one basic tenet: The successful stepmom has exercised her right to run her household the way she wishes. She receives her husband's unconditional support and his full participation in what she does, including the requests she makes of both his children and her own.

Some skeptics may raise questions: Does the stepmother abuse her authority? The answer is generally, perhaps even surprisingly, no. Or how about this: Don't the kids get upset by this? Stepmoms say noses are a little out of joint in the beginning, but on the whole, provided she is seen to be reasonable (see number 8, "Stepmom's Quick Primer"), kids seem to like a well-run home, two happy parents (even if one is a stepmother!), and some boundaries to work within.

Theorists can disagree, but we can categorically say that

based on the anecdotal evidence offered by stepmothers from all walks of life, ages, and income brackets, if this basic premise does not apply, the marriage, and ultimately the stepfamily, stands little chance of success.

He's Still My Daddy

As a biological or adoptive mother, you have the prerogative to raise your children as you think best. You have legal rights to support you and a powerful emotional bond with your kids. As their mom, you are an intimate witness to their experience of losing their dad, if he died, or of how they are handling the changes and disruption resulting from your marital breakup. For the most part, you will probably understand, better than anyone, your children's feelings and difficulties in joining a stepfamily.

If your previous marriage ended in divorce, your relationship with your former husband will be very important to your children. They need to be reassured that their dad will still play a primary role in their lives, if not yours; they need to feel confident that they can love each of their parents without being disloyal to the other and that both Mom and Dad will do their best to establish a working relationship for their benefit.

Assuming you have or share custody when you divorce and remarry, as most biological and adoptive mothers do, it's vital to accept that your kids want and need to continue to spend good times with their father. This is why we encouraged you in Part 1 to do everything possible to get past leftover emotional tensions with your former spouse. Your life will run much more smoothly if you can handle the practicalities of your continued, reshaped relationship with your ex with relative ease, especially since your children are likely to pay close attention.

Delia is a financial planner with a prominent bank. Her ex-husband, Tony, manages a local fast-food restaurant. Their home ran like clockwork, with lists, schedules, and checkbooks balanced to the last minute and cent. Delia was fairly sure that in spite of their rancorous divorce, she and Tony could work efficiently together to meet their children's needs. She approached Tony, suggesting an agreement to limit their discussions to the kids, their lifestyle, and what was best for them.

Reasoned Delia, "We don't need to get personal at all—we both love the kids, and we both want them to be happy." Tony agreed, and they worked out a flexible custody schedule and had a strategy session on managing their finances for future college tuitions. So far, according to Delia, both parents (who are admittedly more logical and businesslike than most) have stuck to their agreement, and the arrangement is working well for everyone.

Few couples find it this simple, though. Jared and Rochelle, who shared custody of their three young children, fought constantly about how much each should pay of their kids' spiraling expenses. What finally helped them decide to compromise, however, was their long-distance telephone bills: the charges, listing the date, time, length, and *cost* of each argument, were enormous! They decided to set up a joint bank account to cover clothes, sports and school equipment, school trips, and any unusual expenses not covered by their divorce settlement. Each parent deposited the same amount in the account monthly, and each consulted the other before writing a check. Explained Rochelle, "We're working on the honor system, but we're both so relieved to stop the fighting that I think it's going to work."

What's Good about What's New

If you are bringing your own children into your new marriage, you will have some support, family members who know and love you and who, in spite of struggling with their own adjustments, will be "on your side." Of course, especially if they are young, your kids are dependent upon you for their happiness and well-being.

Positively presenting the prospect of your remarriage and

future life in a stepfamily will ease your children's transition.
But be sure to have worked out a list of these positive points
beforehand; don't just *say* that stepfamily life is going to be
wonderful

Be prepared to detail the upside of every stepfamily issue.
When your twelve-year-old says crossly, "What's so great about
moving?" be ready with a list of reasons, not recriminations.
If you will settle in another town when you marry, and one
of your kids is a budding pianist, focus on the fact that there
is a renowned concert hall ten minutes away and that you've
already got tickets for the whole family. Your projection of
confidence about the future will help your children feel secure
and encourage their sense of adventure, even if they're far from
happy about impending changes.

Evelyn wasn't sure she would like San Francisco any more
than her three kids, who were already convinced they would
despise it. Prior to her divorce, Evelyn and her sons had lived
in the country, surrounded by lots of flowers and trees to
climb. Marrying Tom, an executive with a computer services
firm, meant getting used to an urban life. To compensate, Tom
promised them weekend trips to the Sonoma Valley. All Evelyn
needed to do, as she saw it, was to persuade her three boisterous boys of the benefits of weekday city life.

The selling points appeared in the form of both unfamiliar
and familiar advantages. Tom's apartment came with a wonderful view of the city, and the building offered lots of youngsters their age to play with. After they made friends with the
uniformed doorman (another interesting novelty), a walk in
their new neighborhood revealed a tiny park, with familiar
flowers, trees, and birds, and, as a bonus, an ice cream shop
just up the hill. The boys fell in love with it. Evelyn's youngest,
who pronounced San Francisco and its environs "awesome,"
said, "This will be our park, Mom—we can come here when
you pick us up from school."

Sometimes you'll need to dig really deep to find the proverbial silver lining, which might not reveal itself until the
new family has settled down together. You'll need to be creative when persuading your thirteen-year-old daughter that

sharing a room with her fifteen-year-old stepsister might actually be fun. You might suggest that when they've had a chance to know each other better, they might want to trade or share clothes, instantly expanding their own wardrobes, or, eventually, have those late-night girl-talk sessions that some sisters who've had to share a room during childhood look back on with great fondness. Try asking your kids for suggestions too: "How do you think we can make this work?"

What's on Their Minds?

Another priority is to spend plenty of time with your children, keeping them up-to-date and involved in every step of your plans, encouraging questions, discussing anxieties and concerns, and letting them know that it's safe to express their feelings with you, that nothing is going to change your love for them. Keep in mind that while you may be in love, your children aren't, nor should you expect them to be.

Dealing with new feelings and new people all at once can be frightening and overwhelming. There will be many strong emotions flying around—anger, fear, confusion, guilt, and sadness about loss. Even if you don't like what you're hearing from your family members—"I hate that kid," "I don't want you to get married," "I can't stand how Dad's wife cooks,"—respect their point of view, and encourage ways of resolving, changing, or accepting things without belittling their feelings.

However, keep your eyes open for behavior that is out of character for your kids. Mood swings, emotional outbursts, and acting up are all normal in these circumstances. But if a child becomes withdrawn, depressed, or secretive; develops erratic sleeping or eating patterns; or becomes violent or abusive, you need to find the cause. An objective professional might be required to help your youngster through a period of his life he finds too hard to handle.

On the practical side, explain what will happen so there are as few surprises as possible, such as where you will live, if your son and stepson will have to share a room, etc. Let your children spend time with their stepdad, meet their stepsiblings, and get to know them in their own time.

Adam, thirteen, and Stevie, fourteen, didn't just dislike each other—these stepbrothers hated each other. They had to share a bedroom, however, when Adam's mom married Stevie's dad. From the day they both set foot in it, they fought over everything—which closet was whose, whose bed should be near the window. The bickering was endless. Stevie even ran away once after an especially bitter argument.

Adam's mom, Christine, was at her wit's end, despairing of the boys ever getting along.

One afternoon everything changed. Stevie brought home a baby bird he had found that must have fallen out of its nest. Exclaimed Christine, "I couldn't believe what happened next! Stevie ran to show Adam his treasure. Together they found a shoe box for the bird, lined it with twigs and grass, and took it up to their room. Then they rode their bikes to the library to find out what baby birds eat.

"From that day on, they were the best of friends, taking care of this little bird, each taking a shift in the night to feed it," recalls Christine. Even now they spend hours together in their room, which they call their 'office,' because they've decided to become veterinarians when they grow up and run a joint practice. They're working out all the details!"

The best strategy to encourage good relationships between your children and stepchildren is for you and your husband to let all your kids know your marriage is sound, strong, and permanent—they will test you on this now that they are experts on death, abandonment, or divorce. Explain that while there are firm behavioral guidelines, which are set by parents, how and when they form relationships with the members of their stepfamily is completely up to them.

The Other Stepmother

If wedding bells are in store for your former husband, your children will be getting a stepmother, too—yet another new relationship! We'll look at this woman from your point of view later, but from your kids' perspective, she might simply represent another obstacle to being with their dad, diluting the already limited time they are able to spend with him. On this basis alone, they may resent her.

Because you're in a similar position in relation to your husband's kids, you can discuss this common ground with some confidence. Explain to your children how their new step-mother may be feeling—because their own mom is feeling the same way! Reassure them that their stepmother will want to get to know them and will more than likely welcome them into her home when they visit their dad. (You should discuss this issue with her directly, before you promise your kids any-thing she can't provide, as discussed in chapter 10.)

Meanwhile, encourage your children to look at their new stepmother with open minds, as another adult with their inter-ests at heart, perhaps with kids of her own who can become new friends to them.

Depending on their ages, this might be another opportu-nity to reinforce how a two-way relationship works—that only by being courteous and considerate to this new person in their lives can they expect the same treatment. Stress the fact that there will be ample opportunity to get to know her better and maybe even to like her, as their dad does.

Fanny, happily remarried and thriving in her own catering business, initially didn't think much of her ex-husband's new girlfriend. Zoe was very young, at least fifteen years younger than her former husband, and Fanny agreed with her son, Jamie, that Zoe, who favored black nail polish and funky clothes, seemed "a little strange." But remembering the anxiety she had experienced while trying to settle into a new stepfam-ily herself, Fanny was determined to keep an open mind.

Jamie, however, continued to come home from visits with his dad and Zoe, complaining about the way Zoe cooked (mac-robiotic), where he had to sleep (bunk beds), and what he felt was Zoe's odd behavior: "She kisses Dad all the time." Fanny, recognizing she wasn't getting an in-depth picture of the new woman in her son's life, gave Zoe a call on the pretext of discussing what Jamie would need for the camping trip his stepmother had planned for his next visit.

Fanny found that Zoe was interested in getting to know Jamie and expressed appreciation of Fanny's show of support, which she hadn't expected, having heard horror stories about ex-wives. Fanny later told her son she thought Zoe was a very nice person. His mother's "approval" had a softening effect on Jamie. Soon he, too, was seeing Zoe's good side: "Mom, she has a telescope and knows all about the stars. She let me look through it last night, and she's going to teach me all the constellations."

Fanny is pleased about her son's budding affection for his stepmom but does admit to a pang of jealousy. "It's a little bittersweet, but I think the reason I can handle some of these unsettling feelings is because I feel secure and happy in my own marriage, and I love my work. Support and fulfillment in your own life helps you be that much more openhearted."

Your Stepchildren: Strangers and Family

Most stepmothers are concerned about balancing their feelings between their own children and stepchildren. Inevitably, because you know and understand (and love) your own children so well, it's easier to relate to them. However, all the stepmothers we interviewed detailed superhuman attempts to be even-handed with both sets of kids.

Initially your husband's children are strangers to you, and months, perhaps years later, you still might not know them as well as your own kids, nor, probably, love them as well. Your husband, on the other hand, feels about his kids the way you do about yours—protective, responsible, and often guilty for the upset he feels he has caused them. What's more, he believes they are near-perfect!

Some stepmothers revealed that their relationship with their husband directly corresponds to the quality of the relationship they have with his children. Is this the case in your situation? In everyday life, when someone isn't your cup of tea, you can walk away. It's hard to do this when you have a personality conflict with a stepchild. Dad loves his children— he doesn't understand your problem. Debi, stepmother to fifteen-year-old Samantha, came across a shoe box filled with old family photos taken when times were good: her husband, his ex-wife, and the two children. "They all looked so happy," Debi said, "I wish I could experience that feeling of solidarity. Maybe if I had known Sam when she was little, I wouldn't be having problems with her."

Possibly. But moms have trouble with their fifteen-year-old daughters too. But relating to your own daughter is very different from relating to a stepdaughter. At one of our focus groups for stepmoms, one woman pointed out, "Do you realize, if we had anyone here who was a mom but not a stepmom, she'd be unable to identify with almost anything we are discussing?"

Your stepchildren have been raised by your wonderful new mate and his former wife, with beliefs and values, models of behavior, and standards that may bear little resemblance to your own personal philosophy. Do not rush to form an opinion about them—you are meeting them for the first time under difficult circumstances, possibly seeing them at their worst, at the lowest point of their short lives.

Although it's natural to worry if you don't even like your husband's children yet, affection has to be earned in stepfamily relationships. In the early stages of stepmotherhood, it's enough to recognize the benefit of constructing a working relationship with your stepchildren, put them in the context of their history, and accept that you will get to know them naturally over time. The initially hard-to-like ten-year-old boy might be handling your investments one day, or repairing your car. Someday, he might melt your heart by presenting you with a scruffy, handpicked bunch of flowers and saying, "Happy Stepmother's Day."

Like your own kids, your husband's children are hurting, grieving, trying to heal. They have major adjustments to make, new people to meet. In addition, they may resent the time their dad spends with you and your kids, which is perhaps more time than they get with him, and they probably won't be as adorable as usual, but defensive and wary.

Simultaneously handling the feelings that come with getting a stepmother and being happy that their father has found love again is simply beyond the capabilities of most children, regardless of their age. Conversely, it can be hard for most fathers to accept that their children aren't as interested in their father's happiness as they are in their own feelings. This common scenario puts you in a very sensitive position.

As a stepmom, you have to expect that your husband will need to deny what looks to you like selfishness in his children. Your kids probably won't welcome him as a stepfather with open arms either. The best way to deal with this lose–lose situation is to make sure your husband wins with you while the kids make their often messy adjustments. Love him, be kind to him, organize as many romantic interludes as you can, and reinforce that his decision to marry you is going to benefit everyone in the long run.

Private Time Is Priceless

Be aware that your stepchildren need time alone with their dad just as you sometimes need your husband all to yourself. Since his kids might already feel abandoned, due to the divorce or particularly the death of their mother, they might see diminished attention from their father as further abandonment.

Be understanding in this area, and get involved in arranging this private time for them, making sure they know you think it's important for them. They might not show their appreciation, but it's something they won't be able to hold against you; you aren't keeping their dad from them. If you know your stepchildren are arriving Saturday morning, suggest activities your husband can share with them during the day, then make time later for just the two of you.

Being proactive will help you avoid any feelings of resentment—so you and your husband can fully enjoy your time together without guilt. Remember, too, to arrange something pleasant for yourself when stepkids and Dad spend their time together. If you simply wait at home until they return, you're likely to feel left out when they walk through the door on top of the world after their fun afternoon. Don't forget to ask what they did; encourage them to talk to you about it; it will reinforce your approval of the time your mate spends with them and afford the opportunity for a stepfamily discussion.

If you have kids of your own, create opportunities for spending time alone with them, perhaps enjoying one of the familiar jaunts you all used to love before the divorce, or another special treat. Reassure them that although life might be pretty chaotic, you love them more than ever, because they are coping so well. Everybody wins—and you organized it!

Equally important is that you and your mate spend one-on-one time with each other's kids. Even a few minutes at a time is a great start—a quick game of catch between your husband and your daughter before dinner, an impromptu invitation to your stepson to help you plant some spring bulbs for an hour.

Drew was in despair at the distant relationship she had with her young adult stepdaughter. She had tried for three years, since she had first married Laine's dad, to spark a warmer rapport with her, but the relationship remained awkward at best. One evening after work, while preparing dinner, Drew poured herself a glass of white wine. She had just sat down to enjoy it, and unwind from her long, busy day while the sauce for dinner simmered, when Laine walked in.

The moment just seemed right. Drew said, "Hi, Laine, this wine is just too lovely not to share. Would you like a glass?" To her amazement, Laine accepted and plonked herself on the stool next to her stepmom.

"What a terrible day I've had," Laine blurted out, taking a sip of her wine. She described her experience in detail. Drew listened sympathetically, astonished at the torrent of words. The two talked for half an hour or so before the rest of the family came home. The next night at around the same time, Laine made a beeline to the kitchen to update her stepmom on the day's events. This brief evening interlude now belongs to Drew and Laine, when they share talk and prepare dinner together. Drew, still in shock at her success, said, "We have a cozy routine now that's just for us. We really enjoy it."

read up Spencer again

Quiet, Alert Observation

Your job in the early stages of your engagement or marriage is simply to observe. We suggest you do very little else, at least prior to your wedding, since you don't really know enough yet to make an informed judgment.

Later it will be your job to show your stepkids that affection is possible between you, but now is probably not the time. Initially, for the most part, make allowances for minor behavioral annoyances—smart-mouthing, untidiness, disobedience, lateness, etc. Simply watch and take note of issues or traits that disturb you, to discuss later with your partner. Refrain from criticizing at this point—unless a stepchild is directly rude to you or does something dangerous or abusive, such as kicking your beloved cat, when you are at liberty to interfere.

Beware of overindulgence, however, which can take the form of showering children with material goodies, allowing certain privileges that would not otherwise be granted, or overlooking behavior that would normally be intolerable. Discuss with your husband the parameters of a cooling-off period or adjustment phase so you won't have to live with a bunch of "professionals" for an unlimited period or be blamed for being the spoilsport. (When a stepmother is unwilling to join in overindulgence, and attempts on her own to return her family to some sort of normalcy, she can become in no time at all a "wicked" stepmother.) The information on the stages of stepfamily development in chapter 5 can help you anticipate what you might experience as your stepfamily develops and can help you set guidelines and a time frame for settling down.

You're Not My Mother

Depending on their ages, degree of confidence, and sophistication, your stepchildren will likely have some difficulty relating to you, especially at first (remember what they have probably heard about stepmothers). Whether their mother is alive or deceased, there will be loyalty conflicts. It takes time for children, even adult children—and perhaps especially adult children—to realize it is possible to have a relationship with you without detracting from the love or loyalty they feel for their mom or her memory.

Frequently, a stepmom who is experiencing difficulty forging a relationship with her stepkids makes the classic mistake of believing she is trying to relate to regular people who simply don't like her. She might also mistakenly believe it is her responsibility to attempt to make her stepkids like her. Not so. In the early stages of stepfamily life, children, whatever their age, are rarely capable of behaving or relating to others normally or rationally. When you meet your stepkids, they might still be in active mourning—or angry, frustrated, depressed, or scared.

Ellen, thirty-three, did everything she could to help her eight-year-old stepson, Nicolas, cope with the death of his mother when the child was four. She and her husband, Gordon, met two years after his wife's death and married one year later. Ellen, who loves children, was thrilled when she met Nicolas, but the child rejected all overtures of affection on Ellen's part, saying "I hate you—you're not my mother."

With the help of a therapist, Ellen and Gordon are resolving what has been identified as Nicolas's fear of losing another maternal figure. Though initially resisting the idea, Ellen agreed that her stepson should call her by her first name, which has helped Nicolas see Ellen as someone distinct from his deceased mother yet someone who cares for him in a special way.

Losing a mother to death, or grappling with divorce or abandonment, is not a state of mind conducive to forming new relationships, least of all with a woman who is ostensibly taking a mother's place. When a mother is separated from her children through divorce or abandonment, she is still mother, regardless of her flaws.

Learning about Grief (when You've Never Been Happier)

If your mate's former wife died, we recommend that you learn more about the grieving process and the way this has affected your stepfamily. It's all too easy for a potential stepmother who is deeply in love with a man with children to believe that she can "save" her stepfamily from their torpor—the rescue fantasy is a trap many fall into. Your stepchildren don't want to be saved, least of all to be saved by you.

If their father has been outwardly distraught over the loss of his wife, his children might wait until he becomes stabler before they start grieving themselves, deferring mourning until it is "safe" to do so, sometimes for many years. Therapists believe the most difficult time for a child to lose a mother is from ages seven to eleven. At these ages children are likely to suppress their feelings and act out in other ways. Because most girls are more outwardly emotional than boys, you might feel your stepsons are coping more easily with their loss. But stepsons report that they lost "their best friend" when their mother died and that their lives, too, will never be the same, though fewer studies have been done with boys who have lost their mother, and the effect it has on them.

Your task, with your husband, is to provide a nonthreatening, secure atmosphere where children can gradually talk about their feelings when they feel ready. Hope Edelman, author of *Motherless Daughters* (Addison-Wesley, 1994), has recommended that couples delay their wedding at least one full calendar year following the death of a mother so children can experience each of the holiday seasons without her before another woman comes along.

It's very, very difficult to mull over a book on grief when all you want to do is dance in the street. But grounding yourself in what the members of your new family are experiencing will, ironically, save *you* grief in the long run. It will help eliminate the "it must be me" syndrome of self-blame and is the best way to be there for your new family.

Do They Know What happened?

Find out from your mate what your stepchildren understand about how and why the divorce, if there was one, took place. Their dad or another family member likely will have told them *something,* but was it the truth? You need to know the details, because if the family tried to shield the kids from something considered unpalatable for them, you will probably be expected to continue the charade. For example, were the kids told that their mother had an affair with a neighbor and took off in the night with him, or were they told a gentler story— that Mom went to take care of Granny in the hospital two states away and decided not to come back? Was it a complete shock when their parents divorced, or were they old enough to suspect that something was happening in their home, because they heard arguments or even fights?

If their mother died, were they told she died in the hospital of cancer, or were they simply informed of her death, with no explanation? When a family tells a child that her mother is "asleep" or has "gone away for a while," the child will, logically, expect her to return or awaken. Similarly, if Mom is currently doing time in jail, it's better that her children know about it and be allowed to visit her, and love her as she is, than to have a fairy story embellished for them.

Today it's generally acknowledged that it's better to tell children the truth about death and other endings, including divorce and abandonment. To try to protect children from what adults think they won't understand might do harm in the long run, since the truth has a habit of eventually coming out.

Give children credit for their resilience; providing the truth also affords you, as their stepmom, a chance to relate to them with honesty from the very start and to help them come to grips with seeing less, or perhaps nothing at all, of their mother.

Special Grief: Girls without Mothers

Interviews with stepmothers of female children have revealed very special problems for girls in dealing with the death of their mother. Hope Edelman maintains that regardless of her age, when a woman's mother dies, her "life is irrevocably altered; that this one fact forever changes who she is and who she will be."

If you have lost your mother, you will understand the emotional roller-coaster your stepdaughter(s) might be experiencing. If you are fortunate enough to still have your mother with you, we recommend you read *Motherless Daughters* for some insight.

With an understanding of your stepdaughter's special trauma over having lost her mother, it would seem your job can only be to assume a sensitive, compassionate role. It's easy to believe that your motherless stepdaughter might look upon you, given time, as at least a friend. But in her chapter "When a Woman Needs a Woman," a discussion of mother substitutes, Edelman paints an extremely unflattering picture of the stepmother:

"It's true that the Evil Stepmother stories I've heard are one-sided, but if even their most basic facts are accurate, many motherless women were raised by stepmothers who were, if not downright abusive, then at least coolly detached, ranging from those who gave preferential treatment to their biological children and turned stepdaughters into domestic servants, to those who restricted a daughter's contact with the father and appropriated the lost mother's possessions after his death. Jealous of a stepdaughter's closeness with her father, unwilling to accept a child of the 'other woman' in her new family, or simply inexperienced at mothering, stepmothers may falter, give up, or turn on a motherless child."

This modern-day perpetuation of the old-fashioned fairy

tale is not good news to the potential or new stepmother. Where does this leave us? Edelman's book is obviously well researched and, from the motherless daughter's point of view, accurate.

Stepmothers Tell Their Side

Research for this book revealed an entirely different story. We listened to stepmothers who detailed well-meaning attempts to show affection to motherless girls and to form relationships with them. An overwhelming majority of the stepdaughters, however, were unreceptive, often all but wrecking their father's new marriage through unreasonable or rude behavior, to which the stepmother objected but which Dad excused "because she lost her mother."

Lisabeth confided, "I was expected to make every allowance under the sun for Della, my sixteen-year-old stepdaughter, because her mother had died seven years ago. Not having a mom is horrible. I know, because I also lost my mother when I was in my teens—I'm forty-one, and I still miss her. But I was encouraged to grieve, cope, and move on with my life, and I'm stronger today because of this. It was explained to me by my grandparents that life deals harsh blows and that my mom would not want me to make her death what the rest of my life was going to be about. Making excuses for Della because she's motherless is not equipping her for her life."

Open a Discussion

It's been implied by Hope Edelman and other stepdaughters that a stepmother, regardless of tact or sensitivity in how she approaches a motherless stepdaughter, is not wanted—only the biological mother will do. The advice passed down from experienced stepmothers in this seemingly lose–lose situation is simply this: continue to play your role the best way you know how, primarily by being a wife to your new husband

and trying to develop at least a working relationship with your motherless stepdaughters, as well as stepsons, by being calm and consistent. Remember "Stepmom's Quick Primer" number 10: This is your life too. If a stepchild chooses to reject you, there is very little you can do. It's just not possible to force people to like or accept you. You can only insist on courtesy in your home.

We also suggest you bring the issue out into the open. Initiate a discussion along these lines: "I know how hard it is for you to get used to me, and I understand how you must be feeling, seeing another woman married to your dad. If you want to talk about it, I would welcome it. But your mother's death was not my fault, and it is not reasonable for you to take your feelings out on me. I have no wish to take your mother's place, but I am your dad's wife, and I'm here to stay. It would be much more pleasant for all of us if you could try to accept that." By doing this you have (a) acknowledged their feelings, (b) indicated that this is your life, too, and (c) shown you are willing to discuss things. It is important to keep the door open for a future relationship. People change; attitudes evolve.

In the meantime, make up your mind not to allow bitter feelings to impact negatively on you. Unhappiness about losing a mother is understandable. But what is not reasonable is that stepchildren be allowed to blame you for their unhappiness. If you believe they need professional help to get them through this particular stage of life, suggest it to their dad and perhaps to them also, depending on their ages.

Entering the Shrine

Be aware, too, that children without mothers are sensitive to the way things were when Mom was alive, down to the placement of every object in the home.

When Hal's first wife died of breast cancer ten years ago, he faced the challenge of raising two young daughters alone. Four years after the death of the girls' mother, when Jacqueline and Jillian (known as Jack and Jill) were twelve and ten, Hal met and became engaged to Catherine.

"I was as careful and sensitive as I could be in taking on my role as Hal's wife," Catherine explained, "but the girls were determined to preserve the house as a shrine, down to the smallest detail and ritual. Vases were placed only where Mom used to put them. Laundry was done only on the day Mother did it. If I tried to do anything my way, I received cold stares. Anything I moved was replaced when my back was turned."

When Catherine repeatedly pointed out to Hal that as his wife she needed to supervise their home, Hal said, "Go easy on them, honey. They lost their mother."

Recalled Catherine, "Their grandmother finally told me bluntly, 'Unless you put your foot down, my dear, these girls are going to ruin your marriage.' When I thought it through, I realized I didn't have much to lose. I called the three of them together that evening and explained, 'Hal, I am your wife. Girls, I am your stepmother. I will never take the place of your mother, but I am going to start immediately to run this house my way. Either you can all accept that and help me, or we will have a problem.'

"Jack and Jill burst into tears and left, but Hal and I had our first really productive conversation on this subject. He was visibly relieved that I had taken charge of the worsening situation instead of continuing to complain to him. He admitted that he hadn't been sure what to do and so had done nothing. Later, though, he talked to the girls and confirmed what I had decided."

A Mother's Abandonment: Suspended Grief

When a mother abandons her family, children's grief can be delayed or protracted, often with no imminent conclusion. Sandi had been married for six years to a man with three children whose previous wife, Barbara, had abandoned the family for her boyfriend, whom she married after her divorce.

Barbara lives in a nearby town, has two sons with her new husband, and refuses any contact with her three older kids.

"The children talk about her constantly, almost as though she is still part of their lives," Sandi told us. "They still love her and live in hope of her return. It's heartbreaking. Every birthday, they expect to hear from her but never do. Christmas is our saddest time, because they still have her tree decorations and continue her traditions."

Sandi's stepchildren have been in therapy, but they have yet to acknowledge the unlikelihood of their mother reclaiming them. "I love these children as my own," this stepmother said. "We get along well together, and I encourage them to talk about her. But as long as they believe their mother will claim them someday—and who knows, she might—I don't know if they'll ever be able to really love me back."

The Catchall Stepmother

Like most of the stepmothers we interviewed, you will probably be quick to learn that typically any difficulties arising in your new family will be determined to be your fault, particularly by your stepchildren, whatever their ages. Teenage stepdaughters may present a particular challenge. In her book *Women and Their Fathers: The Sexual and Romantic Impact of the First Man in Your Life* (Doubleday-Dell, 1993), Victoria Secunda states, " . . . The stepmother is yet another rival for Daddy's love. And because the daughter has no ambivalent biological tie to her . . . the stepmother is an easy scapegoat: she keeps the daughter from hating either of her parents. As one woman, whose mother died when she was twelve, put it, 'When my father married my stepmother, I could let him off the hook by blaming *her* for our distant relationship.' Stepmother becomes the repository for all the daughter's mixed emotions about her biological parents."

Of course, it is not only teenage girls to whom this applies; stepmothers see this attitude with stepdaughters of any age. Jan vividly remembered an outburst by Dina, her adult stepdaughter, who was planning her wedding. Dina had insisted on handling all the arrangements herself—she didn't want her stepmother involved, although Jan had offered her help numerous times.

Dina was overtired, and overwhelmed—nothing was falling into place. Upon learning that her invitations would be late coming back from the printer, Dina screamed, "If Daddy hadn't married Jan, they'd be back by now!" Jan was able to laugh at this later but, at the time, was completely nonplussed. She was thankful, however, that her husband, Bernie, had finally witnessed these hysterics—he had never before seen his daughter behave this way toward Jan, since Dina only yelled at Jan when they were alone. Said Jan, "Bernie just raised his eyebrows, shrugged, took me by the hand, and led me into another room. Then he quietly poured a stiff drink for both of us. Later we just decided to chalk it up to irrational behavior under pressure."

Small Steps Go Far

No family, biological or step, is problem free. To lead a completely peaceful life is probably a pipe dream, but your chances of forming at least a working relationship with your stepkids are good.

Stick with small steps in moving relationships forward. For example, if you've noticed that one of your stepkids is an avid reader of science fiction, ask if he's read the new book by his favorite author. If he hasn't, pick it up as a little present for him. After all, what's the worst that can happen? Even if he receives it sullenly, he'll still have to recognize that you went out of your way just for him. If you know your seven-year-old stepdaughter loves pasta, ask her what her favorite dish is, and suggest she help you make it one evening. She might resist at first, but if you tell her you want to get it "exactly right" and can't do it without her, she might be flattered. Little displays of interest go a long way. If your teenage stepdaughter is rushed or stressed out because of her heavy schedule at school and a part-time job, you might offer to show her how you meditate; perhaps you could even enjoy this calming ritual together.

There is one issue you need to be alert to when forming a relationship with your mate's children: a number of women, too many to overlook, reported that when they had finally achieved an easy companionship with a stepchild, their husband became jealous! This was most common when the stepchild was a son and usually didn't last very long. We'll leave the therapists to analyze *that* one. The advice these stepmothers wanted to pass on is simply to keep the issue lighthearted and point out the obvious desirability of a good relationship over a tense or uncomfortable one.

YES!

Questionnaire

Try to answer these questions in writing in your idea book. It's a great morale booster, when reviewing your answers in a month or in six months, to see how well you've done on matters that concern you now or to note how completely different you can feel about someone or something when you've had more experience with your stepfamily:

1. If you have children of your own, do you believe your mothering experience will help you relate to your husband's kids? How?

2. What kind of relationship would you like to have with your stepchildren? Do you see possibilities for a reciprocal, one-on-one relationship?

3. Based on the research you've done so far, do you see potential difficulties in forming relationships with your stepchildren? If so, what are they?

4. How do you believe your stepchildren feel about you at this stage?

5. In what ways do you think your stepchildren will affect your relationship with your mate? List pros and cons.

6. Do you feel your biological children, if you have any, will affect your relationship with your mate? If so, how?

7. What positive steps do you think you can take to form your new relationships? What specific strengths do you have that will help you in this regard?

❧

Action Box

🦈 As you begin to get to know your stepkids, focus on forming a direct one-on-one relationship. Avoid triangular relationships (dealing with your husband's children only through him). This will shortcut the getting-to-know-you phase and will encourage mutual respect.

CHAPTER 8

Stepchildren at Every Age: From Baby Spoon to Empty Nest

In classes and focus groups stepmothers often debate these questions: What's the "best" age for a stepchild to be when you enter their lives? A baby? A teenager? An adult? Which are easier to cope with, boys or girls?

The answer is none of the above. Each age group and gender raises different issues, no two people are alike, and situations concerning someone else's kids are almost always sensitive. Many women feel that whatever age their stepkids were when they first met them is the toughest.

It might seem less complicated, for example, to "inherit" an eighteen-month-old baby than a sixteen-year-old, since it's easier to form a loving relationship with a cuddly toddler than an adolescent with built-in resentment and mood swings. Offsetting this, though, is the fact that a baby needs intensive attention.

This chapter is a discussion of issues stepmothers have raised about stepchildren in specific age groups. If you wish to learn more about a child's psychological, emotional, or physical development, there are many excellent books on the market and in your local library. Titles on child rearing are now quite specific; there are volumes dealing solely with family rules, teaching the value of money, sleep problems, sex education, bed-wetting, and positive discipline.

Although most of these books were written for biological

families, much of the general advice on raising children is applicable, and brief stepfamily specifics are sometimes offered. A stepmother could spend a very profitable afternoon just browsing.

Full-Time Baby Care

Once upon a time, even up to the turn of the twentieth century, women commonly became stepmothers because a biological mother had died in childbirth or perished from some now treatable disease. A young woman who married a widower often became the primary caretaker of his babies or small children. Today this occurrence is far less common: few women die in childbirth, and the revolution in hygiene and health care means many more diseases are preventable or curable.

In contemporary times the majority of women become stepmothers through divorce, not death. But even when a couple with a baby dissolves their marriage, the father is seldom granted custody unless the mother proves to be unfit or is incapacitated. It is unusual then, for a woman marrying a divorced man to become a full-time stepmother to a tiny child—of all the stepmothers we met, we came across only one case. We discuss the possibility here, however, because of the increasing number of abandonments by biological mothers and the chance that our readers might meet a widower or an abandoned dad with a young baby.

Babies might be one of the few exceptions to our "Stepmom's Quick Primer" point number 3: "Understand and accept that you are not and can never be your stepchildren's mother." If you marry a widower or an abandoned dad with a very young child for whom you assume maternal responsibility, a mother–child bond could be formed, since a baby will naturally love a person who nurtures him or her. Later, if you and your husband agree, and depending upon the circumstances, you might be able to adopt his baby, formalizing the relationship both emotionally and legally. We'll look at adoption in more detail in chapter 18.

On the practical side, infants need active, full-time care, and you must discuss your responsibilities with your partner, preferably before marriage, especially if you do not have children of your own and the word "colic" is not in your vocabulary. Several stepmothers pointed out that their husband assumed all women instinctively knew how to care for children, that mothering was an inborn trait. (If you're already a mom, obviously you'll know what you're getting into.)

For the inexperienced stepmom, a totally dependent baby, especially someone else's, is a daunting responsibility. Just holding, feeding, bathing, and changing a baby can be terrifying. Get some help! Find someone who can work with you until you feel comfortable performing the Baby 101 necessities. Read some comprehensive books on parenting young children. You haven't had nine months to prepare, nor do you have devoted friends, relations, and business colleagues giving you helpful hints, baby showers, maternity leave, and all the niceties that accompany pregnancy. Unless you go after assistance, it will probably not be proffered.

Baby Care, Some of the Time

If your husband's former wife has custody of her baby, Dad will probably be granted visitation rights, provisions that will almost certainly not include you. Stepmoms report difficulties with mothers who are unwilling to let "another woman" near their babies or are reluctant to let Dad have a fair share of time with his child, particularly if the divorce was hostile.

The best a part-time stepmother to a baby can do in these circumstances is be supportive of her husband—and wait. As the baby gets older, his mom may be willing to relinquish some control. Stepmothers also point out that when a mother starts dating, she often welcomes the opportunity to share her child, especially if her new boyfriend isn't keen on kids.

If your husband and his former wife have worked out an informal shared-custody arrangement for a baby, your mate will probably expect you to help him care for his child. Again, as with a full-time arrangement, discuss what will be required, how much time will be involved, what you are willing to do, what fits your schedule, etc.

Consider whether a baby-sitter will be needed—don't grudgingly try to handle everything yourself. A baby needs devoted attention from someone willing to provide it; he deserves to be loved, cuddled, and played with. If you have enough help from others you'll probably enjoy this relationship.

It's imperative to hire someone of the highest caliber if you need day care for your stepbaby. Mandy, stepmother to two-year-old Francis, had "the most awful experience of my life" when she used a neighbor's teenage daughter to watch her stepson one Saturday afternoon. "I came home after just two hours and found my house in an uproar," she recalled. The baby-sitter had picked Francis up from his nap and seated him in his high chair for a snack but forgotten to strap him in. The baby had fallen onto the tiled kitchen floor and was screaming—the girl was hysterical.

"I called nine-one-one, grabbed Francis, and saw he couldn't move his arms or legs. I later realized I shouldn't have touched him in case I made matters worse, but I was terrified." To cut a long, agonizing story short, after several days and visits to the pediatrician, Francis was fine, but, says Mandy, "I still have nightmares about it, and I will never, never, never leave him with anyone other than an experienced, highly qualified, older woman again." To Mandy's surprise, Francis's mother listened to the whole story quite calmly. "I admired her so much for the way she handled the episode. I think she realized how upset I was and how seriously I take the fact that her child is in my care. Ironically, it was a positive turning point in our relationship."

It's also important to be aware of any possibility of child abuse from people within or outside the stepfamily. Media sources and school professionals alike confirm that child abuse (or the reporting of this crime) is on the increase. Some people are not beyond reacting to anger or frustration by striking or

otherwise hurting a child. One stepmom reported finding ciga-
rette burns on her four-year-old stepson's tummy. The culprit
turned out to be a boyfriend of the child's mother, who fortunately was quickly discovered after this incident.

Consider, too, your own response to stress and anger. If
you find yourself upset by a continuously crying baby or dis-
obedient or rude stepchildren, you *must* be able to react in a
responsible nonviolent manner. If you suspect child abuse, are
concerned about your own ability to deal with anger, or want
to learn more about this issue in the interest of your stepchildren's safety, don't hesitate to call your local child-abuse
hot line.

Preschoolers: Everywhere, All at Once

When you become a full-time stepmother to a toddler who is
beginning to try his wings, you may be in for a shock at the
amount of energy he is capable of expending in his quest for
independence. This little one will be wary of you at first, but
as you become a familiar face, he will gradually come to accept you.

As a part-time stepmother to a toddler, you and your husband won't be able to explain the sudden switches between
your house and his mom's so that he can truly understand it,
though even children this young like consistency. Watch him
play, and note matters that disturb you—strong emotions, violent play, etc.

Observe his personality, likes and dislikes, and general
constitution. Is he a timid or a brave child? Withdrawn or
sociable? Is he healthy, or does he seem to have a perpetual
cold? Is he toilet trained? If not, whose job is this? Check out
with his mom or other experienced mothers anything that worries you, and if they're stumped, consult child-care books, or
consider professional help.

The time will come when you'll require him to behave
within the framework you and your husband devise for your
home. Right now your priorities will be centered on keeping

your stepchild safe and providing for his basic needs. Start planning ways to deal with the toddler's continual "no," a word he uses with everyone, not just his stepmom.

More than anything else, a calm, relaxed atmosphere in your home, along with a regular routine, will help a toddler adjust to life in your care and help him feel secure. (An anxious, rattled stepmother or house in turmoil compounds any difficulties.) As your young stepchild begins to talk, spend time chatting and playing with him.

"I find I can't wait to get home from work to pick Charlie up from my sister-in-law's house," recounted Dottie, a newspaper reporter. "And I think he even knows when I'm coming. Last night he was standing by his stroller, and I was sure he was waiting for me—it was so amazing."

Dottie is a part-time stepmom to three-year-old Charlie, who lives with her and her husband every second week, and is very attached to him. During work hours Dottie's sister-in-law cares for Charlie and her own two children. When Dottie picks up her stepson after work, he is all hers for a few hours. Dottie loves her part-time role—for her it's quite enough. "I'm really into my career," she explains, "and I have no desire to have a baby of my own. This is perfect for me. I am madly in love with Charlie, and because I show him that with lots of cuddles and treats, I think he loves me too. I will enjoy watching him grow up, and I think I'll be able to do a lot for him. But now, when it's time for him to go home, I'm always ready to bundle him up and return him to his mom!"

School-Age and Preteens: The Budding Socialites

Don't underestimate the sophistication of the six-to-twelve-year-old set these days. If you're a stepmom without children of your own, you may have little idea of how savvy they can be.

School-age children and preteens are honing their social skills, aligning themselves more and more with their friends, though adults are still quite useful for certain things. On the days they acknowledge your existence, and need advice, the fact that you're *not* Mom or Dad but an adult figure who can be an objective source of information might work to your advantage.

Asked what general advice they could give to a stepmother with stepkids this age, a guidance counselor and a school psychologist at a middle school within a large suburban school system in Westchester County, New York, stressed two vital points:

1. **Do not require them to introduce, address, or otherwise refer to you as their stepmother.** This is generally felt to be a relationship that nobody understands. Allow them to call you by your first name.

2. **Communicate.** Err on the side of explaining too much to both sets of kids—about your "courtship," how the relationship is going, when you've decided to marry, plans for the future. Explain that everyone has adjustments to make, but if everyone works together, problems can be resolved.

Both professionals agree that kids in this age group are amazingly resilient, able to cope reasonably well with changes in their lives if events are explained to them and if the adults involved are of good character. They estimate approximately fifty percent of the kids in their school are part of a stepfamily situation. They also noted that kids in the middle-school years can be very opinionated about roles in relationships. During a discussion on stepfamilies, an eleven-year-old girl who was not a stepchild remarked, "It should be simple to cut the legs from under a stepmother. You just tell her she's not your mother—that should handle her."

Since your stepkids are getting into the "group" phase, it might be a good time to suggest to their dad (and perhaps their mom) that they join a chat group for stepkids. Some youngsters may think this is a great idea—being able to complain about their stepmom in a supportive, solution-oriented environment; shyer kids may need some persuasion to attend. Just the chance to compare notes with others, to see that his own situation isn't as "bad" as another kid's, or even deciding on second thought that you, his stepmom (or dad's girlfriend), aren't so bad after all are among the worthwhile results.

With a talented leader, the group can also help a stepchild understand how relationships work, and offer a chance to practice some elementary problem-solving skills. Be sure you and your husband meet the group leader before arranging for your stepchild to attend. You'll want to know he or she has some knowledge of stepfamily dynamics, has no bias against stepmoms and is capable of directing the discussions into productive areas. We heard of a school-sponsored support group, Kids of Divorced Families, which turned into a brainstorming session on "How to Mess Up a Date"—members of this particular meeting pooling ingenious methods designed to scare away adult interlopers. If you and your mate are not yet married, you might prefer your potential stepchildren not engage in topics such as this. But as with most support groups, generally the positive outcomes by far outweigh any negative aspects.

Some family experts believe when parents divorce, kids often hope that one day they will reunite. This fantasy (which can be held by children of any age, right through adulthood), together with the determination of some preteens to get their own way whatever it takes, provides limitless possibilities for disruption.

Stepmothers have reported that when they were dating their husbands, it was impossible to get through a nice, quiet dinner without the phone ringing several times during the evening, one schoolchild or another calling to ask an unnecessary question or to tell tales—anything to stop the relationship in its tracks as early as possible.

Failing this, their second choice may be to select a stepmother themselves, which in one case worked remarkably well:

Betsy and Tammy, aged ten, were best friends. Both lost one parent to cancer in fifth grade—Betsy her mother and Tammy her father—and their friendship grew out of this shared experience. Two years later, the twelve-year-olds hatched the romantic idea of combining their two single-parent households by playing matchmaker to their parents. Throughout one summer, the girls initiated family "dates"—barbecues, movies, picnics. By September, there was no looking back. Tammy's mother, Mary, now Betsy's stepmom, told us: "It was one chance in a million, but it worked! Sam and I have been married for two years, and the girls believe they pulled off the deal of the century. We think it helped that we all moved and started over on an equal footing in a new home."

Sticks and Stones

The preteen years are a time when there may be an escalation of the classic insults used by stepchildren: "I hate you." "You're not my mother." "I don't have to do what you say." "You're not blood; you don't count." Try not to take childish taunts personally—remember they are directed at their stepmother, Dad's wife—you just happen to be filling the position.

Insults hurled in anger or frustration are common in many families, biological and step; sometimes a child's only means of retaliation. Treat verbal barbs lightly, and respond in a casual vein as you feel appropriate: "I'm sorry to hear that, but it's time for lunch"; "Of course I'm not your mother; you have a mom. I'm your stepmother"; "While you're in this house, your father and I agree you have to do as I ask." With the last of the classic insults, "You're not blood," stepmothers report on occasion a great temptation to respond, "Thank God!" but usually end up rejoining more prudently, "That's true, but you still have to set the table."

Veteran stepmothers advise that unless you have the ability to think on your feet, you need to build up a repertoire of responses to these inevitable insults. Bursting into tears or striking back with an equally hurtful remark will only make it more fun for your stepchild to repeat his performance and perhaps reinforce his negative feelings about you. Better to acknowledge the truth he thinks he's discovered and head off further discussion.

Children at Risk: Stepmoms Are Part of the Solution

Educators advise that school-age stepchildren are *among* those considered "at risk"—those who in the school's opinion may need additional attention—but no more so than kids living with other types of stress. According to a high school principal in a large suburban school system in the Northeast whose career spans twenty years, children are not necessarily affected negatively by being part of a stepfamily. Stepmothers, in fact, are often seen by the school as a positive influence on families, easing a sometimes tense relationship between a child and his or her father. Difficulties for a stepchild frequently relate to other aspects of a remarried family—stepsibling troubles, divided loyalties, emotional pressures from the parents, dissatisfaction with custody arrangements.

Children in the at-risk category also include those whose parents are in the process of divorcing; children suspected of being physically or emotionally abused; youngsters from unstable, unsupervised, or financially impoverished homes; and children with learning disabilities. Other children at risk are those from single-parent families, particularly those with single mothers. Mom is frequently overwhelmed by logistics, by shouldering most of the responsibility for her children and their behavior (particularly if she has a son), and is often worried about money. Kay Pasley, Chair of the Research Committee of the Stepfamily Association of America, adds that research overwhelmingly shows that children who live in a conflict-ridden biological family are also at risk. Says Pasley, "These may be the most common at-risk kids who most professionals [like educators] ignore because we assume that two-parent homes are good."

School professionals also note the disturbing increase in the number of mothers who abandon their children. Under these circumstances, when Dad has "care, custody, and control," the stepmother is often treated in exactly the same way as a mother would be treated, were she around. Adopted children, who in their teens often begin a quest for their biological parents, especially if they find out the facts by accident or were not told of their heritage until adolescence, are also looked upon as "at risk" by schools.

Tipping the At-Risk Scale in Their Favor

Preteens and teenagers should be enjoying some of the best times of their lives. To help them do this, a high school principal, who is also a stepfather, encourages stepmothers of kids in this age group to become involved immediately in their daily lives—to be open to discussing anything and everything.

His belief in the necessity of early involvement is based on his personal experience with his two stepkids; his wife, whom we interviewed, considers herself a successful stepmom to his child. You and your husband can do much to enhance your children's and stepchildren's preteen and adolescent years by being certain they understand, as far as their ages permit, the following:

- that their parents' divorce was not their fault.

- that both parents (if Mom is still alive) will continue to love them.

- that if Mom died, you are not replacing her.

- if the parents are divorced that you're their dad's wife, but will also be there for them.

- that it is possible to love, or at least like, several adults at one time and that liking you in no way detracts from their love for their mom.

- that you are here to stay—their parents aren't getting back together.

Holden Caulfield Up Close

The teenage years are often difficult for any family. Stepmoms say the biggest challenge of meeting stepchildren for the first time in their high-school years is one of timing. While the pulling away from their families toward privacy and independence, often embarrassed by relatives and preferring the company of peers and the telephone, you're trying to get to know them and create a family. They, like their stepmom, are exploring a new role in life, a commonality which may be the basis of an interesting discussion or two.

The difference is that while teens are expected to be self-absorbed, you'll be expected to provide a warm, accepting, non-judgmental environment, complete with a full refrigerator, and an oblivious attitude to the hours they keep, the state of their rooms, clothes, hairstyles, manners, social graces, use of your property (particularly clothing and makeup if you have a stepdaughter) and claims to their dad's possessions, including the family car. While all this may seem natural to a mother who has raised her children since birth, many a stepmom, with or without kids of her own, finds it difficult to nurture and provide for kids who actively dislike her.

Nonetheless, teens can be very interesting if you take the time to get involved in their lives. Try to learn who their friends are, what they like to do in their spare time, how they feel about school, and their plans for the future. Notice their dress code, the sports they play, clubs they belong to, etc.

Teens love to discuss anything under the sun (you may call it arguing), and might be willing to use you as their sounding board. They're trying out the sound of their own voices, and if you prove to be a good listener—they don't actually want to hear much from you—you may be able to form a somewhat uneven, but promising, relationship with them. They are quick, however, to criticize established social systems—school, culture, family, religion—and will also test the boundaries you establish with their dad.

Teens may also enjoy embarrassing a new stepmom, or putting her on the spot, so be prepared for this. At her first Thanksgiving dinner with her new family, Jody's stepson asked her, during a lull in the conversation (unusual with almost twenty people present), "Jody, when did you and Dad first sleep together?" Jody stammered and blushed for a moment, until her husband rescued her: "I don't think Jody or I, for that matter, will discuss that with you."

Jody has resolved never to be caught off guard again. You can rise to the top of a teenager's totem pole by having a few flippant remarks ready. Had Jody been able to zap back with a witty response—"Haven't slept yet, sweetheart, we're having too much fun!"—everyone may well have laughed and Jody would probably have increased her standing in the family, especially with the younger members.

If your teen stepchildren make it clear they don't want to get closer to you, back off. Move on to something else in your life—organizing your new household, concentrating on your career, raising your own children—you have better things to do than be upset by continual rebuffs. Continue to observe and let them know the door's open for a future, more mature, relationship. Also persevere with your research. If you are uncomfortable around your burly six foot teenage stepson because you have no experience with boys his age, find a mother of teens and talk with her. For an understanding of adolescent girls, *Reviving Ophelia,* by Mary Pipher, Ph.D. provides some worthwhile insights.

Teens and Serious Decisions

Older teens face many serious decisions, perhaps for the first time in their lives. What to do to prepare for the future? How to earn a living? Straight to college or take a year off first, to travel or work? Loans, a car, an apartment? On top of all these life-changing decisions, young women and men are dealing with raging hormones and mood swings. It's a time of first love, dating, insecurities. Of acne, weight gain, physical overdevelopment, underdevelopment. Nobody, they're convinced, understands them.

By the time kids are in their mid to late teens they will probably know more than their parents about sex. You may be horrified to discover that your stepteenagers, girls and boys, are sexually active. If you believe this is the case, you and your husband will want to discuss sexual responsibility with them, depending on your position on the issues—abstinence, or protection against sexually transmitted disease and pregnancy prevention.

An unwanted pregnancy can present an emotionally and financially devastating situation, compounded if your teen, you, or your husband is opposed to abortion, or if you and your partner have decided against or cannot have a baby of your own. Not to mention the heartbreak of bringing a child into the world who starts out unwanted and perhaps even resented. Where there are seemingly irreconcilable differences, don't hesitate to bring in a professional, preferably one who has helped resolve similar situations with other stepfamilies. A stronger, more united stepfamily is often the result of constructively handling a crisis together.

Try to bring other sexual issues out into the open, too. Homosexuality is becoming easier for young women and men to deal with—there's a lot more support in society when they do decide to "come out."

Discuss your attitude toward homosexuality with your mate and find out what his views are. In talking with stepmoms, we found it was generally easier for them to accept a stepchild being gay than it was for their husbands.

All Grown Up, but Still Living with Dad

Adult stepchildren (18-24 age range) still living with dad don't need mothering or nurturing, in fact, it wouldn't be surprising to be rebuffed if you attempted anything along these lines. Similarly, say stepmoms of adults, do not make the mistake of offering unsolicited advice; it is unlikely to be considered.

In their dad's eyes, these kids are still his babies, and while you will expect them to pull their weight in the home, perhaps contributing financially, Dad may still think they need to be fed and possibly clothed by him.

If your stepchildren's mother has died, and your mate has been a full-time single parent since her passing, he has likely tried to be both mother and father. Stepmoms report scenes of Dad serving as butler and maid rolled into one, with kids sitting at home waiting for him to return from work to make dinner. Stories abound of Dad sacrificing his personal needs to compensate for the loss of his "babies'" mother. He, and they, forget that he also has suffered a loss, and that life is difficult for him, too.

If a divorce took place, given the choice, older kids may have elected to move in with Dad because he was easier on them, because they were provided more space, more amenities, and less was required of them. In addition, their father may find it difficult to take money from them, not requiring them to contribute to the household financially. If Dad travels on business, his young adult kids are probably left alone in the house to party, practice their increasing sexual skills, or simply enjoy unstructured days. Life is pretty good.

When you appear on the scene, and you and your lover want some privacy, young adults who live with their father are unlikely to surrender their privileges or adapt their lifestyle to include you. Through their eyes you pose an inconvenience. Dad now has less time for them; when he takes you to dinner they are left to get their own, and worse, money being spent on a romantic dinner for two leaves less to be spent on them. That Dad is happy after the pain or heartbreak of the last few years often seems less important to them than the latest change in their lifestyle.

It is important for a potential stepmom to understand that younger children, while often resenting you, actually do need you for certain of their material comforts, whereas adults do not. They can live perfectly well without you. And, unless you are going to tangibly improve their lives, which they rarely perceive as possible, you need to accept that these step-children, more often than not, don't want you around.

This is hard to hear, and usually comes as a major shock to stepmoms. We heard women say many times, sometimes through tears, "They just don't want me!" While it's in your interest to make overtures of friendship to adult stepchildren, many stepmothers reported beating their heads against the proverbial wall trying to form relationships "for the sake of their father," and suffering a great deal of emotional pain. Don't do it. If they reject you, it's their right to do so. It's also their loss, not worth a stepmom becoming sick, suffering guilt, or depression. If you can absorb the possibility of rejection before you marry, you'll be able simply to concentrate on being their dad's wife and focus on other areas of your life.

Some practical-minded stepmoms report being unable to comprehend the shortsightedness of their stepkids who reject them—whatever their age. "They'd have a much better relationship with their dad if they were half-way pleasant to me," explained Darlene. "I don't encourage them to do things with us because, to be quite honest, I'm happier when they aren't around. If they were at least courteous, I'd take it as a sign we could have some kind of relationship."

Depending upon the circumstances, adult stepchildren may have the option to leave Dad's house and live at Mom's when you arrive. Those financially able to do so may elect to set up house by themselves or with roommates when dad remarries—often the best solution for everyone, if working relationships cannot be formed. This may be an expression of disapproval of their stepmom, or be done simply to upset (punish) dad. Unfortunately, it gives any observer who doesn't know better the chance to say of you, "She drove poor Davey out of the house." In a flash, before you can open your mouth to explain that Davey chose to leave, you can become the wicked stepmother.

Your mate, probably reeling from the guilt, arguments, or tension caused by Davey's dissatisfaction with his new stepmother, or his father's new lifestyle, might view his son's departure as a personal failure; you, on the other hand, might breathe a sigh of relief while recognizing Davey may simply be resisting yet another change in his life.

But even if Davey's departure takes place in the heat of the moment, most people his age find living at home restrictive anyway, and it can be considered part of the maturing process. Odds are he will experience tensions in his mother's home, too, if that's where he's headed, unless she is particularly permissive.

Whatever the case, it's important to leave the door open for him, both practically and metaphorically. When the dust has settled, you and his dad can decide how to start the recovery process.

Wanda knew she had made a mistake after only four months of marriage. A corporate woman, single for almost eighteen years after her divorce, she had married Eric, a handsome fireman with two children—a young man of twenty-one and a young woman of twenty-four—still living at home. Neither was working or contributing to the household finances.

"Having been single for so long, I felt I had dated enough to know a good man when I met one," reported Wanda. "I fell in love with Eric because he was so much fun. I knew he had two kids, but I didn't know they would have such an impact on our lives—after all, they're adults. I met them only once before we married, and just assumed they would be pleased to let me restore some sort of order to their lives. The house was an awful mess—the kids, home all day, did no cleaning. I wanted to fumigate the place before I moved in, but thought I could make changes once we were settled."

Wanda's nice corporate salary, and the rent from her condo apartment, all went toward paying off Eric's mortgage and to support his adult children, who insisted they could not find gainful employment. The family's lifestyle could not be more different from Wanda's. As she explained, she had gone from eating off a matching Wedgwood dinner service to supermarket plastic dishes! Eric called Wanda "superficial" and "cheap" when she tried to discuss their increasingly intolerable living conditions.

"Maybe it's shallow of me, but I like to live nicely, and I've certainly earned it for myself. I can't go on like this. His daughter says I have no right to run things my way and Eric refuses to insist on his kids' cooperation, so I seem to have no option but to leave. I'm just relieved I kept my condo."

Preventing a War of Wills

Young adult stepkids commonly resist a stepmother's authority to run her own home. Your only leverage in dealing with this challenge is your mate's support. Regardless of the way they feel about you, Dad needs to support you in developing a well-functioning household and help make sure his adult children know exactly what will be required of them whether they live with you full-time or part-time. One 29-year-old stepdaughter told her stepmom, "We didn't know what the rules were until you got so annoyed that we broke them!" Discuss possible financial contributions and other household responsibilities first with your husband. See chapter 14, "Home Sweet Step Home," for more on setting up house rules.

What Wanda needed to do before making the decision to marry, (and what we strenuously advise based on many women's experience with adult-still-in-the-nest-kids) was to fully assess the household that she was expected to move into and to help finance. Had she researched, Wanda would have known these "kids" were not working, were not required to take on any practical responsibilities around the house, and that she would be expected to provide a substantial financial contribution. She could then have discussed these problematic issues with Eric, and expressed that marriage to him would be predicated on an agreement to make changes or compromises.

Marrying into an Empty Nest

When a woman marries a man with independent adult children, she's likely to be very surprised by the unexpected challenges she'll face.

Most stepmothers assume incorrectly that since their mate's nest is empty, they will have adult-to-adult relationships with his children. Why is this usually not so? Because 20-something, 30-something, even 40-something adults (perhaps only a few years younger or sometimes even older than you) are still referred to and treated as "the kids" by their dad but don't always behave with age-appropriate maturity around him.

Almost to a number, stepmoms are unprepared for this. They meet grown men and women, leading upwardly mobile, two-career, two-car, two-children lives, who appear to believe the death of their mom, or divorce of their parents, followed by the arrival of a stepmom in their lives, gives them grounds for any type of negative behavior they care to display. Again incorrectly, stepmothers tend to expect adult children to be able to cope or to have coped already with their loss, since they too have suffered losses during their lives. It's more diffi-cult to overlook unacceptable behavior or hurtful remarks on the part of independent grown men and women (near-peers) than it is from younger children with less experience of life's vagaries.

Stepmothers report seeing their husband ill-treated by his adult children, which they interpret as punishment for moving forward in his life, finding happiness again and remarrying. "I sometimes cry for Brian," reports Vera. "In twelve years I have never seen my stepdaughter do so much as make her dad a cup of coffee. When we're invited to dinner, upon our arrival, we hear, 'Let's go to the new restaurant in the village,' with the assumption that dad will foot the bill."

Another stepmother recalls an overnight stay with her 38-year-old stepson. "We barely set foot in the door when my stepson presented his dad with a list of repairs needed around the house. Not even a 'Would you like a drink after your long trip, Dad?' I don't expect to be treated like royalty, but I think courtesy to his dad is a reasonable expectation, even if he can't stand me."

Yet another told us, "We were expected to help his thirty-three year old daughter move house but on our own moving day she was nowhere to be seen."

While any sense of consideration of reciprocity seems lack-ing, adult stepchildren's sense of entitlement appears fully de-veloped according to stepmoms. Dad is still expected to pay every time they venture out together—cab fares, meals, theater tickets. Money is expected for private school or college for grandkids, for vacations, toward down payments on homes, in the words of one disgusted stepmom, "he's expected to give, give, give until he's dry." That this may also be the case in biological families is of little consolation to a stepmother attempting to forge adult relationships with her adult stepkids.

Other stepmothers tell of seeing their mate practically beg to be allowed to visit. Nina confided, "We are told we may visit the grandchildren on Tuesday between 2 and 4, then leave because they have something important to do. We live almost 3 hours away, so you can imagine how we feel about this. It's humiliating for me, but worse for my husband."

Nina acknowledged there isn't much she can do about it. "A wise, experienced stepmother took me aside one day and explained that my husband had allowed his kids to treat him this badly over a period of many years and a pattern had developed," she said. "It was not a situation I could remedy instantly, if at all. Since he had permitted it, he must now bear the brunt of it, or make changes himself." As a stepmom in love with this particular dad, witnessing this kind of behavior can be extraordinarily difficult to bear.

Assess your situation very early in this regard and try to accept what you find, protecting your husband's feelings where you can. It's not necessary (or helpful) to bring to a father's attention the fact that his children appear to have little interest in his happiness. Some stepmoms report an eroding of their feelings for their mate in light of his inability to command respect from his kids, but try to see things from another perspective—the poor guy has let things get out of hand, and is understandably reluctant to admit it. He probably feels powerless. Make him feel like a hero when he's with you. Enjoy your life with him for the reasons you married him. Let your husband visit his kids alone, if necessary—you don't need to see him humiliated, or to put up with bad manners yourself.

At some point your stepkids may see things differently. When they visit you (if they do) treat them with respect, make them feel welcome, and set a shining example of courtesy by your actions.

Why Do Adult Stepchildren Behave like Six-Year-Olds?

Stepmoms speculate unceasingly about why they are not welcomed, or at least accepted, as the reason for the newfound happiness of their adult stepchildren's dad, the man these children supposedly love. It seems incomprehensible. Some enlightened stepmothers think it often comes down to whether or not these adults are happy themselves. People, not only stepchildren, who have problems, often feel entitled to make other people's lives miserable, too. When life is going well, there is a tendency to be more generous.

But even when you know this, animosity still confounds. "I would understand it if there was a personality conflict—if they got to know me and decided they didn't like me," declared Amanda, "but not one of my three stepkids has ever asked me a personal question about my likes and dislikes, my background, my opinions, or how I spent the thirty-nine years before I met their dad."

Olivia surmised, "Perhaps they just don't like the thought that their father's having sex again, at his age! They know we're in love, maybe they're embarrassed at the thought of us doing it! They might even be worried we'll have a baby, which is possible, since I'm only forty-two."

"I think it's about money," declared Zena. "Every mouthful I take, every gift their dad gives me, they believe leaves less for them. Little do they know—because they won't talk to me—when my former husband died, I was the beneficiary of his five hundred thousand dollar life insurance policy. I've had that invested and it's almost doubled. Having no kids of my own, I would have enjoyed sharing it, but with their attitude, I decided to set up a scholarship fund in my late husband's name at an inner-city school that can use some help. Not a cent will go to my husband's kids."

An Adult Stepdaughter's Perspective

It's worth seeking out adult stepchildren—other than your own—and asking them how they felt about the appearance of a stepmother. One adult stepdaughter we talked to gave an embarrassed giggle and admitted, "Oh, God, we were so awful to that poor woman," another said her hostility was "par for the course." Rarely is there much regret about unkindness, and only once or twice have we heard a stepchild speak with sincere regret or consider an apology necessary.

Alisa, 44, a therapist with a thriving practice, including counseling stepfamilies, is a stepdaughter. Her parents suffered through a bad marriage "for the sake of the children" until her last sibling married, three years ago. "My father literally walked my sister down the aisle and then left," Alisa remarked. "He didn't even come to the reception."

After her parents divorced, Alisa's father remarried a woman whose attributes are clear, even to her stepdaughter. Said Alisa, "This woman is so good to him—she makes him so happy. He has finally come to life after years of bickering with my mother." A comment about how pleased Alisa must be for her father, however, drew her ire. She banged on the table in front of her and through gritted teeth, exclaimed, "I hate her, I hate her, I hate her!" When she had calmed down, she admitted her reaction seemed irrational and tried to explain why she felt so negatively toward her stepmother. "She really is a nice person, but it should be my mother who is with my father."

The feeling that one's parents should be together is prevalent among adult stepchildren. As fully independent adults, they often begin to turn back to their family of origin for support and encouragement as they marry and have children of their own. Perhaps the arrival of a stepmother—a "stranger," with whom their father has found new love, reminds these adult stepchildren of the unpredictable nature of the future (the impermanence of marriage, the possibility of death) at a time when they are trying to write their own 'happily ever after' story.

An adult stepdaughter, a psychologist, had the most succinct answer. About her stepmother, she said, "She was a lovely woman, but I couldn't like her. She wasn't my mother." Putting on her professional hat, after being pushed further for logic, she responded, "I had an inborn resentment that precluded an objective evaluation of this person." It's probably additionally heartwrenching for kids to see dad content with another woman, if their mom is miserable and alone.

If as stepmoms we're given a "hard time" (which takes many forms) simply because we aren't our stepkids' mother, we can probably do no better than recognize this early on, accept it, and go our own way. Whatever the reason, from a stepmom's point of view, it is the way these feelings are played out that is unacceptable and that needs to be addressed.

Responding to (Childish or Worse) Adult Behavior

It's not easy to rebuke an adult child. During the course of our interviews, we were distressed to hear stepmoms tell of retreating to their bedrooms, of leaving their homes, or of not joining their husbands on special occasions because they could not cope with bad attitudes or behavior on the part of their adult stepkids. A father may resist rebuking his 40-year-old son for belligerence since he is used to it or might have condoned it in the past.

Clearly, it is unacceptable for a woman to be run out of her own home by visiting adults behaving badly. In responding to conduct you find intolerable, it is essential to think in terms of your marital united front—we have a problem. (See chapter 6 for a review of this concept.) If your mate finds this task impossible, you need to say something along these lines: "We understand it must be difficult for you to get used to our marriage. But this is our home and we must ask you to behave courteously while you are here. If you find it impossible right now to conduct yourself with restraint, you'll be welcome to visit us another time when you are able to do so."

It is essential that you and your mate discuss this scenario, and what you will say, ahead of time. Be aware that your husband may see it as an upsetting confrontation. But only when he endorses and enforces your words (or tells his kids the position himself) will the situation improve. Without a

united front, adult children, like young ones, may s
possibility of dividing you, and of their dad siding with _____

Victoria, 44, was just a few years older than her husband's
three children, aged 32, 35, and 37. Their behavior—rude
remarks, referring to Victoria as "she," never by name, lack of
consideration toward their dad, dropping by unannounced at
all hours of the day—reached the point where Victoria knew
she had no option but to stop it, or leave the family.

"My husband insisted he was not able to control them,"
she explained, "so we together decided to handle it my way.
I invited them with their families to our house to celebrate
Father's Day. When they were all gathered, I pulled a chilled
bottle of champagne from the refrigerator and began my well-
rehearsed speech.

"I said, 'Today is a new beginning for this family. I want
you to know we will no longer tolerate any rudeness or lack
of respect toward your father or me. Let's start over. I am
abdicating my role as your stepmother—from now on you can
think of me simply as your dad's wife, and perhaps someday
as a friend. We need a telephone call before you visit, I prefer
to be called and referred to as 'Victoria' and we'd both appreciate a word of thanks once in a while for the nice things we
do for you. Now, please raise your glasses and let's celebrate
our new relationship.'

"There was always the possibility that I would fall flat on
my face after that announcement, but to my utter amazement,
they clinked glasses, quite speechless, and looked at me with
new respect. There was no scene or argument on their part,
and without further ado, I just smiled and asked everyone to
help bring out food for our barbecue. One son apologized to
me later, when we found ourselves alone in the kitchen. After
that day, they turned out to be quite pleasant people."

Adult Transitions: New Roles and Relationships in Your Stepfamily

If you married your stepchildren's dad many years ago, by the
time they reach young adulthood and begin to live on their

own, you will probably have smoothed out the rough edges of your relationships with them. Some of the stepmoms we spoke with had eventually formed what they considered worthwhile relationships with "kids" this age, based on mutual interests, love of the same man, and mutual understanding of the difficulties of stepfamily life.

If this is the case, you have the basis for some lifelong friendships. Eileen, the stepmom we met who decided to claim the role of "big sister" to her stepsons, has shared their experience of watching parents struggle through a divorce. Her own father has remarried at the age of sixty-one, providing an opportunity for her to talk with her now thirty-something stepsons about adjusting to a stepmother.

Stepmothers usually welcome the time when stepchildren they have helped raise leave home and become independent, since day-to-day difficulties with them diminish. It's time for you to have your husband mostly to yourself, perhaps for the first time since your wedding day.

Some report feeling guilty at their delight when their mate's last child finally moves out. This is natural, to be expected after what has gone before. Even if you have a wonderful, affectionate relationship with your stepchildren, the getting there has usually been tough.

"I remember the first time in sixteen years that Jim and I spent the weekend at home alone together," Sallyann told us. "We helped move my youngest stepson into his new apartment on a Friday and were alone that weekend. We acted like a couple of kids, chased each other through the house, naked, made love in front of the fire, had too much to drink and made love again under the dining room table. We couldn't believe what we were doing! We danced to loud music, had pizza in bed on Saturday night watching TV, with a bottle of champagne resting on a pillow. All our pent-up inhibitions evaporated. After years of restraint "because of the children," we finally had our privacy. Of course, we did settle down into our new routine eventually, but we still laugh about that one weekend."

When Stepdaughter Becomes Stepmom

What goes around, comes around! Several stepmothers reported an astonishing change in their relationships with their adult stepdaughters when—surprise, surprise—they became stepmothers.

Leah, mother of four and stepmother to her husband Vincent's five children, had a tumultuous relationship with her stepdaughter, Cindy, while the girl was growing up. Now in her early thirties, Cindy is a stepmother to an eight-year-old girl. "On a recent visit," relates Leah, "Cindy told her father and me the problems she was having with her stepchild's mother." The woman was demanding an increase in child support, even though the girl lived most of the time with her dad and Cindy. Plus, her stepdaughter didn't seem to like her, and . . .

In the middle of her story, Cindy suddenly stopped and stared at Leah, dumbfounded, her eyes welling up with tears. "It hit her like a ton of bricks, listening to herself pour out her troubles as a stepmother," Leah recalled. "She connected with me completely at that moment and started crying, apologizing for her past behavior. Later she said, 'Isn't it ironic that you're the only person I now feel I can turn to for advice? After all these years, I finally understand where you were coming from.' "

. . . And When Stepmom Becomes Stepgrandmother

Once grandchildren appear, adult stepchildren wield yet more power. They only have to threaten to withhold these cherished babies, say stepmoms, and dad becomes putty in their hands.

Many stepmoms we spoke with were told categorically that they should not consider themselves part of the family and will never be looked upon as a stepgrandma to their stepgrandchildren. Others have found that the arrival of stepgrandchildren can be an almost magical turning point in the relationship between a stepmom and her stepkids, providing endless shared opportunities for everyone to coo over and admire the babies, to play silly games together as they grow, and to take older ones on jaunts. A stepgrandmother now has something very precious in common with her stepkids who become parents—the love of their children.

But stepgrandchildren can present a stepmother with another dichotomy. If she finds she is welcomed as a stepgrandmother, she is usually delighted and, particularly if she doesn't have children who will provide her with grandchildren of her own, revels in the family "doting." She takes pleasure in buying miniature clothes and toys, and enjoys the fun of being involved in young lives again, or maybe for the first time.

The other side of the dichotomy has great emotional risk. Several stepmoms confided some anxiety about the long term nature of their relationship with their stepgrandkids. Jade told us, "I'm really scared to invest too much of myself in these kids. It would break my heart to love them, to get really involved in their lives, and then lose contact with them, if my husband should die before I do. My fear is that my stepson won't want much to do with me if that happens—we had such a stormy relationship when he was younger. I think once the will has been read, he'll take the money and run, and I won't see him, or his kids, for dust."

Many older women felt this way, some to the extent that they resisted attachment to their stepgrandkids. One expressed her fear that once stepgrandkids were old enough to understand family relationships, their mother would relate tales of how "wicked" a stepmom she had been, and this would influence their as yet untarnished feelings toward her. Another stepgrandmother decided to take a proactive position and explained her worries to her stepson. Happily, this young father assured his stepmom he enjoyed the improved relationship they had, and promised that his affection toward her, and her access to his children, would continue even if his father was no longer alive.

Spouses of adult stepchildren can sometimes be of enormous help in this area. Barbara Jean, an eighteen-year veteran stepmom put it this way, "If it hadn't been for my husband's daughter-in-law, I would have been afraid to invest so much of my time and emotion in her two children. I got on well with her, and she seemed to understand both my stepson's—her husband's—point of view, and mine. I know my stepson told her about the terrible fights we had when he was younger, but she says she didn't know me until four years ago, so my stepson must adjust. They're her kids too, and she enjoys me being a stepgrandmom to them. He's becoming more comfortable with this, and I'm hoping our relationship can now improve."

❧

Questionnaire

1. Do you believe your stepchildren are aware of the power they hold, whatever their ages? Do they realize their dad may be nervous about losing them or their love?

2. Do your stepchildren blame their father for the break-up of their family? If so, how is this exhibited? How does it affect you or your marriage?

❧

Action Box

- Step back and take an overall view of all these children who will be part of your life. Take your time—don't commit yourself to becoming their best buddy, and don't write any of them off, yet. It's easy to misjudge people, whatever their ages, in the early stages of a relationship.

- Research further the issues of children in your stepchildren's age group if you think you need to understand them better, especially if they have specific problems or challenges not necessarily related to stepfamily life.

CHAPTER 9

A Baby of Your Own

Just as most women grow up never guessing they will become stepmothers, many assume that one day they will be mothers. Since childhood, we've learned that motherhood is a rite of passage, along with marrying and having our own home.

Today, as women delay or skip marriage to pursue careers or to be true to their sexuality, childbearing has become elective—we are deciding not only when we wish to have children, but also whether we want to at all.

The U.S. Census Bureau predicts that fifteen to twenty percent of women in the baby boomer generation will not have children of their own, compared with just seven percent of the previous generation. For some women, becoming a stepmother, inheriting children, takes the place of bearing them. But for many of us, having stepchildren cannot satisfy the desire to be a mom. If you're a stepmother to young children, for example, you may realize you want more than simply performing caretaking duties for kids who have a mother to love elsewhere.

A Stepmom's Special Concerns

Ideally a woman's choice to have children is based on her desire to be a mother and her ability to provide for her offspring. A stepmother, however, especially one with young children already, step, biological, or adopted, has a different set of criteria than other women. As a stepmom, you, with your mate, will have to consider his responsibilities—financial, emotional, and practical—to his existing family, commitments that will profoundly affect the life of your new baby.

From a purely practical standpoint, you'll need to examine your financial picture—is your family income sufficient to support another child, or is your budget already straining at the seams? The estimated cost of raising a child from babyhood through private college is at least $250,000, a figure that increases every year. Will your husband be putting his kids through school at a time when your daughter might need expensive orthodontic work? Will you have to work part-time or full-time while caring for your new baby? Can you organize your time and home to raise another child while accommodating the needs of full-time or part-time stepchildren?

For stepmothers who were previously divorced or widowed, a new baby can be the ultimate sign of a new life. Other stepmothers report wanting another baby to bring unification to a fragmented stepfamily.

But remember: your stepfamily can take a long time to adjust to the changes resulting from your marriage, and a baby presents another major adjustment. It's logical to believe that everybody loves a baby and, further, that the baby you have with your stepchildren's father is a biological link to all members, a happy fact that does have a certain irresistible, poetic quality. This scenario does encourage unity sometimes, but generally if relationships within the stepfamily are not good, a new baby does not improve them and may even exacerbate the already existing feelings of inequity and jealousy. Better that this little one should enter your life when existing relationships in your stepfamily have reached a reasonably stable point, with the marital relationship based on the united front and unconditional support we have stressed.

Baby Talk: Before You Say "I Do"

Deciding if you'll have a baby of your own is one of the most serious decisions you and your mate will make together; it's a discussion that needs to take place *before* your marriage. Underestimating the importance of talking it out before the wedding has contributed and will continue to contribute to the divorce statistics of remarried couples.

If your fiancé doesn't want a baby, you should not imagine you can change his mind once you are married, nor try to persuade yourself at a later date to agree with your husband's negative decision. And, as with so many other issues facing a stepmother, be sure this is not a decision that's made *for* you—your husband's undergoing a vasectomy before you've had a chance to discuss it, for example. Unless you can reach a solid, mutual decision about this issue early in your relationship, you have the potential for an explosive situation later in your marriage.

The Reluctant Dad

Some stepmoms-to-be, especially those who see the end of their childbearing years approaching, feel an urgency to marry and "start trying" hours after they've tossed their wedding bouquet. It can be a great disappointment to find out your man believes he has been blessed enough already and doesn't want to head out on the diaper trail again. Some initially reluctant dads, though, change their mind once they realize how much their wife wants (and feels she deserves) to be a parent to her own child. Once committed, stepmothers report, these once-anxious mates are wonderful dads and relish their second chance at fathering.

Other stepmoms caution against forcing your mate into another round of fatherhood when he is adamantly opposed to it. If he belongs in the "been there, done that, period" category, and you really insist, complete with ultimatums, the results can be disastrous. For the same reasons, "forgetting to take the pill" is not advised. No good can come from marriage to a man who feels trapped. Life is tough enough for a child these days without his being resented by one of his parents.

If your husband's reasons for not wanting another baby are financial, take these objections seriously. Are you willing to be penniless for the sake of your child? How will it affect your relationship with your husband? If money is his only reason, are there financial compromises that can be made?

It's harder on you when you believe his objections are due to selfishness. It is wonderful to hear, "I want you all to myself; I don't want to share you with a baby," if you personally have decided against maternity. But if a statement like this comprises your husband's total engagement in a discussion about having a baby, you'll have to decide whether he's taking your needs seriously enough. If he won't even consider the idea after you've explained your feelings for wanting a child of your own, you need to think deeply about whether or not this man really is the one for you.

A woman who is denied motherhood cannot be expected to be an ideal stepmother to her husband's children. She can hardly be blamed for feeling resentful if she is required to nurture and cater to another woman's kids while longing for her own. It can be difficult at best to feel love toward these children or, in the long run, for the man who refused her wish.

If you reach a stalemate in your decision-making process, consider a visit to a therapist. An objective listener might be able to help one or both of you clarify your feelings.

Are You Marrying for Love—or Motherhood?

One or two stepmothers admitted that as age gained on them and Mr. Right remained elusive, they contemplated single motherhood, decided against it, and determined to marry the next reasonably acceptable suitor, simply to have a baby.

For one of these women, Rene, this decision worked out fairly well, at least in the short term. She found a widower, became stepmom to his two young children, aged four and six years, and became pregnant as soon as practical.

Rene's happiness at becoming a mother has offset the task of caring for her husband's two motherless children. She would not recommend her route to other women, however, partly because of her guilt about marrying without love and partly because she feels unable to give her stepchildren the kind of love she feels they deserve.

She cautions other women to consider the consequences carefully before doing as she did. At the time of our interview, Rene's happiness definitely outweighed her guilt, but she acknowledged that this ratio may change in the future. During the year following her son's birth, she found herself thinking, "I have my baby. Now what?"

Rene advises potential stepmoms considering a "marriage for a baby" strategy to go through with it only if they feel that love in the marriage could grow and if they know the marriage could provide a stable, loving environment in which to nurture their own child as well as a stepchild. In retrospect Rene felt that she had been rather selfish, that she had simply wanted to come first with someone, to have someone dependent on her who would always love her.

Balancing Feelings

It's important to realize that your feelings toward your own children, if you decide to have them, can be quite different from your feelings for your stepchildren. Many women, convinced they should love their children and stepchildren equally, spend a lot of time and energy feeling guilty when they can't.

Reread "Stepmom's Quick Primer" number 11: It is not reasonable for you to expect, or to be expected, to love your stepchildren immediately, or vice versa. The best thing you can do is accept the disparity between your affections—it doesn't make you a less caring person. Loving feelings can take a long time to grow.

Stepmoms who become moms, particularly for the first time, report being unprepared or overwhelmed by the deep love they feel for their new baby. Some said their motherhood helped them understand their husband better. "I've experienced the same protective feelings Joe has for his own kids," Lillian confirmed following the birth of her son. "I know I would kill anything or anyone who threatened him in any way. I want his life to be perfect."

Other women reported having to pull themselves out of their initial total involvement with their own brand new baby. Several said they felt diminished interest in their stepchildren during the immediate post-natal period. Others explained their desire for a child as wanting a "power base." They were not very proud of this but were tired of being outnumbered, of not "having anyone on my side," or of having to arrange their life around their spouse's kids. "Now I have a reason to say no," Maxine explained. "I can't be at everyone's beck and call; I have my own baby to take care of."

Notwithstanding the different degrees of love you feel for the children in your home, however, it's imperative that you and your husband treat both sets of kids fairly, with the same standards, which we'll discuss in depth in part 3.

When What You Have Is Enough

For many stepmoms we came across, raising their own kids from a previous marriage, plus having a part to play in the lives of stepchildren, satisfied the extent of their maternal urges. The women in this category were without doubt among the happiest and most successful stepmothers we came across.

Other stepmothers, who had no children of their own, were content in the role of "earth mom" to their husband's brood, helping to raise them in a thriving, well-run household. These women demolish the myth that child-free women don't understand or don't like or can't relate to kids. Quite the contrary—these highly capable stepmoms felt they had the best of both worlds: the ability to pursue fulfilling, active lives

and careers while enjoying the sense of family they shared
with their husbands and their stepchildren.

When You Want a Baby but Can't Have One

Women often feel vulnerable and wary of sharing their feelings
about infertility with others. When an infertile woman is also
a stepmother grappling with stepfamily issues, she might
choose to remain silent about that pain, too; the infertile stepmom is suffering on two levels.

A stepmom who is having trouble conceiving might need
to seek medical intervention, often an emotional and financial
drain. If the final outcome is negative, the sense of loss and
failure can be devastating. Women saddened to find they cannot have a baby of their own say they feel . . .

- not normal, not whole, incomplete, unfulfilled

- less of a woman, unfeminine

- defective, flawed, anatomically useless

- angry, resentful

- cheated of what is rightfully hers—a "real" baby, not a
  stepchild

- left out of the privilege and wonder of creating and raising
  another human being.

Accepting a Child-Free Life: Special Notes for a Stepmom

Linda Hunt Anton's book *Never to Be a Mother: A Guide for
All Women Who Didn't—or Couldn't—Have Children* (HarperCollins, 1992), from which the above characteristics are
drawn, is a must-read for a stepmother or potential stepmother
who has not yet made up her mind about motherhood or who

finds she cannot have children (either for medical reasons or because she and her mate agree it is ill-advised).

Anton opens a window on the lives of women who, for a variety of reasons, did not have children and includes steps to heal the heartache of infertility while leading a rich, child-free life. The guidance Anton offers might help you make your decision, justify or confirm the decision if it is already made, or expose you to perspectives you might not have considered.

You need to recognize there will be those who question your reasons not to have a child. Unfortunately, on top of the negative connotations associated with stepmothers are those associated with women who do not have children: "barren," "unmotherly," "child hater," "selfish." These epithets can provide a verbal arsenal for "problem people" in the stepfamily: "Well, what does she know? She's not a mother."

Stepmothers reported being on the receiving end of many negative remarks that are often quite cruel. Regina, a forty-something stepmother when she married, was told by her predecessor's sister that her life was "worthless" because she would never experience "maternal feelings." This new stepsister-in-law added, "How could you possibly understand your stepkids when you've never had children of your own?" This affront was particularly painful for Regina, since she was having regrets that she hadn't met the love of her life earlier, in time to have a child of her own.

Child-Free, Not Childless

If you and your partner decide against having a child together or cannot, and you do not already have kids, we suggest you replace the word "childless" with "child-free" (some professionals use the phrase "child-independent") and focus on the positives accompanying not having a baby—more time to yourselves when your mate's kids are with their mother or are old enough to leave home, less financial strain, fewer sleepless nights, etc.

Child-free stepmothers advise having assertive answers

ready in anticipation of insensitive comments and unwanted questions about the fact that you don't have children. Handle this early on; you cannot allow another negative connotation to attach to you.

Leslie Lafayette, author of *Why Don't You Have Kids: Living a Full Life Without Parenthood* (Kensington, 1995, currently out of print), offers a few flippant rejoinders to the invasive query "Why don't you have children?:"

"I forgot."

"I give up—why?"

"Good question. I'll get back to you."

If the flip answer isn't your style, Lafayette suggests another strategy: "You aren't required to give a serious answer to a question that should never be asked of you, but because it will be asked, relax, smile and give the answer with which you're most comfortable. For example:

"We didn't have them because we can't afford them."

"That's a personal issue, and I prefer to keep it that way."

"We think the earth is populated enough. We think we can make more of a contribution by using our time and money to help with environmental issues."

"We're still thinking about it."

Adoption for Stepmoms

If you cannot have biological children and are considering adoption, we suggest you talk to other adoptive mothers and thoroughly research the related issues. The recommended reading list includes some books on adoption that may help you make a decision. One, *The Adoption Reader: Birth mothers, Adoptive Mothers and Adopted Daughters Tell Their Stories* (Seal, 1995), edited by Susan Wadia-Ells, is particularly worthwhile, since it presents all points of view. It does, however, paint a rather negative view of adoption, pointing out the difficulties and bewildering emotions involved. If you are also involved in difficulties with stepkids, you need to be particularly careful not to undertake too much to cope with.

We came across only one stepmom who, unable to conceive, had adopted a child other than a stepchild and she categorically said she would not recommend it. Her reasons were simply that her son had many medical problems, which she had been unaware of at the time of his adoption, when he was six weeks old. When we interviewed her, she was at the "Why me?" stage, feeling way out of her depth. Be very sure you are that special lady who can cope with the issues of adopted children, including adopted children's inevitable request to know about or even find their birth mother.

❧

Questionnaire

1. Are you completely satisfied with the decision you and your mate have made about a baby? Whichever way the decision went, list the positives for you.

2. If you have been persuaded into a decision you are not a hundred percent comfortable with, list the negatives as you see them now. Take plenty of time to think about this. You need to know exactly what your feelings are so you can work out a way to live with this decision without allowing any self-pity to creep in.

3. If a negative decision was based on finances (and you are still not happy about it), have you jointly examined every inch of your budget to be sure you can't cut back or stretch other areas? To what extremes are you willing to go financially in order to make room for a baby? List ways you are prepared to economize.

4. If your joint decision was yes, do you have any idea how you will feel if you are unable to get pregnant? List your anticipated feelings.

5. Do you have any idea how your existing kids, if you have any, or your stepkids will react to the addition of another baby? Speculate a little in your stepmom's idea book—it will be interesting to refer back to once you have had a chance to talk about it with them.

6. Are you and your mate still undecided? Do you need help
   arriving at your decision? Describe in writing exactly where
   you are hung up, and go find someone to help you. An
   hour or two with a professional might provide a new perspective once you yourselves have pinpointed the stum-
   bling block.

✖

Action Box

- ❧ Even if you already have biological children,
  and even if you believe in your heart that you
  don't want any more, go through the motions
  of a discussion with your mate. You need to
  air your thoughts on the subject and hear his
  thoughts just to confirm your feelings and to
  be sure you both agree. It's one more thing you
  can do to prevent a problem down the road.
  Neither of you will then be able to say, "I never
  brought up the subject, because I didn't think
  you wanted another child" or "I've always
  wanted a baby. I didn't mention it because I
  knew we couldn't afford one, and I didn't want
  to make you feel bad."

- ❧ Before going ahead and having the baby you
  want so much, examine your motives once
  more. You need to be very sure you are doing
  so for the right reasons—not just out of the
  selfish need for a power base or for someone
  whose love you can rely on.

- ❧ When you have the all-clear—the agreement of
  your mate, the confirmation that your baby is
  going to be a welcomed, well-loved child—get
  on with it! Don't delay, only to find you have
  medical difficulties to overcome.

CHAPTER 10

The Ex-Spouses and Their Mates

Your Stepchildren's Mom

She used to be your husband's wife. She shared his life and his bed, knows his quirks and habits, even some of his secrets. You're his wife now, but this woman will always be the mother of his kids, whether she died or is divorced from your husband.

Stepmothers claimed more conflicts with their husband's ex-wife, mother of their stepchildren, than with any other person they meet in stepfamily life. It can be a relationship fraught with as many difficulties as the one you need to form with your stepchildren. If one operated solely on logic, it would seem that a mother's motivation to form a working relationship with you is crystal clear—you're a person who'll be spending time with her children in an intimate setting, perhaps even influencing their growth and development.

Logic, unfortunately, does not always preside over this relationship, but that doesn't mean you can ignore your stepchildren's mother. You need to be curious about her, how she died or what caused the divorce or why she left, and the effect any of these endings had on your new family. She's in your life, at least until your stepchildren reach the age of majority, perhaps even long after that.

Your husband's ex has enormous power, with the potential to withhold your stepchildren from their dad, to make unreasonable demands, and even, said some stepmoms, to destroy your marriage. Antics of ex-wives seem amusing within the confines of star-studded Hollywood movies, but when children are involved, bad behavior seems foolish at best and irresponsible or abusive at worst.

Others may have different findings, but unfortunately, the overwhelming majority of stepmothers we spoke with did not report constructive, civilized relationships with their husbands' ex-wives. We hope the ideas in this chapter will encourage you to take a fresh approach to working with your stepkids' mom in the interest of raising healthy, well-adjusted children.

From Silly to Serious

First we need to explore the reports of stepmothers trying (and frequently failing) to forge this relationship. What's happening out there?

Stories related by stepmoms about ex-wives' behavior run the gamut from silly or childish to those verging on violent, even criminal and insane. Amy, a forty-year-old stepmom of eight years, distraught and in physical fear of her stepchildren's mother, speculated quite seriously: "It wouldn't surprise me if, under our judicial system, crimes of passion get light sentences. Seems to me the likelihood of a woman killing or harming her ex-husband's wife and getting away with it is quite high, particularly if she had a good attorney and he could prove it was a crime of passion."

At the time of our interview, Amy was sporting a black eye given to her by her husband's ex-wife and was recovering from a dislocated shoulder, courtesy of her twenty-two-year-old stepson. Amy had married into a physically abusive family, including her husband. Fortunately for her, she is now in the process of divorce.

Eva, stepmom of four years to a nine-year-old boy, recalled many sleepless nights during the first year of her marriage.

Her husband Anthony's ex-wife would call fifteen or twenty times through the wee hours, shouting obscenities or starting arguments with whoever answered—usually Anthony, but sometimes Eva herself. The couple tried everything they could think of to stop her; pleading, getting a separate line, calling the police, legal action. Nothing worked. Her response was either to prevent her son from visiting or to get her attorney involved, which cost them money, since Anthony paid her legal bills as part of their divorce agreement. After about a year the calls suddenly stopped with no explanation.

The mother of Violet's two stepkids had a much less harmful but quirky habit of sending her children for their twice-monthly weekend visit with their clothes stuffed into a black plastic bag, washed but dripping wet. She did this consistently and, when asked why, responded that she "didn't have time to put them through the dryer." Violet said she now expects the wet clothes; it's part of their weekend routine. She greets her stepkids with "Let's have our milk and cookies while we get your clothes dried." She commented wryly, "I think I would miss this now if it didn't happen; I'm used to it."

Pleading Poverty

Stepmoms tell about ex-wives' demands for money beyond the support payments they are already getting, of depicting themselves as poor, overburdened, abandoned mothers, valiantly attempting to raise kids on a shoestring budget. Ex-husbands, on the other hand, are perceived as responsibility-free men who have maintained or even improved their standard of living, which stepmothers are assumed to share in and enjoy.

While statistics show that most divorced women live at a lower standard than their ex-husbands, the anecdotal evidence gathered from our interviews with stepmoms suggests that this may not be true of divorced women with children whose ex-husbands are paying alimony and child support. Actually, stepmothers tell us, it is they who live paycheck to paycheck, while their husband's ex-wife often ends up with the family house, the car, and the greater part of her ex-husband's income and assets, emotionally blackmailing him with tales of his kids' suffering because he won't provide even more. An ex-wife is sometimes able to include in the terms of the divorce continued provision for herself and her children, even after her ex-husband dies, through his life insurance and pension plans. She can virtually tie him up financially for the rest of this life—and the next!

Unless there is inherited money involved, or the husband is fortunate enough to earn a huge salary, one of the most common financial complaints we heard from working stepmothers is that they help support their husband's first family.

Some stepmoms reported losing respect for their new mate as time and time again he gave in to an ex-wife's demands, great and small. Others reported the agony of being unable either to intervene or help while naturally resenting having been put in a submissive position to this woman who can wreak havoc on her marriage.

Ex-Wives: Purveyors of the "Wicked" Stepmother?

Several stepmothers told us that they were convinced that ex-wives were among the chief perpetrators of the "wicked" stepmother myth. Tabitha, a forty-five-year-old stepmother married for twelve years to Willie, recalled the rainy afternoon she and her two stepgrandchildren watched one of the kids' favorite Disney videos, Cinderella.

Partway through the movie, Katie snuggled up to her stepgrandma and said, "Stepmothers are very bad, Grandma." Tabitha spent the remainder of the video trying to decide how to explain to the six-year-old without scaring her, that the grandma she loved was a stepmother—that stepmothers aren't bad. Tabitha had worked hard over the course of twelve years to form a pleasant, if only polite, relationship with her stepdaughter, Liz, and asked the young mother if she was doing anything to counteract her small daughter's belief. "Hell no!"

was Liz's response. "If Tom and I split up and he remarries, I don't want my kids to like their stepmother!" Liz, who sees herself as a potential ex-wife, has already formed a negative opinion of stepmoms which she is passing on to her children.

Stepmothers reported hearing other negative descriptions of themselves: "home wrecker," "bimbo," "that bitch," depicting them as having married only for money or even as being child abusers. Stepmoms who are much younger than their husband's ex are particular targets of these epithets.

Unless you were part of the breakup of her marriage (and, rumors aside, very few of the women we spoke with met their husband while he was still married), you cannot be blamed for anyone's divorce. So why is an ex-wife able to get away with false accusations? Perhaps this behavior is so common, it's become customary. Are we so used to an ex's ranting and raving that it's actually considered normal?

Even more worrisome is the fact that women who behave this way are role models for their daughters, future mothers and stepmothers.

Jennifer grew up as a daughter of divorced parents. According to her mom, no man was ever faithful or had consideration for a woman's feelings—they were all brutish, sex-crazed beasts looking after their own interests. This vituperation was aimed specifically at Jennifer's father, who soon after the divorce moved to another state, making frequent visits with his daughter impossible. She saw him only twice a year, for Christmas and two weeks in the summer.

One Christmas Jennifer found out that her dad had remarried and that she had a stepmom. Jennifer's mom began to include classic barbs against stepmoms in her regular tirades against Jennifer's dad. By the time Jennifer was in her twenties, she was turned off to men, marriage, and, most of all, stepmothers. She dated rarely and was forty-five before a widowed father of five persuaded her to marry him. With her inexperience in relationships, Jennifer's marriage was a self-fulfilling prophecy—this man, in Jennifer's view, turned out to be just as her mother had described all men. And since her stepkids hated her, she had to agree with her mother—stepmoms were undeniably worthless people.

Children as Weapons

Stepmothers we interviewed expressed frustration at their powerlessness in the sometimes devastating struggle that continues between husbands and ex-wives, especially when children are involved. You've most likely made an effort to understand the emotions your husband's ex-wife has experienced over their divorce—anger, pain, resentment, guilt, perhaps rage that life has become so complicated and sad. You know that when people separate, these emotions don't always dissipate once the appropriate papers have been signed. But it's nearly impossible to be sympathetic if for years after the divorce, you've witnessed an ex-wife's acts of revenge for perceived injustices, or have seen her use her children as weaponry.

For weeks before their wedding, Nell and Chet had been discussing how his two sons, aged eleven and thirteen, would handle the big event. Chet and his ex-wife had planned the details for their kids, deciding the boys would wear their blue blazers and gray pants and would arrive the evening before the wedding, with Chet meeting them at the airport.

"Things were going too well," Nell recalled. "I wish I'd suspected their mother might cause some trouble—she'd never been that cooperative before. The boys arrived the night before our wedding, dressed in ripped jeans and baseball jackets, with just a pair of pajamas each! Chet had to rush the boys from the airport to the nearest mall, which, thank God, stayed open till ten, to buy them both completely new outfits—blazers, pants, shirts, underwear, shoes—everything. They came home late, all three of them totally stressed out. The next morning, our wedding day, the poor kids just stumbled around, exhausted. I'll never forgive that woman—she almost ruined our wedding."

Why Are We Adversaries, Anyway?

Your stepchildren's mother might be upset by her ex-husband's remarriage, frightened that she might lose control of her kids, their love, their company, or their attention if they are older. In short, she might fear losing her kids to the affections of another woman just as it appears she "lost" her husband, even though she might have initiated the divorce.

So why are we adversaries, anyway? We know from our earlier discussion that no one can replace a mother, not even the most wonderful stepmom in the world. We know this, but perhaps moms who are ex-wives don't. Stepmoms have described feeling sorry for a woman who seems to have this blind spot, particularly one who has not remarried and must now witness her kids' relationship with their dad's new wife.

Lanese, a lively, outgoing young mom of three, always tried to make visits fun for her husband Ted's three children. Her home was happy and noisy, with music playing and lots of food and drink around—life was one long party. Ted's kids grew close to Lanese and their stepsiblings—all of whom had personalities to match their mom.

Lanese was the first to recognize how Ted's ex-wife might be feeling, left alone when the kids visited their home, knowing that they preferred their dad's upbeat new surroundings. "I feel sorry for her. When I talk on the phone with her sometimes about her kids, she sounds gentle and kind, but she's made herself into a martyr. The best thing in the world for her would be to remarry, but she told me she plans to devote the rest of her life to her children and, hopefully, her grandchildren. I think after the divorce she just gave up on the thought of starting a new life for herself. It's so sad."

Their Mom's Opinion Counts with Your Stepkids

Stepmothers told us they found themselves doing a lot of damage control, especially about an ex-wife's bad-mouthing of her kids' father or his new marriage, behavior that does great harm to children, a fact a mother, almost incomprehensibly, over-looks. Continual criticism of one parent damages a child's sense of unconditional love, makes him feel guilty for still loving his dad, and engenders feelings of confused loyalty. By some people's standards, this constitutes emotional abuse.

A mother's attitude toward her ex-husband and "that woman your dad married" strongly determines how children will feel about and relate to their stepmother.

One weekend Peter's son, Danny, arrived at his dad and stepmom Alice's home for his weekend visit, looking very glum. Taking his son aside, Peter asked what the problem was. "Mom says you won't love me as much now that you're mar-ried to Alice," Danny said. Both Peter and Alice assured Danny that his mom was mistaken.

On his next visit Danny was even more upset. "Mom said Alice doesn't want me to come here anymore." Again Peter and Alice had to convince the boy of his unconditional wel-come. But Danny was torn in two—hearing from his mom that his dad and Alice didn't want him and from Alice and his dad that they did. *Yes, we do; No, they don't.* It took several visits to a family counselor to make Danny's mother see the pain she was causing her son with this tactic.

Stepmothers are usually advised by therapists to be com-passionate and mature in relating to her stepchildren and their mother. We would like to see mothers and ex-wives given similar advice. Once the children and their mom understand that it is not only possible but acceptable, easy, and beneficial to everyone to simultaneously appreciate two adult women—their mother and their stepmother—everybody gains.

The United Front to the Rescue . . . Again

An ex-wife can affect you negatively only if you and your new mate allow it. It is as important for the two of you to form a united front in any dealings with your stepchildren's mother as it is with your respective children. Just like a badly behaved child in your household, your husband's ex-wife is "our" problem. But it means work—you cannot take the attitude "If we ignore her, she'll go away."

Many stepmoms mentioned that where possible their husband avoided contact with his ex, expecting their new wife to act as go-between. This is not acceptable. You can act in your own right, not as a messenger for your husband. Remember, no triangles—one-to-one direct relationships only. However difficult it may be for him, she is *his* ex, not yours (although one young stepmom jokingly called her husband's former spouse "my ex-wife"), and he needs to handle certain issues with her directly. Also, he must be perceived by her to provide total support for you when you need to be in contact with her.

After trying their best to reason with Anna, Zach's ex-wife, about her unreasonable demands without success, Zach and his wife, Vanessa, simply decided to look upon Anna as an unpleasant but inevitable presence in their lives, like bad weather or a traffic jam. "She has tried for four years to get more money from us," explained Vanessa, "but even the attorneys agree that's an impossibility. We simply don't have it! But she's still at it. Terry, my sixteen-year-old stepson, wants a car, and she says we 'have to' buy him one. The week before that call came in, she assumed we'd take my nine-year-old stepdaughter for a month during the school year while she went away with a boyfriend. Ted and I have grown closer over her crazy demands, some of which are truly funny."

Revolutionizing the Relationship

Is it beyond the powers of two grown women to pull together? Certainly custom—the myth of women as natural adversaries—has played a part in making this arrangement more difficult. Just as cats and dogs are presumed not to get along, it is expected that mothers and stepmothers won't (or can't) get along. And yet many people have cats and dogs living together who tolerate one another, respecting one another's boundaries and getting along quite happily.

Psychologist Patricia Papernow advises stepmoms to encourage the relationship stepkids have with their mother. This approach makes healthier kids and in the long run makes life easier for everyone. Try to form a working relationship with your stepchildren's mom. It isn't necessary to perceive your husband's ex-wife as a rival, the way women are encouraged by our culture to see one another in nearly every other arena.

Two adult women acting as integral, cooperative members of a joint-parenting board—what could be more enlightened and, we hesitate to say it, more normal? We're not suggesting a cozy, "let's have lunch" relationship (we're writing nonfiction here, after all), but a business relationship that allows either of you to pick up the phone to discuss some practical arrangement for one of her kids or to discuss any concern you have about your stepchildren's well-being, behavior, or needs.

Some stepmoms have made it work. Caroline is a police officer in a large industrial city, married eight years to Allen, who has two daughters. "Perhaps it was my uniform that did it; I don't know," reported Caroline, "but in no time flat, Allen's ex and I had our relationship worked out. Shortly after Allen and I married, I called her, introduced myself, and told her exactly what I was willing to do for her children.

"I was pleasant, polite, made it clear that I was prepared to cooperate but that I wouldn't accept any disrespect from either her or her daughters. Thinking back, I may have been a little too heavy handed, but it was effective. We have a completely emotionless, practical relationship. I have no idea what she thinks of me—I don't care. I have never met her and have no feelings at all toward her. I am very fond of her kids, though. They are both lovely girls. Maybe one day we'll meet, but that hasn't been necessary yet."

Try to be aware of the stereotypes you might hold about ex-wives too. Thea, a young stepmom, was exasperated by her husband's constant criticism of his ex-wife's mothering and finally told him to quit it: "Once I stepped back from his perception of her and saw her as a real, live person, with feelings and issues and human flaws, instead of the caricature he was painting of an evil, heartless woman, things just got simpler. I made up my own mind about her. I discovered she wasn't a monster after all. Just asking my stepchildren, 'How's your mom?' and showing my concern made a huge difference in our relationship. If my husband still hates her, fine. But I need to deal with her on my own terms. She's just a woman who happens to be the mother of my husband's kids, and I refuse to get embroiled in his emotions about their—admittedly—terrible marriage."

Another stepmom reported with obvious delight how the attitude of her husband's ex-wife became more cooperative once she remarried and became a stepmom herself. Tillie related: "I watched in horror for nearly five years as Jake's ex-wife made life as difficult as she could for my husband and me, doing untold psychological damage to her kids. Once she remarried, the shoe was on the other foot. She had an ex-wife to contend with who was every bit as vicious as she'd been! I hate to admit this, but I really enjoyed it!"

Here are some more guidelines, provided by stepmoms who are working toward revolutionizing this relationship:

• Extend an olive branch. You have nothing to lose and everything to gain. You might hear some classic rebuffs: "I will not share my children with that woman." "I don't need her cooperation." "Who does she think she is?" If so, wait awhile, and try again. You are being proactive. You will feel better about the relationship, or lack of one, if you take charge.

• If your overture is accepted, even grudgingly, keep the relationship on a business level. You don't need a personal relationship with your mate's ex-wife—too much intimacy can backfire if she begins to pry into private matters. (One stepmom recalls the time when, after a couple of glasses of wine at her stepson's high school graduation party, her husband's ex-wife asked her to "rate" him in bed.) Remember, while she is still your stepkids' mother—a fact you need to fully and frequently acknowledge—she is history in almost all other areas.

• Let her know that you think her children are wonderful (this can be considered a social lie if it is not yet true—one day, if things go according to plan, you might really feel this way) and that you would like to know them better. Assure her you have no wish to take over her role of mother, just to be the best stepmom you can be and simply to work with her for the benefit of the kids, whom you enjoy so much (again, this social lie is allowed).

- Convey to her that while you recognize her status as mother, as stepmother you need to be aware of the kids' schedules and be involved in planning for them. She needs to know you will not take a backseat in matters that affect you or your household, nor will you accept being told what to do in your own home, as many stepmoms have reported is the case. You are perfectly willing to work with her, but on terms agreed between you, not dictated by her.

- We recommend she does not visit your home. Some step-moms allow this, but it's better if she does not see your brand-new Oriental rug or Aunt Christina's heirloom silver vase. Nor do you want her comparing the size of the closet her son has been allocated with the one your daughter has, or seeing your kitchen piled high with canned ravioli, which the kids love and you provide when you're too tired to cook dinner. In general you don't want her comments on anything that takes place within your home. Similarly, do not give her a front-door key "just in case," and do not allow her to store her belongings in your basement. Better to help her find storage elsewhere than to allow this. (The same applies to your ex-husband.)

- Under no circumstances should you discuss money with her. Avoid discussing anything other than matters immediately concerning the kids. If she wants to talk about finances, refer her to your husband. This might not be quite as proactive as you wish, but the financial arrangements are between the two of them, although you should be fully aware, through discussions with him, of your husband's financial position and responsibilities toward his previous family.

- Assure your stepchildren that you want a good relationship with their mother, that you will not talk negatively about her, that you understand a divorce simply means that their parents cannot live together, not that they will forget or stop loving their kids. This communication will pave the way for making the family occasions comfortable when it is necessary for you and your husband to come in contact with her, such as weddings, funerals, bar/bat mitzvahs, and other milestone events. It might also make her a little happier, which means she will have less inclination to hatch plots. With luck, in light of all your efforts, your stepkids will feel less stressed and more receptive to your wish to get to know them.

Your Husband's Deceased Wife

If you've married a widower or are planning to, technically you have no ex to deal with. If your husband's former wife died of a long illness, there was probably time for them to prepare the family for her death. Under these circumstances she will likely have talked to him about the kids' future. Any promises your husband made to her will be very serious and important to him.

Even though she is no longer alive, however, you need to consider her effect on your life and the lives of your new stepfamily. Women who marry widowers have said they need to feel they would have liked her, to feel no animosity or resentment toward her. One stepmom said she even thought of her husband's deceased wife as a "beneficent spirit" in their home.

Try not to let comparisons take place. Many stepmoms indicated they felt they came off second best when being compared with someone deified by memory. As many stepmothers to motherless children find, unless the deceased wife had some really outrageous faults or was a child abuser, in the minds of her husband and stepchildren, she usually becomes a saint after her passing.

Hope Edelman, author of *Motherless Daughters,* has coined the term "posthumous perfection" in describing the deceased mother. You might find yourself being compared with a saint or feel you have to tread lightly, vigilant whenever you open your mouth (since you cannot possibly ever say anything negative about a dead wife and mother). You are two completely different people. You will play an entirely different role in the lives of your stepkids as well as your husband.

If you talk to people who knew her, you will find she was just a regular person, complete with faults. It might be satisfying for you to hear from others that his dead wife had imperfections, but you would be wise not to remind him of these. The old adage applies more strongly than ever in these circumstances: "Do not speak ill of the dead." There is no reason for you to feel threatened. She is in the past—not forgotten, of course, but neither is she here to antagonize you as an ex-wife might.

Grace told us, "I feel I would have liked Brett's former wife, who died of a heart attack, partly because she made Brett happy for all those years and gave him his three children. Our mingled fates meant I could marry him. I feel no sense of competition with her, just as though we have a sort of partnership. Sometimes when Brett and I are facing something difficult, one of us will say, 'I wonder what Sue would have done,' and usually it helps us. We haven't managed quite as well with the kids; they've never really taken to me. But we're still working on that."

It's natural, of course, that in the minds of her children, the deceased mother was perfect. As their mom, she might have sung in the church choir, knitted all their sweaters, and read stories to them every night. As their stepmother, you might be a horticulturist par excellence, bake homemade scones for breakfast, and know where to buy discounted Nikes. Neither one of you is better than the other. The important thing is she was their mother, and we know mothers are special and irreplaceable.

You also need to understand that your stepkids will still have a relationship with their mother after her death. They will talk about her, air their memories of her. It's good to encourage this, as long as your stepchildren are recovering from grief, not stuck in it. One stepdaughter whose mother died fourteen years ago told us, "It just gets worse. I miss her more every day."

Fourteen years is too long for active grieving, according to psychologists. The stepmom needs to assure her stepkids that it is fine to talk about their mom, that judging by all the good things she has heard about her, she feels she would certainly have liked her, had they been able to meet. Ask questions—about the time their dad said they all went swimming and the dog ran off with their clothes. Ask to see photos they took on vacation in Europe. You can afford to be generous in this way. Your stepchildren's mom would want her kids to be happy, and she would be grateful to you for all you are doing for them.

A stepmother living with the memory of a deceased wife and mother not only needs to form a positive "relationship" with her predecessor but needs to ensure that her new stepfamily can accept their living stepmom and move on with their lives. As with almost everything else on the relationship level, talk about this to your husband and your stepkids.

Don't Say It . . .

There are two mistakes stepmoms reported making when their stepchildren's mother is deceased, usually in times of stress or frustration. Avoiding them is in your best interest in the long run:

a) When angry, one of the easiest ways to hurt your step-kids whose mother has died is to say, "Your mother would be so ashamed of you" or "Your mother would turn in her grave if she heard what you called me."

These barbs are not constructive, although they might momentarily relieve your anger. You cannot suppose what their mom would have thought or felt. Besides, since his kids are behaving so badly, perhaps their mother allowed, or even contributed to it. You can't ever really know what went on when she was alive, because those talking about her will always have their own slant. You can only express your own opinions, not those of a deceased mother.

b) Avoid blaming your stepkids' mom for whatever you find unacceptable. This is a no-no when she is alive, and out of the question when she is dead. Stepmoms have reported having done this during disagreements with their husband: "How Cheryl [his dead wife] could have allowed her flesh and blood to wear that skimpy skirt/that revealing tee shirt/all that makeup is beyond me" or "I can't believe Cheryl never taught the kids to hold their fork properly/use a table napkin."

Your Husband's Ex-Wife's New Mate

Your husband's former spouse will probably be happier if and when she finds a new love of her own. The relationship your stepfamily has with her might improve all around, too, and with luck your mate's financial obligations will decrease. When your husband's former wife marries, her new husband becomes stepfather to your stepchildren. Interesting!

While this will certainly be a time of jubilation for you, the effects on your stepkids might not be positive. Their mom will be involved with her own life, in love again, perhaps seeing less of her kids or paying less attention to them. She might even request custody changes to accommodate her new man, which can be devastating if her kids feel she is trying to get rid of them now that she has found a new husband. You'll need to be very sensitive and gentle with your stepkids, who are again going to experience a trauma not of their making.

Although it is unlikely you will have much contact with this man, it is to your advantage to welcome him. Knowing what you do about stepmotherhood, you can understand his difficult position. You have something in common; you're both stepparents to this particular set of children. Encourage your stepkids to attempt to form a relationship with him—it will probably feel like déjà vu! Talk positively about him for the

sake of your stepkids, and when the opportunity arises on a
family occasion, you can genuinely say, "Nice to meet you!"

Your Husband and the New Guy

This time, however, it will be your husband who might have
a difficult time accepting his former wife's new husband, and
for exactly the same reasons his ex-wife had accepting you.
Everybody now has something in common! If you play your
cards right, you can initiate discussions within your own stepfamily on how ironic and interesting this is and how hard
forming new relationships can be. This is an ideal opportunity
to bring feelings and difficulties out into the open (always the
best place for them) so they can be examined and addressed.

Your mate will need lots of reassurance from you that this
new man is not going to overshadow him with his kids, regardless of his accomplishments. This is admittedly difficult to
do if the new husband is a multimillionaire race car driver or
has just won Wimbledon for the second time. If the new man
in his ex's life is six foot four and in superb physical shape,
your shorter, slightly paunchy husband might feel a bit piqued,
especially if his ex chooses to flaunt this aspect. Be sure to
show that you love him exactly as he is, regardless of your
bank balance or the fact that you (secretly) have to admit that
his ex's new beau is rather adorable!

Your mate will need to spend lots of special time with his
kids while they're adjusting to life with a stepfather. The kids
will need assurance they are not losing their mom, your mate
will need assurance of his kids' love, and vice versa. A difficult
time all around, but you can be a heroine by understanding
everyone's fears and opening up discussions about all these
complicated relationships.

You might even want to bring out the family tree you
started making while reading chapter 4 and add the new
names. Trees grow! Perhaps your stepchildren's stepfather has
kids from a previous marriage. Encourage your stepkids to see
them as future friends. It can be very exciting to have all these

new people as family, provided there is the assurance of a basic love from their two biological parents.

Your Ex-Husband

This is the guy you once promised to love and honor until death parted you. Along the way, something went wrong and you or he or both of you decided to call it quits. After living together, perhaps having children together, he probably knows you very well. But like your new husband's ex, he is history. If you do not have children together, there is probably very little need for much contact once the matters arising from your divorce are settled, unless you both wish to attend extended-family occasions with your new spouses. Once each of you has what is rightfully yours in the material sense, memories, both good and bad, are all that's left.

We've talked about the importance of this man to your children and recommended that you develop a working relationship on issues concerning your kids. Keep your fingers off dangerous emotional buttons, and relate in a strictly professional manner. No question, this is difficult, especially if bitterness remains, but for the sake of your new mate, the benefit of your kids, and your own sanity, you must try. It is fruitless to hash over the past.

Many stepmoms report animosity between the two men in their lives—past and present husbands. It's not necessary for these men to like each other, but you can insist on courtesy if and when they have contact—competitiveness between them is pointless. Your ex does not need to come into your home, for the same reasons you do not want your new mate's ex-wife in your home. It feels invasive, and you don't need his comments on the way your new life is turning out or your new financial bracket, especially if he is paying child support. If your new mate is paying child support, your home might be more modest than the one you shared with your previous husband. There is no reason to encourage comparisons.

Your Ex-Husband's New Wife

This woman is stepmother to your kids, if you have any. Sisterhood! Unless she proves totally unreasonable, she will welcome your overture toward forming a working relationship. Because you understand her difficulties so well, you can take direct steps to help her by discussing with your kids ways in which they can cooperate.

Stepmothers facing this situation—that of dealing with another stepmother—reported far fewer problems than those dealing with plain-vanilla ex-wives. None had formed a cozy relationship, become buddies, with their children's stepmother, but most had worked out a way to coexist. Some reported pangs of jealousy when their ex-husband's new mate exhibited more acuity in one area or another—if your daughter comes home raving about her stepmom's peach flambé while you're the hamburger-on-a-roll type of mom, you might feel a twinge! You might find yourself feeling sorry for your children's stepmom, on the other hand, now she's the one dealing with your ex-husband's gambling problem.

Even though we've recommended seeking out other stepmoms to discuss the common issues of stepmotherhood, this particular stepmom—your children's—is sleeping with your ex-husband, a fact that may preclude friendship. But certainly on a practical level you can work together.

Fanny, whom you met in chapter 7 as the wise stepmom who gave her son's stepmom, Zoe, a show of support, never regretted this initial contact. Zoe opened up a whole new world to Jamie with her unusual lifestyle, not to mention her eccentric friends. Fanny said, "He would never have been exposed to all these people without her—he's meeting astrologers, painters, writers, musicians, a lot of bohemian types. He met a chess wiz the other day who's teaching him to play. I have to say, if it were not slightly odd, liking your ex-husband's new wife, she's the sort of person I'd like to have as a friend."

Questionnaire

1. Given what you know so far of your mate's ex-wife, in which areas do you see the potential for cooperation? What, if any, problems do you foresee? Go into some detail on these two areas so that when you refer back, you can see the improvements.

2. Identify two distinct areas of difficulty, matters over which she might present specific challenges. What can you do to reverse these issues?

3. Put yourself in the shoes of your mate's ex-wife. How do you believe she sees you? Is she accurate? If her view is negative, what can you do to turn her opinion around so you can form the basis of a working relationship?

4. At this moment, do you feel that she is beyond reason and that a working relationship is out of the question? If so, you are in the majority, so don't worry, but do list your reasons for this belief. Later, we'll ask you to come back and reexamine these feelings.

5. If your mood and energy allow it, list five things you would like about her, were she not your mate's ex. List five things you dislike about her.

6. What effect does the behavior of your mate's ex-wife have on the relationship between you and your stepchildren? Make two lists: positive effects and negative effects. What can you do to move some issues from your negative list to the positive one?

7. Do you believe she is sabotaging your relationship with her kids? If so, how?

8. Is she a good mother to your stepkids? Do they have a close relationship? Can they take any and all of their problems to her? Does she provide good advice? Is she fully part of their lives?

9. Do you foresee any difficulties with

- the new mate of your husband's ex-wife?
- your ex-husband?
- your ex-husband's new wife, your children's stepmom?
  If so, list them, and consider if they are reversible.

CHAPTER 11

Other People:
Friends and Foes of the Stepfamily

Drawing on tried-and-true relationships, making new con-
tacts, knowing your opponents or competition—these are
the basics of social savvy, whether it's your first day at a new
job or the start of your campaign for the school board.

These are strategies you can use as a new stepmother to
observe and evaluate the people important to your stepfamily—extended relatives, friends, and what we call "problem
people," those who are not supportive of the new marriage and
resulting stepfamily but who impact it in some way. Whom do
your husband and stepchildren depend on, and how much
influence do they have? Are you marrying into a loosely knit
group or a closely controlled dynasty?

People close to your stepfamily will have been personally
affected by the death or abandonment of your stepchildren's
mother or your husband's divorce. Be prepared for almost any
kind of welcome. To some you may seem a savior; to others,
a brazen intruder. All these people have their own memories
of, connections to, and opinions about your stepkids, your
husband and his former wife before you came on the scene.

Family Circus

Joining a stepfamily means getting to know a lot of new people
besides the ones in the immediate stepfamily circle. People

tend to stay close to those they enjoy, whether related by blood, marriage, or proximity, and you will probably not wish to disappoint relatives or friends who are used to seeing your stepfamily often.

With your husband, try to set a comfortable pace for meeting everyone. Pru's first encounter with her fiancé's huge family was nothing short of a family circus. "I had no sooner become engaged to Jay and moved into his house with my two kids than Jay threw a surprise welcome party for us," she recalled. About two dozen relatives, who were all very friendly, descended on Pru's new home and commandeered the kitchen, setting up appliances, reorganizing the refrigerator as they assured her with hugs and endearments that they already knew where everything went.

"I was completely overwhelmed," Pru remembered. "My kids hid in their rooms most of the day; Jay's kids were jealous of their having a party and acted up. With so many people, I didn't have a chance to get to know anyone, and I had no control over their first impression of me, which was that of a hapless guest in my own house. I really would have preferred to meet them well prepared and dressed to the nines."

Especially in the early stages of stepmotherhood, you need to control your schedule when you're simultaneously moving house, working, and trying to spend some one-on-one time with the most important new people in your life—your spouse and his kids. If you have kids of your own, you also need to protect them from too many people all at once. Even if your nine-year-old daughter is a social butterfly, she needs time to adjust to her stepbrother first.

Shedding the Outsider's Shell

All of us would like to consider ourselves a part of our new family from the start. But let's be honest: as your husband's new wife and as a stepmother, you'll find it hard to feel like an insider when so much family history has taken place before your arrival.

You might meet people who see you as an outsider or a "replacement," perhaps an unwelcome one. You can expect to be scrutinized, even compared to your husband's former spouse, and you might possibly overhear the odd ambiguous comment "She's younger than I thought she'd be." Everyone you meet will have his or her own agenda (as do you) and will be alert to the potential effect you will have on their continued relationship with your stepfamily. Some people might have been very attached to your husband's ex-wife— their former daughter-in-law, mother to their favorite niece, or their friend. Even if they weren't bosom buddies, she was at least familiar, while you're an unknown quantity.

Marital dissolutions disturb everyone close to a family. Since the time of your predecessor's death or your mate's divorce, relationships in his extended family will have been tempered, adjusted, to reflect that change. If your stepchildren's mother abandoned her family, it will have caused outrage and sadness, and the extended family might have been split down the middle; those sympathizing with her, those rejecting her. Your fiancé's relatives and friends might have feelings about his readiness for marriage to you or your suitability as a stepmother or worry about your motives.

All this is understandable—and stressful. The best way to deal with a perhaps unprecedented personal examination, stepmothers have said, is to convey confidence—in your marriage, in your rightful place at your husband's side, as mistress of your new home. Regardless of how others feel, you're a pair building a life together. Think of yourself as a valuable addition to your stepfamily. They are lucky to have you and particularly fortunate that you are eager to nurture good relationships all around. You bring with you all the talent and skills you acquired before joining this new group of people.

On Whom Do They Depend?

Stepmothers often found that after the breakup of their husband's former marriage, other people—relatives and friends—

became important in his life, providing emotional support, practical assistance, or both.

Your husband's next-door neighbor might have been given a key to the house when she began looking after the kids for a couple of hours after school. Perhaps a coworker has taken his daughters shopping for clothes or cooked an occasional Saturday supper for them all. These can be completely platonic relationships, simply the efforts of a generous-minded friend to help a guy who seemed out of his depth.

A few stepmoms discovered, however, that some offers of generosity by other women were prompted by hopes of romance as the men these stepmothers eventually married recovered from divorce or adapted to widowerhood. Some stepmoms have reported listening to their lover's telephone ringing incessantly in the early days of their relationship with women calling their mate, "to see how you are" or "to see if there's anything I can help with." Widowed or divorced men who have daughters, in particular, might have welcomed a mature female mentor or confidant into their daughters' lives.

If another woman appears to be a factor, you and your fiancé will need to clarify her role. If a would-be female suitor is a business colleague, you won't want to damage a working relationship, and you'll have to tread gently. Discuss any other highly sensitive emotional transitions that might need to be made as a result of your marriage.

If your spouse has siblings living locally, more than likely they, too, will have pitched in. Aunt Susan who lives three blocks away might regularly pop in for coffee on Saturday morning, bringing homemade blueberry muffins with her. She'll probably want to include you and your kids in this ritual. It would not be appropriate, however, for her to confine her visit (and the number of muffins) to your stepkids now that you have moved into the house.

Upon your arrival, some helpful relatives and friends might be relieved to find they can phase themselves out and form a good relationship with you. Bottom line: there are many people who can be great allies in helping to build a new family— if they want to help your husband, they'll usually want to see you succeed too. Consider some likely candidates for friend-ship, and seek them out.

Finding Allies: Begin with Grandma

Most grandparents positively dote on their grandkids, and being able to spend time with them free from responsibilities (other than their safety) seems a perfect reward for all the long, complicated years of parenting. Your stepkids' grandparents have a vested interest in being your friend—continued comfortable access to their grandchildren.

These mature individuals include your spouse's parents and his ex-wife's parents—your stepkids' paternal and mater-nal grandparents. (There might also be a further set if your husband's ex-wife has remarried, plus your own parents if these seniors consider themselves stepgrandparents.) Have an-other look at Chart 3 (page 92) to keep the stepfamily tree straight in your mind. Or, better still, create one of your own (see chapter 4).

Your husband's parents have watched their son cope with either the death of their former daughter-in-law or his divorce from her. They have supported him emotionally and practi-cally. Now that he has remarried, your husband's parents will probably embrace you as the source of his newfound happi-ness—for this reason alone you might become a favorite of theirs. Once you indicate that you welcome their support and involvement with your stepkids, it's more than likely all will go well.

In fact, you might have to gently persuade them to ease up on responsibilities they have assumed in the aftermath of their son's previous marriage. Granny might have become too involved for your liking with the running of your household—buying new sheet sets when she thought her son wasn't up to it, for example.

Your husband's parents have known the man you love longer than anyone and can fill you in on much you don't know about him and the rest of the relatives. They might also have suggestions for handling "problem" people you might encounter, a group we'll discuss later. As a bonus, your husband's mom and dad might become fond of your kids and vice versa.

The Maternal Grandparents

The parents of your husband's former wife might find it difficult at first to form a relationship with you. Especially if their daughter died or if she has abandoned her family, watching you at their former son-in-law's side, striving to forge a relationship with their daughter's kids, can be a bittersweet experience for them.

Be very gentle and understanding with these folks. Their grandchildren will be even more special to them now, and they might resent you simply because you are there and their daughter is not. Do your very best to welcome them and create some happy times for them with your stepkids, providing them time alone together. Be sure to encourage your kids to enjoy them, too—they probably can't have too many grandmas!

You might find, however, that you have a fine line to draw between sensitivity and encouraging your stepkids and their grandparents to move on with the creation of a new family, instead of lingering in the past. Be aware that the maternal grandparents might not share this wish, especially if their daughter is deceased.

If your mate and his ex-wife divorced, maternal grandparents will probably see their grandchildren more often in their daughter's home, particularly if she has custody. Other than encouraging your stepchildren to talk about these folks in your home, you might have little contact with them, except at large family gatherings.

If your relationship with your mate's ex-wife is amicable, this should ease any tension for maternal grandparents in their relationship with you. But if your stepkids' mom feels hostile toward you, her parents probably will too. There is nothing much you can do about this until they have the opportunity to get to know you. Focus on building healthy relationships with your stepchildren, your primary concern. There's always a possibility of good news spreading!

Your Children's Grandparents

If you were previously married and have children, your parents and your ex-husband's parents will more than likely wish to remain close to their grandkids, which is to your children's advantage. This might pose a strain if you and your ex-mate endured a bitter divorce and his parents sided with him against you. If you share custody of your children with your ex-husband, for practical reasons perhaps together you can arrange a schedule that allows his parents to see their grandkids while they are visiting their dad.

The many accompanying changes caused by your new marriage—relocation, strict visitation schedules, perhaps less time, less money—might prevent anything more than an occasional get-together with grandparents from either side of the family. Phone calls, letters, and even e-mail can become an important way to enrich relationships. One year for Christmas, Gigi's parents gave her new stepfamily a computer, complete with an Internet service plan. "It was the greatest gift they could have given us," she exclaimed. "Now, we can e-mail notes to each other all the time, even if it's just a little 'hello, we love you.' The kids have learned how to use the technology, and the writing back and forth has improved their spelling too. My stepkids think it's awesome, and they're able to stay in closer contact with their whole extended family. It's been a good lesson in sharing for all the kids."

Problem Solving in a New Family: Your Role

One of the many strengths you bring to your new family is your fresh perspective on issues and relationships that are routine to the rest. In this way your initial outsider status can be an advantage. By diplomatic handling, you can even help ward off what might otherwise have become a family crisis.

For several weeks, Rosie had not been as keen to visit her grandparents as she used to be. "I don't feel like it," the girl kept telling Kristen, her stepmom, who recalled, "I knew something was wrong, so I didn't insist—I just made excuses for her."

One afternoon Rosie decided to confide in Kristen. Apparently her granddad had started to feel her chest for signs of developing breasts, pretending to hug her. "Rosie just pulled away but didn't say anything," Kristen related. "But she has lost all affection for her grandfather, and I haven't told Craig, Rosie's dad, yet—he totally reveres his father."

Kristen decided the best approach was to talk with her stepdaughter's grandmother first, whom she felt close to. Nana had suspected something was upsetting Rosie and assured Kristen she would talk to Grandpa. She also promised to be present at all times if Rosie decided to resume her visits. The two women agreed to monitor the situation closely and decided to seek professional help if necessary. By intervening at the right time, Kristen helped avert a full-scale war between Craig and his parents.

In many circumstances, your new role can help you build a bridge between members of your family, making transitions easier for everyone.

Daisy's stepdaughter, Rhoda, who was fourteen at the time Daisy married her dad, was a bright girl but an underachiever who was performing poorly at school and seemed deeply troubled.

Said Daisy, "I intuitively believed that this girl was grappling with the fact that she was gay. My husband and his family were prejudiced against homosexuality." Over the years Daisy took every opportunity to change some minds on the subject. If she was wrong about Rhoda, she reasoned, no harm done, and if she was right, an ongoing positive dialogue would have a lasting effect.

Rhoda revealed her homosexuality to her family when she was in her early twenties. "Rhoda's dad is very worried that his daughter is going to have a difficult life," remarked Daisy, "but he's determined not to make it more so. My husband says if it weren't for me, he couldn't have handled the fact that his daughter is gay."

In-Laws from the Past

If this is a second marriage for you, you will know which of your ex-husband's family, if any, you wish to remain in contact with. Grandparents are special because of their close relationship with the kids, but stepmothers have reported that when loyalties lie in different camps, ties to most past in-laws are hard to maintain or become redefined. If there are people you will truly miss, such as your ex-husband's sister with whom you shared so many shopping trips, you can try to keep these relationships alive.

Robin was very close to her sister-in-law, Gail, during her marriage to Gil. The two had a lot in common and looked after each other's children, cousins close in age. The two women hoped their friendship would continue even after Robin and Gil divorced. "I don't blame you for divorcing my brother; I wouldn't want to be married to him either," claimed Gail. But Gil was jealous and interrogated his children for details of what their mother and Aunt Gail discussed or did.

Before long brother and sister had stopped speaking to each other following weeks of arguing about Robin, and the kids were upset about their father's constant questioning. Weary of the contention, Robin and Gail reluctantly decided to put their relationship on hold.

"I miss her," reported Robin. "I'm hoping we can be friends again when feelings about the divorce have cooled."

New In-Laws, New Friends?

Beverly was delighted when, soon after her marriage, her husband's sister, Arlene, invited her to lunch: "I'd like to know you better, and I have two friends who are stepmothers. They have a hunch you might like to chat!"

Beverly jumped at the invitation, and the four women have become close friends, the two other stepmoms providing an instant support group for Beverly.

Other stepmoms, frankly, have not been as fortunate as Beverly. Many women have reported that once the initial checking-out period is over, they feel left out. They wonder about this: Is it shyness? Awkwardness about how to relate to a stepmother? Some new stepmoms interpret standoffish behavior as "they just don't like me," which can be the beginning of the downward spiral we've talked about, compounded by rejection or problems with stepchildren.

You need to initiate new family relationships yourself. Everybody is so busy these days, it isn't really surprising that no one's knocking down your door (which you don't want all at once anyway). Here are some interesting tips veteran stepmoms suggest to help you break the ice and ease yourself into the family:

- Refresh your memory about how you wish to describe yourself and your new role as stepmom (see part 1) so you are prepared for questions or negative comments.

- Find out which relatives have children the same age as your kids or stepkids. Try to arrange a multi-family trip to the zoo, a barbecue, or ice-skating in the park—any outing you'd all enjoy.

- Do the reverse of what Arlene did for Beverly. Find out if there is another new extended family member or changed family circumstance—did your mate's brother recently marry, did a cousin adopt a child, did Grandma just become a widow? Any of these folks would appreciate a lunch invitation.

- Try a "combination" supper—invite a couple of your husband's relatives over with a couple of yours. Choose people you are pretty sure will get along. Propose a toast to each

of the families now uniting. Do the same with friends—
some of yours, some of his.

- If you hear a family member is sick, take a casserole to her
home for the kids' dinner (don't just offer; actually appear
with it), or send her some flowers from you and your
new mate.

- Offer to do some reciprocal baby-sitting with relatives who
look as though they need a night out alone. They can do
the same for you in return.

- Offer to share anything you have too much of—herbs from
your garden, the three coffee makers you received as wedding gifts, the extra coffee table or lamp you don't need
since you've combined two homes.

- Start your own coffee klatch on Sundays. Make it known
that you always serve coffee and bagels-with-all-the-trim-
mings from noon to one-thirty on Sundays, and invite your
new relatives.

You can't hope to please everyone, but think of these invitations as "cold calling" when you have something to sell. You
can expect a certain percentage of rejections. These people
don't yet know you, so it's impossible for them to dislike
you—if they believe fairy tales or are listening to the family-
problem person, you won't want to bother with them anyway.

If you have one taker, great—you're not sitting, waiting
for the phone to ring. Those willing to get to know you will
be the people you can ask about who's who and what's what
in the family. Many stepmoms have found that their husband's
relatives are reluctant to discuss an ex-wife—the mother of
their nieces and nephews—but you might find out more about
your mate's cousin Augustus or your stepdaughter's boyfriend
who concerns you. Just remember, though—if they talk about
others, they will certainly talk about you.

Your Side of the Family: A Mixed Bag of Concern and Support

You will naturally assume that your own relatives and friends will be behind you when you meet and marry your life partner. It's reasonable to expect that people who love you will want what you want and will delight in your happiness.

Perhaps surprisingly, this is not always the experience of a woman marrying a previously married man with children. Some people close to you might see this union as *not* being in your best interest. If your nearest and dearest have been involved in a stepfamily themselves, they might worry about what you'll have to contend with. Many stepmoms, for example, said they would never wish stepmotherhood on their daughters, or their stepdaughters for that matter. Some said they didn't think these younger women would be able or, most significantly, *willing* to handle the rigors of the role.

People who've known you since babyhood might think you deserve to be the bride of a man as unencumbered as you are, rather than see you enter marriage with the burden, both emotional and practical, of someone else's children. Others might object on religious grounds to your marrying a divorced man. Citing love and concern, family and friends might attempt to talk you out of marrying him.

This can be upsetting, particularly if you are very young. Stepmoms who have faced a bevy of worried aunts and siblings have suggested you firmly remind them that your choice is based on not only love but information about what your life will entail. Make it clear you need their support and love for the reasons they've pointed out—you have many challenges ahead as a stepmom.

Myrna's dad found it impossible to accept her decision to marry Brian, a divorced man with a small son. When forbidding the wedding didn't work, Myrna's father said she had to choose.

"It broke my heart that my father didn't walk me down the aisle," recalled Myrna. Her mother visited her newly married daughter alone. Two years later, when Myrna's son was born, she sent photos of the baby to her dad, but he didn't respond.

"When my child was two years old, I just decided to visit my parents with the baby and found Dad mowing the lawn," Myrna recalled. "As we got out of the car, the baby just toddled, arms outstretched, to his granddad. The whole feud was over—Dad scooped the baby up, and we all cried! He's apologized to Brian and me and now relishes his love for his grandson. I get chills thinking of what we could have missed."

Surround Yourself with Friendly Faces

You might find it helpful to invite your family members to your house, often. They'll see how things are going for you, and, more important, you need friendly faces in the house. If you have no children, it's comforting to surround yourself with people who know and enjoy your style, your personality, even your cooking. The bonus is that your stepkids will get to know your side of the family. You might find your mother and your stepdaughter have an instant chemistry, which can only help. If possible, suggest visits to your relatives' homes with your stepkids too.

Ask your family for their opinions—they might have suggestions for resolving any difficulties you are experiencing, especially since they might, to some extent, have a more objective view. At the very least, you'll feel good knowing there are people on your side you can trust.

"It's easy now to see what I did wrong," related Betsy, a stepmom with no children, married nine years to a man with four kids whom she met when they were all in their teens. "I was so embarrassed by the kids' behavior—their lack of respect, the profanity they used—that I didn't invite anyone over."

Betsy advises any stepmom to fill the house with friends and relatives so stepchildren can see her functioning with people who love her. "I realize now that the kids saw me as someone with no outside support, and I believe it made it easier for them to treat me badly. It's important for your stepfamily to see you as a well-liked person valued by the rest of the world—it might make them reconsider their own perceptions."

Problem People

We all know people who've caused us trouble. In fact, it's hard to imagine life without them (but what a lovely fantasy). People without the experience of stepfamilies tend not to understand the limitations automatically placed on a stepmother who is trying to run a home or take her place in the family. A stepmom often doesn't have the support she needs to say and do what she considers necessary—a fact that makes dealing with problem people that much harder.

Stepmoms say their list of difficult people is topped by the ex-wife and stepchildren. Other members of your stepfamily, and your mate's friends, will probably pale beside these primary people, but since the cornerstone of this book is preparation, you need to be aware of others who can cause problems for you:

a) *Those who don't want you around, try to get rid of you, or make a decision not to like or welcome you, often before meeting you.*

Among these people will be those who believe the myths and fairy tales about "wicked" stepmothers or have heard negative stories of other people's stepmoms. Some of these problem people, maybe even most, you can turn around, given time. It might seem irritating to be in a position of proving yourself, but it's worth the experiment if it results in changing a negative opinion.

When you've taken your best shot with someone who is not receptive to your overtures of friendship or who rejects your efforts to discuss your mutual relationship, or lack of one, leave them alone. But be sure to verbalize this decision to them: you've received the message they don't want a relationship, so you're backing off. Now it's up to them. You cannot force people to like you. You can, however, insist on being treated with courtesy.

Don't spend too much time on these problem people. Adjust your attitude toward them, and accept that they are among the few people who don't recognize your value. It happens in other kinds of families too. You might not like your new brother-in-law, because he's just not your type. That's perfectly acceptable as long as you don't do each other any harm.

b) *Friends or members of your new family whom, after doing your research, you decide you are better off avoiding as much as possible, due to their attitude, behavioral characteristics, or a personality conflict.*

This species of problem person relates to you but does so negatively or in a way you find unacceptable. A common root of this kind of trouble, stepmoms have reported, is that some family members or friends are unable or unwilling to reconcile themselves to the fact that you're here and your husband's former wife isn't.

Edie flinched when she recalled the comments made by her husband Bill's best friend, Greg. Greg had been very fond of Bill's former wife, Jean, who had drowned in a tragic boating accident three years earlier. Greg still missed his best buddy's first wife and never really took to Edie, though he continued to visit after Bill's remarriage.

Remembered Edie, "The same thing happened every visit. Greg would look at Daphne, Bill and Jean's daughter, clap Bill on the back, and say, 'Well, old boy, Jean will never really be gone while Daphne is with us, will she?'" Daphne was a child replica of her pretty, gray-eyed mother.

Fortunately, Edie didn't have to make an issue of Greg's awkward remarks, since the comments made Bill uncomfortable too. Bill began making plans to see his friend alone, away from the house.

Stepmoms have reported other kinds of negative affronts. Younger stepmothers have heard themselves referred to as the new "trophy" wife, been called "the wicked stepmother" (just as a "joke," of course), and had to put up with other denigrating comments about their marriage or their role as a stepmom. Others have had their home treated disrespectfully or have witnessed other bad behavior either designed to provoke or done because the instigator didn't know any better.

Whatever you do, don't seethe in silence. If it makes you uncomfortable, it has to stop. Decide whether you want to remedy the trouble a problem person is causing or you want your mate to do it for you. If you feel that you have to fight your own battles or that hostile people will consider you "weak" if you ask someone else to do your dirty work, plan your strategy. Give some thought to responses you might make to put-down comments: "I may be young, Tom, but I'm not inexperienced. I know a put-down when I hear one. And I don't need any more, thanks." You can always ask your husband to help if you don't have success.

Try shaming those whose behavior you object to: "Why don't you put your feet on the stool, Tom. It will be more comfortable than the table. There doesn't seem to be room for your drink and your feet." You can try being more aggressive with your comments if that doesn't work: "You know, Tom, we're trying to teach the kids how to behave socially; I'd really appreciate it if you wouldn't use the table as a footstool."

c) *Family members who have personal problems of their own that might have an impact on you and your stepfamily.*

Carrie's fifteen-year-old stepdaughter, Natalie, suffered from extreme mood swings and erratic behavior; she was unpredictable, unreliable, and hostile, erupting into screaming or crying jags seemingly without provocation. This stepmom found it impossible to form a relationship with the teen. Carrie tried talking to her husband and Natalie's siblings, but all maintained that Natalie's outbursts must be Carrie's fault, and suggestions about therapy were dismissed. Carrie resolved to simply avoid Natalie as much as possible.

Years later one of Natalie's siblings admitted that the girl had always been "unstable" and had had problems long before her parents had divorced. Out of loyalty to Natalie, the family hadn't wanted to reveal her history, believing it would make matters worse. "You should never have expected rational behavior from her," her stepson said.

A stunning entry in the now-you-tell-me category! Carrie's husband, too, finally acknowledged the truth. Said Carrie, "It was so unfair of this family to keep me in the dark. Had I known of Natalie's instability, instead of everyone denying it, I would have related to her in an entirely different way."

Be alert to clues: if friends of the family ask, "How are you getting along with Natalie?" often enough, you can be sure you need to find out what is prompting such intense interest.

d) *Medically ill or dependent people for whom you are partially or completely responsible.*

You will know, prior to your marriage, if your husband has children who are ill or otherwise incapacitated and who will become your stepchildren should you decide to join the family. But it is one thing to help care for disabled stepfamily members, quite another to be totally responsible for them. When we interviewed Greta, she had just been widowed at age seventy-two, left entirely in charge of the welfare of her forty-five-year-old severely retarded stepdaughter.

"I'm not able to take care of her by myself," this elderly stepmother admitted. "She's completely dependent, has to be bathed, taken to the toilet, fed—everything. Phil left me a little money, and she has some medical coverage, but it's not enough." In her younger years, Greta and her husband, Phil, coped well together, financially and practically, but she wasn't prepared for Phil to die first. Be sure you are aware of your responsibilities to dependent stepchildren if your mate dies before you do (see chapter 18, "The Stepmom's Legal File").

Find out, too, what your mate's relationship is with physically or mentally handicapped relatives in your extended family and what sort of commitment to them he wishes to have now that he's remarried. You might find that your brother-in-law has a child with Down's syndrome who eagerly awaits his uncle Joe for their weekly visit to the duck pond on Saturday mornings. Your husband's mom might have Alzheimer's disease and is used to his company on Thursday nights, when he stays over to give his dad time to go out with his cronies.

If you know about these commitments, decide to accept them, and build them into your new life, you'll be ready to give of yourself too. To hear about them the day you return from your honeymoon isn't fair to you or this loved one. If you are not equipped to help willingly, it is unjust to do so grudgingly.

Six months into her marriage, Peg was shocked to discover someone on the sofa in her living room one morning. She rushed back into her bedroom, screaming, to wake her husband, Len. He calmed her down, explaining, "Honey, it's only my brother, Johnny—he comes here to crash every few months." Peg was appalled. It turned out Johnny, an alcoholic, used the front-door key tied round his neck to let himself into his brother's house to dry out from time to time.

There was no way Peg, whose dad was an alcoholic, could handle this—it brought back too many painful memories. She told her husband, "Either it stops, or I'm out of here." Len refused: it had been Johnny's routine for so long, he said, it would kill him. Peg left. She says in retrospect: "If I'd known about Johnny, I never would have married into that family."

Maud told a different story. She was a nurse, trained to work with substance-abuse patients. When she learned that her husband's brother, Felix, age twenty-eight, had been doing drugs since he was fourteen, she felt she could help. When she married Jerry, she willingly "took on" Felix, too, and encouraged the family to attend a support group for relatives of drug abusers. After two years of drug rehab, Felix has a new lease on life, a fact his family gratefully attributes to Maud's patience and knowledge of the problem.

e) *The behind-the-scenes saboteur. It might take you longer to discover them, since they do not work overtly. But they can cause a great deal of damage to the stepmother and her family.*

One of the most common kinds of saboteur, stepmothers have reported, is the person who tells lies, either about the stepmother or her actions. If a liar is young, you might be inclined to call her stories "fibbing" or the product of "a vivid

imagination." As the child grows into adolescence and adulthood, however, lying becomes more destructive.

It took Margaret quite a while to discover that Kay, her
twenty-seven-year-old stepniece, had been lying about her
since she'd first joined the family. Kay had a repertoire of
"stories" about Margaret—things her stepaunt had supposedly
done, thought, felt, and said: "Margaret hates kids" (although
Margaret was the devoted mother of two children and stepmother of three); "Margaret says James [her stepson] is spoiled
and rude"; "Margaret doesn't want everyone there for Thanksgiving"; "Margaret thinks we're too religious."

Over several years, Kay gradually built up an unflattering
image of Margaret that made her seem critical of her new
family. Margaret accidentally discovered the alter ego created
by Kay during a conversation with her mother-in-law, who
asked what her problem was concerning Thanksgiving, when
in fact Margaret was looking forward to hosting the celebration. "I didn't understand how there could have been any
confusion about it at first," Margaret admitted. "We ended up
on the phone for almost two hours, unraveling a litany of
outlandish things Kay had said about me. After that call, my
relationship with this family changed overnight."

It is humiliating for a stepmother to have to correct misin-
formation about herself, to deny whatever it is she's been accused of, particularly if it happens frequently. Often it's a case
of a stepmom's word against the perpetrator's: "Yes, you did";
"No, I didn't." Frequently, perhaps usually, the family will side
with the relative, since the stepmom is a stranger—perhaps
she is critical and unaccepting. It is unthinkable, however, for
a stepmom to call a stepchild or any other member of her
new family a liar; it is equally unlikely that his or her dad can
concede that his baby has trouble with the truth. One stepmom who complained to her husband received the response
"My son does not tell lies. Period."

If you find you get no help from your mate in dealing
with a liar, all you can do is set the record straight through
clear communication of your ideas and feelings, followed up
by your actions. Say, "I think Kay misinterpreted my position.

I'd absolutely love to have Thanksgiving at our home this year—I'm so thrilled you're coming" or "I'm afraid Kay hasn't read the relationship between James and me accurately. I think he's a charming boy—I can't wait to get to know him better."

If by chance you think you have a receptive listener among your step relations, you can hint, "Am I imagining it, or does Kay have a tendency to exaggerate?" You are more likely to find support in your new family if you approach the problem on the basis not that your reputation is being damaged but that you are concerned about a person who is obviously crying out for help.

Most saboteurs can be discovered and helped, even though with their potential for damage you might not feel they deserve help. When the truth comes out, in fact, you and your stepfamily might ultimately decide you need to avoid the saboteur as much as possible.

Amalie became a part-time stepmother to three preteen boys four years after their parents divorced. Trying everything she could to make friends with them, she was met with the silent treatment or outright rejection. Amalie and her husband, Jon, were mystified by this lack of progress. Quite by chance, Amalie overheard the kids discussing Therese, their mother's sister:

"Aunt Therese told me she couldn't understand how Dad could be so cruel to us, marrying Amalie," said one.

Said the youngest, "Well, we don't have to like her. Aunt Therese told me we should never let Amalie try to be our mother."

Once Amalie realized the extent of her sister-in-law's negative influence on the boys, Amalie and Jon actually felt relieved, the mystery revealed. Jon gathered his sons together and explained that Amalie wasn't trying to be their mother, just his wife—their own relationship with Amalie could be anything that they felt comfortable with. Amalie later talked to them as well, explaining that she cared about being part of their lives, as a woman who loved their dad and could offer them support, advice, and friendship.

All five of them discussed how sad it was for Aunt Therese

to feel so bitter about Amalie and to be mean to her, when they could have been friends. The boys, presented with this alternative point of view, gradually began to feel protective of their stepmother, and Amalie heard through the family grapevine they had begun defending her when their aunt made unfair and uninformed remarks. For their own part, Jon and Amalie decided to limit their association with Therese to major family occasions.

The Family "Bosses"

While the notion of a matriarchy seems old-fashioned, the occasional stepmom reported a similar system, fully operational, within her own modern stepfamily. These stepmothers described their new families as being "run" by someone, usually a female, who is looked upon as "the boss," her approval and blessing sought to keep the peace.

Anita reported that while she and Dale were dating, whenever she visited his home, where he lived with his three children following their mother's death, she knew as she entered the house whether or not the oldest daughter, Rachelle, was present. If she was, there seemed to be a dark pall over the house. If not, the house seemed brighter and more cheerful.

"Rachelle managed to dictate the mood of the entire family," marveled Anita. "The rest of them, including Dale, just revolved around her. I can remember having dinner with them one evening when Rachelle was in one of her foul moods. There was practically no conversation at dinner, everyone taking the lead from her hostile, rude attitude. When she wasn't around, they were quite lively. I tried to find out the reasons behind this phenomenon, but Dale's only explanation was that she was having a rough time."

To this day, said Anita, Dale's oldest daughter still manipulates her family's mood, even now that her siblings are independent adults, two with kids of their own. Anita, who is strong-willed, yet recognizes a losing battle when she sees one, accepts this as a family eccentricity. "To be honest, it's easier to go along with the rest of them when we're together—it's not important enough to argue about anymore."

Like Anita, you need to find out who "the boss" is and determine whether or not, or how, you can relate to this person. Some stepmoms report liking or even admiring "the boss," or of being able to laugh with her, about her role. One stepmom worked up the courage to ask her formidable mother-in-law how she came to have the job and received the response, "They're such an indecisive bunch. Someone had to take charge!"

How Not to Be Your Own Problem Person

In Part 2 you spent time getting to know yourself better. Now that you're halfway through your research, you need to take another, slightly different look at yourself.

Some stepmoms we spoke with admitted that they became a problem person to themselves—sometimes their own worst enemy—during times of crisis. We've said that preparation is part of being a friend to yourself as a stepmom—we can unequivocally promise that all the reading you're doing now will prevent many of the most common difficulties stepmothers face.

But how will you respond when crises do occur—when you can't prevent problems? When life becomes really tough, as it can for every stepmom, it's tempting to walk away and blame the people who are making your life difficult. You can do this, of course—it's undeniably reasonable all too often—but we think it's important to present a worthy alternative.

Sandi is the stepmom we met in chapter 7 in our discussion of mother abandonment. Her predecessor had left her kids, Sandi's stepkids, but since they still fully expected their mom to return, they were unable to love their stepmom. Sandi, who was devoted to them and determined to succeed, mentioned that her grandmother advised her to "bloom where you are planted."

This lovely phrase is appropriate for the many stepmothers

who find themselves on rocky ground but choose calmly and methodically to handle each issue as it arises, each problem person as he or she makes an appearance.

Make up your mind to develop a positive, can-do attitude: Shrug off what you cannot change, deal with what you can, and move forward. The stepmothers who succeed are the ones who refuse to look upon themselves as victims. If we sink into depression and self-pity as many stepmoms we interviewed did, stepfamily life becomes harder, and we can be of little help to anyone else. Everyone in the stepfamily needs to bloom where they are planted, not just the stepmom, but Dad and the kids too. You'll be setting an example for all-weather hardiness, nurturing relationships within your stepfamily and with the people important to your husband and stepchildren.

❧

Questionnaire

1. Can you name three people you have met within your new circle of family and friends that you really like? List in your journal their names and the reasons you like them.

2. What can you do to further foster a deepening relationship with these three?

3. How can they positively influence your role as stepmom? What do you need to do to help them in this?

4. List three people in your new extended family (if there are this many) whom you believe you will have difficulties with. Detail your reasons.

5. Do they have the ability to complicate your role of stepmom in this family? If so, how?

6. Is there anyone in your biological family who has a problem with your marriage and to your taking on stepkids? List his/her reasons as you understand them. If you don't fully understand them, ask him/her to clarify.

7. Is there anyone in your biological family who has a problem with your marriage and to your taking on stepkids?

List his/her reasons as you understand them. If you don't fully understand them, ask him/her to clairfy.

8. Do you believe there is justification for the problems your family member sees? Can you do anything to alleviate his/her fears for you or to remedy their cause?

Action Box

  Attempt to make friends with only two or three members of your new family at a time. Try grandparents first, then add people who live nearby. It makes more sense to feel comfortable with your husband's brother and sister-in-law who live three miles away than those who live in another state whom you'll see only once a year. When you've had a chance to meet new people, consider whether you think they will become good friends or just family members with whom you'll share a courteous relationship.

  Keep an open mind regarding people you currently believe should be on your "problem" list. People and their circumstances change, and it's possible you have made a mistake about them or have met them at a bad time. You need to give everyone the benefit of the doubt, just as you deserve a grace period. If your problem people later try to remedy or revise their behavior, be receptive to a change of heart.

PART III

Lifestyle and Practical Matters

OVERVIEW

Unlike relationships, which take a long time to develop, have no set time frame, and are dependent upon unique personalities as to whether they fail or flourish, practical solutions and decisions about how your step home will operate can be enacted by you and your husband right away, in some instances before you marry.

Making informed, practical choices about your lifestyle—from how stepfamily members will meet one another to planning your wedding, deciding where you will live, organizing moving day, and running the stephousehold—provides a strong structure for everyone while personal, perhaps erratic relationship adjustments are made. If you can start out on the right foot in the practical arena, relationship issues can only benefit.

Also included in part 3 are suggestions for blending two sets of traditions and rituals into one stepfamily, as well as for integrating your stepfamily into the larger sphere of school, church, and community. Finally, the last two chapters offer stepmom-tested advice about managing stepfamily finances and your legal must-know list. As always, the questionnaires will help you pinpoint your specific concerns.

CHAPTER 12

The Wedding and Other Formalities

Social graces smooth our way. A sparkling introduction or a warm invitation is worth its weight in gold, especially in delicate situations—which, you'll realize by now, stepmothers have no lack of. For us, the right words or gestures are more than usually helpful.

You've thought about what you want from your role and from your relationships as a stepmom. Now it's time to express your position clearly and with style, from the time you're introduced, through your engagement, wedding, and setting up your home. This chapter is all about etiquette that makes life easier for a stepmom.

Seize the Day—But Plan It First

For most stepmothers, meeting their mate's children for the first time, and making the best possible impression on them, is a great concern. We highly recommend planning in some depth for your first meeting. Timing is important—if your husband has younger children, for example, a counselor (court appointed or selected by one of their parents) might already be working with them as they cope with their mother's death or their parents' divorce, and he/she may help determine when they're ready to meet you. Accordingly, avoid sensitive dates—

their mom's birthday or the anniversary of their mom's death or their parent's wedding.

Your first get-together should be action packed, fun oriented, and very casual—no formal dinners leaving everyone uncomfortably trying to think of something to say. Arrange an activity you think will help break the ice and encourage positive impressions. Outdoor events are best for this—a picnic or a barbecue where everyone pitches in or an afternoon ice-skating, followed by a pizza party. Whatever you decide, plan every detail. Consider every angle. Anticipate everything. What if someone refuses to go? What if someone throws up in the car? What if it rains? What will you do—what's your backup plan?

Try to avoid unexpected first meetings too. Dana and her husband, Frankie, still regret how she met her stepchildren. "Frankie's two kids were with their mom for the weekend," Dana explained. "Saturday night Frankie and I were alone, brewing up a pot of spaghetti, barefoot and splattered with marinara, kissing and giggling, when in walked Frankie's kids, followed by their mom. Dead silence. His daughter burst into tears, his son ran out of the house, and his ex-wife screamed, 'Who the hell is *this*?' It was one of the most embarrassing moments of my life."

Unfortunately, Frankie's ex-wife still had a key to his house "just in case, for the kids" and was known to turn up at odd times before Frankie had begun dating again. It would have been more sensible to have rendezvoused at Dana's place until the "key" issue had been resolved and the children had had the chance to meet Dana the way she and Frankie thought best.

If you have children of your own, and it feels right, include them in this first group date. Don't surprise them—make sure you've told them first about the man you've been dating and the state of your relationship: "We like each other very much, and I think you'll enjoy him too." You can tell older kids, who understand the dating process: "We're getting serious, and I want you to meet him and his kids."

Keep your expectations low to moderate. Mention to your children that whatever they think on first sight, you want them to be polite, that this meeting is important to you. If nothing else, at least you've made them feel part of what's happening and asked for their help. If they refuse to participate and are old enough to be left out, leave them alone, and try another time. You may have to keep trying, especially with teens.

How Do You Do: Introduction Tips

- Your united front starts *immediately*. If possible, arrive to meet the kids together, and drop them off afterward together. Show them you're a pair, a "we." Assuming you two are committed, the sooner they know and can try to accept this, the better.

- Remember "Stepmom's Quick Primer" number 2: Start as you mean to go on. While you want this first get-together to be a relaxed affair, agree with your mate ahead of time on standards of behavior. Resistance, acting up, sullenness, and moodiness can be ignored. Direct rudeness is not acceptable and must be addressed, ideally by your husband if it's from his kids or by you if your kids are the offenders. Only by insisting on courtesy from day one do you have any chance of becoming a successful stepmom.

- Unless his kids are outrageous terrors at the first meeting, try to convey how much you want to get to know them: "Your dad told me you have the lead part in your school play. Is it hard learning all those lines?" Don't ask to see the play, just to hear about it. Express interest, but don't be pushy.

- Do not visit Dad's home on the first few occasions with his kids. If their mom died, this is the old family home and will be sacred. When they know you better, you'll visit, but until you marry, you should behave like a guest in Dad's home when the kids are present. Do not take control of the kitchen because you are the only one who can cook—Chinese takeout is great. Don't inspect the house or handle their things, and don't make intrusive comments—other than how nice you think their rooms are (if you're invited by the kids to see them).

• Invite his kids to your home only when you feel you know them a bit; otherwise, this can seem too formal. Make this visit feel impromptu—if you're all on your way to the movies, just invite Dad and kids to pop in for a minute because you need to feed the cat/birds/fish or grab a sweater. But plan this "spontaneous" visit ahead of time so that your place looks the way you want it to. It's nice to be able to show them something interesting too: "This is my herb garden/electric guitar/map of ancient Egypt"—anything that tells something personal and intriguing about you.

When the Day Is Done

If your first get-together—or even the second, third, and fourth—feels like a disaster, don't worry. (Yes, we really mean that.) It's not the disaster that's important but how you handle it.

Always, always, always build in time, somehow, for you and mate to discuss these get-togethers later, to talk about what went well and should be repeated or what your concerns are. You need intimate time to reinforce your love for each other and to express support, particularly if the event *was* a disaster. Find the humor in it, and above all don't blame each other for anything. If you had problems sticking to a united front, now is the time to talk about it. Together, you'll try again.

If there is anything positive you can focus on, however minor, do so. Perhaps his ten-year-old thought your twelve-year-old's sneakers were "cool," even if it's the only time his kid opened his mouth all day. Maybe they *all* liked the pizza place you picked out, even if they fought over who got the biggest slice.

Be extra attentive to both sets of kids after your first meeting. They might think (especially if you presented a spectacular united front) that they are being further abandoned as a result of their parent's new couplehood. You and your mate can each talk to your own children, alone, afterwards. Express interest in their opinions, even if they're negative, but make it clear to your kids that your mate is important to you and will remain so and that courtesy is expected. Let your children know how much you appreciate their attempts at friendship to your mate's daughter, who wasn't very nice back: "Yes, she seemed angry—maybe something is bothering her that she can talk to her dad about." Dad should tell his son how great it was of him to lend his favorite comic book to the little boy he just met, your son.

Talk, talk, talk. It doesn't matter how many times your kids make fun of your wonderful husband-to-be's regional accent or how much your mate hears from his kids that they "hate" you. Continue to talk positively about each other.

How to Say, "We're Getting Married!"

Once you've made the decision to marry, you and your mate have the task of telling family and friends. But a word of caution: some parents believe they are being sophisticated, progressive, or sensitive by asking their children for "permission" to marry. We strongly advise against this. Suppose they refuse—are you going to cancel your plans? While there's no question your life will be easier if your children support your decision, it is inappropriate for them to make it for you.

Plan and rehearse with your mate how you want to tell the children about your engagement. Ideally you should tell them as a couple, all of yours together, then all of his together. It's better not to tell each child individually; this avoids the "you told Billy before you told me" problem. This might not be possible with adult children, who might be scattered, but kids living in your home or seen regularly need this approach. Be sure to reinforce the news often. Several stepmothers mentioned that their stepkids had denied knowing about the proposed wedding, maintaining, sometimes years after the wedding took place, that they hadn't been told until the last minute.

Expect any kind of reaction to the announcement. One child might initially be polite but then shut himself in his room for two days. Another might have instant hysterics but settle down and accept it after an hour or so. Whatever happens, remember— it is not personal; it is a response to yet another change when they might not have become used to the last one.

After his kids, your mate needs to proudly introduce you to the rest of the world—"This is my fiancée/wife, Judy"—the moment he suspects there is anyone present who has not yet met you. Ten minutes later, an "Oh, by the way, this is Judy" is not acceptable—those present will perceive that you're not very important and relate to you accordingly. (Immediate and glowing introductions should apply even if you're still in the just-dating phase, in case this turns out to be a permanent relationship.) Once he has introduced you, he should remain at your side until you are comfortable. Family and friends will get the message— you are a precious commodity, his wife-to-be, future stepmom to his children. You should perform the same, proud introductions of your mate to your friends and family.

Spreading the Good News

It's becoming increasingly popular to send a wedding announcement noting the formation of a stepfamily, similar to birth or adoption announcements. Your news can be delivered in the form of a printed card, as creatively or simply as you like, including the facts:

Mary O'Connor and John Valentine
announce with much pleasure that on July 1
they will marry and form a new stepfamily.
Their address, together with
Susie and Tommy O'Connor
and
Joseph and James Valentine, will be . . .

Others prefer a simple phone call to pass on the word. Whatever feels right for you is perfectly fine.

What's in a Name?

We've discussed alternatives to the title "stepmother," but even if better descriptives elude you, decide early on how you want your husband's kids to refer to you personally, if not your role. The vast majority of stepmothers prefer being called by their first name. A few stepmothers reported conflicts with stepchildren who refused to comply, using a nickname or other unacceptable term or an anonymous pronoun—"she" or "her." This is disrespectful and needs to be corrected immediately. Get your husband involved in doing this, if you have to.

Stepmom Showers and Parties

Some stepmoms told of being embarrassed or uncomfortable having an engagement party, a bridal shower, or a lavish wedding when stepkids or other family members were opposed to the marriage. Our advice is to go ahead and celebrate with a full heart. You'll have to make other compromises once you are married. Enjoy every precious moment as a bride-to-be.

Traditionally pregnant women or those who adopt are given a baby shower. Women acquiring stepchildren, however, are deprived of this attention. Let's start a tradition—if you have a friend who is becoming a stepmother to children she'll have responsibilities for, throw her a "stepmom shower." There is no reason why a woman "getting" a young stepchild or two should not be included in one of life's traditional passages. Both full- and part-time stepmoms would enjoy receiving some age-appropriate books or toys or some Disney bed linens for when little Jimmy comes for the weekend. This would be a wonderful show of support (especially from other women) for a new stepmother, who deserves all the perks women who give birth to or adopt children receive.

Living Together or Apart before Your Wedding

Some people contemplating marriage are opposed to living together for moral or religious reasons. Others believe it's foolish to enter marriage without a trial run.

Perhaps the most usual reason to live with your potential husband prior to marriage is to get to know him up close before making a decision about a permanent commitment, to judge if you are compatible under the same roof. About half the stepmoms we interviewed had lived with their fiancé before their walk down the aisle.

Before her marriage, Dora, a therapist and veteran stepmom, was encouraged by friends (also therapists) to move in with Quentin, father of two teenagers, a boy and a girl who visited on weekends, along with her two young teenage boys, to see how they all got along. Quentin's city apartment seemed to have plenty of room for the four of them, six on weekends, and they lived together for five years before their wedding.

While her marriage is a happy one, Dora said in hindsight that she would not recommend living together before marriage to anyone with children. "We reduced the importance of marriage in our children's eyes," she explained. "When we were just cohabiting, my kids saw Quentin as my boyfriend, and they weren't really comfortable with it. I vividly remember an argument I had with my fifteen-year-old son during this period, which escalated until he finally shouted at me, 'And how do you think I feel, hearing you and your boyfriend having sex in the next room?" I was devastated. He ran out in tears, and I cried, too, from embarrassment. He still talks about this scene, and he's in his thirties now."

A number of stepmoms who lived with their mate before marriage found that this trial run was not a reliable barometer for how things would be after the nuptials. In fact, relationships with their stepchildren changed dramatically after the wedding. "Dad's girlfriend," for children of any age, is a vastly different concept from "my stepmother."

Daia was stunned when her husband's teenage daughter, with whom Daia felt she had a good relationship while she was living with her father, had to be practically dragged to the wedding. "The whole day, she acted as though she didn't know me," Daia recalled. "It hurt me so much. My husband was surprised too—he just hugged me and refilled my champagne glass. I felt I had to start getting to know his daughter all over again. Things are much better now, seven years later, but I still can't forget the shock and sadness I felt." Would she have done it differently, though? "Absolutely not. I needed to ease into this family gradually—there were a lot of leftover problems with my husband's ex-wife, including financial messes, and I wouldn't have known about these things or perhaps seen them resolved as quickly unless I had lived with him first. And, to be honest, I liked knowing I had an escape route, if necessary."

If you do decide to live with your mate and his kids, either those who live with him full- or part-time, here are some thoughts and suggestions from stepmoms who did:

- Remember, this is a temporary arrangement, one you have considered very carefully both from your perspective and that of any children you may have. At any time, either you or he can decide to leave, and you are back to being single, or a single mom.

- Retain all your outside interests, hobbies, friends, routines.

- If you have full-time custody of your kids, consider the stress of forcing them to change their lifestyle, their home, schools, friends, etc., only to move again if the relationship doesn't work out for you.

- While it's now more socially acceptable for couples to live together without marriage, it can add yet another negative connotation to your already negatively loaded role. As a "live-in" stepmom, you might come to feel you have even less status than a married stepmom.

- Do *not* pool any of your assets (e.g. buy a house together) or make any other major financial commitments to your live-in mate. Don't lend him money or pay to move his stuff from his ex wife's house until you're married.

• Realize that living together affords you none of the legal and social protection that marriage provides. Don't give up your job (unless you get another where you're going) or medical insurance for yourself and your kids. Consider this living arrangement only if you can continue to support yourself and your children if it doesn't work out. It's far from ideal to be financially dependent on a husband, and it's impossible with a live-in lover.

Your Wedding Day (Emphasis on "Your")

Opinions vary widely about what is appropriate for a second marriage. Wear white or not? Religious or civil? Accept from the start that you will not please everyone, whatever choices you make. The most important thing to remember (and to keep reminding yourself about) is that your wedding day is *your* wedding day.

In retrospect, some women who married men with children have resented and regretted having had modest or low-key weddings out of concern that children and stepchildren would be unable to handle the ordeal of seeing their parent remarry: The kids' feelings were accommodated. The bride's, all too often, were not. That makes no sense. Before making your plans remind yourself of "Stepmom's Quick Primer" number 10: Don't forget—this is your life too. Getting married on Saturday, staying overnight in a hotel, seeing the kids for dinner on Sunday, and being back at your desks on Monday is not an acceptable plan when your dream was a beautiful, romantic wedding on the beach, a week cruising the Greek islands, and another week settling into your new home.

Your wedding should be arranged exactly how you want it, down to the last detail. At the risk of horrifying critics who believe stepmoms should give way for the sake of the children, we recommend, "Go for it!" By the end of the day, you will be a stepmom, having accepted, not chosen, the related duties and responsibilities. While you want to start off being the most positive, optimistic person, wife, and stepmom you can possibly be, that doesn't mean sacrificing your dream wedding day. Plan it, save money for it, figure out how you're going to do it, and make it happen. Do *not* accept second best for your wedding day.

When Willow became engaged to Ivan, whose previous wife had died giving birth to Brenda, now four years old, he was still paying off medical bills and wanted to economize on the wedding. Willow confided, "He made me feel guilty having a wedding at all, because it was costing so much—I even agreed to have his previous wife's wedding ring, instead of one of my own. He said it was silly to waste it. But my giving in so much has backfired. I think I've conveyed that I don't deserve the best, because I've been willing to accept so much less."

Wedding Jitters

Most brides get wedding jitters—second thoughts, wondering if everyone will behave, praying the flowers will arrive on time. A woman marrying a man with children has the same worries, and more. What if his ex-wife shows up? What if our kids fight? What if his daughter refuses to come to the wedding?

By the time your big day arrives, we trust, you've done as much research as possible about your new stepfamily and, to the best of your ability, planned the wedding you've always dreamed of. After that, you can do no more. Relax, enjoy, and hope for the best.

If something unpleasant happens on your wedding day that you've been unable to anticipate, your attitude toward it is what will make it either a major catastrophe or simply an annoying little wrinkle in the day's proceedings. Your cool and calm response to any calamity will save the day and is what will be remembered.

Wendy had done her research. She knew her eight-year

old-stepson, Timmy, was unhappy about his dad's remarriage. Sure enough, as she walked down the aisle, Timmy, sitting in the front row of the congregation with his grandmother, cried, "There she is—I hate her," and burst into loud sobbing.

Without preparation, Wendy could have burst into tears herself, crying that her day had been ruined. She could have bravely ignored her stepson's sobbing as she took her wedding vows. But what she did do was a result of practical planning. When her stepson started crying, Wendy slowed in her tracks, turned gracefully toward the howls, and said to his grandmother: "Nana, why don't you take him on to the reception ahead of time so he won't have to sit through this?"

Actually, Wendy might have been able to prevent this kind of scene altogether. The controversial question is this: Should Timmy have been there? He certainly didn't want to be there. This was not the first time he had said he hated Wendy, and she correctly anticipated that he would have a problem coping with the day, particularly the ceremony. His dad, however, had insisted his son attend. "I want my son at my wedding," he said. "It will look bad if he isn't there."

Wendy came out of the experience receiving admiration for having handled it well, but she was disappointed that the scene had occurred. Her husband was embarrassed by his son's display and later admitted that he would rather have had to explain his son's absence than endure what actually happened.

To Be There, or Not to Be There—That Is the Question

Ideally your children and your mate's kids will all be present at your wedding, prepared to wish you and your husband well and be part of the formation of their new stepfamily. Some stepmoms enjoyed creating a ceremony of unification in which the new family is formed and blessed. If this is your style (and wish), be as creative as you can be, make room for them all, and enjoy it together.

Often, however, that's not how it goes. One or more of

the kids might either feel forced to be there and walk around, glum, all day or threaten to boycott the wedding as a show of disapproval. This is understandable—it's just not very pleasant.

Whether or not parents should insist on their kids' presence at the wedding is an emotionally loaded debate. Our advice is to sanction nonattendance if they do not want to be there. Recognize that a sense of loyalty to mom might be behind this wish, or even a mother's reprimand: "How can you be so disloyal to me, going to your father's wedding?" Since it's impossible for a child in this position to please both parents, you'll make his life much easier if you allow him to make this decision for himself—an important gesture on the part of you and his dad that's a long-term investment in a good relationship.

Discuss the issue of attendance in depth with your mate before and after your talks with the children about this. Adjust your attitudes, accept the child's decision, and do not allow this issue to become an emotional firestorm. Try not to be influenced by your parents, his parents, or your stepchildren's mother. The only people this question involves are you, your husband-to-be, and the children—your stepfamily. Keep everyone else out of it; it's not their business.

Regardless of the reason children refuse to attend, however, be sure to express how much you would like them to be at the wedding. Let them know you want them to feel part of the new family, even if it takes them time to accept their dad's remarriage.

If a child is not old enough yet for rational discussion, make the decision for him or her, based on behavior to date. Have a strategy ready to handle a child who might be too upset to sit through the whole ceremony—either have somebody bring her briefly and take her out the side door if trouble starts, or just arrange for a babysitter to take her to the zoo during the wedding. A brief appearance, possibly at the reception or before entering the church or synagogue, is a good compromise.

Children of any age who refuse to attend the wedding should be welcomed later, no questions asked, when feelings change. The "prodigal son" might feel guilt, uncertainty about his welcome, along with a sense of responsibility for the major decision he made months or years ago not to countenance the happiest day of your life. But your support nevertheless for that decision formed a foundation of trust you can both build on. At least you have that, if not a photo of him in the wedding party.

Details, Details

Books on planning a step wedding, along with etiquette tips, are beginning to appear on the market—some of the best are listed in the recommended reading list.

Whatever kind of wedding you decide to have, plan carefully. If you've ever been an intimate witness to wedding arrangements in your family, you'll be aware of how easily relatives can be hurt over the minutest detail and how much trouble an imagined slight can cause for years to come. It's just as easy, perhaps more so, to inadvertently upset someone in a stepfamily, even after you've conscientiously done your research.

Etiquette guides, at least, can tell you who stands where and why. If your plan includes children and stepchildren of any age, be certain they know what they are expected to do and, just as important, what they are expected *not* to do. Review their part in the ceremony repeatedly with them to be sure they have it right. Even then, you can probably expect mistakes, deliberate or accidental.

Expect the Unexpected: Sadness and Strange Behavior

The happiest day of your life might be the saddest day of your stepkids' lives, and perhaps your children's too. Few children are able to be happy when their parents remarry, and they usually dwell on their own feelings of loss. Today their family of origin permanently changes shape and style, and emotions are in overdrive. Even if they've seemed fine until now with the idea of your marriage, prepare yourself for almost any reaction.

Several stepmoms—enough to be a mini-phenomenon—said their teenage stepdaughters arrived looking like the bride, dressed from head to toe in white. (One of these girls even had a little veil!) None of these women was able to determine if their stepdaughter was simply trying to outdo the bride or just didn't know any better.

For many remarrying couples the wedding day is an ordeal. We heard stories of stepchildren who refused to participate at the last moment, refused to wear what had been decided for them, cried (always loudly) throughout the ceremony, ran around during the reception, disrupting people and spilling drinks, made ugly faces during the photos, etc. Because of this kind of unexpected bad behavior, several stepmoms advised women not to include the children in their wedding ceremonies.

Other stepmoms told stories of a blissful day when everyone behaved beautifully, and the kids smiled and actually seemed happy to be there. One ex-wife even sent a congratulatory note. Another stepmom fondly recalled the lovely toast her stepson made at the reception. Other stepmoms took the long view: plan as best you can, include the kids, shrug it off if they act strangely, and concern yourself with the marriage, not the wedding.

Just Do It: The Quick and Painless Route

A number of stepmoms admitted to wanting to get the wedding "over and done with." If you're the unsentimental, efficient type, this approach can work really well. Tamara, a working mom who had two young children and married a man with two of his own, took this route: "My husband's daughter wasn't speaking to him, and his son was acting up. My kids were angry and depressed about our engagement.

"Bob and I just couldn't face the hassle of a full-scale wedding with all that was going on with the kids, plus our jobs. Fortunately, my parents have a condo in Florida, so we just took off one weekend and, with only our parents present, were married by a rabbi on the deck. Bob and I went to a hotel in Sarasota for the weekend, had a wonderful, romantic mini-honeymoon—no phones, no kids, no complaints—and returned home as a married couple. It was great."

The Honeymoon: Room for Two

Some couples reported a temptation to take the children on the honeymoon trip. We strongly advise against this. You may have heard of the wonderful trip to Niagara Falls that your friend's brother's sister-in-law took with her three kids and her new husband's two—everything was perfect. Forget it. Except in the most unusual case, this is fiction. It might be hard to find someone to take care of all your children while you're away, but try—try very hard.

Honeymoons are for newly married couples—they're not family vacations. After the wedding you need some downtime alone together to sleep late, play, make lots of delicious, uninterrupted love, plan, discuss, psych yourselves up for what lies ahead. Real life, kids and all, begins when you get home.

Questionnaire

1. If you and your mate are considering living together, or are doing so now, which of you is unable to make a commitment to marriage? Why? Explain in writing to yourself exactly what your position is and how you see your mate's position. You need to know precisely why you are willing to set up home without marriage.

2. List in detail what you personally are going to achieve from this test run. Also, list any negatives you see for yourself, short- and long-term.

3. List what you believe are the advantages for your mate of living together. List any disadvantages you see for him.

4. Have you established a time frame for the wait-and-see period? Have you agreed on a "deadline," when you will get married or call it quits? Or would you rather play it by ear? Do you agree on the strategy?

5. If you decided to leave your live-in lover, could you afford to do so and reestablish the lifestyle you enjoyed before?

6. If you're planning your wedding, is it going to be the wedding you always wished for? If you're already married, was it the wedding you hoped for? If not, why?

Action Box

> Are you having trouble taking the reins and doing exactly what *you* want for your wedding? Or are you allowing your lover to call the shots on your arrangements for moving in together? This won't do; you're on the brink of a brand-new life. Splurge on a few sessions with a therapist to resolve what might be a problem of self-worth. Do it now—once you're married, you become a stepmom, a role that requires a fifty–fifty partnership to have a hope of success.

CHAPTER 13

Custody and Visitation: What You Need to Know but Didn't Know to Ask

"Do I have any rights?" Annie queried. She had recently learned that her husband Joseph's ex-wife wanted her fifteen-year-old daughter, Patrice, to live permanently with her father and Annie, her stepmom. The mother, who had won full-time custody at the time of the divorce, now found herself unable to control the teen, who was failing academically, staying out half the night, and mixing with the wrong crowd.

Joseph did not have a good relationship with Patrice, who blamed her father for her parents' divorce. Over the years, Annie had made many attempts to encourage the girl to visit, without success. "I would have liked us to have had a better relationship with Patrice, but I don't feel we can possibly take on full responsibility for her. I married Joseph accepting his child-support commitment. I would have been comfortable with a visitation schedule if Patrice had been willing to stay with us. But do I have to go along with this new plan? Doesn't what I want count for anything?"

The Fallout of Divorce

If divorces can be vicious, battles between ex-spouses over which parent gets the kids can be worse. Children are bartered and bargained with as the last currency divorcing parents have to get what they want from the other or to inflict more hurt. There could hardly be a worse time or climate in which to make child-care provisions.

Unfortunately, many attorneys fan the flames in negotiating the best deal for their clients. One family-law attorney advised a divorcing mother to "make choices on the assumption that your husband is: a) waiting to gain custody of the children; b) thinking it is cheaper to put them under his roof than to pay for them under yours; c) aware that you want to keep the children, so that's what he doesn't want you to do."

Traditionally a stepmother is expected to stand by and watch while her husband continues to fight with his ex-wife and, without comment or complaint, to fall in with whatever is decided. If the stepmom—who often can see more clearly than anyone that the children are the ones losing the war—attempts to intervene, a common reaction from all parties is "Butt out."

But hostility years after her husband's divorce and well into her marriage and changes in the kids' living arrangements or petitions from the kids' mother for more money certainly *are* a stepmother's business. Her life and her children's lives are profoundly affected by an angry, emotionally wrung-out husband, disturbed stepchildren who, often at their mother's instigation, become hostile toward her, and the required back-and-forth between two homes. The expense involved in legal fees and the emotional trauma incurred are immense. You have every right to intervene when conflict takes place in your home. You can and should voice your opinions, make your wishes known, and offer suggestions.

Regardless of what your husband and his ex-wife agreed to at the time of their divorce, you need to recognize that things can change even after your marriage. A woman might, for a number of reasons, unexpectedly find herself becoming a full-time stepmother. A mother might die, leaving the children with their dad. Together the parents might feel a child needs the influence of her other parent for a time. Or a mom, as in Annie's situation, might decide she can no longer handle her kids. (One stepmom returned from her honeymoon to find her husband's three children waiting on their stoop with a message from her mate's ex-wife on the answering machine, saying: "They're all yours. I'm on a plane to Europe."

Children, too, might decide they'd rather live with their other parent if things seem too rough where they are. As each possible scenario plays out, it often seems that the power others have over a stepmother's life grows, while the control she has over her own life decreases.

What Kind of Arrangement Are You Living With?

It's hard to make generalizations about custody and visitation. Much depends on the attitude and goodwill of those involved. Legal imperatives can work magnificently when ex-spouses put their malice aside and pull together for the sake of their kids. Or it can be agony if the ex-spouses are still bitter and use their children to hurt each other.

There are an increasing number of custody and visitation arrangements a stepmom might have to live and work with. The important thing is that you know and fully understand the details of the arrangements that apply to your stepchildren (and of course to your own children if you have any). Sole custody, joint custody, shared custody, split custody, and all the variations on visitation rights—find out from your mate if possible, or from his attorney if he's unable to explain, which are applicable in your case. Some children change homes every few months, others are shuffled back and forth, perhaps Monday to Wednesday at one home, Thursday to Saturday at another, alternating Sundays with each parent. You cannot operate efficiently, and to everyone's best advantage, unless you fully understand these legal requirements.

If It's Saturday, It's Dad's House

Unmarried weekend dads are pretty easy to recognize around town. They're the ones wandering through parks and malls, sitting in fast-food restaurants, a couple of kids in tow, trying to fit a week's worth of fatherhood into a couple of frenzied afternoons. Dad usually picks the kids up from the old family home with instructions from his ex-wife to have them back by a certain time on Sunday.

Visitation schedules might have been set in concrete following the divorce. If Mom has been awarded sole custody, Dad usually gets visitation rights. Some ex-wives stick to the letter of the agreement, refusing any flexibility at all.

Hannah, a stepmom for three years, and her husband, Ted, wrote formally to Dougie's mom in November, requesting custody of the twelve-year-old for two specific weeks in July the following year so he could join them on a trip to Europe. Ted's ex-wife demurred for several months while the couple awaited the mother's decision (her right to make, according to the custody terms). Finally she made up her mind: *no*. No reason given. Dougie was inconsolable. Ted was furious. Beyond the terrible disappointment for the boy, according to Hannah, "Dougie is starting to realize who is making life difficult for everyone and that the stories his mom tells about us aren't true."

Some ex-spouses will bend a little, some not at all. The agreement usually loosens up as the children get older and become more independent or when Mom starts putting her life back together and wants more time to herself. Upon remarriage, and the creation of a new home, many dads request joint custody, with a stepmom's agreement. Often this paves the way for more legal battles—stepmoms say mothers are usually opposed to the idea of her kids falling under the influence of "that woman your dad married" or being cared for by "the bimbo" in Dad's home. Contributing to an ex-wife's antagonism might be an attorney who is encouraging her to fight to regain custody.

Co-Parenting: A Welcome Addition to Postdivorce Life

Co-parenting, or joint parenting, are options with many advantages, the primary one being that a spirit of cooperation exists. Under these arrangements, both parents together are responsible for raising their children on a daily basis. This is easier when parents live near each other and have worked out a civil postmarital relationship. Mom and Dad devise a schedule that suits them, building in their own personal commitments, preferences, and other responsibilities. One parent can pick up the slack if the other has unforeseen plans, is sick, or has a crisis. Most important, their willingness to cooperate can help eradicate the most damaging effects of the divorce on their children, who have the opportunity to thrive without constant contention. Finances also can be mutually worked out according to each parent's ability to pay.

Unfortunately, in spite of looking hard, our interviews for this book did not reveal one couple who were co-parenting. Instead, most were allowing themselves to be drained by expensive and emotionally destructive legal battles. Melinda Blau, author of *Families Apart: Ten Keys to Successful Co-Parenting* (Putnam, 1994), who has operated happily under this arrangement with her own ex, writes, "Co-parenting, which concerns parents' responsibilities, has little to do with custody, which concerns parents' rights." She also contends, "The legal process works against cooperative co-parenting."

If your mate is one of those rare dads who has a coparenting agreement with his ex-wife, you will need to be a very understanding stepmom. He will be in frequent contact with his kids' mom, on the phone and in person, organizing their day-to-day issues. You might be seeing more of his kids than you would under a formal custody arrangement. Although this might take time away from you, in the long run you will have a happier husband, happier stepkids, and, however you feel about her, a happier ex-wife. For you, this means there will be fewer problems all around, as long as you can handle the constant interaction.

A Stepmother's Rights

As it now stands, stepmoms have few rights. Fortunately, however, legal professionals are advocating change. Joel Tenenbaum, partner in the law firm Waloshin, Tenenbaum & Natalie, in Wilmington, Delaware, asserts, "The Family Law Section of the American Bar Association recognizes the need to address the position of stepparents in areas such as their duties, responsibilities, and rights to their stepchildren and has promulgated a Model Act in order to address and bring attention to these needs." (A Model Act suggests legislation to states. Family law varies from state to state.)

Other organizations, representing fathers, are working to raise awareness of the needs of second families and single parents. These groups strongly reject the negative image of the "deadbeat dad," a label too many divorced or remarried dads receive as a result of the nefarious doings of some divorced fathers, just as stepmoms reject the image of the "wicked stepmother."

Mediation: The Law of Common Sense Applies

It's a lawyer's job to get (or keep) as much for his client as possible. Many stepmoms believe that under our current laws their mate frequently comes off the all-around loser, parting with more of his assets and/or seeing less of his children, than he'd like to. An adversarial divorce and continued litigation can leave him impoverished for years to come and takes a huge toll in time and emotion.

Along with co-parenting, the use of mediation—managed or facilitated negotiation—is becoming more widespread as a less punishing method of handling divorce, custody arrangements, and other areas of dissension. Dr. Robert Singer, a psychologist and a mediator, operates as one half of a family dispute resolution team with an attorney in New Haven, Connecticut. Dr. Singer offers another layer of insight when working with stepfamilies, that of personal experience. He and his wife both have been previously married and have four children between them.

Dr. Singer maintains that as long as people "come in clear-headed," with a "willingness to be fair and open to negotiation," almost any practical issue can be handled through mediation. He stresses, however, that you can't mediate an attitude, such as a stepchild's lack of respect for his stepmom. Dr. Singer also points out, "People deal with divorce in the same way they deal with marriage. They have the same qualities."

A mediator represents the needs of each person in the room—a couple, ex-spouses or an entire family—equally. Does it work? On average, says Dr. Singer, if a stepfamily has a list of about ten issues to negotiate, some weeks later six or eight of the agreed solutions might be in operation, while the remainder might have fallen by the wayside.

Here's how it works: Two ex-spouses want to negotiate custody issues for their children. If one parent wants the kids for the whole Christmas vacation and the other balks, the mediator might say to the reluctant parent, "What will it take, what do you want, to let your ex-husband have the kids for Christmas?" Perhaps she'll take them for Thanksgiving and New Year's and alternate the following year. Compromise presides, disagreements become narrower, and ultimately everyone wins. With severe problems the mediator will focus on the slightest, remotest area of agreement and try to build on that. (See our discussion of conflict resolution in chapter 15 and tips on how to choose the right mediator in chapter 20.)

Advantages of a mediator over an attorney:

- The spouses select and hire the mediator together. He or she represents the couple. There is no winner or loser.

- A mediator costs less and takes less time.

- Parents know their kids better than any lawyer or court. Through mediation, parents can consider what is best for their children, their personalities, social lives, needs. An arrangement can be tailor-made to fit the special requirements of the family.

- A custody and visitation schedule that has been negotiated by both parents provides the bonus of flexibility—unusual in many litigated divorce arrangements—to accommodate a crisis, an unforeseen event, such as a business trip, or an exciting invitation. (Under a more hostile, formal custody arrangement, Mom might not be willing to give up her son for an evening or might present problems in delivering the boy to his dad.) When both parents have taken part in making the arrangements there's more likelihood they'll pull together.

It doesn't make sense to pay legal fees while deciding where your children should spend spring break or where Billy should keep his bike, his mom's house or yours. Once arrangements have been worked out with a mediator, an attorney can put the details in contractual form. (Some mediators are also attorneys, others also therapists.) Some stepmoms use a mediator on a continuing basis, instead of a therapist, when they run into conflicts they are unable to resolve themselves.

Marya, married for ten yeas, has two stepsons, aged thirteen and nine, and a son, aged four, with her husband, Dick. Marya, a successful therapist, and her husband are great believers in mediation. "In the early days, while we were having problems with Dick's ex-wife, who lives nearby, we would run to a mediator twice a month," Marya recalled. "Over the years, Dick's boys have worked with her, too, about house rules and problems with their mom. One of Dick's boys once told me he thought I needed her to decide what we'd have for dinner! But I don't know what I'd have done without her. When a relatively quick fix is needed on a practical matter, mediation is the answer."

Annie's Answer

Let's go back to Annie. Although she has no legal rights in a decision about whether or not her stepdaughter will come to live with her and Joseph, she has moral and practical rights within her household. She also has the ability to see the situation realistically, along with a firm commitment to Joseph and the sincere wish to resolve their conflict.

Annie knew she was faced with the potential of being tagged a "wicked stepmother" if she refused to accept Patrice into her household. She could not, however, be expected to fall right in with a sudden reversal of the position she had accepted when she married, without being included in this discussion.

What can she do?
1. Annie's first priority must be to protect her relationship with her husband. He feels torn apart and guilty. She is feeling shut out and wants her concerns acknowledged—that she will not be dictated to in her own home and that she has the right to be part of the solution for Patrice, since she will be affected by it. She and Joseph must vow to meet this crisis together.
2. Discussions between Annie and Joseph should establish what each partner needs and wants. Annie would like a better relationship with Patrice, both for herself and for Joseph, who she knows regrets the current status. Joseph, who feels he has not been an ideal father and does not want to turn his back on Patrice now, would like to make amends.

What did they decide?
Joseph and Annie both admitted they were used to their free lifestyle, and neither felt equipped to handle a girl with serious problems. They decided to present a compromise to Patrice's mom, who the couple acknowledged needed some slack.

Patrice will stay with Annie and Joseph for occasional weekends to start with, then for a couple of weeks during school vacation, perhaps longer in the summer. This will allow everyone to get used to one another gradually, give Patrice's mom some downtime, and, everyone hopes, help Patrice feel that all the adults in her life care about her. The discussion remains open about Patrice's moving in permanently with them.

Joseph and Annie asked for time to talk with Patrice's teachers and for her mom's cooperation in providing some background about the girl's difficulties. They suggested that Patrice receive some counseling if necessary.

Annie was able to encourage this compromise by remaining calm and acknowledging the position and feelings of each of the three adults, as well as Patrice. A less reasonable person might have refused to consider a change of custody for Patrice and probably wrecked her marriage, along with any chance of working with Patrice or her mother. As it was, she received credit for having orchestrated the discussion, made clear to all participants that she would have to be a part of any decision, strengthened her relationship with Joseph, and formed the basis of a new relationship with Patrice and her mom.

Had Annie felt unable to accomplish this alone, an alternative for her would have been to suggest mediation, when all three adults, and perhaps Patrice, too, could have negotiated an arrangement acceptable to them all.

When You Can't Change Things

Stepmoms who marry when a tightly regulated custody arrangement is in force can't change much.

It is possible your home is governed by two differing schedules operating independently—one for your kids and one for your mate's. With luck it's working well, but a rigid schedule is rarely a happy one, and stepmoms reported the lack of flexibility very troublesome. They reported feeling out of control, having little time for themselves or their mate and limited freedom in their own life.

Some stepmoms we met ran mini travel agencies, dealing with tickets and reservations in commuter custody situations with children plane hopping from one coast to the other—jet set custody!

Being prepared for these circumstances, which are admittedly not the best, is essential. Preferably prior to your marriage you reviewed the terms of your mate's divorce and custody or visitation arrangements (if you didn't do it then, do it now). You will need to arrange your married life around this framework. If your mate is granted custody every second weekend, a month in the summer, or three days a week, other plans will flow from that schedule, in addition to the arrangement you have in place for your own kids. You and your husband need to agree that this framework is your business and to make it clear to everyone concerned that if any further negotiation is required, you need to be involved. Encourage your mate and his ex to view you as someone willing and able to see both sides of the equation.

Tips to Keep the Peace

In the early stages of your marriage, particularly if you work and don't have kids of your own, you'll probably relish your two free weekend days alone with your husband to catch up on chores, see a movie, and have dinner out. But if he has custody every second weekend, you've got stepkids. If your relationships are not yet in good shape, this will probably not be your idea of a great weekend. What a coincidence—the kids would more than likely prefer to spend a nice, fun time alone with their dad, without you!

In Dr. Singer's view, visitation is an unstable arrangement. Kids grow older, become more independent, schedules change, Dad's or Stepmom's job changes, Mom presents difficulties. "It's the perfect place for people to play out their issues," comments Dr. Singer. The "leftovers" from the divorce and "resistances" to accepting it are in full swing. He finds that for those who have a "need for chaos," the visitation arena is fertile ground.

What would Dad prefer? Don't put him in the position of having to speculate. Here are some suggestions to make life easier for everyone:

- Encourage your husband's dependent children to view your house as their home, even if you only see them every other weekend. Adjust your thinking: they are not visiting you; they are living with you for whatever length of time they are in your home. They have two homes, and they are family. Older children, married or single, who have established their own homes or families will *visit* you.

- Help your stepchildren feel at home. Arrange a special space that's theirs; give them a private place to keep their stuff. Make sure they know where they can find things they might need, depending on their age, and familiarize them with your household routine.

- Let stepchildren know what is expected of them, what they will be responsible for, so they can relax and enjoy the time they spend with you and their dad and vice versa. See page 287 for "house rules."

- Fill them in on what has happened since they were last there—the new tree you planted (better still, wait and let them help you plant), what the kid down the road did, the new kitchen china, etc.

- Do not comment on the routine or rules of their other home—what Mom decides is her business. Don't discuss Mom either, except to ask briefly how she is. You don't want to be accused of interfering in or being nosy about matters that don't concern you, specifically her new boyfriend. If your stepkids bring these issues up, listen. Respond only to questions; volunteering what you think she should do is a no-no (even though you know how much money it will save in maintenance payments if she ends up marrying the guy.)

- Encourage private time with their dad. Discuss this with your mate, and arrange it with him ahead of time. Plan with the kids on one weekend what they will do next time they are there—it will give them something to look forward to. If you don't have children of your own, it can be disconcerting to watch your husband become less of a lover and more of a dad. While Dad is enjoying his kids, take the opportunity for part of the time they're living with you to do something that pleases you, either alone or with a friend. This gives you a sense of control—over something!

Transitions and Turnovers

Before they know you well, your mate's children will be nervous about living with you. Professionals advise a transition routine—so the same thing happens each time they arrive and leave, depending on the time of day and their ages.

Maybe you can start a pizza-for-lunch tradition. Perhaps they'd rather just go to their room for quiet time, putting their stuff away and settling in. It's quite an ordeal to move from one house and its customs to another house with different routines, so allow some adjustment time. Professionals advise that, given time and clear explanations, children are very resilient and can adapt to the differences between two homes.

And remember, you don't know what they have just left. Perhaps Mom will be on her own while they are with their dad, and they're worried about her feeling lonely. Or they might wonder if their mom and new husband, their stepdad, are glad to be alone. Maybe Mom pumps them about what goes on in Dad's house when they return, and this makes them uncomfortable. In any event, children are grappling with divided loyalties, which they don't fully understand when they're young and which when they're older cause untold stress.

If your stepchildren reject you or seem barely to tolerate your presence (the "I hate you" phase, perhaps, or the refusal to do as you ask because "you're not my mom"), you're going to need some rewards for endurance, to get you through the time they're in your home. Make plans with your husband for dinner at your favorite restaurant the night they leave or for something equally nice to look forward to. One stepmom also spoke of "stocking up" on lovemaking before the kids arrived, as she felt inhibited while they were in her home.

Stepmoms who experienced a particularly difficult time

with their stepkids talked of this romantic interlude with their mate as a lifesaver. Make a pact that you won't, at that particular time, discuss the kids but will focus on the two of you. Analysis of what went right and what needs work for next time the kids come needs to take place, but at another time. Together time is imperative now, after your emotional few days, to rekindle your priority twosome.

Questionnaire

1. Do you understand the commitments, moral and financial, your mate has to his children? Can you discuss these comfortably with him and feel a part of arrangements that are made—e.g. do you think in terms of what *we* are committed to, when the kids come to live with *us*? Describe to yourself how you feel about these commitments.

2. List what you believe are your responsibilities toward his kids, recognizing that you have no legal rights or responsibilities to them.

3. Describe to yourself the degree of comfort you currently feel when your husband's kids are in your home; e.g. excited, anxious, overwhelmed, happy?

4. Picture an ideal weekend with your mate and your stepkids. Imagine these two days in detail. What makes this fictitious weekend so successful? List the reasons you enjoy it. List the reasons your mate enjoys it.

5. Would your stepkids enjoy the weekend you just pictured? If so, why?

6. What is the one issue that, if resolved, would improve your overall satisfaction about the custody and visitation schedule you work with? What could you or your mate do to resolve that issue?

7. Can you talk with your husband about how he feels when his kids are with you? Does he feel he gets enough private

time with them? Does he like to see you spending one-on-one time with them (or is he a bit jealous)?

8. Do you know how each of you feels when his kids leave? Is he unhappy? A little relieved? How much does he miss them?

9. If there is a great difference in how you each feel when the kids leave—e.g. he's despondent and you're thrilled—can you discuss this comfortably? Are you able to accept that difference?

10. Can you visualize a time when both of you will happily anticipate their arrival and both miss them when they leave? What will it take for this to happen? Is there something you can do now to work toward this?

Action Box

- Prepare some responses to negative comparisons between the way your house is run and the way Mom's operates. Use "our" instead of "my," and "we" instead of "I," reinforcing that you and your husband are in agreement. Say: "In our house, we clean up our own messes after snacks. While you're living with us, we need you to do the same."

- Hang up a special calendar, and circle in red the dates your stepkids will be in your home. Plan some interesting activities the whole family—including both sets of children—can enjoy, and write them in so you won't forget.

CHAPTER 14

Home, Sweet Step Home

The first night spent together under one roof is a milestone in every stepfamily's life. Perhaps more than your wedding, the intimacy of sharing a home, even if it's only every other weekend, says you're a family. Whether you move into your husband's home or your place or to a new location, this address becomes "ours," combining any number of kids, possessions, and pets. You'll also be blending the emotional, aesthetic, and lifestyle preferences of two subfamilies, everything from whether the dog is allowed to sleep on the bed to the color of paint for the kitchen.

Organization and planning will help you and your mate create a new step home that meets everyone's needs. Again, we advise against winging it.

Blending Possessions: A Mix-'n'-Match Job

Combining households to form one step home often means blending and sorting two sets of almost everything.

Before you start, remember that your husband and his kids are probably as attached to their stuff as you are to yours. Lola didn't understand why her stepkids are still angry at her after six years. When she moved into her husband Harry's established family home with her two sons one month before the wedding, she wallpapered the kitchen, bathrooms, and living room, removed all the "clutter," and moved her furniture in, displacing what was there. "It was so much nicer," she claimed. "I made a scrapbook of the old wallpapers for Harry's kids so they wouldn't forget how it used to be." Certainly this was small compensation for the virtual demolition of their family home!

With your mate, plan how you'll blend your possessions into one household. You'll save yourself a lot of time, energy, space, and grief if you make these decisions before you move. One upwardly mobile couple arrived separately at their new home on moving day, parking "his and hers" moving vans in the driveway. Each oblivious to how much the other owned, they tried to fit into one house two full sets of kitchen equipment, eight sofas, twenty chairs, two dining room sets, and five televisions (all of it in colliding styles). "It was awful," said Arnell. "Nothing matched, and we lived there for ten years, stuffed to the rafters, and never finished unpacking!"

Make a list of all the major furniture pieces and appliances owned between you, and allocate them on paper to each room of the home you will all live in, taking measurements into account. Then, item by item, decide what moves with you, what goes into storage, and what should be sold or given away.

There probably will be a few items you cannot compromise on. His beloved beat-up recliner, however ugly you think it is, might be a keeper. (Perhaps he'll let you reupholster it.) Same with previous wedding presents. If he has come to cherish them, don't try to talk him into giving them up, even though this might be difficult for you. Be flexible. He might not love your pink velvet armchair as much as you do, but you know you won't feel at home without it.

Organizing the Kids

Your kids and stepkids need space for their treasured possessions too. Again, figure out how you'll combine their stuff into one home, and make the necessary compromises. If your stepkids are already living in the home, persuading them to consolidate and share with stepsiblings is no easy task. Get the kids involved as much as possible in your decisions about dividing rooms equitably, and consider some inexpensive but effective space savers.

One stepmom strung brightly colored nylon fishnet across a ceiling to store stuffed animals and other toys. "It looked nautical, and the kids loved it," she said. Another installed large, sturdy hooks to get book bags, clothes, and other hangable items off the floor and invested in some colorful, stackable box shelves that took up little space but provided storage nearly to the ceiling.

What Kind of Move Are You Making?

Moving to a new house, with rooms free of memories and associations, automatically creates a level playing field—everything is new to everyone. It's the best of all scenarios, if financially possible or where there are no overriding reasons to stay where you are.

On the other hand, if you and your children are moving into a home where your mate has spent years with his former wife and their children—often the case when death or abandonment has taken place—more emotional adjustments need to be made by the residing stepfamily members. Physical changes to the home—painting, combining some of your furniture with some of your mate's, or reorganizing the use of space—will help make the house feel new to everyone, essential if the moving-in family members are to avoid feeling like intruders. These changes should be made after a family discussion, chaired by you and your husband in the spirit of compromise.

Stepmoms who didn't initiate changes reported, years later, feeling like a lodger in her own home, relegated to a modest corner. Said one stepmom with no kids of her own who joined a ready-made family in their home, "I've got one tiny closet for my clothes and a small chest of drawers—everything else is used by my husband or his kids." Another, who favored bathing rather than showering, found that her husband's home had only a small hot-water tank that provided barely an inch of water in the tub. "He tried to persuade me to take showers, but I couldn't adapt," she recalled. "It practically took an act of Congress to get him to have a larger tank installed."

Among the stepmoms we spoke with, it was rare that a husband moved into his wife's home, and in those few cases we came across where the stepmom had her own kids, Dad had no children living full-time with him. His kids were either adults or in the custody of his ex-wife. It's easier for a stepmom in that situation to combine possessions, because unless a man has an exotic hobby (one stepmom's husband had a huge gun collection that he moved into his new wife's apartment), most marital property stays with the ex-wife. Women found that possessions acquired by their husbands during his bachelor days were minimal.

Absolutely Essential Changes

Master bedroom: Unless you are very unusual, you probably won't want to sleep in the same bed your mate and his ex slept in for ten years. It is reasonable to insist on a brand-new bed or at least to bring your own! Don't compromise on this unless for some reason it's low on your personal priority list—even if you can afford nothing else, buy a new mattress and bed linens. Your bedroom is your love nest—it cannot have belonged first to another woman or remind your husband of his previous marriage. If possible, repaint or repaper the bedroom and adjoining bathroom, too, if there is one. Be sure to present these changes as a fresh start to your new marriage. Avoid disparaging the previous color scheme or implying you don't want anything his previous wife owned or used.

Mom's things: If your husband's former wife is deceased, be tactful about having her belongings put away—these are sacred mementos and must be treated respectfully. (You will not be forgiven if you forget this.) On the other hand, Mother's portrait, hanging in your hallway or bedroom, has to go. Kylie, a new stepmom, reported sleeping with her husband's dead previous wife's photo in her bedroom for weeks before she suggested that her stepdaughter take it into her room. The girl was delighted and Kylie's husband agreed that it belonged there now.

Giving a mother's possessions to her children usually works for most items you do not want, even larger items of furniture. Suggest, "This is so nice, we must save it for one of the children. Let's pack it up carefully and store it." If the children are older and have homes of their own, you can off-load almost anything you don't like with "I'm sure Yasmin would love to have her mother's armchair/crystal vase/Oriental carpet."

Household items, that Mom and Dad once shared (unless bequeathed elsewhere) become your mate's when she dies. When you marry these become yours to share, just as your possessions are his to share. (If there was a divorce and possessions were split, it's still a sensitive area, but perhaps less so.) Usually, if his kids are old enough, he will consult with them on the disposal, but otherwise these items become part of your new household when you marry.

Be aware that it might be difficult for your stepkids to see you use objects they once saw their mom use. Much heartache and conflict can be caused by the mishandling of this one issue, since emotions run high.

Talk about these items, and find out if they hold any special meanings you should know about: "I love this platter your mom and dad used at parties. It must bring back some happy memories for you." If your system in the kitchen is different, a few words can ease the transition: "I know your mom kept the frying pans in that bottom closet, but I'm left-handed. Here, they're easier for me to reach."

Don't seethe in silence if someone returns to their original home things you've moved: "I guess you put the pans back there because you are used to doing that. Please try to remember their new place." Your stepkids will adjust, given time and plenty of patience from you.

Other Basic Blending Tips:

- Don't be negative about anything you find, however much you don't like it. Someone else loved this particular item, and you will indirectly insult its previous owner by being critical of it.

- Treat all items with care, and express your wish that your mate and his kids treat your possessions the same way. (Many stepmoms reported that their stepkids took out their displeasure with her on her furniture or treasured items.)

- Any of Mom's personal items still in the house should be put aside and not used, especially if she has died. Intimate belongings, such as clothes, grooming items, and jewelry, should already have been dispersed by your mate, but knickknacks, recipe books, notebooks, etc., that might have been overlooked should be carefully preserved for her children.

Our House: Moving Day

If possible, both full- and part-time members of the new household should be present on moving day, pitching in. That way no one unfairly stakes claim to the best of everything— closets, windows, bookshelves. (For this reason alone, you might be able to persuade the child who refused to attend the wedding to show up on moving day.) Part-time stepkids who are not involved in setting up the stepfamily home are liable to feel like visitors when they finally see it and might have more difficulty adapting to stepfamily life. As with possessions, try to have made all necessary decisions and compromises about assigned space prior to your move date, to avoid major squabbling over turf while you're trying to direct movers and phone company installers. (If one of you is moving into the other's home, be sure you've already made provisions for moving out the things you've decided should go, to accommodate those moving in.)

Afterward, a celebration is in order—perhaps eating out or popping a bottle of champagne (Shirley Temples for the kids!) while sitting on the unpacked boxes—whatever feels right. Moving day will be one of your first new stepfamily memories—you might even want to have fun during the day, taking turns with a disposable camera to fill the first page of your stepfamily scrapbook.

It's a good idea to have a short family meeting on moving day, if anyone has the strength left, or soon after if not. You and your mate should discuss what you want to say beforehand. For example:

- We're a new family, living in a new home (or a changed or evolving home if you are moving into yours or his).

- Even though we don't know one another well yet, we have a lot in common—everything is new and strange for all of us. We need to help one another settle in and to realize that everyone is going to be making adjustments to living together.

- It's our job as the adults to organize this household, but everyone's needs are of equal importance. We want you all to be happy.

- We're proud of all of you and our new home, and we love you very much.

The House Guidelines: A Written Agreement

Shortly after moving day, you and your husband will need to start setting the standards family members will live by in your new home. Developing a written list of house rules or guidelines, which everyone in your stepfamily knows about and agrees to, will help you avoid the role of the "heavy," which is often commensurate, said stepmoms, with the title of "stepmother."

These guidelines should apply to *all* members of the household, including Dad, Stepmom, residential children, and children living with you part-time. Do not treat children living with you only part of the time as "guests." Residential kids will resent them for getting away without chores or responsibilities, and the part-time kids won't feel they belong.

One stepfamily with two working parents and a very busy teenage household devised an interesting house rule. Every Thursday evening all five stayed home to clean the house from top to bottom. They worked hard, but it was all over for the week in three hours (fifteen hours of combined step power.) Afterward, they rewarded themselves with dinner at the local Italian restaurant to keep the kitchen clean. Except for some unavoidable scheduling conflict, everyone stuck to the Thursday-night commitment. A bonus for the whole family was that their weekends were relatively free of chores.

Ideally, your master list of house guidelines should be developed with input from each stepfamily member. Have a family meeting for this. Explain that you want good ideas to keep your home running efficiently and fairly so that everyone is clear about what they are expected to do and not do, to eliminate nagging or arguing. Appoint someone to write down *all* the suggestions, no matter how far-out, suspending criticism or comment. The ideas can be as detailed or as brief as necessary and can incorporate anyone's pet peeves—maybe you dislike the wearing of baseball hats inside the house or the leaving of toys in the yard overnight. Perhaps your stepson is tired of always waiting for your daughter to get out of the bathroom and wants a time limit. When everyone's had their say, review each contribution and discuss its viability.

Tell the kids that you'll select those ideas you believe are fair and will work, and at a second meeting allow everyone to look over the guidelines you've chosen and discuss them. Some might again be amended or rejected. Try to make a compromise if anyone strenuously objects to a rule. Children can be very creative and willing to cooperate when they are part of the process—otherwise, the whole scheme probably won't work.

If there are some ideas you want to experiment with on a trial basis, make a temporary list containing those items. When you believe you have a final version, write it out, and have every member of the family sign it as an indication they accept *all* the rules. Post copies around the house—on the refrigerator, in the bathroom, laundry room, garage—wherever you think reminders are needed.

Official house rules save hours of arguing and explaining for a stepmother, particularly when Dad is not there. When your stepdaughter leaves puddles in the bathroom after her shower, you don't need to get into a hassle with her. Just remind her of the house rule, which she has already agreed to, that says everyone must tidy the bathroom for the next person.

Your kids and stepkids, particularly teenagers, will enjoy testing you about the rules. Sometimes their arguments might even strike you as sensible. Flexibility is a virtue. When a house rule clearly has become inappropriate or needs changing because it is outmoded, being able to say, "You're right; that's silly. Let's do it your way," earns respect. But be sure the kids understand your reasons for the original rule and for your change of heart in a particular case.

Sample House Rules: One Stepfamily's List

(This stepmom had a four-year-old son, Tony, and three stepkids, a boy of nine and two girls, eleven and fourteen.)

General
- We will treat one another with respect and courtesy, using "please" and "thank you."
- We will acknowledge one another's presence with a "hi" or "good morning."
- Nobody makes a telephone call after 10 P.M. unless there is an emergency. Friends will be encouraged not to call us after 10 P.M.
- TVs, stereos, and radios are to be kept at a moderate volume (not disturbing others) unless we are all listening or watching together.
- Toys must be picked up by owners and put back in rooms before bed. We all help Tony.

Bathroom(s)
- Nobody will hog the bathroom—fifteen minutes maximum. Girls will dry their hair in their own bedrooms.
- Leave the bathroom dry and tidy, with soap back in the soapdish, puddles cleaned up, wet towels removed for laundering. Use rags under the sink for wipe-ups.
- Whoever finishes the toilet tissue replaces the roll. New ones in linen closet. We all help Tony when he asks.

Family Areas
- Last person to go to bed plumps up cushions on sofas, turns off lights, closes downstairs windows, and locks outside doors after making sure everyone is home.
- No food or drink upstairs (except water) unless you are sick, or ask first.
- Everyone home by 6:00 P.M. on Thursday night for cleaning.
- Everyone home on Sunday night by 5:00 for family dinner.
- Nobody goes near Dad's gun collection unless Dad is with them.
- Kids under ten must let a parent know if they go to play outside. We all help Tony remember this.

Kitchen
- Anyone having a snack clears up afterward. Food back in refrigerator, cans or bottles in recycling bin, dishes in dishwater. Nothing left out.
- If you use the last of any item, add it to the shopping list on refrigerator.
- Kids under ten may use stove *only* with adult supervision. We all keep an eye on Tony in the kitchen.

Individual Responsibilities

Besides house guidelines or rules, each stepfamily member needs to have assigned chores and responsibilities, adapted to the various ages of the kids, their abilities, or their special needs in the case of a handicapped, "slow," or sick child.

These chores should be discussed, agreed to, put in writing, and signed. You and your mate can judge how much work each child can handle, making sure there is an equitable distribution.

Try asking the child what she thinks she is good at and would like to do, or prompt suggestions. It makes sense to allow a child to perform tasks that suit his personality. Your neatnik ten-year-old might be a natural at keeping the recycling bin organized. Your fifteen-year-old stepson might be the outdoors type and take pride in mowing the lawn. Your resident animal lover might want to be in charge of feeding and walking the stepfamily dog.

When you're living with people you don't know well, it's tempting to try to change not only ways of doing things but even people's personalities. Try to avoid the impulse. Dr. Harold H. Bloomfield, author of *Making Peace in Your Stepfamily* (Hyperion, 1993), states, "Fundamental to creating family is first recognizing each family member's need to feel appreciated and accepted exactly as that person is."

Likewise, don't pit stepchildren and children against one another: "I wish you would behave at the table like Susie does"; "Why don't you keep your room as neat as Billy's?"

If children don't or won't volunteer ideas for their own individual responsibilities, you or their dad will need to assign them.

The D Word

The subject of discipline has probably caused more debate than any other in stepfamilies. Some family therapists suggest that each parent discipline his or her own children and that a stepmom (or stepdad) never discipline stepkids. We disagree. Some parents might have difficulty getting used to their spouse sharing this task, but there are few options to this in a stephousehold and what options exist simply don't work.

With your mate, you need to jointly enforce the house

rules, individual responsibilities, and other standards of behavior for all the children in your home. While each of you might have had dissimilar parenting styles in the past, it's vital you "match" now. Kids love to play one parent off against the other. If there is disagreement, or the possibility that one parent will override the other, the kids will immediately hone in on that rift in your united front.

Having different sets of rules—one for your kids, another for his—or having one parent act as sole disciplinarian while the other looks on is asking for trouble, including rivalries, confusion, a perception of favoritism, or the perception that one parent's (usually Stepmom's) opinion doesn't count. You can't have Dad allowing his kids to take food into their bedrooms when you don't allow yours to do so—while neither rule is necessarily right or wrong, you and your mate will have to decide which mutually applicable standard will prevail.

Stepmom, May I?

Some stepmoms report being bashful at asking children they don't yet know well to do as she asks. Don't be. You're running a household—knowing about and approving of what goes on in your home is your responsibility and your right.

Once your mate has taken charge of guiding his children and granting permission for requests they make, there is no way you can suddenly decide to step in. You *must* be a fifty percent partner immediately, however difficult you find it. A reminder: the reason many stepmoms don't succeed is that they failed to do this. Anything concerning the running of your home, from where the salt is kept to whether one of your stepkids may have a friend to stay for the weekend, has to be checked with you and receive your approval.

Stepchildren may balk at asking "permission" of their stepmother to do something, but they'll get used to it. If it's a problem, change the wording—use "check it out with me" or "run it by me first." Likewise, we prefer "guiding" or "explaining rules of the house" to "discipline."

Briefly tell your stepchild why you need to know what they want to do. (See "Stepmom's Quick Primer" number 8.) You are one of the people—Dad is the other—who will be responsible for your stepkid's visiting friend, for example, while she is in your home. Her parents need to be assured she will be safe and taken care of. It's basic courtesy to check with you first that it's OK, convenient, that you don't have plans to have someone else stay over that night, etc. It's your mate's job to insist that his kids think of you as his parenting partner. The sooner the requirement is made, the sooner everyone will become accustomed to it.

Clarity—the Key to Positive Behavior

If you find you need to remind one of the kids to do something, try using the who/what/when/where/why method. It works both for getting the kids organized and for keeping them within the house guidelines.

Sometimes, in the interest of being tactful, you might risk the possibility that your request seems open to interpretation. Be specific so there is no question what you are asking, and go for the end result rather than worry about how they achieve it.

Example: *Dinner is almost ready and you want everyone to wash their hands and sit down at the table.*

Non-specific: "I think it would be nice if you got ready for dinner. It's almost done."

Whom are you talking to? What does "I think it would be nice" mean? Does "Get ready" mean put your toys away, change your clothes, take a shower? Is "almost done" ten minutes away, twenty minutes?

Be realistic with your request. If they are outside and will need major cleanup time, give a ten-minute warning. One stepmom, Maria, had a ship's bell installed in their kitchen. She devised a system of five bells for a five-minute warning;

one bell meant dinner was being put on the table. Everyone loved it!

Specific: "David, kids, please all wash your hands and sit at the table. I'm putting dinner on the table, and I don't want it to get cold. You have five minutes."

Who? David and the kids.

What? Wash your hands and sit down.

When? In five minutes.

Where? At the table.

Why? I'm putting dinner on the table, and I don't want it to get cold.

In the specific request there is no question that anyone who has heard you will know exactly what you want them to do, or why. If someone is lagging behind, follow up with "We can't start eating until you're here," throwing in for good measure a lesson in good manners—nobody starts eating until everyone is sitting at the table. Your mate should back up your request. The fact that Tommy "forgot" to wash his hands is immaterial (just this once, assuming he isn't covered in mud), as long as he arrives on time. The end result of your request is what's important—everyone is there, ready to eat. (Of course, be sure that you live up to your own statement about having dinner ready, or you lose your credibility.)

In the early stages of stepmotherhood, if you find it helps, you can invoke "Dad's wishes" in guiding your stepkids:

Example: You want Joey to get ready for bed.

Specific: "Joey, it's almost eight-thirty, your bedtime. Put your toys away now, then put your pajamas on, brush your teeth, and come and say good night. Your dad and I decided that if you went to bed when I asked you, you could read for a while."

If Joey dawdles, some positive encouragement might help. "Your dad will be so proud when I tell him you did what I asked the first time." If you encounter outright refusal, express what the consequences will be—being grounded for the next day, forgoing his favorite TV program—and be sure your mate backs you up (even if his preference in consequence is slightly different) when he comes home.

Consequences

You'll need to be prepared for inappropriate behavior and ways to handle it immediately, not wait for Dad to do it. Consequences are a major part of nurturing and guidance. Professional advice to stepmoms, which we wholeheartedly endorse, however, is *never* to use physical punishment. You cannot risk even the suspicion of child abuse. Make sure your mate understands that you will never physically punish his children. Secure the same assurances from him concerning your kids.

You and your mate should discuss what will happen if one of the kids, yours or his, fails to live up to her agreement about house rules or her personal responsibilities. Try to agree on general guidelines for meting out consequences, both in terms of severity and what you wish the consequences to accomplish, perhaps reinforcing a logical cause and effect. That way, if one of you is not present, you can be fairly sure the other would have reacted similarly. Say your stepson forgets to walk the dog, resulting in a dirty carpet. Can you and your husband agree that cleaning up after the dog would be a just consequence for his transgression? (You might also decide to assign an additional chore to help him remember in the future.) Also, make it clear to the child that it is his behavior you have the problem with—you still care about him very much even though he forgot to walk the dog.

More serious incidents—e.g. stealing, drug abuse—will probably require discussion between you and your husband: "Your father/stepfather and I will have to talk about this. We'll let you know later what we decide."

When guiding children and stepchildren, you also need to be able to admit when you're wrong and to apologize. An admission of a mistake reinforces your goodwill and sets an example of fairness and consideration.

Bedrooms

Bedrooms are worlds unto themselves; depending on the ages of your kids, you're probably better off leaving them out of your house rules list. The likelihood of a teenager's bedroom being tidy and clean is remote. There is no point fighting over it—it's a fact of life. Instead, perhaps an option that worked well for one stepmom can work for your family.

Andrea, mother of two teens, stepmom to preteen boys, remembers her brothers' rooms growing up as "squalid" and her own as only slightly better. But Andrea's mother made it clear that their bedrooms were their responsibility. "She would close bedroom doors and not look, rather than argue," recalled Andrea. "She would not clean them, nor launder anything left around. Eventually we got tired of the squalor and started bringing dirty clothes down and keeping our rooms reasonably tidy so we didn't lose anything or harm our possessions. Now I'm using my mom's approach. Right now the kids' bedrooms are disgusting, but the doors are closed, and I don't have to see it."

If bedrooms get so bad you suspect the family might contract typhoid fever, try a major spring cleaning once in a while, in partnership with the offender, when everything is removed from the room and virtually sterilized before it is returned.

Sex in the Step Home

Especially if you're living with teens, you and your husband will have to establish the sexual mores of your step household and the degree of personal privacy you believe is appropriate. Some parents and stepparents have a laissez-faire attitude about sex under their roof, emphasizing only birth control and protection from sexually transmitted disease.

Others permit no premarital sex at all, anywhere, and no closed bedroom doors when girlfriends and boyfriends visit. Wherever you and your mate fall on the permissiveness spectrum, you must make your wishes very clear—preferably before you find out your stepdaughter's boyfriend has been climbing through her window every night!

Also consider a dress code governing acceptable nudity. Do you really want your teenage daughter walking around in a bra and panties when her stepfather and stepbrother are around? Decide if you want to include sexual standards in your family guidelines or leave them as verbal agreements.

Hilda is a young, first-time bride with no children of her own. Her husband and his three teenage sons had lived in a male-only household for several years before Hilda's arrival, and a locker-room culture prevailed. After she moved in with them, she was horrified by the boys' habit of running naked from bedroom to bathroom and vice versa, dripping, from the shower. They also frequently used the toilet without closing the door. "I was really embarrassed, but I told them I needed more modesty in the house," recalled Hilda. "Fortunately they're good-natured kids, and I haven't run into any more bare behinds since I asked them to cover up."

Physical attraction between the "wrong" people in a step-family is best prevented. Before you discover your sixteen-year-old daughter is pregnant by your husband's seventeen-year-old son, lay out firm guidelines for the teenagers in your home. If space permits, you might want to regulate as much as possible the times your kids and stepkids meet in intimate settings, such as bathrooms and bedrooms, particularly at the age they start noticing the opposite sex.

❧

Questionnaire

1. How well is your home functioning on a practical level? What are you satisfied with? What needs improvement?

2. Which single household issue is currently presenting the greatest difficulty for you? Why does the problem exist? What resources can you draw on to ease the difficulty?

3. Do you feel you are running your home in partnership with your husband? If not, what's holding things up?

4. What needs to be done—by you—before you will feel you have reached an ideal partnership?

5. What do you need from others before you will feel you are regarded as the female head of your household? What can your mate do to help? What can your own kids or stepkids do (or not do) before you will feel secure in this position?

6. How can you initiate these changes?

7. Which function of stepmotherhood, at this point, do you enjoy most?

Action Box

- Every year, celebrate moving day, your "inauguration day." If the kids are old enough, let them decide how you'll commemorate the event.

- Have the children take turns choosing and help preparing a favorite dinner. If the kids are older, let them help shop for it too.

- If you have never put a meal on the table that you cooked yourself, learn. It is impossible to buy in or eat out all the time with stepchildren. At least make sure you are capable of making macaroni and cheese, spaghetti and meatballs, and other child favorites. From day one, get stepfamily members to pitch in.

- Develop a tradition for birthdays that involves the entire household. Maybe other family members can take over the birthday boy's chores for the day, or he could get one big wish fulfilled that the whole family can take part in and that doesn't cost money.

- Have an economy meeting every few months to discuss ways to cut back on expenses and save money in the family budget. Or administer a "family savings box," into which everyone contributes a small amount each week or month, even a few cents if allowance is small. Then every six months, blow it on a family treat—a new household item that everyone wants, or dinner out, depending on how much has been saved.

CHAPTER 15

Smoothing Out the Wrinkles

All families experience disagreements, personality clashes, and wars of will, which can disrupt any marriage, family, or home when combined with the additional challenges of stepfamily life.

Exhausting as conflicts can be, try not to regard them as totally negative. As the stages of stepfamily development show, a conflict can be a growing experience and lead to change for the better.

Says Dr. Bloomfield in *Making Peace in Your Stepfamily,* "Other people's behavior depends as much on the emotional environment you generate as on their personality traits." In other words, you and your husband have the job of setting the emotional tone for your stepfamily.

On the following pages are some of the most commonly expressed sources of conflict for stepmothers:

1. disagreements with her mate about how to run their household, guidelines for their combined children, money.
2. disagreements with, or concerning, her mate's ex-wife or her own ex-husband.
3. disagreements between her own children and her stepchildren.
4. disagreements between a stepmom and her step-children.

5. disagreements between a stepmom and her own children.

Conflicts often result from a perceived lack of some precious commodity—space, privacy, time, attention, acceptance, love, money, or freedom. In stepfamilies there's often less of everything to go around. The kids might have to share bedrooms, when they used to have their own. There might be fights about where to display favorite objects, objections to virtual strangers using what is familiar or sacred. Money, a major concern in any family, often has to stretch twice as far in a step home.

Everyone is working within new boundaries. Old habits have given way to what some members may see as more rigid do's and don'ts. Your kids might have enjoyed leisurely lunches on Saturday with you—now you're running around, doing errands for an extended family. Even your mate, although he might not admit it, probably feels he isn't getting as much of your undivided attention as he would like.

There are a number of tools stepmothers have recommended to resolve conflict in a stepfamily:

- First choice: quiet, calm discussion with your mate, with a focus on your united front.

- Consult books on conflict resolution or negotiation, and apply the suggested exercises to the conflict your stepfamily is experiencing.

- Outside intervention: consult an objective friend, minister, or other stepfamilies with experience in the area troubling you.

- Mediation.

- Therapy.

- When all else fails and you need protection, hire an attorney.

1. Conflict with Your Mate

Since marital disagreements take place in your home, with the person from whom you need to receive the most support, these conflicts probably have the most personal impact on a stepmom. Disagreements between you and your mate must be resolved as swiftly as possible. You can't live with battles within your primary relationship—you have too many responsibilities to tackle together. If you find yourselves unable to reach a peaceful settlement, having tried quiet, reasonable discussion, first try working through some of the suggested exercises in the books we recommend on conflict resolution, then consider mediation. If either of you believes you have emotional resistances to finding a peaceful settlement in any other way, consider a visit to a therapist.

2. Conflict with Your Ex-Spouses

If you or your husband is still dealing with a contentious ex-mate—because of leftover grievances, resistance to the divorce, jealousy, anger, or current practical matters—do what is humanly possible to stay out of the courts and away from attorneys, due to the time and cost involved.

However, in situations where other means of resolution seem out of reach, where you feel the ex involved is unwilling to compromise, sometimes there is no alternative to seeking legal help. Dr. Singer, the psychologist and mediator we met in chapter 13, suggests using an attorney when protection is needed, when an ex-spouse is being underhanded in some way, e.g. hiding assets, or when either physical or mental abuse is taking place or is threatened.

Often a mediator can help resolve the difficulties without the necessity of legal help, since a mediator equally represents each person taking part. All parties involved must want to reach resolution and be willing to compromise to reach any agreement, or it won't work. (If it is discovered that one party is being underhanded, mediation has to be terminated.)

If you have children, your ex-husband's new wife will be their stepmother, faced with similar challenges and emotions as you. You're in an ideal position to understand her and her difficulties and to attempt to forge a working relationship with her. If we have done our job well in this book, you will be looking at your overall role very differently now: you are becoming an enlightened stepmother. For the sake of the healthy development of your own children and for the sake of peace in your new family, make overtures to this lady. Tell her you want to work with her, not against her, and offer her a copy of this book.

If your mate's ex-wife has remarried, the same approach *might* work with her, too. You can understand, if you have children of your own, that it's hard to see another woman involved in an intimate family setting with them. But again, two intelligent women should not be wasting their valuable time and energy on antagonism.

3. Stepsibling Rivalry

You already know better than to expect instant love among stepsiblings. In dealing with rivalry, it's especially important to recognize your natural bias and protective feelings toward your own children and to accept that your own flesh and blood are as capable of creating trouble with their stepsiblings as your husband's kids are of starting trouble with yours.

Along with normal sibling competitiveness and jealousies, children in blended families experience extra rivalries induced by stepfamily circumstances, including the perceived loss of Mom or Dad to an adult not their parent. Try to teach all the children in your home that they must respect one another, that they are all equal, and that before fighting, they should try to listen to one another. Conflicts among children and stepchildren are difficult to avoid, and it's wiser and certainly easier to let kids settle their own disputes, as long as they aren't physically hurting one another or being otherwise unacceptably abusive, when adult intervention is essential.

Usually, if you've had personal experience of sibling rivalry, seeing it in your own step home won't unnerve you as much, and you'll be better equipped to put it in perspective. June, a veteran stepmom of eighteen years, recalled being very upset and even frightened by the fighting between her three kids and her husband's two during their early years together.

"I was an only child and had never seen sibling rivalry in

action—I had nothing to compare it to," she said. "it didn't trouble my husband at all; in fact, he claimed our household was relatively calm compared to the home he had grown up in with his four brothers, where fistfights, bloody noses, and violent play were everyday occurrences. I took his word for it, but I can't help feeling relieved that all our kids survived to adulthood."

If you find that one child always comes out the loser, you might want to intervene—not to take sides or decide who's right and who's wrong but to discover why one kid consistently is the tormentor or the tormented. You might need to help a child who shows signs of being too submissive to stand up for himself or to find out, before his behavior gets out of control, why a child has become a bully.

In stepsibling situations where there is no willingness to resolve conflicts or where there appears to be outright hatred, consider professional help or the possibility of changing the custody arrangements for one of them so they don't have to live together. Perhaps a teenage stepdaughter would be better off living with her mother for while until she and your daughter get a little older. Perhaps an older child is wildly jealous of a new baby. Several stepmoms reported they were not comfortable with or were even scared of leaving a baby alone with a particular older child for fear of what she might do to an unwanted new half-brother/sister.

In the case of adversarial stepsiblings in whom you sense a wish to resolve problems, mediation can work well. Susan Norwood (no relation to the author of this book), a family mediator, and president of the Family Mediation Counsel of Louisiana, describes most family disputes she encounters as "no worse than I have in my own house," but as an objective third party and skilled negotiator, she is often able to bring two warring parties to agreement.

According to Norwood, kids enjoy mediation. "Each is regarded as an equal partner in the mediation process, and perhaps for the first time the focus is on them and what they want and need." Although mediation doesn't address emotional problems, she frequently finds that once kids realize they can coexist on a practical level, they often begin to think, "He isn't so bad after all," paving the way for a positive relationship. Norwood sees "managed negotiation" as preferable to the possibility of violence or avoidance.

By demonstrating how to resolve problems through peaceful means and enabling a child to see another person's point of view, the mediation process can equip him with important social skills that can last a lifetime. If you suspect a child has emotional problems that you believe cannot be resolved on a practical level, however, seek the help of a therapist or family counselor. (See chapter 20.)

4. Conflict between Stepmom and Stepchildren

Much of the friction between stepmothers and stepchildren is caused by a mutual feeling of unacceptance, made worse by living together. The fact that the stepmom needs to nurture and provide guidelines for her stepkids adds insult to injury for both parties.

If a child refuses to abide by your family guidelines or her personal responsibilities, having originally agreed to them, and you and your mate have exhausted your own remedies, try talking to the child's teachers or guidance counselor. They might have made some objective observations about your child and be willing to share their ideas on how to help her.

For more serious, confrontational conflicts, try some methods others have found to work. One book, *When Families Fight: How to Handle Conflict with Those You Love,* is especially useful. Written by a husband-and-wife team, Dr. Jeffrey and Dr. Carol Rubin, and published in 1989 by William Morrow & Company, this guide follows the entire life cycle of a family (not a stepfamily) dealing with all varieties of family conflict, "from the physical to the long-smouldering to the petty."

When all else fails, try family mediation, which can often quickly resolve practical matters and even clarify expectations about house rules or roles or behavior. A combative atmosphere in your home is hard on everyone—children, and stepchildren. It needs to be dealt with as soon as possible, not tolerated simply because you don't know what else to do.

5. Conflict between Stepmom (Mom) and Her Own Children

For all the reasons you already understand, your own children, whatever their ages, more than likely found it hard to see their mom remarry and devote so much time and love to a man other than their dad. Kids they don't know well, and might not like are also taking up your attention and possibly living with you. Besides being forced to share you, they're expected to behave courteously toward these people—it's almost too much for many kids to bear.

If you're dealing with acting up, rudeness, withdrawal, even running away, you might be hurt, disappointed, or frightened by these developments, feelings compounded by love and the nagging question: Are their dad and I at the root of their behavior? Additionally, you might be embarrassed by what you imagine your new mate thinks of them. On the bright side, this might be one time that you'll welcome the bad behavior of your stepkids—at least yours aren't any worse!

While this kind of conflict is par for the course, you still have to do something about it. The united front can help. Explain your feelings to your mate. More than likely he feels exactly the same way about his children. After you've sorted out your emotions (with his support), arrange a "heavy" discussion between just you and your kids: "We're all in this together. We can all be miserable, or we can try to get along." Talk to them as a group and individually. Listen to what they have to say; explain that change is hard for everyone. Tell them that you love them, that you appreciate their good efforts. Ask for their help in resolving problems; make them feel part of solutions. The most important goal of these discussions is to let your kids know you're available to them when they need you.

If you think any or all of your children can benefit from professional help, read chapter 20 for some suggestions.

One (Unusual) Way to Defuse Conflict: Over-the-Top Attention

Whom are you having the most conflict with in your stepfamily? Your ten-year-old stepson who "hates" you? A sixteen-year-old stepdaughter who refuses to cooperate about anything because "you're not my mom"? Perhaps one of your own children who feels neglected?

A number of stepmoms have used a strategy that sounds truly strange but has worked in some cases. Focus on the person you're having a conflict with, grit your teeth, and shower them with beneficent attention, unconditionally and outrageously. Within the bounds of decency, agree with everything they say; compliment them on the way they look, what they wear, how they behave. Thank them profusely for whatever they do—even the most minor positive act. Take an undivided interest in them; ask them to explain things to you. Inquire how they feel; ask about their day. Bend over backward to be flexible and helpful; when they complain, be understanding and sympathetic.

In short, go overboard. All this is being done, obviously, with tongue in cheek and with your bottom line in mind—it falls into the same category as the social lie. You want peace, to get on with your own life and enjoy your marriage. If you can achieve an end to conflict with this odd but relatively little effort, go for it. Chances are your nemesis is feeling unloved, unwelcome, uncertain, un-everything. Maybe over-the-top attention will help. Do it for a week, and see what happens. Bizarre as it sounds, this strategy has been known to turn people around very quickly (providing you don't seem phony)—perhaps because it is so completely unexpected.

Of course, you might get an unexpected response too. A stepmother who tried this tactic one weekend told us that her young adult stepdaughter was shocked, even dismayed apparently, to encounter solicitous smiles and interest from her stepmom. When the young woman found she couldn't get a satisfactory rise out of her stepmother and was met only with sweetness and light for twenty-four hours, she simply decided to leave before the weekend visit was over. You might find that smaller kids, once they find they can get lots of positive attention, stop being disruptive and combative. If the over-the-top strategy doesn't work, or makes matters worse, give it up.

Family Meetings

Many professionals recommend regular family meetings as the forum to discuss problems, make suggestions, ease conflicts among family members, air general complaints, or (bravo!) assess the issues that all of you, as a family, are handling well. They suggest that all family members attend, and that the meeting be conducted by the two adults in a formal manner. Some even recommended a "suggestion box," where ideas can be contributed on a regular basis. We have suggested at least two or three family meetings in the early stages of stepfamily life. That way everyone knows from the beginning how the new family will function and nobody can claim not to be aware of the changes that will occur. (Remember the kids who said they never heard their dad was remarrying?)

If you have a bunch of articulate, outgoing children, and you and your mate are that way yourselves, you might find regular family meetings a perfect communications venue. But if one of your kids is shy or reserved or doesn't like to speak up in front of others, you might find the meetings dominated by the more verbal ones. Also, for the child-free stepmother, these meetings can be uncomfortable, since she usually feels outnumbered on most issues.

Depending on your stepfamily's personalities, you might find that one-on-one meetings work better. You are more likely to hear a child's true feelings, fears, wishes, and suggestions in a private discussion, which can take place only once you have won the child's confidence. This kind of conversation with a stepchild, especially the first time, can be particularly rewarding for a stepmom.

What most stepmoms consider more beneficial than family

meetings is a time of family togetherness, such as a special meal at least once a week when all stepfamily members are present. Often issues will come up for discussion spontaneously. (Or you and your mate can plan to bring up a matter for discussion "spontaneously.") This takes the pressure off those who are uncomfortable at a formal family meeting.

Famly Values: Integrating Yours and Theirs

As you begin life with your new family, you might come across some standards, rituals, or values that you didn't discover in your initial research—things impossible to know until you're living together. An activity that seems quite normal to the rest of your stepfamily—your stepson's penchant for tending his ant farm at night—might make you nervous. You probably have no grounds to discourage unusual (to you) behavior, however, unless it is dangerous or affects others negatively. Miranda, stepmom to two boys, aged eight and ten, didn't find out until she was married that her husband, an ex-combat veteran, insisted upon sleeping with a loaded pistol under his pillow. "I never got a wink of sleep with that thing so close," she admitted. Her marriage ended over this single issue.

Several stepmoms reported being surprised that their stepchildren were vegetarians, although most found it to be the basis of an interesting relationship as the child explained her beliefs and helped Stepmom with food preparation.

Josephine joined a family who enjoyed "moon gardening." They spent hours poring over planetary planting guides, and then, when the moon was just right, they planted their seeds. "I was fascinated by this, and I have to admit, the vegetables somehow tasted better!" she marveled.

Six-year-old Sami played the cello. Sheila, her stepmom, fully expected to have to endure "the most ghastly sounds." She was amazed when the little girl turned out to be a virtuoso, carting off prize after prize at musical competitions.

Another stepmom learned on moving day that her stepson had a beloved pet snake that subsisted on still-live tidbits.

After an initial fright, Gayle realized she could never insist on banishing the little boy's pet, so with some ground rules (the snake *must* stay in Bobby's room) she coexists peacefully with this creature, which receives lots of visitors from her stepson's classmates.

Cindy, who was single prior to joining her stepfamily, was used to a great deal of solitude and personal space. Living with a boisterous family, which she enjoyed, meant less time for her own single-life rituals. The scented baths she had taken every morning before work were out of the question with one bathroom and three children rushing to catch a school bus. Same with her after-work hour-long meditation—that time slot now held carpools or organizing homework. To accommodate her hectic family lifestyle, she just reversed her rituals—taking her bath at night and meditating very early in the morning.

As Stepmom, you can introduce some of your own favorite rituals or routines to stepfamily members. The aim eventually is to create your own stepfamily values, incorporating those from both sides of the new family, but this takes time and much creativity. For the first year or so, you will be exploring what your mate and his kids are used to and how they fit in with what you and your kids hold dear.

Established Family Traditions

Be sensitive to established traditions, which fall into two categories: everyday household routines and those surrounding the holiday seasons, which may be more formally observed and have a religious slant.

You might love to serve spaghetti and a delicious Bolognese sauce on Friday nights with a bottle of cheap red wine—your idea of a perfect pre-weekend family party. Continuing that tradition with your stepfamily (since your own kids would miss it if it stopped) means one night you don't have to think about dinner. Before you know it, your teenage stepson might be asking if he can bring a friend to join your boisterous

Friday spaghetti night. Next Friday you'll know to include him in the routine.

On the other hand, you might discover that your step-daughter's deceased mom used to serve fish on Fridays and that she'd miss it if you didn't continue this tradition. Your mate confirms how much this meal means to her, so perhaps you can designate Thursday or Saturdays as your famous spaghetti night instead.

Special Family Occasions

In the early days of your life as a stepmother, you might be so involved in carving out your place in your new family that you have little energy to organize special occasions. In all likelihood, however, this role will probably fall to you. You'll find that a few occasions are extra-sensitive for stepmoms:

Events Your Stepchildren's Mother Has Always Organized

If you married a divorced man, do not try compete with his ex-wife by either outdoing her efforts or undermining them. She has already made her mark on her family and will probably want to continue handling certain family occasions.

Mother's Day

Unless you have children of your own or fall into one of the "exception" categories discussed in chapter 3, this day is not for you except in context with your own mother. Many step-moms make the mistake of expecting some acknowledgment from their stepkids. Forget it. No matter how good your relationship with your stepchild is, no matter how much of a parenting or nurturing influence you have, you're not his mother. Get this fact out in the open. Let your mate know you don't expect his kids to fete you, their stepmom, on Mother's Day and that he should not persuade them or force them to do so. Stepchildren often try to avoid their stepmother on Mother's Day, or are careful not to mention the day in their stepmom's presence, because of the uncomfortable feelings involved. Very few stepmoms reported having received so much as a card from a stepchild until many years had elapsed.

You will feel much more at ease with Mother's Day if you are able to ask your stepkids what they are going to do for their mom. If your stepchildren are young, and it's geographically practical, encourage your mate to arrange a visit for them with their mother, complete with a bunch of flowers, which he should purchase. Make this easy for him. You don't want him buying flowers for his kids to give behind your back, thinking it might hurt you. If he is unable to perform this task because of bitter feelings, persuade him to ask another family member to handle it. The kids need to acknowledge their mom. If they aren't encouraged to do this, guess who is usually blamed?

If your stepkids' mom died, the holiday can be even more sensitive. Even though you are a full-time stepmom, it is still unreasonable of you to expect acknowledgment. Mother's Day will be a very sad event for your stepchildren, and for your mate too. Ask him what would be the most comfortable way for them to spend the day. Try to make it easy for them to talk about her, if they are so inclined. If they seem reluctant to reminisce about Mom in your presence, encourage Dad to take them to lunch or a long walk. Generous suggestions on your part, although perhaps not appreciated by the kids, will be welcomed by your husband.

Many stepmoms we interviewed described Mother's Day as "agony," "the worst day of the year for me," and similar terms. Yes, it is grossly unfair to be responsible on this day for so many mothering duties with none of the recognition, but by now you know that a stepmom doesn't get a fair shake in many areas. With our continued aim of preventing problems for you, our strongest recommendation is that today you expect *nothing*. Make your own plans, especially if you have no kids of your own. Go spend the day with your mother, if you still have her. Pique is a reasonable response to this holiday, but give yourself reason to commend yourself for the way you are handling it.

Stepmoms have told some heartwarming stories regarding Mother's Day, but acknowledgments of a stepmother's nurturing contributions are usually not expressed by stepchildren until after many years. When Fay married her husband twenty-seven years ago, he had two children, aged ten and twelve. Fay's stepson, now well into adulthood, called her one recent Mother's Day and left a lovely message on her answering machine: "I don't believe I have ever thanked you for all you did for us when we were kids. I thought this would be an appropriate day to do so. Happy Mother's Day, Fay."

Another stepmom, after fifteen years of helping to raise her husband's daughter, recalled having received her first Stepmother's Day card—which are beginning to appear in a very few stores—with a similar note of appreciation. Much depends on the age at which you inherit your stepkids. If your husband's children are adults, it's very unlikely you will receive acknowledgment, since you won't actually have done much for them. If you acquire very young stepchildren and have time to build up a relationship, you might be in for a pleasant surprise—after a decade or two.

Your Wedding Anniversary

This day might be uncomfortable or unpopular in your household, at least in the early years. Stepkids are not known to break open the champagne on the anniversary of their father's remarriage, but having said that we want to suggest you make sure they are aware of the day—you don't want to hide it. For you and your husband, this is a happy, special occasion, and you can celebrate alone. If the kids are little, hire a baby-sitter, and have a wonderful evening together. If they are older, let them get their own dinner and know you are out together, having fun. Don't allow stepchildren to denigrate your anniversary—no snide remarks are acceptable. Unlike Mother's Day, this *is* your day.

Father's Day

Most stepmoms expressed astonishment at the lack of attention their mate received on Father's Day, particularly in view of the importance of Mother's Day and the fact that their stepkids wanted and were assisted to do something special for Mom. These stepmoms, feeling hurt on behalf of their mate, encouraged their own children to show appreciation to their dad on his special day, even after a divorce. It's usually best not to interfere with the way your new family handles this holiday—to express annoyance or hurt to your mate will only emphasize his kids' omission and possibly upset him further. Stepmoms interpreted kids' lack of attention on Father's Day as punishment—"He married her, so he doesn't want us." If a gentle suggestion or query to his children is shrugged off with a "We never do anything," you have to accept it.

A Stepchild's Wedding
When your husband's child marries, your role will probably be low-key, unless you are invited to be an integral part of the wedding. Otherwise, you are Dad's wife, attending as his partner. You can offer to do anything that is needed, but you should not insist on participating.

Similarly, if your ex-husband has remarried, your daughter's stepmom is also simply Dad's wife, although if your daughter likes her, she might wish to involve her. As a stepmom yourself, you will probably not object to this. Your husband, your daughter's stepdad, should be included as your partner. If your mate became her stepdad when she was much younger and they have a good relationship, she might want him to take on a greater role. Step occasions are becoming more flexible and creative. Sometimes two dads, biological and step, give a daughter away at her wedding; sometimes neither, and her mom handles this role. Whatever you are comfortable with is acceptable, as long as it is respectful to all participants.

The guiding principle for planning step occasions is simple: who plays the starring role, and what do they want? Often if relationships are not good, decisions about inclusion or exclusion are based on anger or revenge, such as a stepdaughter insisting that her dad walk her down the aisle but refusing to allow her stepmother to attend the wedding. Will your mate refuse to give her away unless you are there, or will you both agree to take the easy way out and accept her wishes? Opinions in your stepfamily will probably vary widely.

Stepmothers who experienced this unpleasant conundrum have advised that you don't force your mate to choose between you and his child. Nobody wins—and who wants to be where they're not wanted, anyway? Opt instead for an all-day shopping trip, lunch with a supportive friend, a date with your own daughter—whatever makes you happy.

The only request you should make of your mate is that he express to his child his disappointment about her discourteous behavior and that he is not condoning it. Also, be sure the story behind this unpleasant scenario is told *accurately* to all concerned, by him. Do what you can to prevent his telling a "doctored" version—that you couldn't come because you had the flu or were called suddenly out of town or became otherwise indisposed.

It is almost impossible to plan a stepfamily event—a wedding, graduation, bar mitzvah—without someone being put out or upset in some way. Remain calm and gracious, and refuse to get involved in arguments. Do not allow yourself to be put in an uncomfortable position; maintain your dignity, and decline attending any event that portends trouble for you.

Holidays and Vacations

Holidays and vacations often include the entire family and perhaps extended family members too. Hurt feelings, disappointments, conflicting wishes, and opposing ways of celebrating the holidays occur in biological families, but in stepfamilies these problems are often compounded by divided loyalties. Stepmoms often felt the holiday spirit was nonexistent with members wishing they were with their "real" family, celebrating the way it "used to be."

There can be much sadness for you too. Perhaps your own children will be with their dad, while you're trying to put a happy face on your favorite family holiday with stepkids who are eyeballing your stuffing with suspicion. Holidays, generally recognized as being difficult when life is fairly normal, are much more difficult when everyone is suffering losses and changes.

To successfully unite two families with different sets of traditions, religions, and routines might seem almost impossible in the beginning. Stepmoms have told of having a stomach in knots for weeks before major holidays as they anticipated any kind of disaster or hysterical scene. The problems, real and anticipated, need to be acknowledged by both you and your mate.

Try to integrate existing routines and traditions into your new stepfamily holiday plans, making compromises and trade-offs when necessary. Said Mona, "Gerry's kids thought it wouldn't be Christmas without flashing lights on the tree, while mine loved our generations-old teatime ritual of lighting candles. We thought we were doing beautifully, having both, until we saw the results! It looked like Coney Island gone haywire. We decided to do it their way one year, our way the next. We all laugh about that first Christmas now, and it has become one of our funniest stepfamily stories."

If you have different custody arrangements for each set of kids—and perhaps a new baby, too—scheduling holiday gatherings can be a nightmare. Since there's very little you can do about legal imperatives, remind yourself that a calm atmosphere and the welcoming *spirit* of the particular holiday you provide are what become most important, not battling over who goes where, when. If your celebrations take place when the kids are with their other parent, celebrate without them. Or make arrangements for your family celebration to take place when you are all together. There is no reason you can't have Christmas dinner a couple of days later, a week later, or in the middle of January.

One stepfamily we met had "Christmas in July." Children and stepchildren were living in different parts of the country, spending the holidays under different custody arrangements, and July was the only time everyone was available at one time. Explained Aurora, "Each July we get together at one of our homes, exchange gifts, have a wonderful celebratory feast, and laugh a lot, pretending we are Australians, who have cookouts on the beach on Christmas Day."

Gifts: It's the Thought That Counts

Many stepmothers reported awkward inequities over gift giving on any occasion. This was more noticeable at Christmas, because generally everyone opens gifts at the same time. Stepmoms on the receiving end of cheap, thoughtless gifts, after having given much more generously themselves, quickly learned to adjust their spending. High-priced gifts can't buy love, but gifts given without any feeling or care behind them are insulting. One stepmom recalled her corporate-executive stepdaughter giving her a generic business gift she had received from a vendor. "My stepdaughter's name and corporate address were still on the package; she hadn't even bothered to remove it—just stuck a tag with my name over it and put it under the tree." Others recall inappropriate gifts, obviously worn or utilitarian gifts. One woman's adult stepson gives her a cheap kitchen tool every year.

If you have a good relationship with a child and know exactly what he or she would like (and it's within your price range), then go ahead and get it. Otherwise, if you'll be planning, buying, and wrapping the gift Dad gives his kids anyway, your name might as well be on the tag with his: MERRY CHRISTMAS, FROM DAD AND SUKI. Just don't expect equal thanks. Stepmom after stepmom mentioned they had shopped for and chosen the joint gift, but Dad got the big hugs and kisses, while they were ignored.

Other stepmoms mentioned that their stepchildren "forgot" or gave away the gifts given to them. Stepmoms, quite fairly, interpreted this as disrespect or an indication that their stepchildren weren't interested in a stepmother's gift. Again, if this happens to you, just put your name on Dad's gifts to them. But first bring the issue into the open—it's better to know where you both stand: "I see you left behind that lovely sweater I gave you. I've noticed you've done this before with things I've given you, so if it's making you uncomfortable, I'll stop. I don't like wasting money." Try to keep the door open to a change of heart, however, since you don't know if a problem person is behind this behavior ("Don't you dare wear anything that woman gave you.") You can always add, "I'd like to talk about it, if something is bothering you. You can let me know when you're ready."

Holidays are stressful. Expectations are high—often too high. The desire for everything to be perfect is compelling, even in biological families. As a stepmom, you need to be aware of this tendency—for you this fantasy is especially undesirable, on top of all the other stepfamily stresses you are likely experiencing. Recalled Adrienne, "I had knocked myself out, trying to make a perfect Thanksgiving for Kelly's three kids and his parents the first year we were married. When I finally sat down, I realized there was only one person at the table who was glad I was there—my husband. Nobody else talked to me. I might just as well not have been present. I couldn't wait till they all left." This scenario is common in step households when a stepmom doesn't have children of her own or any members of her family of origin at the gathering. To ease the tension Adrienne could have enlisted Kelly's support ahead of time, making sure he included her in the conversation throughout dinner, or arranged to sit next to her husband at the table.

Other helpful tips for holiday gatherings:

- Plan ahead with your mate. Discuss your personal preferences and traditions. Devise a plan you can both agree on, incorporating as many of the traditions and routines from both sides of the family as reasonably possible. Discuss the guest list and any idiosyncrasies people might display. Keep control of organizing the celebration—you must do this, especially if it's your first year as a stepmom—but delegate tasks so all the labor doesn't fall to you.

- Discuss the celebration with your children and stepchildren, explaining that you want them to enjoy this first holiday together and that you need their help to make sure all goes well. Ask for their input, what they would like to do. Perhaps a teenage daughter can help make pies, or your stepson can learn to carve a turkey. Smaller children can help set the table, or make table decorations.

- Include extended stepfamily members in the preparations. Make it known (unless you specifically want to handle everything yourself, which is not advised, as you run the risk of being regarded as the maid/cook) that you need all the help you can get. If Grandma usually brings her sweet potatoes, wonderful. If there are vegetarians in your midst, suggest they make something meatless and delicious.

- Find out if anyone on your guest list has a food allergy. You don't want someone keeling over in your home (imagine the opportunities here for the family saboteur!).

- Be certain there is at least one person present who is totally understanding and supportive—perhaps some of your own family members—so the celebration will feel familiar to you, too. Try not to attend your own party "alone," if you can avoid it.

Stepfamily Vacations

What's your idea of a vacation? Two weeks at a luxurious hotel, spent alone with your mate? If so, you've got company. Noted Yolanda, "I take care of my stepchildren for fifty weeks a year. Our life revolves around their activities and what they need. And they don't even like me. At vacation time, I need some off-duty time away from them."

While this is a reasonable feeling, you might find that if your husband sees his kids only on crammed, breathless weekends during the year, he might want to spend his vacations with them. The kids might also look forward to a long, uninterrupted period of time with Dad.

Compromise, is usually the best solution. One week alone, one week with the kids, might work for you. If you can't afford two separate getaway vacations, take turns. One year the kids get the going-away one; next year you and your mate do. The other week can be spent at home, going out for day trips and excursions you don't normally have time for.

Stepmoms warn against trying to combine your, his, and "our" kids when it's vacation time. Not only is it logistically risky—trying to coordinate custody schedules, hoping everyone will stay healthy, praying for good weather now that you've made such an enormous financial investment in having everyone at once—but it's impossible to fulfill everyone's idea of a great vacation; there are bound to be "casualties." Keep it simple.

As Judy's two stepsons grew older, she encouraged her husband to take them away, without her, for the odd weekend—sometimes together, sometimes one at a time. The remaining boy spent time with his mom, stayed with a friend, or occasionally stayed home with his stepmom. Judy recommended this idea to other stepmoms. "I got a lot of credit for initiating this 'treat' for the kids," she explained. "It was a complete win–win situation. The boys loved taking turns having Dad all to themselves, my relationship with them improved as I spent occasional weekends alone with each boy, and I enjoyed a weekend alone once in a while. Tim, my husband, enjoyed it too."

If you decide to try this arrangement, be sure to ask Dad and kids to tell you about their weekend when they return. Show your interest, and enjoy their enthusiasm, especially since you started the new tradition. Another bonus: it will be easier for you and your mate to take a weekend break together if everybody else gets his turn with Dad.

Step Pets

To many people, their animals are their babies. A beloved family pet needs as much welcome into a new family as do the children. But because there is so much else going on, this doesn't always happen, causing a lot of hurt feelings and ferocious protectiveness.

Tonya had serious allergies. In spite of her condition, she married Noah, a man with three cats and one son. When the couple was discussing marriage, they hardly thought about the cats, preoccupied as they were with their kids' adjustments. But on moving day, Noah's cats came too! The very first night, the kitties hopped on the bed, ready to curl up around their beloved owner as usual.

"We fought for a full week over those damned cats," reported Tonya, who eventually insisted that Noah keep them in the basement. "Noah is heartbroken and spends most of his free time down there with them. I let them come up in the evening, and they spend some time outdoors, but I can't stand being near them." Tonya was amazed to find Noah more concerned about his cats than about her children. But since she was banishing his "babies," he saw no reason to pay much attention to hers.

Decisions and compromises have to be reached about step pets before you move, preferably before you marry. Do not anticipate you can change anyone's mind once you are living together, nor should you let others believe you will become used to a pet that gives you allergies. Stepmoms reported ongoing conflicts because "their dog chases my cat" or because "my stepdad won't let Fluffy sleep in the chair she's used to." Animals deserve to be loved and well cared for and to be treated with kindness and consideration by all members of a stepfamily.

For children who have never had an animal, a step pet is a wonderful opportunity to form a special bond. But watch out for cruelty, unintentional or not. Children unused to cats might not understand they don't like to have their tail pulled and, unlike some good-natured dogs, rarely want to be dressed up! Children need close supervision before they can be allowed responsibility for a precious animal.

You might need to invoke a leash law for the dogs in the house, and a special time for the cats to go in the yard, when they won't bump into your mate's "killer" dog. It is possible to blend pets, but this task requires a lot of sensitivity, not only for the pet's sake but for the emotions of the owners too. You can't expect a child (or adult) to be willing to compromise in other areas if her pet has been relegated to the sidelines.

We saw this happen repeatedly to stepmoms who had no kids but brought an animal to their step home. Outnumbered, both the stepmom and her pet became second-class citizens.

⟡

Questionnaire

1. Are there any special occasions in your stepfamily that cause you anxiety or concern? Which one(s)? Why? What do you think will help you enjoy the occasion more?
2. Are you experiencing conflict with a member of your stepfamily (or with ex-mates?) Who? Do you know why? Is there anything you can do to defuse some of this tension? Detail what you think might work.
3. Do you (or any member of your stepfamily) have any ideas for integrating family rituals/traditions? Does the potential exist for any new stepfamily traditions? Detail.

⟡

Action Box

☙ If one of your children and one of your mate's are having trouble getting along, take the two of them to lunch together two Saturdays running. One week one will choose the place to eat, the next week the other. Nothing elaborate, perhaps fast food restaurants where they'll have to sit together for a maximum of thirty minutes. Initiate discussions on subjects you know they both agree on—like their mutual love of pizza, or the wish they share of seeing the latest Disney movie. Show them they can agree on something—you're laying the foundation for an improved relationship.

☙ Don't forget how important one-on-one time can be during this critical settling in period for each member of your stepfamily. When you notice someone is particularly despondent, pay them a little extra attention—a glass of milk on the deck together; for an older teenager perhaps a glass of wine in the den. Encourage discussion on how they feel the stepfamily is coming together.

~ Continue to talk, discuss and explain. Only by repeatedly initiating exchanges of ideas and thoughts you can ensure each person feels like an important, validated and secure member of your new stepfamily. Be especially sure to do this with your mate.

~ Be as creative as you can with new stepfamily rituals—events that fit your unique circumstances and step schedules. If your stepson's mom wants him to spend his birthday with her, don't argue about it, simply create an "official" birthday for him too on an entirely different, more convenient day. He spends his "real" one with his mom, and his "official" one with you and his dad. He gains all around and will love it—he gets two birthdays! Be sure he has two birthday cakes and you're a winner too.

CHAPTER 16

School, Church, and Community

Outside their private lives with their stepfamilies, stepmoms often felt they had to "prove" their good intentions again—to members of their community, those they meet socially or at work, and the members of various organizations they became part off. Bringing your young stepson to his first day of day care, you might find yourself listening to a beat of awkward silence upon introducing yourself as "Bobby's stepmother."

In the public arena, as in the private, stepmothers are scrutinized, judged, and rated, often before anyone has a chance to get to know them. People who expect you to assume the form and shape of the mythological wicked stepmother won't look for your positive traits.

Stepmoms also face "second wife" prejudices, described by Glynnis Walker in her book, *Second Wife, Second Best?* (Doubleday, 1984): "She comes in two basic styles: 'the full-chested floozy,' who sets out to lure another woman's husband away from hearth and home, dangling her physical charms like a carrot in front of a donkey, or 'the scheming, conniving gold-digger,' who seeks not so much a healthy man in her bed as a man with a healthy account in the bank."

Given these circumstances, you need to act in two seemingly contradictory ways. First, be proactive. Don't isolate yourself just to avoid scrutiny—you should be as visible as you want to be in your community, adopting roles you want to play. Second, be protective of yourself. Act as your own "public relations" expert, offering people the information you choose to release, cutting off speculation. You won't win everyone over, but at least you'll steal some thunder from the rumor mill. Getting your message out will also relieve some of the confusion of having two "Mrs. Smiths" in your community, if your husband's ex is still living nearby, especially if you're involved with your stepchild's school.

Stepmom at School

If you become a full-time stepmom, or if your mate and his ex-wife share custody and your stepchildren live with you during school time, for the sake of a smooth-running household, you'll need to organize your schedule to accommodate the kids' school and extracurricular activities. At the very least you will have to be aware of the school calendar—social events, seasonal breaks and vacations—and what your stepkids need day-to-day, including lunches, school supplies, clothes for sports events, cookies for the bake sale, etc.

In many ways, handling school-related issues will be much easier if you're a full-time stepmom, since your home will follow a consistent routine. And if you have children of your own and are already involved on your kids' behalf, encompassing your stepchildren's activities, too, will be relatively easy.

With your mate, discuss the depth of your participation, if any, in your stepchildren's school events. Be realistic—don't commit time you really can't afford in the hopes of being the "perfect" stepmother. Consider activities that appeal to you, fit your schedule, and don't conflict with the involvement of your stepchildren's mother. If you haven't had much to do with school since your own childhood, you might find it fun to help with an occasional after-school crafts project or to chaperone the annual holiday dance.

School Formalities

Schools are often willing to view a stepmom as a parent for practical purposes, but each school system might have a different policy, and it's important that you check.

In circumstances when a mother lives far away or is deceased, it is essential, both practically and for the safety of the kids, that you be named in school records as an alternative responsible party, called "in loco parentis" (which means "in place of a parent"), to act on behalf of the children when their dad is unavailable. It would be unfortunate if a child became ill at school and could not be released to you (while Dad's on business in Chicago, and Mom lives 200 miles away) simply because the paperwork was not completed. If you have stepkids in more than one school, you'll need to make these arrangements at each school. Be sure to thoroughly research the details about what in loco parentis status—which may vary among states or school systems—will mean to you.

If your ex husband's ex-wife has sole custody of their children, she can refuse to allow you in loco parentis status. When Dad has shared custody, she can't refuse—dad has fifty percent of parental authority, and can designate the stepmother to act in his place when he is unavailable. Either way, to prevent problems or confusion, your husband should discuss this issue with his ex-wife—obtaining her permission if necessary, pointing out the security this would provide their kids, or simply informing her of your in loco parentis status.

In our current litigious climate, schools need to protect themselves. The guidance office or the principal can tell you what the school requires so you can make decisions regarding your stepchild in the absence of the biological parents, particularly in a critical situation. They may need a copy of a power of attorney or other legal document, your daytime phone number, a record of your signature, your photograph, etc.

Whether you are named in loco parentis or not, you and your husband should meet your stepkids' teachers and principal to explain your remarried situation, to inform them of the different surnames you might use in your stepfamily, and to provide any other background details you believe they should have.

Ask Teachers to Teach You

If you don't have children of your own in school, you probably won't be well-versed in current routines and methods. Seek out your stepkids' teachers, and explain that the best interests of your stepchildren are a priority and that you want some pointers. Most educators will be very happy to do this. Teachers love parents and guardians who care; it makes their job much easier. Ask questions about anything you don't understand—school policies, classes, safety, homework, social development, and culture among children your stepkids' age. Elicit ways the teacher thinks you can best become involved, depending on the time you have available.

Ask school officials—including guidance counselors, school psychologists, and social workers—if they can recommend any tried-and-true ways for handling stepfamily issues that might concern you, including issues you (or we) might not have considered. Have they made any observations about the effects of stepfamily life on kids? Some school facilities are experienced in, sensitive to, and conversant on the subject of stepfamilies. Others categorically reject the idea that stepfamily life has any effect on school life at all.

What You Can Teach Educators

While most schools recognize the difficulties of divorce for their students, few know enough about stepfamily issues. You might want to enlighten them specifically from a stepmother's viewpoint. We met highly qualified and well-intentioned faculty who had simply never been exposed to the perspective of a stepmom. Invariably these educators were intrigued.

We need to give teachers the opportunity to engage in an on-going dialogue with us, to absorb a well-rounded view of stepfamily life and recognize the contribution we make in helping to raise our stepkids, as well as the difficulties we face in doing so. We cannot expect our schools to be responsive to the needs and concerns of stepmothers if the faculty at large doesn't hear from us.

Protecting Yourself from Tall Tales

A number of stepmoms mentioned finding out that their stepkids had told "stories" about them at school. Sometimes the fib had been told weeks, even months, before it was discovered—by then it was nearly impossible to set the record straight. "Look what my stepmother did . . ." (brandishing a bruise or scratched limb) was a common one. "She made me do that . . ." and "She wouldn't let me do this . . ." were close seconds.

If you think your stepchild might have a tendency to misrepresent your actions or character—out of anger, dislike, revenge, or any other number of reasons—you must address the problem immediately. First and foremost, see if you can, together with your mate and possibly school personnel, find out what lies behind the child's behavior, and take steps to help the child who is obviously unhappy.

School officials must handle accusations of child abuse very seriously. If a teacher spots a bruised arm, or if the child points it out, and the teacher has the slightest doubt as to its cause, she is legally required to report it to the principal. If the parents and stepmom are "known" and appear at school for meetings and functions, perhaps a telephone call would be made to the parents to discuss the matter. This is one advantage of making yourself familiar to your stepchild's teacher.

If a satisfactory explanation is not received, the principal might decide to take the matter to the school superintendent. An investigation would likely be made within the school: Is there a troubled history in this family? Is the child frequently absent? Does he show signs of other problems? If, after the school's investigation, it is believed abuse might be taking place, the incident will be reported to the appropriate child-protection agency.

To protect yourself from tall tales, act with extreme caution. If your eight-year-old stepson trips on his skateboard in your yard and falls, badly scraping his leg, you should not only get him immediate medical attention but also inform school officials of the incident, detailing how the injury happened and the treatment your stepchild is receiving, and provide the doctor's name and phone number. Leave word also where you and his dad can be contacted in case your stepson is in pain or doesn't feel well during the day.

These precautions are particularly important if your stepchild has the potential to be a storyteller. An injury can easily be blamed, by an unhappy child, on a stepmother. If a story like this is believed, the ramifications can be horrendous for you and your husband.

Some troubling facts emerged from our discussions with school personnel:

- A biological mother is as capable of child abuse as a stepmother, but the latter will usually head the list of suspects.

- According to one superintendent of schools in Connecticut, "It is not unusual in divorce situations that the biological mother will condition her child to dislike his or her stepmother, based on lingering hostilities toward her ex-husband and his new wife." Be aware of the possibility that an ex-wife might be behind a fictitious scenario.

While it can be extremely difficult for a stepmom to point out to school authorities the delicate position she is in, your mate, the child's father, might feel it appropriate to mention in confidence any fears he has over his ex-wife's possible misrepresentations. For the child's benefit, it is important they know what is going on at home, particularly details about the stepmom/biological mom relationship and the possible effects it might be having on the child.

Your School Role as a Part-Time Stepmom

When your stepchildren's mom still lives in your neighbor-hood and is active at her kids' school, or if she has sole cus-tody and your mate has visitation rights, making you a part-time stepmom, your participation in your stepchildren's school lives will be more low-key.

In any case, you'll need to clarify or establish your relation-ship, if any, with your stepchildren's mother and what roles each of you will fulfill in the kids' school lives. Discussing this with her directly is ideal and builds on your goal of a working relationship. But if your husband's ex is still at the "I don't want that woman near my kids" stage, it's in your best interest to back off. If a mother does not want you to be involved with her children's school activities, she can notify the admin-istration, and they will be required to abide by her wishes. Of course, if your mate shares custody or is a co-parent, he has the right to be involved himself and to attend any function or meeting at school that he wishes.

Often if a mother is dating or has remarried, she might understand that just as she would like to take her new partner to school functions, her ex-husband might want to take you. Perhaps the school can be persuaded to issue two sets of tick-ets for the school play. It's good for children to have both parents witness the precious times in their lives, good for you as a stepparent to be part of them.

If relationships among ex-spouses are not civilized, then maintaining your dignity and behaving graciously is probably as proactive as you can be under those conditions. Don't be tempted to be more forceful—you'll only promote (more) ani-mosity between your mate and his ex-wife and exacerbate your stepkids' feelings of divided loyalty. You can only insist on your right to know your stepchildren's schedules and how they will affect you and your household. Do not allow yourself to be perceived by an ex-wife as "awaiting instructions" from her, a position many stepmoms inadvertently and resentfully fall into. Make sure you and your husband receive duplicate copies of whatever information the school sends to your step-kids' mom.

Helping with Homework

One school guidance counselor we queried, who views home-work completion as a "contract" between student and teacher, recommended that stepmoms avoid supervising stepkids' homework but instead simply act as a facilitator, making sure they have a quiet place to work, setting a time frame for com-pleting assignments, praising when it's done, sympathizing when it's difficult or boring. This educator believes the step-children will not benefit if a stepmother is a disciplinarian in this area. If the homework is not done, it is up to the teacher to be displeased and mete out the consequences.

Discuss this idea with your mate and your stepkid's teach-ers. Obviously you and your husband want to instill a sense of responsibility, and homework is one of the first for many children. Not all stepmoms and their husbands agree with this method, believing that parents and stepparents should be involved in ensuring that homework is done properly, that it's a parental responsibility. Whatever you decide, it's best to establish a house rule or guideline for homework, encouraging a regular routine acceptable to the children, stepmom and mate, and teachers.

Parents who opt out of the homework battles, placing the responsibility firmly on the shoulders of the child, report a calmer atmosphere in their homes. In his book *Familyhood* (Simon & Schuster, 1992) Dr. Lee Salk suggests that a parent "be available to help if your child has trouble sitting down and getting started." Doing homework for the child, however, according to Dr. Salk, is "the unpardonable sin."

In a shared-custody situation, it makes sense, for consis-tency's sake, that a homework routine be worked out with the kids' mother—another reason for the joint-parenting board we previously discussed. See page 208.

Houses of Worship

The increase in interfaith marriages is seen by some as the death knell of tradition and by others as an opportunity to teach children tolerance and acceptance of those who are different.

Prior to marriage, if possible, discuss with your mate how you will worship as a family or if you'd rather continue separate traditions. Many stepfamilies have successfully blended religious traditions and rituals, but it's vital to know the depth of your new mate's convictions—and he yours—to assess if they are compatible.

Finding out after your marriage that your husband insists on attendance at mass not only each Sunday morning at 7:00 A.M. But every day during Lent might not be a welcome surprise if you and your children attend church only on Easter Sunday and Christmas Eve. You'll need to consider whether you and your kids will join him or if your husband and his children will continue their observances as a subfamily.

Especially important is discussing how you will raise an "ours" baby in context with religion. If your mate is Jewish and you're Catholic, how will you raise your interfaith child? If religion is important to both of you, you can't wait until the child is born to discuss it.

Noreen, a Catholic stepmom, had been married for three years to Stephen, who is Jewish. Although in the Jewish tradition a child inherits the religion of the mother, Stephen wanted any child of their union to be a part of his family's Jewish life, including participation in his religious holidays. Noreen insisted on a Catholic Baptism and religious instruction, as well as the receiving of Sacraments and attendance at Mass. Stephen decided he could not participate in any Catholic ceremonies involving his child but acknowledged that any child of their union would become a Catholic. Said Noreen, "We began this discussion before we married, but we've never really finished it. We're continuing to answer each other's questions about religious imperatives and subtleties, making sure we can agree or compromise, even on the smallest detail."

Find out all the little ways religion affects your new family's day-to-day lifestyle. In time you might find yourself accepting some small spiritually oriented customs and enjoying them. Does your new family say grace before meals? Will you merely tolerate this as you observe, or would you like yourself and your children to be included in this ritual?

Consider how you will integrate various religious holidays and feasts. Jewish–Christian couples have many more family occasions to attend but no conflicts about whose "turn" it is at Christmas. Other stepfamilies might find it a nightmare in logistics to be fair about who should go where, especially when there are ex-wives, ex-husbands, their new mates, grandparents, and stepgrandparents to please.

When you and your husband have decided how you wish to worship as a family, if your plan varies from the way you worshipped prior to your marriage, your minister, rabbi, or priest might help you resolve doubts or concerns or negotiate remaining incompatibilities. Chances are your clergyman has come across similar circumstances and might even be able to put you in touch with stepfamilies with similar issues.

Tips for Blending Religious Convictions

- Don't criticize or condemn the religious beliefs of your new family, however unusual their spiritual practices might seem to you. One stepmom has never lived down the time she responded, in a stressful moment, "Oh, for God's sake, shut up," when her stepdaughter had for the thousandth time suggested, "Why don't you pray for the answer?" to some minor indecision.

- Don't allow members of your new family to comment negatively on your beliefs. Notwithstanding a lively philosophical debate about your faith with those of different persuasions, criticism or belittling of your chosen spirituality is not acceptable.

- If you take your religion more seriously than your new family does theirs, be sure you don't inflict your beliefs on them unless you know they are willing to hear them.

- Make certain you understand all the social ramifications of your mate's religion. The media have detailed some extraordinary stories of mothers' searches for children kidnapped out of the United States by their father during a custody battle and brought to a country where mothers have no legal rights to their children. If you are considering an interfaith marriage, it is vital you research these customs thoroughly before making a commitment.

Meeting the Community

How do you, as a stepmom, become visible and respected in a community where families are still measured by the standards of the biological family? Where friends of your husbands's might also be his ex's closest friends? A few tips:

- Remind yourself again, as you participate in social or community activities, that you are your husband's *wife,* not "the second wife," not "the new wife," not "the other Mrs. Smith," not a "stand-in" for your stepchildren's mother. Review with your husband how you'd like to be introduced to people in your community, including a detail of interest to the person you're meeting: "This is my wife, Sara. She was a member of our town's school board/a volunteer with the ambulance corps/involved with our community theater when we lived in Ohio.

- Do not react to anything your mate's ex-wife does in public unless it is physically or mentally dangerous or abusive to your new family. If she wishes to publicize her version of her divorce from your mate, that's up to her. Do not adopt a defensive position of denying or correcting rumors, but simply let people in your community get to know you through one-on-one interactions. The truth will reveal itself.

- Use positive (enlightened!) language about your stepfamily (see chapter 4) with both sets of children to counteract any negative phrases some people might use around them. Casual epithets they might hear—"broken home," "divorced parents," "failed marriage," "split family"—might upset them. You are an interesting, proactive, striving group of people living, learning, and growing together. The children in your home need to hear this frequently.

- Check out the prevailing attitude toward stepfamilies held by the school administration or any other organizations your children and stepchildren participate in—from Sunday School to dancing lessons. Do any of these community leaders imply a bias against stepfamilies by the language they use? If so, consider ways to amend this. (Perhaps you are the first stepfamily they have met and they are unsure how to handle the difference.) If bias continues to prevail, consider finding another class.

- When you're settled in—after your wedding, subsequent move (if there was one), and organization of your household—do some research about your community and its organizations, and consider where you'd like to become involved. Target a world that is undisputably yours, where you will meet people with similar interests, who know and value you in a context other than stepmotherhood. Do you enjoy gardening? Call the local gardening club. Do you love politics? Plug in to your local chapter of the League of Women Voters or chosen party headquarters. If you are among the many stressed-out stepmoms we met, perhaps a local yoga class will help you meet like-minded people and relax at the same time.

Helping Kids Explain Different Surnames

Some stepmoms reported that their kids and stepkids were teased because of the different surnames in their step home. If this happens to yours—preferably *before* it happens—discuss a satisfactory positive response: "Obviously my stepsisters have their dad's last name—just like I have my dad's. We think it's funny, letting people figure out who's related to whom, then we tell them our last names."

Laugh about it, and encourage the kids in your home to treat it as just another interesting feature of stepfamily life. It might be complicated for some people, but they'll get used to it. Once surnames are made clear to those who need to know—schools, churches, and organizations you join—you'll probably have to repeat the explanation only once in a while to the curious.

❧

Questionnaire

1. Does the school your stepchild attends understand step-family dynamics? Is the staff aware of your role? If not, what steps can you take to help them understand?

2. Are there any other stepmoms with stepchildren at school with whom you could compare notes, pick up some tips, or who would join you to correct any negativity in your community toward stepfamilies?

3. Is there a support group for children of divorce, children who lost their mom, kids with stepmoms? If not, would the school be willing to start one? (Would you be willing to help?)

CHAPTER 17

The Stepfamily Checkbook

These days many women view themselves as an equal financial partner with their husband. Without a doubt this is a healthy, clear-eyed attitude and, for proactive stepmothers, essential.

While you don't want to enter your new marriage with a completely mercenary outlook, neither do you want to end up on poverty row through lack of information and planning. If "problems with the children" is the number-one reason remarriages fail, money surely runs a close second.

Every stepmother has different financial priorities and concerns. You might be a rising executive, with savings, a stock portfolio, and a home of your own, concerned with protecting your hard-earned assets. Or you might have been unemployed or sick, forced to deplete any savings you had to keep body and soul together as a single mom, saddled with some serious debts. Your worries might center on paying bills so you can start saving for your child's education.

No matter what your current monetary profile looks like, it is your right and your responsibility to have a working knowledge of the financial situation you are marrying into, preferably before you marry. Without an accurate, fully disclosed economic picture, your stepfamily household budget cannot be realistically administered, nor your financial future together planned. Your comfort zone about who controls what money must be discussed very frankly and in specifics. Perhaps you'll want to make future investments together but keep separate checkbooks. Maybe you'll decide to split the household bills down the middle but manage your own mutual-fund accounts.

If your husband-to-be doesn't bring up the subject, it's essential you do. No doubt it's a sensitive area—stepmoms worry about seeming pushy or embarrassing their mate if he is worried about his strained financial position.

Still others worry about playing into the myth of the "gold-digging" stepmother. But overwhelmingly we found that women preferred to make their own money and sought marriage for love. Not one woman we spoke with had married for money. Of course, two incomes are better than one, but in the cases where a stepmom considered herself "well-off," she either had brought her own money to the marriage or was earning it herself. While undoubtedly there are people out there—men and women—who marry for wealth, overlooking love entirely, gold-digging stepmothers are the exception. Fortune hunters go after the money—not, clearly, the role of stepmother.

If you do feel uncomfortable, raise the topic by pointing out your mutual concern that all the children in your new family have a secure future, with adequate medical coverage, education plans, and appropriate insurance, not to mention a well-functioning household: "Why don't we talk about all of it this weekend, and get it out of the way."

If you're already married, don't put off your research into money matters any longer.

Sticker Shock

Many stepmoms we interviewed experienced some unpleasant emotions—resentment, panic, complete outrage—upon their discovery of unfair, even bizarre, financial and legal predicaments they had married into. Some of these situations had all the earmarks of bankruptcy and ruin, which a woman with her wits about her would normally avoid. Why would an intelligent woman have taken on these inequities? The usual reason—she didn't know they existed. When people are basking in romance and love, they don't like thinking or talking about money, debt, support payments, taxes, insurance, and wills.

You might find, as did several women we spoke with, that your mate has been financially bound and gagged by a brilliant attorney hired at his own expense by his ex-wife—that the mother of your stepchildren has claims on him and his estate long after he dies. Your might realize, only months into your marriage, that your husband is still paying his adult children's rent and living expenses. At tax time the first year you file jointly with your wonderful new mate, you might discover that he has maxed out his credit lines—and owes tens of thousands of dollars—to pay for his kids' college tuition. Any of these scenarios can be a terrible shock. You think: "Why didn't he tell me?" The same reason, more than likely, that you didn't ask.

You must ask. As you conduct your research into your stepfamily's business affairs, however, try not to place blame. You might believe your mate has done some stupid things, but they're done, and you have to accept that under pressure he was not as wise as he could have been. Very few stepmothers will not face some kind of economic horror story. Perhaps you, too, have done some silly things.

The $64,000 question is, what can you do about it now? Maybe you can improve some things, perhaps not all. But what you don't know can hurt you, and being able to fix something is better than doing nothing. Can your husband consolidate his credit-card debt into one lower-cost home-equity loan, or transfer the balance to a lower-interest account? Perhaps the two of you can identify a number of small ways you can be thriftier or plan a better budget. Part of becoming a success story is how you handle your strong feelings about unpleasant checkbook surprises and your willingness to become proactive, together, about what you find.

As you discuss money with your mate, keep in mind that you're coming from different perspectives. While you understand your mate's commitment to his children, for example, you will want to be sure you and your children, too, are provided for, both while they are living in your new stepfamily and after your death.

The Truth and Nothing But

The legal and financial complexities of a stepfamily are impossible to untangle without an atmosphere of total trust between a stepmom and her new or soon-to-be husband. With your mate, try to schedule a quiet weekend, preferably when you can be alone together, to lay on the table all the details of your finances. Both of you should be prepared to divulge these facts:

- Total assets. Include homes, owned vehicles, savings accounts, and other investments, stocks, bonds, T-bills, etc. along with estimated annual income from these; pension/retirement funds, valuable possessions.

- Annual earned income, including bonuses and company profit sharing.

- Total debt, including mortgages, credit cards, bank or other loans.

- Financial commitments, present and future, to previous family, including legal and off-the-record obligations.

- Taxes—those you know of now and expect later.

- Current living expenses, including rent, mortgage, food, clothing, out-of-pocket medical expenses, utilities, telephone, commutation, travel, luxuries, etc.

- The status of wills and all types of insurance (see discussion in chapter 18).

Ask for a copy of your mate's divorce agreement (show him yours, too, if you have one). All of your partner's legal obligations to his children and ex-wife will be there, including the terms of custody and how much and for how long he will be paying alimony/maintenance, child support, college tuition, and living and medical expenses. If there's anything in this document you do not understand, and your mate can't answer your questions to your satisfaction, call his lawyer or yours for clarification.

Besides listing the facts above, tally your anticipated major expenses for the next five, ten, even twenty years: a home together, a new car, children's and stepchildren's college expenses, wedding expenses, care for elderly parents. Discuss your financial goals, and set a time frame for each. Your husband might be tied up now with outstanding bills, supporting two families, but what is his future potential? How long will you, as a couple, be in debt to his first family?

Take a look, too, at any anticipated income—perhaps you have a T-bill coming due in the nick of time to pay for college tuition or some other expense you planned for.

Most stepmoms we spoke with did not bring huge bills to their marriage. But since he's showing you his, it's only fair that you reveal yours. Together you'll need to integrate all these expenses, yours and his, into a brand-new stepfamily budget. Consider getting professional advice if this task seems overwhelming.

Alimony (Maintenance) and Child Support

It is logical and probably unavoidable that a man, even one making a high salary, will not have a great deal of money left after a divorce. If his children are minors, upon his remarriage, more often than not, the lion's share of your mate's income will continue to go to his first family.

While there's no question that children deserve to be well taken care of by parents, many stepmothers strongly resent that a great part of their monthly budget goes to their spouse's past life, especially if they are working and contributing, directly or indirectly, part of their own paychecks to these payments.

Darlene, who took over the bills of her new family when

they started receiving collection notices, complained, "I get a knot in my stomach at bill-paying time. I write the check to his ex-wife first, almost with my eyes closed. It's a huge part of our combined household income and will continue for another fourteen years. I know that she needs it and that the kids must be provided for, but it makes me ill to think of what we could do with that money ourselves. And the final straw is sticking a stamp on the envelope!"

Reva, a stay-at-home mother of two boys and part-time stepmother to her husband's three teen daughters, was making dinner one evening for all seven of them when Rob's ex-wife called, furious. Apparently her support check had not arrived. Reva, who naively assumed that her husband could put off payments, since he was laid off from work, explained that the check would be a couple of weeks late. Rob's ex-wife threatened legal action, and the next day Reva had to withdraw money from her sons' college fund to cover the debt.

Once alimony and child-support payments have been made, you and your mate have no control over them whatsoever. His ex-wife can spend the whole amount any way she sees fit. Dads often worry that child-support money is not being spent on the children. However, the fact that stepchildren arrive at your door in old, torn clothes does not constitute neglect but might be part of a strategy to imply that the payments are insufficient. If you and your husband suspect neglect, get advice from your attorney about how to handle this.

Veteran stepmoms have suggested that you consider as your household disposable income the final dollar amount remaining not only after tax deductions but after payments have been made to your husband's previous family. That way, although you know a great deal of money is leaving your household, you won't dwell on it each month. Your mate might be left with very little after these deductions, but that's what *belongs* to both of you. Focus on what you still have rather than what's going out the door.

Your Money Heritage: Emotional and Practical Points

If you are a working woman who has built a career, complete with savings, investments, and a pension fund, consider very carefully how you wish to administer these when you marry. With his existing family, your fiancé might have trouble making ends meet and might not have assets himself. How do you feel about this lopsided financial position? Will you decide to pool your resources or operate independently?

Stepmoms who had more money than their husband generally wanted to be generous to their spouse and stepchildren but during courtship worried, "Is it the money that's the attraction?" and sometimes opted for a prenuptial agreement (discussed in chapter 18). Prenup or not, a wealthier stepmom will have to consider how this financial imbalance will affect the step household. If your family's century-old trust fund will pay the future college expenses of your sons, how will your husband and his daughter feel when it's her turn and there are scant funds for her education in your combined household budget?

Inequities like this should be discussed as early as possible, while there is time to look for other sources of money, to set up a college savings plan, and to research scholarships or other alternatives. Don't leave the matter unaddressed and allow a full-blown crisis to develop when your stepdaughter is a senior in high school.

Consider your mate's attitude toward your money—both what you bring to your marriage and what you earn during it. What he considers his, he might easily consider is his kids' too. If you have children of your own, you might be uncomfortable with this—a good reason to consult an attorney about a prenuptial agreement.

Our advice is that you do not rush to rescue a financially strapped husband-to-be. Your money is too hard-earned to be sacrificed for what you consider a less-than-compelling reason, particularly one that involves an ex-wife. One unusual stepmom, Lorraine, admitted she gave her husband her nest egg to pay off bills left over from his divorce, including money due on his ex-wife's credit cards, for which he was also respon-sible. "It was worth it to me," she insisted. "He still makes hefty maintenance and child-support payments but can handle these himself. I bought peace with my money—I don't have to get phone calls from his ex-wife about old debts anymore."

Not many stepmoms would either be willing or have the resources to do this. Some said they would lose respect for their mate if he found it easy to accept money from them. Based on the experience of other stepmoms, we suggest that, at least in the early days, you keep your name planted firmly on your assets until you've learned more about your mate's philosophy toward money and his spending habits.

Generally, if you bring your own money to your mar-riage, you might be more likely to escape the resentment stepchildren tend to have about inheritance issues when their dad remarries. Eileen Simpson, in her book *Late Love: a Celebration of Marriage after Fifty* (Houghton Mifflin, 1994), states, "I think it is safe to say that it is easier for adult children to accept a rich stepparent than a poor one." She commences her chapter on money with, "If it is not the first question many adult children ask themselves when they learn of a parent's marriage plans, the second is, 'Will the inheritance we took for granted, money that is rightfully ours, be left instead to the new spouse?'" (See section on preexisting assets, on page 344.)

If you have always earned your own money, you might also need to consult your tax advisor to review the effect of your marriage on your tax position, which is shortly to become a joint tax position. Are there steps you can take to lessen your tax burden? If you sell your home to buy a home together to accommodate your kids and his, you might be caught in a down market at the time you marry. If you're not willing or able to ride it out, living apart until you can afford to live together, it's possible you won't get as much for your home as you paid, which means you might have to find some money to pay off your remaining mortgage.

When Your Husband Has More Money Than You

Similarly, if you are marrying a man who is wealthier than you, you'll need to find out if he is willing to share it once you're married, or if you and your children will continue to live according to your own means. We found both instances operating in stepfamilies, as well as stepmoms who felt their wealthier husband's money should play as low-key a role as possible in their children's lives.

When Siobhan married into a wealthy family, bringing a daughter, aged twelve, and a son, aged seven, she and her ex-husband, Randy, were managing a harmonious, though financially stretched, joint-custody arrangement following their divorce. Siobhan did not want her children overly influenced by her husband Brian's money. "Randy and I both thrived with very little money growing up," she explained. "We expect our kids to get a scholarship or work their way through college, as we did—I won't have Brian paying for them." This stepmom felt her stepsons were spoiled by money and wanted her own children to develop a strong sense of independence.

Kawana's perspective was much different. When this working mother of three boys became engaged to Enrique, an independently wealthy father of three sons only slightly older than hers, she felt it would be impossible for her poor boys to live with his rich boys in harmony. "Before we married, I insisted Enrique provide equivalent education funds for my sons, too, which he did, quite happily."

If your mate's family is accustomed to giving expensive presents to their grandchildren—a car at graduation time or globe-trotting trips and does not wish to extend this generosity to their stepgrandchildren, you'll have to accept this. Some stepmoms have demanded equality for all the kids in her home, which does not seem reasonable to us—grandparents should be able to give whatever they want to their own flesh and blood. Wise stepmoms need to have a long talk with their kids about disparity under circumstances like this, explaining that while extravagant gift giving is the custom in the family they married into, it cannot be extended to them. It doesn't mean they are loved any less, just that one family has more money than another.

Preexisting Assets: Reasons to Keep Them in Your Name

Some couples decide to keep a stepmom's assets in her own name, fully protected from an ex-wife. You might also wish to consider ways to keep any future assets you and your mate accrue together out of the reach of his previous family—such as putting them in your name only. (Get professional advice about doing this; even if you shrink at the thought of incurring yet another bill, the cost in the long run will be worthwhile.) Your husband's ex-wife had her day of reckoning when the two of them were divorced; it is not reasonable that she can now have claims on money or assets accrued during *your* marriage, over and above the ongoing payments detailed in the divorce settlement.

Our strongest advice to both you and your husband is that any assets you acquired before your marriage to each other remain yours, an arrangement employed by many successful stepfamilies. Keeping your preexisting assets in your own names has several mutual advantages:

- It's an equitable arrangement for everyone. Money accrued while your stepchildren's mother and father were together stays with their dad (or was already split at the time their parents divorced). Any remaining with their dad can be left to whomever he wishes. See our discussion on wills in chapter 18.

- It entirely eliminates the suspicion that either one of you married for money.

- Your preexisting assets provide you with the security of an emergency exit option if life as a stepmother doesn't work out. Even a small nest egg in your name can make you feel secure, just knowing it's there, and gives you options, which are sometimes in short supply for a stepmom. Interestingly, stepmoms who had the means of leaving usually didn't want to, while stepmoms who felt trapped (those who did not have some money to fall back on) were among the ones who wanted to bail out.

Your Name on Financial Documents: Official Savvy

Aiming for as much financial independence as possible within the working arrangements you make with your partner will give you a sense of security, especially in the early stages of stepfamily life. To this end, maintain your own credit record, as well as your legal name. If your credit cards as a single woman say "Mary Bloggs," upon your marriage keep your maiden name and add your married name: Mary Bloggs Jamieson.

You can change all your official documents this way, including social security records, bank records, passport, driving license, etc. If in doubt, talk to your attorney. Don't use your husband's credit card with your name included only as "Mr. and Mrs. Frederick Jamieson." You cannot risk becoming a financial nonperson. It will take too long to reestablish yourself financially if necessity demands it. If you and your husband want to use a joint credit card, specify Mary and Frederick Jamieson.

The Stepfamily's Daily Budget

If you decide to work with our suggested system for preexisting assets, then money made or received after your wedding day becomes "our" money, and your partnership will govern what you do with this income.

If you were married before, perhaps you and your previous spouse were both high earners, had no kids to worry about, and spent the majority of your time building careers. Now perhaps you are considering marriage, or are already married, to a guy not earning as much who's providing for a previous family. This will take some getting used to. Or the reverse might be true. It might be a happy surprise to realize that, even with his support payments, your new mate is left with a comfortable income.

For your initial business meeting together, you and your mate both calculated what you spent either on a monthly or annual basis, before you got together. Comparing these numbers to your income should give you an idea on entering marriage of whether you need to cut back or loosen up a little. If you're fortunate, what you'll learn from this exercise is that both of you are capable of living within your means.

Once you have decided where you are going to live when you marry or live together, estimate the new costs involved. Expenses will shift. Maybe you'll save a little on rent by moving in together, but your combined food bill might be a lot more. Maybe you'll save on taxes by filing jointly, but four kids in one house might mean a much higher electric bill than you're used to. You won't know exact dollar amounts until you have been living together for a year or so, but starting out with a good estimation is a wise, healthy strategy. If you have a home computer, you might want to check out some of the software programs available to help you plan a budget—they're easy, and even fun, to use.

The Three-Checking-Accounts System: Yours, His, Ours

Many successful step households found it worked well to have three separate checking accounts. Find out if there's a bank in your area that will give you free checking with no minimum balance (sometimes hard to find).

1. A Joint Account or House Account.
From this account all your household bills and expenses that you and your husband decide to share are paid. If you work, both of you can transfer, monthly or biweekly, an agreed-upon

percentage of your salaries to this account. If your husband is the only breadwinner, and you're a stay-at-home mom/step-mom not receiving outside income, he will be paying the total amount.

If you don't work but receive child-support payments from your ex, you'll need to decide if these funds will be deposited in this account. Several stepmoms reported squabbles with their mate over this—husbands felt child-support should go toward household expenses, since his stepkids were part of the household; some stepmoms felt it should go into her personal account to be used specifically for her own children's clothes, hobby, and sport items. Arguments aside, just remember that enough money needs to be in this account to pay *all* your household bills.

Either one of you can take care of writing checks from your house account to pay the household bills, or you can sit down and pay the bills together each month, using this task as an opportunity to discuss any necessary cutting back. (Another advantage to this method is that you'll both be aware of your bank balance. If two heads are indeed better than one, with luck you'll find a surplus growing.)

2. Your Account

These are your personal, private funds. If you work, your salary goes here, along with any income you receive from investments, with your agreed-upon contribution to the house account paid from here. If you've opted to be a stay-at-home mom/stepmom, you need to negotiate some funds, however small, that go into your account on a regular basis—money that belongs only to you. We were very concerned to hear, in one or two of our interviews, about stepmoms who had to ask their husband for money for a haircut or to have lunch with a girlfriend. That is humiliating, and it is an unacceptable position to allow yourself to get into.

Linda, mother of two, full-time stepmom to her husband Matt's four children, was constantly worried about money Though she herself held two jobs, Matt's job security in the construction business was always in question. During three years of marriage, Linda kept no money of her own and gave up all luxuries and even a few basic necessities, like panty hose. Instead, to save money, she wore pants she had owned for years.

One day Linda and Matt shouted for hours, dredging up all the major and minor resentments they had long kept to themselves, including Linda's sacrifice of stockings. After this blowup, their differences were irreconcilable. Whether they would have muddled through without the panty hose crisis, we can't know, but nobody can be expected to work as Linda worked without allowing herself something as basic as stockings.

If there is very little in your joint budget for you to have more than a few dollars of discretionary money, perhaps you can find a way to make some more. Even if you have decided to stay home to take care of the kids, there may be paying work you can do from home. You'll need to discuss with your husband what percentage of this income goes to the house account. Perhaps you can supply the local bakery with your homemade apple pies or care for a neighbor's child, along with your own. There are many stories of women who set up "kitchen table" businesses—use your imagination and your skills and become an entrepreneur. (Ask your local librarian for help in finding information on community or women's business groups and small-business seminars.)

3. His Account

Same as yours. His salary goes here, and he pays alimony and child support and his agreed-upon contribution to the house account from this account. This is also his discretionary fund—if he wants to send a hundred dollars every now and then to a son in college, or buy a new fishing rod, that's his business.

Paying the Fare: What's Fair?

When you have been living together for more than a year, you'll be able to anticipate with greater accuracy the costs of running your household. But deciding how to apportion what percentage of your salary each of you contributes if you both work might take some negotiation. Tinker with ideas, making adjustments here and there, until you arrive at an amicable position. Stepmoms reported that complaints—"Your daughter is on the phone half the night"; "Your son never stops eating— as soon as I put groceries away, they're gone"; "You're always leaving the lights on, but I'm the one who pays the bill"— died down as time passed. In the long run, with give-and-take, and a willingness to succeed, the three-account system usually works out better than any other. Who gets what evens out eventually.

What is not acceptable, however, is for you to find that your mate has been sending his son a regular hundred dollars each month from your joint account, unless you have agreed on this together. The issue is not the money, which might be well within your means, but the fact that you were not consulted. You might feel that with all the support he is already paying, this extra is overkill, since now your household must spend that much less in order to accommodate it. On the other hand, you might reason that the hundred dollars is only for a short time and is fine by you. It's essential you have the option to express an opinion on joint money. Similarly, if your daughter needs a new winter coat, and you want to pay for it out of the household account, it's only reasonable to consult your husband first.

You will probably still find financial issues to disagree about, but the important thing is to discuss them and resolve them as soon as they crop up. Try to remember that a warm, loving home, even with just a small chicken in the pot, is infinitely preferable to living in a cold, hostile environment with more money than you know what to do with. You might also find that as time passes and as you move through the stages of stepfamily development described in chapter 5, you will start to think in terms of "we" and "our," rather than "I" and "my."

The fact is, few stepfamilies have enough money to meet

everyone's needs until the children have grown up and left the nest.

Off-the-Record Promises

You feel confident—you and your husband have discussed all your combined financial IOUs and bank documents, down to the very last T-bill. Great, but you're not done. Now it's time to discuss all those off-the-record promises your husband might have made to his children years before he met you. We heard about a multitude of odd arrangements and deals between fathers and children that weren't written down, or even legally binding, but nonetheless not forgotten. You need to know what these are.

Your husband's promises to his children, both formal (legal) and informal, will directly affect both your lifestyle and what you will be able to provide for your own children. How will you feel when you have to help your husband pay for a promised graduate school education for a twenty-six-year-old stepdaughter (who refuses to get a summer job to help out) when your six-year-old needs braces, which you now realize you won't be able to afford? Imagine having to contribute to a long-promised European trip for your stepson when he turns twenty-one that means, ultimately, that your ten-year-old can't join his friends at summer camp.

In his efforts to "get away" from an angry and bitter soon-to-be ex-wife, your mate might have made promises he hardly remembers. Men have been known to walk away from a marriage with almost nothing simply because they became tired of hysterical scenes or pitiful recriminations. Did your mate promise to send his ex back to school during a late-night, depressing phone call when he just wanted to end the conversation? "Look—after the divorce, I'll pay for you to get your master's, then you'll be able to get a better-paying job." He probably didn't think at the time that this would include not only tuition but books, babysitters, meals out before class, and many other etceteras that she might now be enjoying at your expense.

One dad, newly divorced and guilt-ridden over the pain his children were feeling, promised all three of them a new car on their sixteenth birthday, complete with a gas credit card. Six years later, this dad and his new wife, Sophia, receive monthly bills for "astronomical" amounts of fuel, according to their stepmom, who is driving an eight-year-old used car.

Sophia bitterly regrets not having asked more questions. "I knew about the alimony and child-support payments—I couldn't imagine there'd be anything else." In order to assess your future, you need dollar amounts on these promises, written down. It's possible that some of these off-the-record deals can be renegotiated. Sophia and her husband might have offered "previously owned" cars to the kids on the condition that they get part-time jobs to pay for their own gas.

Past Life Finances: Tying Up Loose Ends

A man whose previous wife is deceased might still be paying off medical bills if a long illness was involved. Obviously, this is a very sad burden for your husband, but it is not reasonable for him to expect you to take on part of this burden unwittingly. If medical bills are outstanding, you must know about them and factor them into your budget.

Legal bills from your mate's divorce might also still exist. Many husbands are required to pay an ex-wife's legal costs, which, in addition to his own, can amount to several thousand dollars, especially if the divorce was adversarial. While your mate might think it well worth the money to be out of a bad marriage, you need to know how much you're talking about and for how long.

Also, make sure that you tie up any financial loose ends concerning what your ex or your husband's ex has access to. Your husband's divorce attorney should be able to advise you on this. Susan, a new stepmom, told of her husband Will's ex-wife presenting him with $25,000 in credit-card bills. Will, furious at himself for not having anticipated this and canceling the cards, unfortunately was responsible for paying them off. Recalled Susan: "We went into shock—this happened right after our honeymoon. She said spending money had 'made her feel better' during the divorce proceedings."

Will's five adult children, disgusted by their mom's irresponsibility, ended up paying her bills, because Susan and Will couldn't—the only alternative was bankruptcy. "Will still had legal bills to pay. And I certainly wasn't going to help subsidize her spending spree," Susan said.

What You Lose When Your Remarry

Don't forget to take into account what you will be giving up, financially and materially, when you remarry, particularly if you were divorced. Does your alimony or maintenance payment cease at remarriage? What about child support? If you are not working, in order to raise your children, you might suddenly find yourself with only your child-support income from your ex-husband and facing the prospect of having to rely on your new husband. Is he willing? Is he able? If dependence is unacceptable to you, will you be able to work at least part-time? What else did you receive under your divorce settlement? Was it conditional on your remaining single? Those little words "in the case of remarriage" will suddenly become very important, because this is *it*. Be sure you review everything.

Pension Plans, Life Insurance: Financial Security for the Future

If you work and have a pension plan, check to see if your marriage will affect it. Some plans provide for a spouse in the event of your death, with varying distributions. If you don't fully understand how this works, perhaps together you and your mate need to consult a representative from your company's personnel department.

Review with your mate the terms of his pension plan. His ex-wife might be the beneficiary under the terms of the divorce, which you might find acceptable if you have a plan of your own, but if you don't, what other arrangements can be made? You might need to start a personal retirement plan. Social security is looking dubious, and it's become very difficult to survive solely on this anyway.

Like your mate's pension plan, his life insurance might be part of his divorce settlement, with his ex-wife and/or children listed as his beneficiaries. This means that he will still have to pay the premiums or that his company will, and as these costs are high, it might not be possible to afford insurance for you.

If you have children and need to take care of their future in the event of your death, and their dad is still around, perhaps the two of you can work something out for your kids. If he can't or won't help, you might want to consider getting a policy yourself and naming your children as beneficiaries. Get some first-rate professional advice about doing this.

Teaching Kids about Money

Even in the most frugal, well-planned step homes, money is often tight. Most kids will absorb their money sense, and their attitude toward this necessary evil, according to how you handle finances in your home.

Some thoughts on the difference between "needs" and "wants" might help you handle perceived financial inequalities between your biological and stepchildren. Because one child requires four thousand dollars' worth of dental braces doesn't mean you have to spend the same amount of money on each child to show you don't have favorites. Another child may want a brand-new four-hundred-dollar bike, which you decide against. Orthodontics is a need; an expensive bike is a want.

While you and your husband will naturally try to meet everyone's needs, the children in your home should have an idea of your financial priorities and understand that if there's any money to spare, wants come second. As your children become older, introduce them to the family budget. You don't have to give them complete details, but they should know what utilities cost, why they should not waste food—the basics of home economics.

You might wish to encourage your children and stepchildren to earn money of their own at an appropriate age. Believing it is each child's responsibility to pitch in, we discourage paying children to fulfill chores around their own home, but there is no reason your stepson can't be paid for mowing lawns or clearing snow for other people, baby-sitting, or other neighborhood jobs. If you can afford it, you and your mate might feel it's appropriate, to match any money your kids make themselves when they wish to save up for something important to them, such as a new bike, or a car for college.

Children can be introduced quite early to the concept of saving money—even children as young as six or seven can be thrilled to discover that their money "grows" in a no-minimum money-market account. Teenagers, too, often have an entrepreneurial spirit, once they get a driver's license and want a car of their own. Kids can be very competent handling money when they understand the rewards.

To help them make their money go further, introduce them to the many "almost new" stores that are springing up. Almost-new roller blades will cost a fraction of what brand-new ones cost. The same applies to most sports equipment. You'll find that teens typically love to prowl around in thrift shops and secondhand clothing stores.

༄

Questionnaire

The following questions will help you identify areas in your financial life that might need attention, including how satisfied you are about money matters, whether or not you feel secure, and whether you have any concerns. You'll find this exercise helpful at any stage in your stepfamily life—try repeating it once a year or so and noting the progress your family is making.

1. Do you know what it costs per year to achieve and maintain the lifestyle you need/would like? If you were to marry into the stepfamily you are considering, would this amount be available? Or will you have to "pass" on some aspects?

2. Do you and your husband share a similar financial management style? Is one of you "easy come, easy go," with no idea of whether you're living within your means, while the other accounts for every penny? If there is a difference in style, does it cause conflict?

3. Is there any possibility that the two of you could be brought to a closer financial working style by consulting a financial advisor or delegating specific business responsibilities?

4. Have you worked out a family budget together?

5. Have you discussed or decided on short- and long-term family financial goals? What are they?

6. Do you have a joint bank account?

7. Does each of you have an individual bank account?

8. Who handles bill paying in your household?

9. Is your partner paying maintenance and/or child support? What are these expenses per year? Describe your feelings about these costs.

10. Are you working now? Do you have money of your own to do what you wish with? If you want a new sweater, dental checkup, or a birthday gift for your mother, does this cause a problem?

11. How are the household expenses divided? Are you satisfied with these arrangements?

12. Do you have an equal voice with your husband concerning the day-to-day spending habits of your family?

13. Is your family of origin wealthier than your husband's, or vice versa? If so, is this troublesome in any way? Describe.

14. Do you and your husband argue about money? What are the major issues? What can you do to ease or resolve them?

15. Are all family members having their current financial needs met? If not, describe the reasons.

16. If you are on a very limited budget, do all family members share reasonably well in the amount available?

❧
Action Box

❧ Have some smart retorts ready for people who assume you're a gold-digger. They don't even have to be true; anyone rude enough to make these implications deserves to be told untruths. For example:

"If only that were true. But with our bank balance I'm lucky to get lunch."

"Yes, I'm just loving it. We were in Tahiti last week. Bangkok will be next. And we've decided on Jamaica for Christmas."

"Bring a flashlight around one night. We keep the gold in the basement—the same place I've chained my stepkids. I'll give you a tour."

Do what it takes to satisfy yourself on as many financial fronts as possible. Better to spend money now, while you have the opportunity to correct anything that needs it, than to suffer more-expensive consequences later. Consult a tax professional, an attorney, a financial advisor—all three, if necessary. Your personal financial, tax, and legal positions will change when you live with or marry your lover. It's up to you to find out how.

CHAPTER 18

The Stepmom's Legal File

Your legal concerns as a stepmother will be specific to your circumstances and will vary depending on the state you live in. We've offered a legal checklist of ten points to make your research easier, but understand that this is a general overview only. It's important that you evaluate with your own attorney your legal position in your state.

1. Stepmom's Legal Rights
Discuss with an attorney the legal rights, if any, you have as a full- or part-time stepmom in your specific situation.

You may be shocked to realize you have few, if any, legal rights as a stepmother since the relationship between stepmom and stepchild is considered a social rather than a legal one. In some states stepmothers are unable to automatically pick up a child from school or from an airport, without prior written arrangements being made. Nor will you be able to provide consent for medical attention in the absence of a biological parent.

Once you get an idea how you plan to play your role as stepmom, check with your attorney and other appropriate authorities, such as the school, to determine what they require. If you move to another state during your marriage, check again; your new state could have different provisions.

2. "Alienation of Affection"
Consult an attorney regarding the status of this law in your state and the possible ramifications for you and your husband.

Be aware of activity taking place under the old "alienation of affection" law, still on the books in 12 states. This law allows an ex-wife to sue a current wife (who might be step-mom to her kids) for "stealing" her husband away. In one particular case, heard in North Carolina, an ex-wife was awarded $1 million, which, according to press reports of her reaction, was of less importance than receiving "vindication" that her anger toward her ex-husband and his new wife was justified.

It is too early to know if this practice will proliferate, but if it does, it could be yet another situation in which a stepmom needs to be cautious. The courts and our society have a tendency to view an ex-wife who has been divorced by her husband, particularly if they have children, as a victim. When you talk to your attorney about a stepmom's rights, ask about this law in your state.

3. Prenuptial Agreements
Whether you plan to marry or live together, consider the benefits of a prenup as soon as you commit to each other.

"Prenups" waft in and out of fashion, increasing in popularity when a celebrity pair splits up and news of their prenuptial arrangement hits the headlines.

Some stepmoms we spoke with refused to consider the idea of a prenuptial agreement, believing it tainted the spirit of the marriage or of the family atmosphere they hoped to establish. "We looked at the possibility of a prenup but felt that discussing how we'd divvy up everything in the event of a divorce made a mockery of our wedding plans," Cicely, now married eight years, recalled.

If either you or your new husband has substantial assets, however, it might be advisable to consider a prenuptial agreement. If you plan to live together, rather than marry, you can enter into a "cohabitation" agreement, detailing financial arrangements (who pays for what) and how possessions will be handled in the event of a split.

Generally, a prenuptial agreement lays out how property and assets will be divided—particularly those brought to the marriage—if a couple divorces or if one spouse dies. Almost anything can be included—who is responsible for supporting the children, who gets the family pet, who gets the time-share in St. Thomas—in addition to the disposition of bank accounts, stocks and shares, and real estate. Prenuptial agreements are enacted at the state level, with the ability to enforce them varying from state to state.

Sometimes people who have been financially hurt by a previous divorce rush to execute a prenuptial agreement so they don't get "cleaned out" a second time. Having one might make you more comfortable if you wish to protect assets for your children, but some attorneys believe only significant assets make a prenup worthwhile. Discuss the details, including your state's laws, with an attorney specializing in these agreements.

One great advantage to be gained from considering a prenuptial agreement, perhaps the greatest advantage, is that the process encourages a couple to fully discuss their financial position and priorities early on, even if they ultimately decide against signing one. You cannot know too much about the financial pluses and minuses of your new family.

4. Renegotiation of Custody or Financial Arrangements for Stepchildren

Check the possibility of a reassessment of your mate's child-support payments to his ex-wife, based on his increased household income following your marriage. An attorney can advise whether this is likely and/or suggest some steps to prevent it.

At the time you and your mate marry, either he or his ex-wife, or both, might think there is reason to renegotiate existing custody and/or financial arrangements.

Once he has remarried and has a stable home environment with you, your mate might, if his ex-wife currently has custody of his kids, wish to petition to share custody with her. If you agree to this, unless an informal, cooperative arrangement is in place, it would mean going back to court and going through the legal process again. Odds are his ex-wife would resist, and some expensive and unpleasant times could ensue.

In addition, there's always the chance that an ex might request an increase in child-support payments now that the father of her children has a working wife and a larger household income. Some courts might go along with this, seeing no further than the fact that Dad's expenses have been reduced due to the contribution of his new wife, making more of his income available for his previous family.

If you have children yourself or are considering bearing or adopting a child (and even if not), you may resent your income being assessed to help support his former family. Be prepared for this possibility by talking to your attorney. Review your position and determine if there's any way to prevent this from happening.

5. Power of Attorney
Consider the advantages and disadvantages of giving each other this authority. These can be simple or complex, depending on your situation.

A power of attorney, governed by state law, appoints another person to act on your behalf as attorney-in-fact on certain chosen issues, including business and financial matters or medical decisions. Extending this authority to each other will enable each of you to act on the other's behalf if one of you is absent or becomes incapacitated.

Note: You might not be comfortable granting your husband the power to make *every* important decision for you until you know he's capable of handling the matters you are considering giving him authority over. You need to be confident that he can and will serve your interests and those of your children, if you have any. Likewise, he needs to feel secure in these respects before granting power to you. It is possible to grant each other authority in some situations but not others.

Talk to your lawyer about the advisability of revoking a

previous power of attorney if you or your mate still has one in effect that was enacted during a previous marriage.

6. Stepfamily Adoptions
These require consultation with legal professionals who know your state's current adoption requirements. A counselor experienced with step adoptions can probably offer good advice about coping with the emotional issues you may face and help a child and his stepfamily through this difficult process.

In chapter 9, we raised the issue of adopting a baby of your own who is not a stepchild. In some stepfamilies the opportunity to adopt stepchildren might present itself. You might wish to look into this possibility if (a) you marry a widower and become a full-time stepmother to his young children, (b) your mate and his ex have divorced and she subsequently dies, or (c) your mate and his ex either co-parent or share custody and she becomes incapacitated, either mentally or physically, or it is proven she is neglectful or abusive to her children.

In the last circumstance, at your mate's request, he might (depending on your state's law) be granted full custody, paving the way for you to adopt. Your mate could consider adopting your children, if you wish, under similar circumstances.

It's important to note that when the biological parent is alive, unless they are incapacitated and unable to do so, they need to grant permission for their child to be adopted by a stepparent. This can be difficult to obtain, for instance, if you are an abandoned mother who cannot locate the father of her children. Should your husband want to adopt your children as his own, you will need first-rate legal advice to proceed.

Adoptions of stepchildren by stepfathers are quite prevalent in the United States. Current estimates suggest that only about half of divorces where children are involved include a child support award, but if you are a mother who has been awarded such payments, and receive them sporadically or not at all, the father of your children might be happy to formally (and legally) end his responsibility and approve his kids' adoption by your new husband. This doesn't necessarily mean he will want to end his personal relationship with his kids—a factor you will all need to discuss in depth before going ahead.

A stepmother adopting her stepchildren is less common, since more often than not the children's biological mother is reluctant to grant permission. In cases when a mother has abandoned her family and her permission cannot be obtained, legal advice is essential.

Adoption is not an easy transition for children. If they are old enough to understand and be part of the decision, include them and take their thoughts and feelings into account.

Advantages to adoption within a stepfamily:

- All members of the household have one last name. Children sometimes feel embarrassed at school or socially, having to explain the reasons for different names within their family. (In most states members of a stepfamily can use the same name without the necessity of formal adoption, if they wish.)

- A permanent, legal relationship is forged. Often this provides emotional security and eliminates doubts about a stepmom's or a stepdad's commitment to them. A child becomes "ours," just like any other child born of your union. However, if the relationship between stepparent and stepchild was not good before adoption, adoption is unlikely to improve it.

- Anxiety about permanence is eliminated for both the stepchild and the stepparent. Even if this marriage doesn't work out, both spouses still have legal rights and responsibilities to any child they adopt. This usually does not apply when the child remains a stepchild.

Disadvantages:

- Severing ties to a parent who has given up his or her rights to function as their parent can have a negative emotional effect on a child. For many children, the realization that their other biological parent "gave them away" can be devastating.

- If the father of your children gives up his legal rights to them, granting permission for your new mate to adopt them, you will lose any child-support payments you are receiving, which can tip the scales negatively for your stephousehold finances. This can be of particular concern if your new mate is paying both alimony to his ex-wife and child support for his children.

- Although willing to give permission for their children to be adopted at the time, biological parents have a tendency to reappear later in their child's life in an attempt either to reclaim him or to rekindle the relationship, which they regret severing. Some may simply be curious, wanting to know "how the kid turned out," with no serious intentions at all. But bear the possibility in mind before making the decision to adopt your stepchildren or allowing your mate to adopt your children.

Another word of caution: Throughout *The Enlightened Stepmother* we have stressed that you cannot look upon yourself as your stepchildren's mother, barring three exceptions—when you marry a widower with a tiny baby who has never known his mother and for whom you will provide all the mothering duties, when your stepchild's mom dies after divorce from your husband, or when you have a stepchild of any age, whose mother is either dead or alive, who chooses to look upon you as his mom.

In each circumstance, if adoption has taken place, you will need to discuss with your child, as he matures, the facts surrounding his adoption.

A child not formally adopted by you who considers you his mother simply might not have a good relationship with his biological mother and considers you his mother in spirit, if not in flesh. As with any adoptive mother, however, you face the possibility that the child will wish to seek out his biological mother or that an absent biological mother, now recovered from her problems, might seek him out.

Examine your feelings very carefully before you either adopt or react to the child's wishing you to be his mom. Prior to making a decision, you might wish to talk it over with a professional experienced in the nuances of adoption.

7. Legal and Financial Provisions for Minor Stepchildren

Working with an attorney or a financial advisor, make certain you fully understand your mate's obligations (governed by state law) toward his children in the event that he dies or is disabled before they become self-sufficient. Be sure he has made or is willing to make provisions for his children, your stepchildren, if these circumstances should occur.

Where appropriate, provisions could include either life insurance or some sort of trust fund or other vehicle that, regardless of the beneficiary, will cover his kids until adulthood for costs such as college, weddings, and particularly the care of a handicapped child. Your husband should also make some provision, perhaps disability insurance, in case he becomes injured on the job, has an accident, or for some other reason is unable to make money to support his children. Additionally, make sure your stepchildren have medical insurance now and in the event of their father's death. (If his ex-wife is working, find out if they are covered by her policy.)

Learn what your responsibilities, if any, would be toward your stepchildren if your mate should die or becomes disabled. Would you be responsible for their support if he was a widower or an abandoned dad?

Unless you choose to, you cannot be expected to financially support your stepchildren if your husband should die before you, especially if you have kids of your own to take care of. If his ex-wife is listed as a beneficiary on his insurance policy, his will needs to state loud and clear that the money is intended to cover care of their children. If his ex-wife mismanages or decides to spend the money on herself instead her kids, that is her responsibility.

Ruth, mother of one teenage son, married Vincent, father of a teenaged daughter. "Due to our previous marriages, we were financially strapped from day one," Ruth said, "but I was particularly worried about the future, as Vincent is twenty years my senior. Statistically, I knew there was a good chance he would die before me, yet Vincent resisted taking out life insurance. We discussed what would happen to his daughter if he died before she became self-sufficient, and I assured him it would mean she wouldn't have a college education or much of a wedding, because I wasn't willing to spend what little I had on her—I had my own son to consider. When I told him I planned to sit the girl down and explain that her dad hadn't provided for her future, it scared him, and he took out a policy."

8. Wills
Both you and your husband need to make one. Divorce and/or remarriage probably invalidates all or part of any will you already have.

Roxanne was only twenty-five when she was swept off her feet by Dave, forty-four. Six weeks after they met, they married, much to the concern of Roxanne's family, who knew little about Dave except that he had two teenage sons who lived full-time with his ex-wife.

Within three years, Roxanne gave birth to twin boys of her own—her joy was boundless. Then, at the age of fifty, Dave was diagnosed with a swift-spreading form of cancer. In little less than a year, Roxanne was a widow.

Devastated by her husband's death, Roxanne had yet another blow to absorb. Dave's will revealed that no provision had been made for his second family. His former wife and two oldest sons were designated as beneficiaries of his considerable life insurance. His will allocated all his assets to them. Fortunately, Roxanne's parents were able to lend her money so she could return to school and support her children. She is now an attorney, specializing in family law, and recognizes that she probably could have contested Dave's will, since most states require that a father provide in his will for the care of minor children.

Unlike Roxanne, many stepmoms might have to cope with financial and legal matters alone if their husband should die suddenly. It's essential, particularly if you are older and have older children and stepchildren, that you make formal, binding preparations while you and your mate are in good physical and mental shape. Writing a will is an important task which needs to be handled early in your marriage due to the financial complexities of stepfamily life. (If you subsequently change your mind about something, you can make amendments.)

A will lays out exactly how you wish to dispose of your financial assets and physical possessions when you die and can provide any special instructions you wish about even relatively minor, but to you important, matters.

You have the right to prepare your will without your husband knowing its contents, and vice versa, in which case you will need separate attorneys. Some couples do this, but it might make more sense to coordinate your efforts to take maximum advantage of our current (often changing) tax and inheritance laws. Talk to your attorney. Writing wills can be incredibly sensitive—quite a few stepmoms claimed they were "on the verge of divorce" from their husband over who would get what, should one of them die.

Marital disagreements about wills frequently hinge on perceived inequities. Your priority might be to ensure that you and your kids have enough to live on if your husband should die. His might be that all his children—those with his ex-wife and those with you—are taken care of in a way he considers fair. You might feel he has forgotten you in his efforts to consider the kids.

Many a stepmom asked, "Why should I leave my stepkids anything. They didn't like me when I was alive. Why would I want them to have my money when I die?" Your mate might feel that if he leaves money to you and your kids, you should reciprocate by leaving money to his children. And on it goes.

Sometimes, it seems more advantageous *not* to have any money.

Since a will is such an important document to produce, the soundest advice we can offer is to find the best attorney you can.

If possible, find one who is a stepparent or who at least has had experience with the complexity of stepfamilies and can understand the sensitive nature of your wills. (An attorney who is at war with her own ex-husband and his wife, stepmom to her kids, might find it hard to provide you with unbiased advice.) Your wills need to be well constructed so they cannot be overridden if your mate's first family attempts to contest them.

One particular issue that concerned a number of stepmoms we spoke with—inheritance of the family home. In some cases, a husband's will required that the home shared by the couple be sold in the event of his death, in order that the proceeds could be divided between his wife and his children. This was often the situation whether the couple had jointly purchased the home and each owned 50%, or if a stepmother had moved into an already existing family home with or without children of her own.

As a result of this kind of provision, a stepmother can find herself homeless (usually a grace period is allowed for a stepmom to make alternative arrangements) after the death of her husband. Be sure to check that the title to your home allows you to inherit it completely in the event of your husband's death, unless there are some very specific circumstances making this impossible or unreasonable.

Also, in light of your new marriage, both you and your mate need to review and if necessary amend the beneficiaries of your IRAs, pension funds and any trust funds you may have.

9. Miscellaneous Items
In handwriting, list intentions for the inheritance of any miscellaneous items not in your wills.

A number of stepmoms dreaded their husband dying before them, predicting bad behavior from their stepchildren over items not in the will but nevertheless considered inherited property. Bettina, stepmom to five "very needy and greedy" stepkids, said, "His body won't be cold before his eldest daughter arrives at the house with a U-Haul. I can just see myself grieving for my husband while his daughter drags furniture out of the house."

One stepmom suggested that you list any of your husband's miscellaneous possessions not included in his will and ask that he insert alongside each item the name of the person he wishes to inherit it. Ask him to do this in his handwriting, not on computer, so that stepchildren know you are not tinkering with his intentions. There can then be no doubt in their minds that this is what Dad wanted. (This would help stepmoms like Bettina.) For example:

> Gold watch.................................son Tommy
>
> Wedding photo album................grandaughter Susie
>
> Onyx cufflinks.............................grandson Fred
>
> all carpentry tools ....daughter Gracie
>
> rocking chair ....niece Luann

This list would then be formally executed (signed and witnessed) and kept with his will so it is not overlooked.

We came across a surprisingly common experience concerning adult stepchildren—the "family silver" phenomenon. For some reason silver, whether sterling or plate, assumes a symbolic role in stepfamily life. We have heard of more disagreements over possession of the silver (crystal is a close second) than any other prize, regardless of its financial value. Stepmothers have reported disgraceful behavior over this trophy.

After finding odd pieces of cutlery disappearing from her home and enduring many snide remarks at holiday meals from her stepdaughters as to who they thought should own it, Jeanette simply packed up the silver one Christmas, substituting her stainless steel at the semiformal family gathering, and handed it over to her husband's two adult daughters.

"They were embarrassed, but I was not about to go

through another holiday meal feeling as though I were eating off stolen goods," Jeanette said. Since both stepdaughters were in college at the time, they were unable to use the silver, and it remained in boxes under the stairs for many years.

In the early days of her marriage, Chauncey found her two stepdaughters taking an inventory of anything in her household they considered valuable, with particular emphasis on the silver, which was worn plate. "They said their mother wanted to be sure her daughters got what was rightfully theirs," explained Chauncey.

Many stepchildren don't realize it, but often the family silver is quite meaningless to a stepmom. Said Chauncey, "I didn't even like the pattern, and besides, I have my own. I use theirs only because it's familiar to my husband and his kids, and they like it. I would never tell them I prefer mine."

Depending on the quantity, value, and emotional attachment your mate has to the family silver, consider giving it to your stepkids now, if you're like the stepmoms who told us it means nothing, and your mate agrees. It will be one more annoyance you can remove from your life.

It's a different matter if your mate won't eat Sunday dinner unless it's accompanied by a full show of his family's heirlooms or if you entertain on a grand scale. One or two stepmoms dug in their heels as a matter of principal—"It belongs to my husband, and we both enjoy it." In this case your mate needs to make it clear to his children that the silver is his—and yours to share—and that you plan on keeping and using it for many years to come. If he wishes, he can let them know who will inherit it when he dies.

10. Living Wills
Consider making one for each of you at the time you make your will if it is appropriate in your state. A living will covers your wishes in extraordinary medical circumstances.

While you are working on your will, your attorney might suggest you consider a living will too. This can be a simple, standard form appointing a health-care agent whom you trust and with whom you can discuss your wishes in the event that you are unable to make medical decisions about your own care. (Some states offer other ways to determine the future management of your life/death.)

This document covers such matters as whether you wish to be kept alive by life-support systems, what medical care you would like to have provided, and what you want withheld. This is not specific to your status as a stepmom but simply another chore to get over and done with.

11. Funeral Arrangements—Yours and His

These are difficult to face, but you need to know what to do if the worst happens. Designate others to handle your affairs in the event that you both die together. It's vital for all the children in your care to be able to rely on someone who knows your wishes and could handle arrangements in a disaster.

As soon as possible, explain to your mate that although you never want to be parted from him, to put your mind at rest, you need to discuss the unpleasant details of funeral arrangements with him "so we never have to think about them again." It's all too easy to postpone this chore, but it's irresponsible, even negligent, to do so, particularly if you have children. You both need to do this, anticipating the three different scenarios that could occur—your death, your mate's death, and a tragedy in which you both die.

Lorna, a young stepmom, was taken aback when her husband of just six months presented her with a file called "In the Event of My Death." "He told me to read through it and ask questions about anything that wasn't clear," Lorna explained. "The file contained complete details of what I should do if anything happened to Bart: names and phone numbers of attorneys, people at the bank, insurance handlers, everyone I should talk to; where things I would need were kept—keys, documents, a checklist of matters I should attend to. He had even made his own funeral arrangements, right down to which hymns he wanted at the service. He left instructions about his children's education, what I should pass on to his ex-wife.

There was nothing he hadn't thought of. I was upset at the time, but now I respect his sense of responsibility."

You might find out about some strange preexisting arrangements concerning a mate's death, best unearthed (no pun intended) as soon as you can. Nina discovered quite by accident, several years into her marriage, that her husband, Juan, had promised his family of origin that when he died, he would return to his homeland, Argentina, and be buried in the family grave, alongside his ex-wife! Nina said this made her feel she had only "borrowed" Juan, that he really "belonged" to his previous wife, since they would lie side by side throughout eternity.

If funeral arrangements already exist, you need to know about them, so ask questions. Should your husband have an accident on the way home one night, you would be grateful you knew his wishes, should he die. You don't need to add to your suffering, for example, by giving his ex-wife the opportunity to contest your arrangements by announcing, "I know what he wanted; we discussed it when we were married." It's considerate, too, for you to put his mind at rest by detailing your preferences should you die first.

⟡

Questionnaire

1. Have you and your husband prepared wills, taking into account your new marriage? If you're procrastinating, list your reasons.

2. If your husband predeceases you, does his will . . .
   adequately take care of you and your children?
   adequately take care of your stepchildren?
   If there is a difference between the way your mate has provided for each family, can you accept it, or are you uncomfortable? Describe your feelings.

3. If you predecease your husband, does your will . . .
   provide for your children?
   include your husband?

include your stepchildren?
If not, detail your reasons for not including them.

4. Does the whole family have adequate medical insurance? If not, why? Is there anything you can do to remedy this?

5. Do you and/or your husband carry life insurance? Who are the beneficiaries? If insurance is not in place, are you worried about it? Do you have plans to take care of this?

6. Do you understand what your responsibilities, if any, to your stepchildren will be if your mate dies before you? Are you comfortable with the arrangements? If not, what do you need to do?

PART IV

Is This What I Want?

OVERVIEW

We all have moments in our lives when it seems the right time to take stock—to contemplate the past, both accomplishments and regrets, to consider changes we'd like to make or different paths we might have chosen. Besides all the other crossroads you'll come to during your life, the "moment of truth" in stepmotherhood will come too.

You may be at that point now, or not. In *The Enlightened Stepmother*, however, we've come full circle. In part 1, you examined your needs and goals in taking on this role. These final chapters will help you evaluate your satisfaction and progress, as well as guide you to a variety of support resources that can benefit you and your stepfamily at whatever stage you're in.

CHAPTER 19

How Are We Doing?

There is no question that women who flourish in the role of stepmom—those who feel they are successful and are enjoying the experience—are able to put into perspective the challenges and difficulties they face. These stepmoms generally recognize that their down days are caused more by circumstances than by any personal lack or mismanagement on their part, and they refuse to allow themselves to become immobilized by negative emotions, instead taking action to alleviate problems both current and anticipated.

This kind of attitude—an ideal one, surely—probably falls into the "easier said than done" category, but it does provide stepmoms with a positive, attainable model for their own lives. One veteran stepmom, firmly focused on her hard-won success in nurturing a strong, thriving stepfamily, declined to be interviewed about her tough times, saying, "Those awful years are over. I don't want to think about them anymore."

Another stepmom, Alexandra, explained how she was able to look beyond her own feelings to where painful problems originated. In the early years with her stepfamily, one stepson had treated her cruelly, with taunts and bad behavior. When she'd asked him why he'd wanted to hurt her, he'd replied, "Because it's fun. Because I hate you."

Alexandra understood her stepson was the one with the problem, not her. This perception helped her deflect hurtful words, and demonstrate to her stepfamily, particularly to this boy, that she was there to stay and that she would be available for a relationship when or if he changed his mind.

Some who flourished drew support from other stepmoms who shared common stepfamily issues. Knowing they were not alone, they were determined to function "as well as the next woman."

While it's easier to thrive as a stepmom if you're naturally an upbeat, confident, positive person—character traits that some people have and some don't—we firmly believe that attitudes conducive to successful stepmotherhood can be learned. You can make up your mind to adopt an "enlightened" approach, using the insights and advice from this book and other sources.

Failure to Thrive

The reverse situation, "failure to thrive," is a term medical professionals use to describe infants whose bodily needs are being met but who, due to some deprivation or another are unable to sustain normal development. During one poignant interview, Jilly, a stepmom married seven years, with five stepchildren, used this phrase to sum up her painful existence: "It is almost impossible to explain to someone who has not experienced it, the feeling of being unwanted by a group of people who are supposed to be your family, of being unwelcome in your own home, a place that's meant to be a sanctuary.

"Day in and day out, whatever I do is somehow not right. Not one of my stepkids has ever asked my opinion, asked how I felt, or thanked me for something. I'm convinced all five would be happier if I were not here. It is humiliating to find myself hoping for a scrap of acknowledgment, which I rarely find, even from my husband."

Continued small slights, too, can add up to a feeling of "failure to thrive." Explained Carla, "One night we were sitting at dinner when my teenage stepson made a toast to his new girlfriend, announcing, 'You are the nicest addition to this family we've ever had.' I was expected to raise my glass, even though I'd been an unacknowledged addition to the family eight years earlier."

Taken one at a time, barbs like this seem trivial. But hearing a number of them each day, from different stepkids, and with a lack of support from her husband, Carla was beginning to think there were perhaps more reasons to leave than to stay.

Dr. Lee Salk, in his book *Familyhood,* explains that children need more than basic bodily necessities, "to attain the best and brightest of life's treasures." But this statement easily applies to the rest of us too. He cites three factors crucial to well-being: to feel you have options and maintain some control over your life; to feel significant in the life of at least one other person; and to feel accepted as an individual "in a society that tends to encourage conformity, rather than welcome differences."

Far too many stepmoms admitted that these essentials were missing from their lives. They simply struggled through each day. Jilly and Carla were not alone in having let their dissatisfaction continue unaddressed for so long. We were deeply concerned to hear about a host of physical and emotional ailments a number of women suffered as a direct result of stresses related to stepmotherhood. Some were taking antidepressants. Several had been hospitalized for what they termed a "nervous breakdown." Others complained of sleepless nights when they either rehashed the day's events, wishing they had handled some incident more assertively, or dreaded some event due to take place the next day.

An unsettling number of stepmoms, badly depleted of energy and self-confidence by the rigors of daily opposition, neglected to do anything about it, fearing that their expression of unhappiness and a demand for change would only make things worse. Until some crisis forces action, on either the part of a stepmom or her mate, it is common for stepmoms to keep quiet and "make the best of it," indefinitely.

Actively seek out support resources as soon as possible, before you become overwhelmed (see chapter 20.) Friends, family, support groups, professionals—any or all of the people you reach out to can help you make changes in your life when you believe they're needed. It's easy to be persuaded that what you are experiencing is something all women involved in family life experience and tolerate. Dismiss this as another myth. A host of issues stepmothers are required to handle are unique to stepmoms—hard to identify with and misunderstood unless experienced firsthand.

The Return on Emotional Investment

Stepmoms we spoke with differed widely on the question of emotional commitment to their stepfamilies. Many believed that a successful stepfamily demands a total commitment from a stepmother. "I want to be part of this family. I am going to do what is necessary to stay the course, whatever it takes." Others felt that their "underdog" status required that they kept a bit of heart and soul (and funds) in reserve and made sure they always had an escape hatch and "exit money."

According to these diverse opinions, there's probably no one right amount of emotional commitment stepmoms should make to their new stepfamilies up front. Again, personality is a major factor—the outgoing, confident, take-charge types we met were able to give it their all. Those less confident needed a backup plan, which they fantasized about during difficult moments. Many a stepmom related sleepless nights spent mentally packing up and leaving home. They knew exactly what they'd take, where they'd go, what they'd do, some concluding this mental trial run with visions of stepfamily members begging for forgiveness and for her to return.

There's a catch-22 on the emotional front. While it seems unreasonable to expect stepmoms to commit to a life so fraught with complications and difficulties—we heard the word "tenuous" quite often—it is hard to make something as challenging as stepmotherhood work without a commitment.

As you evaluate your position on emotional commitment, perhaps what we all need to ask ourselves are these questions:

- What has been my return on this emotional investment I've made?

- If I'm giving my best in care and concern with no response, should I pull back a little, focus on other things?

- If I can see a growing positive response on some fronts— relationships with my stepkids, more cooperation in practical matters—should I open my heart a bit more?

- If I'm of two minds over this, is it because I feel committed to my mate, but not his kids?

- Have my feelings toward my mate changed? Has the original relationship we shared been affected?

- Can I improve my perception of how matters are evolving?

- Should I modify my expectations?

Evaluating Negative Emotions

As you evaluate your satisfaction with life as a stepmom, it is important to understand any negative feelings you have. It's better to head them off before they set in and possibly cause health problems than to attempt to recover from them.

Many upsetting emotions are easier to prevent when you understand that they are a result of *circumstances* (the fact that you're a stepmom) and that they can be considered fairly normal in this context. Anger, anxiety, jealousy, confusion, hurt— a whole array of complex feelings are often caused by what we perceive as unreasonable, even wretched predicaments. Not one stepmom we spoke with had sailed through stepmotherhood unscathed.

Every stepmom has a different emotional pain tolerance, just as we all have a physical pain tolerance. Some women can brush off repeated hurts without any long-term, serious damage. Others wither day by day. How you respond to negative feelings is a great determining factor in whether you will ultimately thrive in your role.

Knowing your threshold, understanding your emotions and the events that cause them, and being able to share them with other women who are stepmothers can help you adjust both your approach and response to unpleasant feelings and put them in perspective.

Here are some of the most common negative feelings step-moms have and their possible cause. Don't be surprised if you feel all of them at some time or another—perhaps at the same time.

Unappreciated

Your stepkids don't want a stepmom; they want their own mother. Many kids take their mom for granted—why would they be expected to show appreciation to Dad's wife? Don't look for appreciation. Simply insist on practical help when you need it. If appreciation comes at all, it will come from our husband.

Excluded

Your stepkids try to exclude you because initially they don't know you, are unsure how to relate to you or what to expect from you, or are just being nasty. Feeling excluded is normal. But explain how you feel to your mate, and ask him to make every effort to include you in conversations, plans, etc. This is a marital-relationship difficulty, not one with your stepkids. Dad needs to help out.

Powerless, Lacking Control

You have joined a family where there are established routines and rituals, where each family member knows what to expect from the others. You are the new kid on the block, trying to fit in with your new ideas. Strange as it seems, you will not be viewed as powerless. Your stepkids might see you as having too *much* power. This is a case of fact versus feeling. You actually *aren't* powerless; you just feel that way.

Lonely

This is one of the worst feelings, since you married your mate to feel close and secure with him. You have to share the man you love; his concern and loyalty are divided among you and his children. Having few friends and family around you, especially if you don't have children of your own rooting for you, intensifies feelings of isolation. If it helps, remember, you're not the only person feeling this way. Your stepkids at one time had the full focus of two parents, then only one at a time. Then Dad met you. Now that he's remarried, they think he spends too much time with you, while you're feeling lonely because he spends too much time with them. Jump in and join them. Explain how you feel to your husband and to your stepkids, too, if you feel able to do this. It is a feeling you all share.

Rejected

Your mate chose you. His kids didn't. It is almost inevitable that initially your stepkids will reject you. They don't want you; they want their mom, or just their dad to themselves. It is the rare stepmom who is welcomed into her stepfamily with open arms. It's your mate's job to make sure his kids are courteous and respectful—all you can expect, to start with.

Overburdened

As with almost any new job or role, feeling this way is inevitable. Are you working too hard trying to please everyone, trying to be the perfect stepmom? Talk to your mate about the need for everyone to pitch in—if you don't ask for help, you won't get it. Ask kids and Dad to help prepare meals. Teach kids and Dad, if necessary, to do laundry. Do what you can, no more. If you are working outside the home, bringing in money, your job is as important as your mate's. He's as capable as you of doing chores; if he isn't, teach him, along with the kids.

Disillusioned

Most stepmoms feel this way at some point, due to unrealistic expectations or being unprepared for joining a stepfamily. Re-read chapter 3 for a list of common unrealistic expectations—

you can't be disillusioned if you're being realistic about step-family life.

Forced to Subjugate Needs and Feelings

A stepmom's needs and wishes are usually at the bottom of the priority list. While a common phenomenon, this is intoler-able for a stepmother who is attempting to help other family members adjust and must be remedied. Bear in mind that most mothers complain about it too. It is actually your own fault for allowing it. Since nobody else will take care of you, it's up to you to look out for yourself.

Angry

Quite common, often frightening. These feelings are serious and need to be handled correctly. Compare notes with other stepmoms, let off steam, write down your feelings. If you are overwhelmed by these two volatile emotions, talk to a therapist.

Jealous

Again, common among stepmoms. Jealousy can be very de-structive. See our discussion of facts versus feelings (page 385) and also chapter 20 for suggestions.

Guilty

This insidious emotion can keep women from taking action about other negative emotions. For example, if you feel guilty about being resentful, you might opt to do nothing about it. Stepmoms can experience guilt over anything that is going wrong in their stepfamilies, from feeling negative emotions they've not had before to not liking their stepkids. Try to find the source of the guilt, and work to resolve the cause, whether it's a feeling or a fact.

Resentful

With so much expected of you, yet receiving little or no ac-knowledgment or concern for your well-being, resentment concerning the unreasonableness of your situation is inevitable. See our discussion on fact versus feeling.

If you believe you cannot handle any of the above feelings alone, go posthaste to someone who can help you—your mate, another stepmom, or a therapist. See other suggestions in chapter 20. If you do not deal with these emotions, recognizing that they are a reasonable reaction to your experiences in a stepfamily, you can find yourself immobilized by them. Unaddressed, destructive feelings such as these can build; you might become depressed, withdrawn, or violent as emotions struggle for recognition.

Marital Disloyalty: One Thing Too Many

Compounding a stepmom's struggle with negative emotions is the accompanying strain on her marriage. Many stepmoms spoke about the indignity and the pain of seeing a mate repeatedly side with his kids, support them or their wishes over her needs, stand by while his kids verbally or even physically abused her. Several stepmoms reported that their stepsons hit or pushed them, that stepdaughters spat at or on them.

No apology or compensation can make up for disloyalty between spouses, even though we might understand a father's own difficulties with divided loyalties. A mate who continues to put his children ahead of his wife is perpetuating an intolerable situation and a continual erosion of the marital relationship.

One father of three, married eight years to his kids' stepmom, shared a thought he had recently come up with: "Seems to me it is up to the kids' father to instill in his kids a positive attitude toward their stepmother. I think that would probably help her."

The stepmom in question, however, said she'd been practically begging her mate to help her with his kids in this way for the entire eight years of their marriage. He seriously believed his idea was a fresh revelation!

It often takes dads a very long time to recognize that they

can actually help their children accept their stepmom. Even when they see the light, they often fail to recognize that it's a *responsibility they have toward their wife,* not an afterthought or a generous favor.

So many stepmoms complained that their mate put his kids' needs ahead of her own that it can only be considered a common syndrome that possibly needs to be given a formal name. But what to do about this impossible position from which a stepmom is expected to operate?

We questioned the dad discussed above about how he had arrived at his conclusion, why it had taken so long, and how could we convey "his" idea to other dads. He replied: "A father has to see that being united with his wife, making his wife's needs and wishes a priority, helps his kids, too, that in the long run the whole family benefits. He needs to understand that his wife can be expected to feel generous toward his kids only when she is accorded the security of her position."

This father suggested that a dad, *prior* to his marriage, have a talk with his kids along the lines of "I love this woman, and I hope that you will like her. I need your help in making her feel welcome in our family. However you feel about her in the beginning, you need to be polite and respectful to her, just as you would to any adult. I know and she knows you've had a very difficult time, but we can't accept bad behavior because of this. Your feelings will get better gradually, and we will both help you."

The dad added, "This will work *only* if dad feels his new wife has the good of his kids at heart. If he believes she doesn't like them, is criticizing them, or is trying to get more of his attention than they get, he won't be able to accept this. He has to believe she cares about his kids' happiness."

Based on the unlikelihood that a mate will have this revelation himself, it is up to every stepmom or potential stepmom to start talking in this vein with him early on. No point in her sitting around, feeling hurt or excluded. Get to work explaining the importance of his kids and yours seeing a good working marital relationship, with an indivisible united front, providing the security and framework in which the whole stepfamily can thrive. Just as important, you are a role model to these children—denigration of you as a woman or your role as a stepmother is unacceptable. If you think it will help, suggest he read this chapter, or maybe just these few paragraphs.

Assure him that you will make every reasonable effort to befriend his kids, that you think they're great, and that you want them to be happy. This is what he needs to hear. It's a trade-off—you try to like his kids and be good to them; he'll try to help them like you and behave respectfully toward you. Happy kids behave better than unhappy ones. Dads are happier when their kids are happy. And in the long run you'll be happier, which is the whole idea. Simplistic? Yes, but it's the only way it will work.

Facts versus Feelings

Often negative emotions can be defused by separating facts from feelings and reacting to the facts in a positive, proactive way.

Let's examine one of the worst feelings—jealousy. Early in her marriage a stepmom can feel jealous in any of several areas—time, privacy, attention, display of love. Seeing a fourteen-year-old stepdaughter, almost a woman, flirting with her dad, hugging him, sitting on his lap, talking intimately, holding hands when they are out together, can seem like having another woman competing for your lover's attention! Jealousy is frequently accompanied by a feeling of helplessness or shame as stepmoms find themselves reacting in ways they would normally consider demeaning. They told of being "mean" in little ways, "just to get back at her," and were appalled at themselves, recognizing how childish they were being.

So separate the facts from the feelings. Your stepdaughter is a young girl, your mate's daughter, who might not have seen her dad for a while. They are delighted to be together, particularly after the bad times they experienced during the divorce. They are a little too physical for your liking. Is this because you come from an undemonstrative family? Were you not hugged as a child? Do you need a hug yourself right now? If you were the girl's mother and the same behavior took place, it might not bother you, since the girl would love you, too, as a parent. Or you might be able to say, with a parent's authority, "Knock it off" or "That's inappropriate."

Because you are a stepmom, you think you can only seethe in silence as witness to (in your opinion) this near-incestuous scene.

Not so. You're an enlightened stepmom. Even the most mature, self-assured women feel jealous sometimes, so don't beat yourself up. The fact is your husband and his daughter obviously need some time together. Suggest an outing without you—a walk by themselves or lunch out. This will (a) make you look like a good guy, and none too soon, because you could not have held your tongue much longer, and (b) get them out of the house so you can calm down. Before they leave, ask your mate for a big hug and a kiss, which he will be happy to give you, because you have just displayed the understanding, generosity, and the independence he loves you for.

This is a major accomplishment. If you have a stepmom friend, call her and discuss it. Drop everything, get together, or give yourself another nice reward—because you deserve it. You turned an issue that could have resulted in a major ugly scene into a very positive experience for everyone. Your husband and stepdaughter will have a wonderful time together, and you will get all the credit.

It's worth mentioning that many stepmoms reported that their mate could take only a certain amount of time with their teenagers. A couple of hours together usually satisfied everyone.

Adding Up the Good Feelings Too

You'll achieve a balanced perspective on how you are doing if you can evaluate the good things that are happening to you too. Most stepmoms, no matter what kind of crisis was going on at the moment, usually could find *something* that had improved with life in a stepfamily over time. Focus on the positives; build on what's working. Look back a year, two years, and note the improvements. Some will be of your making, some are probably circumstantial, some might be due to others as everybody begins to settle down and adjust.

Congratulate yourself for your part in the successes, however minor they seem. And share them! Point them out to your mate and the kids in your home, both biological and step. Have a party to celebrate what's working, even if it's just that you made it through one visitation weekend without a single argument.

We enjoyed hearing stepmoms report on some areas in which they saw the seeds of success, sometimes quite small but, considering the framework in which they occurred, major signs of progress. Something as simple as a stepson's asking for another helping of her homemade pie made Jenny ecstatic, since he previously had been rejecting her. The first time a teenage stepson included her in the routine family good-bye hugs was described by teary-eyed Leslie as "making her week." Colleen was thrilled by her stepdaughter's request to borrow her dressy black sweater for a special date.

Some stepmoms spoke with pride of their accomplishments, citing specific examples: Achieving an understanding with an ex-wife. Gaining the trust of a stepchild. Performing some task for a stepchild that brought joy to a mate. The day a daughter and a stepdaughter finally saw eye to eye on something, however minor. The contentment of watching the whole stepfamily enjoy a movie and popcorn in the den together for the first time, when it was her idea.

Some stepmoms were gratified by their husband's notice of their interest and kindnesses toward his kids. Others felt satisfaction in knowing that due to their contributions, even though unacknowledged by others, the stepkids were thriving. Several mentioned the pleasure of knowing they were doing their job well. Relish the progress you see.

Forgiveness

We've all heard the phrase "forgive and forget." It's an issue that's passionately debated among stepmothers trying to move forward in spite of past hurts. Just how much can you forgive? When do you draw the line on what is reasonable to forgive? Turning the other cheek ad infinitum, while a saintly goal, is not possible or desirable. Is it right to continue to forgive those who repeatedly cause you pain?

Stepmoms not only questioned whether or not they were capable of forgiving but whether it was reasonable of others to expect them to do so. Said Delia, "There is so much pain experienced by stepmoms, made worse by their own silence about it. Who would understand my feelings when it is the kids' needs our culture insists I put above my own? Commitment is not enough. I never had a hope. I came, I participated, and I left without leaving my mark." At the time she spoke the words, Delia's husband had recently told her that he wanted a divorce. "After all I went through and put up with, he's the one who wants out!"

Some stepmoms felt they could forgive "only when there are signs of regret" and the "willingness not to repeat the hurt." Others doubted that apologies would ever be forthcoming, that stepkids (and society) consider it their birthright to treat a stepmom badly. Perceiving it to be reasonable, society condones this, and stepkids' families, absorbed with how much the children are hurting, don't consider the importance of teaching them not to hurt others.

Stepmoms sometimes saw a change of heart among stepchildren when they themselves became adults and stepparents. Recognizing either their damaging behavior toward their stepmom or the negligence on the part of their dad in correcting them, they were sometimes able to express regret for the past. This experience proved to be the positive turning point in a number of stepmom–stepchild relationships.

Some stepmoms stopped short of forgiveness, saying they could only *understand* the reasons their stepchildren behaved as they did but never forget. When you are repeatedly hurt

by someone, by several people, it is one thing to und
intellectually that they are in pain themselves, quite another
not to let it affect you and your future interactions with those
who have caused injury.

"After all," said one stepmom, "if they've done it once,
they are capable of doing it again. My stepson's parents never
taught him to handle his problems in a reasonable, mature
way. He's eighteen now and may never learn. I've had to bear
the brunt of their negligence toward him, and the odds are it
will continue." Another stepmom said she would never "turn
her back" on one of her stepsons, because she had been (metaphorically) stabbed so many times. One said she would never
again talk alone with a stepdaughter, because the girl had lied
so many times about their conversations.

We marveled at the stepmoms who unequivocally were
able to both forgive and forget, seemingly with no damage to
themselves, in spite of their stepkids' anger and spite toward
them. This ability to forgive and move on is a common trait
among the stepmoms who flourished. When prompted for details, Helen explained, "I don't take anything my stepkids do
or say personally. I don't allow them to take their problems
out on me. If anyone is rude to me, I say, 'You must be very
upset about something to be so nasty. Please go away now,
and when you can talk about it calmly, come back and we'll
see if we can't work it out.' Then I get on with whatever else
I'm doing."

Other stepmoms reported variations on the same idea. Said
Angie, "People who are hurting are looking for an outlet. They
don't want to dump on their dad, but it's OK to be rude to
his wife, whom they consider inconsequential."

Noted Laurie, "Once you start being hurt by bad behavior,
you're sunk. If one of my stepkids refuses, say, to set the table
when I ask, I'll say, 'Then please ask your dad to help me,
because I need someone to do it. And if you want to eat
dinner, please be sure you're in a better mood. Nobody wants
to be with you when you're acting like this.' Then I ignore
him and don't respond to anything else he yells at me. I'm
certainly not going to get into a hassle—I'm not willing to

waste my energy like that. I don't consider I have anything to forgive—it's just not relevant."

Nancy said, "If I let them hurt me, I will start expecting apologies, and I know full well nobody is likely to say they're sorry. I'm a sitting duck, so I just dodge the slings and arrows. Actually, I think it annoys the hell out of them that they don't get any reaction. Everything they throw at me misses."

Looking Five to Ten Years Ahead

Uncertainty about the future was a common source of anxiety for stepmoms. Will my marriage last? Can we make a success of our stepfamily? If nothing improves, can I go on in this way? What if anything happens to my husband? Will I continue to see my stepkids? Should I let myself love these kids when there's the possibility their mom won't let me see them? What about growing older? If I don't have kids of my own, who will "be there" for me?

The answer to many questions about what's in store is that your life will probably be what you make of it. If you decide to be a vital, active, interesting woman, you will enjoy your life and those around you, attracting the friendship of similar types, quite possibly your stepkids among them. If you become an introverted, bitter stepmom, who will want to share that with you? Certainly not stepkids, nor anyone else.

We have stressed before that stepmoms *allow* unacceptable circumstances to befall them, not deliberately, but because they are overwhelmed and don't know how to exercise the few options they have or how to claim their rights. Because you are experiencing the negatives of stepmotherhood, you cannot afford, for your own sake, to become a self-pitying victim. It's up to you!

Consider where you would like to be in relation to your stepfamily in one year's time. How do you want your circumstances to evolve over the next year? What's possible? What can you do to make your wishes a reality? Do the same exercise for a five-year period. The kids will be older. How do you see them changing? How do you see yourself changing? And how do you see your mate's perspective altering—with your help?

Finally, look ten years down the road. Draw up some goals with your mate—not financial or practical but emotional goals. In another decade how would you like to be relating to your stepson, who will be twenty years old? What about your fourteen-year-old stepdaughter, who currently can't stand the sight of you? How would you like your relationship to evolve over the next ten years?

People change. Circumstances change. Your whole life can change—take charge of it.

Stress-Buster Strategies

Your day-to-day antistress strategies will be unique, as you are. One part-time stepmom, still struggling with an awkward relationship with her twin teenage stepsons, focused on what she would do immediately following the boys' departure on Sundays—brew up a fresh pot of coffee in solitude, watch an old movie, curled up on the sofa with her husband, take a twenty-minute nap—anything rewarding to look forward to following a weekend that felt like work.

One of the most effective techniques is just to be yourself. Simplistic as that sounds, many stepmoms are *not* doing this. Lisamarie had struggled for two years, trying to please, putting up with stepkids' bad manners and nonresponsiveness, until she'd had enough. "I decided that since whatever I did would be considered wrong anyway, I might as well do things my way, come hell or high water, instead of constantly trying to replicate life in their previous family. I just let go of that impossibility. Life and relationships were instantly easier."

Another common self-protecting strategy was withdrawal. This can help you only over a current hurdle; it is not a long-term solution. Also, only a part-time stepmom can do this. One stepmom, Franny, who had begun to see herself as pathetic, wanting so much to be liked and accepted, was finally rejected one time too many.

"My reaction was to withdraw myself, my feelings," she said. "I have completely uninvolved myself with my stepchildren's lives. I don't ask questions; I don't volunteer help or interest or pleasant conversation when they're around. Right now I can't be hurt. This is not where I want to be, but for the moment it's working. I hope to make overtures of friendship again, but not yet. I'm working on my relationship with my husband—my heart and soul are employed there at the moment."

Sometimes doing nothing else but stepping back and becoming an observer for a while when things are difficult can be quite helpful. You'll notice personalities and relationships with a cooler, more objective eye and possibly see a solution where before you saw only a problem.

Bobbi, a part-time stepmom to three stepkids, found herself "in attendance," expected to provide when things were needed—dinner, clean laundry, a full refrigerator—but otherwise ignored. One day one of her stepkids, on the phone in her kitchen, stood looking directly at her saying to his friend in Kentucky on the other end, "I'm here at Dad's house in Ohio," instead of "Dad and Bobbi's house."

She realized she had become the Invisible Woman. "The kid looked right through me, a nonentity in my own home." Bobbi decided to abdicate. "I definitely wanted to continue my marriage to their dad, but I began to do exactly what I pleased when the kids were with us—my own chores, errands, shopping, evening movie and dinner with a girlfriend. I left everyone to their own devices. My husband found it hard at first, having to organize all the meals and the kids' activities, but he had to agree that his kids were treating me as the unpaid help."

Permanent "abdication" is far from ideal. It can and does erode the marital relationship. But as a temporary measure, it can be a lifesaver if you want to remain married. In effect, you are putting your stepfamily on "hold," providing yourself with some small sense of control and time to consider what you want to do next. It can backfire, though. Lena told us she "heard the laughter level increase. They all—my husband included—sounded so relaxed and happy when I wasn't with them."

Would You Do It Again?

This question, often the final one asked during our interviews with stepmoms, was frequently met with a "No." These women affirmed their love for their husbands but felt their life was diminished by external pressures—finances, arrangements dictated by others, constant conflict. A response heard more often than we would have liked was "I'll deny having said this if you ever quote me—I would never want my husband to know it—but no, I wouldn't. It's just too difficult." Still others said they might do it but would handle their situation very differently. "If I'd known then what I know now . . ." was often speculated. From stepmoms in an especially volatile period of stepfamily life, we heard variations on "If you'd asked me yesterday, I would have said 'absolutely not,' but today things are calmer, and I'll say 'Probably, yes.'"

Interestingly, the younger stepmoms, who had been married the shortest amount of time, were the ones who responded with the quickest "No." Once time passes, as stepmothers build on their roles and become more experienced in stepfamily life, many women can look back on difficult times with a grain of salt and be proud of what they've accomplished.

The happiest response, one we'd like to have heard more often, came from Cami, a thirty-eight-year-old stepmom who said she would do it again, in spite of the challenges. She explained that she had become a stronger, wiser person because of the tough times and that she and her husband had deepened their relationship as well. She revealed, "Mike and I fought tooth and nail in the early years. His kids resented me, I was miserable, clueless and angry, and Mike was torn. It took a long time and many tears before we all trusted one another and realized we had something worth keeping. But when the person you love goes through that kind of hell with you and comes out the other side still holding your hand, you can consider yourself a very blessed person."

Your Answers to Questionnaires, Then and Now

If you've been answering the questionnaires throughout this book in writing, you'll have an interesting record to look back on later.

One rainy Saturday afternoon when you can be assured of a few hours alone, review your original answers. Whether it's a matter of months or years that have passed since you set out as a new stepmom, respond to the questions again from your new perspective. You might be amazed to see how your feelings have changed, at the progress you have made in a relatively short time.

Particularly pay attention to the questions in part 1. Have you been true to yourself? Have you fulfilled the promises you made to yourself? If not, why? Can you recommit to any of them now? Some of these, you listed as "necessities." If you've dropped any along the way, there must be a good reason—what is it? Why are they not as important now as they were when you started out?

If there are still issues you need to address, things that haven't worked out as you'd like, our next chapter, "The Stepmom's Resource Guide," may help you resolve some.

⟨⟩

Action Box

On paper, make three columns with the following headings:
1. What I bring to this family
2. What I'm losing/sacrificing/missing out on
3. The positive things I'm receiving as a stepmom

Take as much time as you need, perhaps over a week or so, and jot down your thoughts in each column, for example, I don't have time to plant a garden anymore for column 2, or I love it when Clive (stepson) comes and sits on the bed and chats to me while Dave (mate) is shaving some mornings for column 3.

How does your personal balance sheet work out? Is there a serious imbalance? Is one column much longer than the others? If you have a nice, long list for column 3, good for you! If the negatives outweigh the positives, what percentage of the time does this happen? Can some of the negatives be eliminated with corrective action?

☙ List your three major areas of concern—those that jump off the page following your introspection—in order of priority. Evaluate them one by one, decide who can help you resolve them, and reach out to take action right now. For example, if your concerns are:

- I have very little time with my husband for romance or to talk about the family's finances.

- I can't handle my ten-year-old-stepson—he's rude and untidy and ignores my requests.

- I'm just not making any headway in forming a relationship with my fourteen-year-old stepdaughter.

  Your action might be:

- Arrange a "talking" date for a night that's best for
  you and your mate to chat, undisturbed. Suggest
  continuing this weekly or nightly date, discussing
  whatever concerns either of you. If money's the
  most critical topic, start with that. Try talking for
  thirty minutes or more at a time until the problem is resolved.

- Call your stepson's teacher. Tell her you're exploring ways to help your stepson, since he's having difficulties at home. Inquire how he behaves
  at school, and ask her for advice. If the teacher
  has no time now, make an appointment. Talk to
  your husband about this at your new meeting
  time.

- Call your neighbor, who also has a daughter
  around fourteen and whom you'd like to get to
  know. Ask her to lunch, letting her know you're
  looking for some pointers concerning fourteen-
  year-old girls. In one of your nightly chats, let
  your mate know what you're doing.

  Taking some positive action over matters that
  trouble you should give you an immediate psychological boost. But don't expect problems to go away
  overnight. If the action you are taking has no effect
  over a reasonable period of time, move to a more
  serious level, perhaps with outside intervention.

CHAPTER 20

The Stepmom's Resource Guide

Stepmoms told us about many kinds of "therapy" that encouraged and supported them through difficulties or helped them aid members of their stepfamilies. Therapy, defined in Webster's as the "treatment of disease or of any physical or mental disorder by medical or physical means, usually excluding surgery," in our context can include a wide range of resources—support groups, psychotherapy, self-help books, as well as the less structured "therapies" we use every day to stay physically and mentally healthy: exercise, hobbies, good friendships. We include mediation in this section too, because although not strictly therapy, it can be therapeutic.

Often something as simple as reading a book can trigger an idea that gets you over a hurdle; discussing a particularly thorny issue with a friend can illuminate a perspective you hadn't considered.

For many reasons, including time and money, most of us have a tendency to seek help only in an emergency situation. By now, however, you'll realize the importance of prevention and preparation. If all seems well at the moment in your stepfamily, bravo! But do not become complacent: at minimum, continue to read about the subject of stepfamilies just in case there is something you can do better, something you are unaware of, or something you can prevent from happening in the future.

Use what works for you, progressing to more serious levels of therapy as your circumstances require. Helping members of your stepfamily understand and deal with their difficulties can indirectly relieve you of additional pressure, so consider therapies that might benefit them as well. Here's a summary of therapeutic ideas, from the mildest to the more drastic.

Your Husband: Make Him Your Best Friend

Your husband is probably more important as a support resource than anyone or anything else. You are in your stepfamily, dealing with the issues you have, solely because you fell in love with and married your mate. If you allow this relationship to fend for itself, take it for granted, or don't pay attention to it, you will be ill-equipped to handle stepfamily life.

Kay Pasley, chair of the Research Committee of the Stepfamily Association of America, in a talk at an S.A.A. conference, said: "One of the things we know from the research and clinical literature is that the marital relationship is the real key in keeping a stepfamily together. The issues around the stepparent–stepchild dynamics get played out in the marital relationship. If the marital relationship is not cohesive, is not strong, then the day-to-day stuff that goes on between stepparents and stepkids begins to tear away at that bonding, that relationship."

Stepmoms assured us that almost any issue—even deciding on a bedtime for your ten-year-old stepson—is simpler when the couple's relationship is strong, close, and trusting. If your sex life is a disaster, the question of how and where to spend Thanksgiving can seem insurmountable.

Your mate should be your best friend and closest confidant, the person from whom you receive (and whom you provide) the greatest comfort and nurturing. Nowhere is your promise "to love, honor, and cherish" more needed than at a difficult stage of your stepfamily life. A supportive word or gesture from your mate might be just the therapeutic touch you need. Help in finding solidarity within this important relationship area can be found in John Gottman's book *Why Marriages Succeed or Fail* (Simon & Schuster, 1994).

Advice offered by veteran stepmoms about the marital relationship is "choose your battles." Bedtime for stepkids is an issue you can afford to compromise on, while making time for just the two of you is worth insisting on.

Your Stepmoms' Support Group

These groups have received rave reviews and are our number-one choice of outside resources for stepmoms. We are very much in favor of support groups as one of the tools that can help you stay the course. They can be tailored to meet the needs of the stepmoms attending, can be as formal or informal as desired, and can take place as often as required.

Meeting regularly, women gain a sense of camaraderie hard to find elsewhere, providing insights unlikely to be offered by professionals they might consult—and all without cost. Support groups are particularly valuable in the early days of step-motherhood, when a stepmom's unrealistic expectations are breaking down as she recognizes how unprepared she is for her new life. This feeling, difficult to explain to those who are not stepparents, is something she has in common with other members from the start.

Nan Baver Maglin, in a book she and Nancy Schniedewind edited, *Women and Stepfamilies: Voices of Anger and Love* (Temple University Press, 1989), devotes a chapter to an examination of a group of six professional women, stepmoms who met for only a couple of hours once a month. She describes issues that emerged immediately: "How do I maintain my own sense of self, my integrity, my feeling of competence, and at the same time be a good stepmother? We sensed the system was stacked against us."

Our own stepmoms' support group started out in a conference room at the local library, with women gathered from ads in local papers and through word of mouth. Originally we had few rules, except that attendees must be stepmoms. The group thrived on a regular two-hour monthly meeting, and attendance varied from a high of eighteen to a low of two, depending on the weather and on members' personal crises. Confidentiality was required—"What is said in this room stays in this room"—and each person had a limited time to speak.

After a few months, when everyone had vented sufficiently, we wanted more. Venting was wonderful, but we needed resolution. We started inviting speakers on various subjects—financial advisors, therapists, attorneys, and teachers of parenting classes.

Another group of five women we met were less issues oriented, focusing on sharing a fun, intimate stepmoms' night out. They met monthly at a different restaurant for a long dinner. Among them they had four stepsons in the six-to-eight-year-old range and three stepdaughters, the oldest fourteen years old. Three of them had also become mothers since the eighteen-month-old group had formed. They compared notes, cheered one another's successes, and examined the "problem of the day," usually determined by whoever needed the most help at the time.

When asked what they each received from the group, the responses were as expected: "support," "laughs," "validation," "respect," and "understanding" (of incalculable value when lacking at home), feelings of "gratitude that my situation isn't as bad as Jane's," "I don't feel alone anymore," "I've made friends I know will be there for me if I need them." Their husbands, too, were supportive, caring for their children during these meetings and forming a limited friendship themselves.

These five women moved heaven and earth to attend their monthly outing. Said one: "It would take a major act of God to prevent me from meeting the group."

Here's what you need to consider in setting up a support group:

• First, someone (or two stepmoms jointly) needs to organize the group and attract members. You can place ads in local papers—in most communities there is no charge for an entry in the calendar or the self-help section. Make telephone calls to women who you know are stepmoms or who might know other women who are. Put up flyers or three-by-five cards on local notice boards (at the Y, library, community center, church, local merchants) announcing the formation of your stepmoms' support group.

- Be prepared to explain what your aims are when inquiries are made. You'll want to sound positive and encouraging to possible members. Suggest they come to the first meeting to check it out, and let them know there is no commitment and no charge, except, perhaps, coffee money. For some stepmoms this call to you might be the first time they have sought a sympathetic ear. Some might be nervous; others, simply curious, wondering what other stepmoms' lives are like.

- Arrange for space, which can be a member's home, a room at your local mental-health clinic or hospital, local library, or community center. Anywhere comfortable, central, and free is satisfactory.

- Consider how often you will meet. Once a month in the early stages is probably not enough. If you want to bond and get some resolutions to difficulties, you should probably get together weekly or biweekly, for an agreed-upon length of time—e.g. once a week for ten weeks. Then, if attendees wish, take a break and start over again, targeting different issues.

- Coffee or some sort of refreshment is desirable. It's comforting and makes the meetings more informal and enjoyable. Women who work in an office don't need another formal meeting in the evening. Members can alternate picking up coffee from a local takeout or take turns bringing cookies.

- Occasional speakers are worthwhile when stepmoms indicate they need a professional's input on a common issue— for example, dealing with an ex-wife's demand for increased child support or financial inequities. But keep in mind that the main purpose of a support group is to share, to air opinions and problems, to provide moral support and insights, and to learn from one another, not to listen to a lecture. Stepmoms want to *talk*.

• Keep the number of members to a maximum of ten—we found eight ideal. More than this, and stepmoms don't get enough time to speak. Six might be fine if the women are particularly articulate, but it's important to have enough to provide a range of views and ideas for handling issues that are raised. It's also important you are not all known to one another. If you're all bosom buddies, odds are you're not going to hear anything fresh.

• A format, however casual, keeps you focused. For example, each meeting might have one major topic for discussion, depending on the ages of the women and their stepkids, and what they need: "How to handle teenage sexuality," for example, or, at your meeting just before Thanksgiving, "How to have a stress-free holiday season." The subject should be agreed upon ahead of time so the stepmoms have a chance to think about points they'd like to discuss. Also effective is giving each stepmom a few minutes at the start of the meeting to describe from her perspective the most important event that has taken place in her stepfamily since the last meeting—either good or bad. Other members might have experienced a similar issue, and the group could decide to discuss that.

• If all members have the time and wish to do so, choose a book from the stepfamily literature (see the recommended reading list), and have each member read it over a period of time in preparation for a specific date—say, a month ahead—on which you can all discuss it.

• Finally, you need someone to lead the group, to introduce new stepmoms, to organize the topics for discussion, to prevent everyone from talking at once, to move things along so everyone gets a chance to speak. You can take turns at moderating, or have the stepmom who put the group together handle it.

Books: Therapy off the Shelf

The Enlightened Stepmother's recommended reading list includes books other stepmoms have found useful—those that brought them solace in difficult times, those that provided good ideas and told stories similar to their own and helped them take action. Also included are some you can recommend to other members of your family.

We suggest you read as widely about the subject of stepfamilies as your time permits. You'll find that early books tended to look on the stepfamily configuration as an unnatural one, attempting to "correct" it and make it conform to the more "normal" biological family, an approach we now know is undesirable and impossible. Others insist on referring to the "real" or "natural" mother, to differentiate her from a stepmother, instead of calling a mother simply "mother."

Trust your own experience to evaluate what you read. Pay heed only to ideas or insights that sound right to you; dismiss or skim through what bears little resemblance to your life or what you simply don't like. Books written by psychiatrists, psychologists, or social workers might have used their client/ patient base (people who have found it necessary to seek professional help) for their research, perhaps not accurately reflecting stepmothers-at-large or your own experience. Those written for the stepfamily as a whole often fail to take into account the special needs, viewpoints, and precarious positions of the stepmother, instead focusing on what is best for the children.

Even if you found one useful idea, your reading will have been worthwhile. The more widely you read, the more you will understand how complex stepfamily life is, enabling you to see the positions of other members of your family, which may guide you toward new ways of relating to them or their behavior.

Self-Therapy: Feeding Your Soul

In part 1, we asked you to focus on yourself, to assess your future needs and wishes as you became part of a stepfamily. By now you understand much better why this is crucial. Many stepmoms mentioned how their personal dreams and satisfaction were superseded by those of their stepchildren and mate.

Whatever else is happening, insist on time for yourself to gaze into space, listen to music, keep your journal up-to-date, seek out new experiences and personal challenges, and, of course, smell the roses! If you have to, explain that this will make you a better person, a better wife, and a better stepmom. A person whose soul is deprived of attention will inevitably begrudge helping others function well in their lives. This is an essential form of self-therapy and doesn't cost a thing.

Family and Friends: Strong Shoulders, Warm Embraces

Don't forget, friends and family can be one of the most important safety nets in our lives, letting us vent when things get rough, offering an honest opinion about what's troubling us. Even confidants not involved in a stepfamily can offer an objective idea or two.

It bears repeating that it's usually best to seek our your *own* relations and friends loyal to you, since they'll be most receptive to your perspective. It won't do you any good to talk to someone who can't think further than "those poor, hurting kids," which, although it might be true, does nothing to recognize or empathize with your feelings.

Join or Start a Stepfamily Association of America Chapter

The Stepfamily Association of America is a nonprofit educational organization founded in 1979 by Emily and John Visher to promote personal and family support through information, education, and advocacy for stepfamilies. S.A.A. has almost fifty chapters located around the country, although some states don't have one at all. California currently has fourteen (one chapter holds its meetings in the corporate offices of a major firm, following the discovery that there were so many stepparents among its employees) and is actively seeking more.

For a nominal fee, S.A.A. will provide a chapter start-up kit, detailing steps toward becoming affiliated with S.A.A., a manual, stationery for leaders, and resource catalogs for members. Chapter structure is fairly informal; leaders are volunteers (often laypeople, but sometimes therapists) who set the agenda, usually discussing one topic per monthly meeting.

There is generally no charge for attendance, but members are encouraged to join S.A.A. which, in return for annual dues, offers a ten percent discount on purchases; a quarterly magazine, *Stepfamilies,* which contains excellent articles and reports on current stepfamily research; plus an annual conference, held in various parts of the country. Couples can attend together, but where one spouse (usually the man) is unwilling to attend, the other may be welcomed alone, depending on the particular chapter leader. Some chapters hold family events—picnics, outings, etc.—but meetings usually are attended by the parents.

Two-by-Two Therapy

Stepfamily couples' groups are often an eye-opener for a husband as he hears other men, perhaps for the first time, talking about difficulties that may be very similar to his own. These groups vary enormously, sometimes being run informally by another remarried couple, sometimes more formally by a therapist or other professional.

It's good for you and your mate to recognize together that what is going on in your household is not unusual. Additionally, your mate needs to know that other stepmoms feel as you do, that your thoughts and feelings are not unusual, or perhaps that you are doing extremely well compared with others he meets. With luck, he might hear of ways to make your job a little easier!

After the meeting the two of you have an excellent opportunity to discuss in private issues that were raised by other members of the group. Often a husband is able to consider a solution more easily when it concerns other couples than when it involves his own relationship.

There are a few drawbacks to couples' groups. In the experience of some stepmoms, husbands unaccustomed to sharing their feelings remain speechless throughout the first few meetings. Sometimes, too, a stepmom is reluctant to express herself on issues concerning her stepkids, or her marital relationship, with her mate present. She might not want to admit to negative feelings or admit she is not coping well under the stress and strain of being a stepmom. And publicly complaining about her stepkids, with her mate sitting right next to her, can seem disloyal. Over time, however, as couples feel more comfortable with each other and with the group, husband and wife tend to open up more.

Keep in mind, though, that a couples' group can't replace a stepmothers' group. Which stepmom could possibly explain why "my twelve-year-old stepson is driving me crazy," while the boy's dad was present?

Other kinds of couples' groups—parenting, marriage enrichment, religious oriented, etc.—may be more readily available than those focusing on the stepfamily. (If there isn't a stepfamily couples' group in your area, consider contacting S.A.A. and starting your own.) You may find any of these other groups helpful also, since a strong marital relationship is at the heart of a successful stepfamily.

Seek Out Community Resources

You might be interested in other self-help groups for specific issues of concern in your stepfamily, for you and your mate to attend either together or separately, or for other members of the family.

Self-help or support groups are available in most communities, and your local paper or phone book probably lists many other kinds of social services as well—including government agencies, and other community organizations, crisis center and hot lines—free to the public.

School Resources: Guidance Counselors, Teachers, Social Workers

Trained in child development and education, school officials can often provide a beacon for a stepmom confounded by the behavior or needs of school-age stepchildren. These professionals see your stepkids in a different light, interacting with different people and in a different environment, and may provide guidance on how you can either help a child or relate to him. Bear in mind, though, that we found many educators who were not well informed about stepfamilies. You may find a negative bias against stepmoms from school personnel not familiar with your role. This is something we need to work to correct.

Spiritual Support: Call on Your Clergy

Some stepmoms find great spiritual comfort and practical help in talking over issues that trouble them with their priest, rabbi, or minister. A talk with a spiritual leader you trust is especially helpful if he or she has some experience with stepfamily dynamics and has been schooled in counseling techniques.

But remember, while clergy can help you reaffirm your faith in a higher power—a source of tremendous strength, comfort, and serenity for many people—it is almost impossible for an unmarried religious leader to have a true grasp of how a stepmom feels, the relationships she is involved with, or the issues she needs to deal with, unless he or she has observed or counseled other stepfamilies.

Spiritual support groups that offer something beyond practical advice and guidance are becoming more available. While not appealing to everyone, such groups may offer an interested stepmom the means to discover her own unexplored depths and strengths, from which she can draw in dealing with difficulties that appear to be insurmountable.

Professional Help: How Do You Know You Need It?

When you face violence, either mental or physical, substance abuse, or any other circumstance in which you are frightened or feel out of your depth, do not hesitate to use outside intervention as quickly as possible. A serious situation, such as how to respond to a stepson on drugs, might mean working with a team of professionals, finding a rehab center, family therapy, or couples therapy for you and his dad. You might additionally believe that you, personally, need to work with a therapist who can help you uncover resources within yourself or provide new insights to help you deal with difficult issues.

If you're not in an emergency situation but sense a lack of progress in your stepfamily, feel your situation is "tenuous," or if you are experiencing situations in your home that make you uncomfortable, do something about it. Complaining, or suffering in silence, is useless; there is no reason to continue to endure days of unhappiness or sleepless nights. If you or anyone in your stepfamily isn't happy and thriving, seek some help and guidance. It is usually the woman in any family who reaches out when things get difficult. Get on with it!

Daphne's twelve-year-old stepson, Toby, functioned well when living with her and his dad but was having trouble coping with life at Mom's house. Toby's mother, bitter and depressed following her divorce, treated him like a baby, complete with baby talk. Daphne and her husband had encouraged Toby's mom to seek help, but she insisted they were the ones who needed therapy, since they were the ones who were upset.

Said Daphne, "Toby behaves like a reasonably well adjusted boy with us, until the day before he goes back to his mom, when he reverts to babyhood, wrapping himself in his security blanket and feeling sick."

Unable to reason with the mother, Daphne and her husband decided to have Toby see a child psychologist. "Within a few sessions, he began to see his mom and her problems in a new light and could talk calmly about how he could help her," this stepmom said. Toby also admitted he found it hard to live in two households where he was treated so differently. Several more visits to his doctor helped him become more confident in handling this.

Mediation: Finding the Right Pro

We reviewed mediation as a practical and cost-effective alternative to legal recourse in our chapter on custody. While mediation is not geared toward handling the emotions that accompany the issues, positive feelings often do follow a practical resolution.

How do you decide whether mediation or therapy is appropriate for your specific concerns?

First, consider the outcome you want. If your goal is to have your stepson relate well to you, consider therapy, because that's an emotional/relationship issue. But if you simply want mealtimes together to be less stressful, by replacing your stepson's bad manners and rudeness at the table with acceptable behavior, mediation might be the way to go, since your goal is a purely practical one that can be negotiated. Other issues might be your stepdaughter's use of the family car or her not doing agreed-upon chores. Mediation doesn't attempt to change anything but behavior; it can eliminate discord and handle practical matters related to home management. Once your stepson sees that both of you can enjoy a pleasant dinner-table conversation about his school activities or the local baseball team, he might come gradually to relate better to you anyway.

How do you find the right mediator? If you believe your stepfamily might be able to use mediation to resolve a practical issue, Susan Norwood, president of the Family Mediation Council of Louisiana, suggests you seek one with a background in either social work or counseling, who is more likely to have knowledge of family dynamics and relationships and be accustomed to working sensitively with people. Few mediators are familiar with stepfamily dynamics, although you may manage to find one. Try, because it helps if he or she understands the specifics involved. Some mediators come from a legal background and may be more helpful in legal disputes than practical domestic issues.

Try to get a lead on a good mediator through word of mouth. A recommendation from someone you respect who has worked with a particular mediator is ideal, although it doesn't necessarily mean you, too, will feel comfortable with him or her. Check with your local professional associations, a counselors' association, or a social workers' association. Even your local bar association may have a listing of family mediators. There may also be a family mediation council in your particular area of the country that can provide you with a list of names.

Qualifications for mediators are determined at the state level; some states don't have any pertaining to mediators. Some states require licensing; others do not. One of the associations you call can tell you this. Ask the mediator you are considering about his or her background and qualifications, but above all, feel certain you can work comfortably with the person you select.

Individual Therapy

When would a stepmom seek individual therapy? Gail Chandler, a marriage and family therapist in Wallingford, Connecticut, is a stepmother with personal knowledge of divorce, remarriage, children, and stepchildren issues. Upon this foundation she designed and teaches a course on divorce and remarriage as part of a master's degree program in marriage and family therapy.

Chandler advises stepmoms to consider individual help not only for major issues—infidelity, violence, physical, mental or sexual abuse, alcohol or drug problems—but also when she is experiencing feelings that are alien to her, that are unusually disturbing, long-lasting and out of proportion to the situation, particularly if these feelings are causing conflict within her stepfamily.

Chandler believes that if a stepmom's mate makes light of her feelings, belittles her, and refuses to try to understand, and if he is also overwhelmed by inappropriate behavior from his kids, perhaps defending them, he needs to attend therapy sessions with her. She affirms that the couple relationship must be strong, with most marital issues handled before bringing in the children for family therapy. Other therapists might work in the reverse, wishing to see the whole family initially to assess where the difficulties lie. Once they see a possible source of the conflicts, they zero in and will work with the individual family member most troubled by the situation.

Sheila Pakula, a stepmother and a therapist who specializes in stepfamily issues and practices in Weston, Connecticut, adds that you might decide you need some help when you have unusual reactions to others—for example, bursting into tears when a twelve-year-old stepchild is rude to you. She points out that most twelve-year-olds are rude from time to time, particularly to a stepmom, and in this context (though very unpleasant) their behavior would not be unusual.

To better evaluate what's happening in your stepfamily, particularly the disturbing issues, Pakula suggests that stepmoms attend a support group to learn what other stepmoms are experiencing and how they are coping. If you find you're having persistent trouble dealing with common issues—those experienced by most stepmoms—you probably can benefit from skilled professional help. If a checkup with your medical doctor turns up no physical reason for ills such as stomach and digestive problems, anxiety, headaches, or poor sleep, and you are experiencing a difficult period in your stepfamily life, it's another signal that you might need outside help.

Family Counseling: the Big Picture

The goal of family counseling is to help create a viable family. It is particularly effective in stabilizing family dynamics and tying up loose ends over the dissolution of previous families— for example, when children and parents perceive the divorce differently, when guilt is felt over Mom's death, or when the kids have been encouraged or allowed to believe their stepmom broke up their parents' marriage.

Family therapy can also help to clear up misperceptions by airing and discussing them. Kids might believe their stepmom doesn't like them or want them, while a stepmom might be convinced that her stepkids hate her. In this arena kids are able to express their feelings and to hear from a third party when and why their behavior is inappropriate. A family therapist can bring all the feelings out into the open, where they can be addressed and resolved. Another aim of the family therapist is to find some common denominators among stepfamily members in order to help create mutual goals toward bonding and understanding.

Pakula points out that in some cases, from a purely practical point of view, it makes more sense for a family to work together rather than individually. If you had various family members working with individual therapists, due to confidentiality, you would not get the overall family picture and be able to discuss issues affecting all family members.

We continue to stress that from the stepmom's perspective, very little will help until she has a sound, secure, and supportive relationship with her mate. Focus on this primary relationship first.

Selecting the Right Therapist

A friend or colleague who has worked successfully with a therapist might be as good a recommendation as you will find in your search for the right professional for you or your stepfamily. Second choice might be a referral from someone you trust—perhaps your doctor, teacher, minister, another stepmom, or another parent—who respects the skills of a particular therapist.

Pakula recommends shopping around when seeking a therapist. During your initial call or visit to the therapist's office, explain that you might be contacting other recommendations before making a decision, and describe what you are looking for: "I need some guidance on being a stepmom, and I'd like to find out why I'm having such a difficult time [with my stepson/helping my husband understand my position/with my negative feelings about his ex-wife], because I want this marriage to work."

It is essential the therapist you are considering has received training in remarried family issues. Whether or not you need a therapist who is also a stepparent is debatable: if a therapist has had disappointing personal experiences, with a negative outcome—e.g. divorce—this person might have some residual personal bitterness or bias, perhaps not an ideal frame of mind for advising a stepmother. On the other hand, a therapist who has been married three times and divorced twice and has several biological kids with different mates and a range of stepkids covering a twenty-year age span, though seemingly unsuccessful in his or her own relationships, might well offer an excellent trove of personal experience from which to work.

The most important issue, once you are satisfied with a therapist's qualifications and experience, is that you be comfortable with the person you are going to discuss your innermost thoughts and feelings with. Don't be influenced by an office with a tight schedule or by one who can fit you in the following day—your instincts and intuition about your therapist are what matters. Similarly, if your child declares he hates his therapist, and you insist he continue with this particular person, you are wasting money and are not honoring his judgment and needs. After a session or two, if you or a member of your family is not happy with a particular therapist, there is no need to return. Move on, and find another.

Some therapists charge for an initial consultation; others do not. Some will also work on a sliding scale, depending on how much the patient can afford to pay. If your funds are low and you believe you or a member of your family needs therapy, don't despair. Check your state mental health center, which may have various offices around your particular state, and ask what facilities it has for someone in your position. Connecticut, for example, has a team of psychiatrists, psychologists, and social workers at the state's New Haven office, who can work with patients on a walk-in basis. They work on a sliding scale, believing patients prefer to pay *something* when they can afford to. The services offered vary from state to state.

Locally, in your town or city, you might find a church, synagogue, or school that runs group therapy for either adults or kids or both, often led by a psychotherapist. Remember, too, your kids or stepkids can often receive help from their school guidance counselor or social worker. Also, sometimes groups are run by the school for kids of divorced parents, or you might be lucky to find one for stepkids. If this is not the case, ask the school to consider forming such a group. Until we ask for these services, and it is recognized that they are needed, no one is likely to offer them.

Seeking Help: Use Caution and Common Sense

It's common these days to talk about "dysfunctional" families. Some people actually joke, "What can you expect—my family's totally dysfunctional," often without the slightest notion of what it means. It's also somewhat fashionable to have a "shrink," as in, "My shrink thinks I'm too serious."

Take care not to become overly absorbed in therapy, oblivious to anything but your difficulties or those of your stepfamily. One of the points made by Mary Pipher in her book

Reviving Ophelia (Ballantine, 1994) (concerning adolescent girls) is that psychology sometimes tends to have a negative view of families. Be sure you are able to evaluate the good things too. Notes Pipher, "Good therapists work to shore up family bonds and to give hope to flagging families." If yours does not, you don't need him or her. Move on.

Unfortunately, as we learned during our research, stepmoms have been harmed by some bad advice given to them by therapists not familiar with the particular challenges of stepmotherhood. While we recommend that you work with a therapist when you feel no other resource can provide what you need, we were delighted to hear therapists we spoke with suggest caution and common sense in seeking out professional help.

Pipher, in chapter 6 of her book *The Shelter of Each Other: Rebuilding Our Families* (Ballantine, 1996) explains: "For the most part, we therapists are well-meaning people with honorable intentions. But we work with theories developed for a different world. Experts with good intentions can do harm. We need to be as scrupulous about the effects as about the intentions of our behavior." Later in the same chapter she says: "We are trained to focus on the client and ignore the people in the client's life. This can contribute to an 'I am the center of the universe' mentality. At its most superficial level, therapy teaches that feeling good is being good and that duty and obligation are onerous chains, better off broken."

We recommend that a stepmom involved in or considering therapy for herself or a member of her family read Pipher's full chapter. To have one member of a stepfamily being taught by her therapist the reverse of what a stepmom and her mate are attempting to instill in their family can be more than counterproductive—it can be dangerous. Therapy must be used with care.

⌘

Questionnaire

1. Where are you right now in your quest for resolution to your most pressing difficulties? Examine the worst issue you have, and describe what you have done to alleviate it.

2. Are you pleased with the way you have handled finding a remedy for this issue? If not, what else can you do?

3. List the resources—perhaps taken from our suggestions above—that you have tried. Which has been most helpful so far? Why do you believe this particular suggestion has helped?

4. If you are not satisfied with the way you are working to resolve your difficulties, describe what you think you could do better.

5. Have you joined or attempted to form a stepmoms' support group? If not, why? This will contribute to your success. What is preventing you?

6. Consider very carefully whether you have an in-built resistance to seeking therapy (many people do). List your fears and prejudices. Why do you prefer to live with your unresolved issues rather than take action?

7. What advice would you give to a friend in your position?

Action Box

- Next time you have a fight with your mate that isn't resolved by bedtime, first thing next morning ask him out on a "date"—your treat. Find the most romantic restaurant your budget allows, dress as though you're still dating, and spend the evening making love talk. Avoid the topic that's causing you trouble. On the way home, after telling him how much you have enjoyed the evening, suggest a date a few days in the future to discuss and resolve your problem, giving you both time to consider your positions, now that a romantic evening has mellowed things a bit. Agree that as a backup you will seek out a mediator if you still can't resolve the problem.

- Review the difficulties you believe each member of your immediate stepfamily is experiencing. If you think anyone could benefit from one or more of the above resources, suggest/recommend what you feel would help, either directly or, in the case of a child, to his dad. Do it confidently; do it now. Traditionally and statistically, help for other family members is usually initiated by a stepmom.

CHAPTER 21

The Enlightened Stepmother:
Breakthrough or End Game?

In the final analysis, only you know if you and your husband can sustain your marriage and if the life you are leading in your stepfamily is the life you wish to lead. Only you, in your heart, know whether the possibility exists for improvement on issues that trouble you and whether you are willing to work to resolve them.

If you have read through this book, answered the questionnaires, performed the tasks suggested in our action boxes, attempted to resolve your most bothersome issues with or without outside help, by the time you read this final chapter, you will probably no longer be indecisive on the question Is life in a stepfamily what I want? (if indeed you ever were):

Yes, this is the life I want. I can build on what we all have together and make it better still. I love my husband and want to be with him.

No, this is not what I want. I can see no future for us together as a stepfamily or for me personally with this group of people. My mate and I cannot or are unwilling to resolve our difficulties.

For the stepmoms who have begun to take advantage of some of our suggested therapeutic ideas and are still hanging in there, congratulations! We hope you're feeling more encouraged to work toward a firm, happy commitment.

If your decision is *no*, we suggest you move on as soon as is practical and not waste any more of your precious life. As long as you feel confident you've tried everything and stepfamily life is still not satisfactory, and you are unhappy most of the time, it's time to leave.

Your Backup Plan

The vast majority of stepmoms we talked to had contemplated the course of action they'd take if their stepfamily didn't work out; a few had made very detailed plans.

One woman we met during our research subsequently left her stepfamily and put her plan into action. She moved to Vermont, took a job managing a gift shop owned by an old friend, and used her nest egg as a down payment on a small cottage. "I don't need much—just a few extra dollars a week to get by," she said. "What I want most of all now is peace."

Another soon-to-be-ex-stepmother lined up a move back to her hometown, Santa Barbara, California, where several of her siblings still resided. Yet another, who had visited Colorado many times on vacation with her husband, vowed to return there if stepfamily life failed. Many more had considered at least short-term alternative living arrangements for themselves and their kids.

In terms of backup plans, this is where fulfilling, or having fulfilled, your personal goals, discussed in part 1, will provide security. Stepmoms who had returned to school, had always worked, or had increased their professional skills felt more confident about becoming the sole head of household and providing for their children, should separation or divorce be the outcome.

Whatever your plan is, if it becomes necessary, put it into motion. For any number of reasons, you will have become one of the majority—the sixty-plus percent of stepparents who gave it their best but did not make it. If you are child free, the world is your oyster once more. If you have children, take time with them until they are settled into their new life, and be sure you seek support resources for yourself as well.

Sitting on the Fence?

If you are still undecided, perhaps reviewing the progress you are making will help. Consider your responses to the following:

- Am I feeling physically better than I did previously? Have headaches and stomach knots begun to disappear? Do I find myself thinking happy thoughts, instead of obsessing on the negative behavior of my stepkids or lack of support from my mate?

- Have I started doing "normal" things again, no longer immobilized by my negative emotions?

- Have I ceased to dread the visits of my stepkids, instead looking forward to and planning for them? Am I taking an interest in their lives, their opinions?

- Can I now accept that each member of my stepfamily has his or her own perspective on a situation or issue?

- Is my martial relationship less stressful? Do we argue less?

Realizing that things aren't quite as bad as they used to be might help you see you are further along the path to success than you thought.

Enlightenment Comes Slowly

Common among the stepmothers who decided against remaining with their stepfamily and opted instead for divorce was the assertion that their decision to leave had crept up on them gradually until one minor incident had tipped the scale. Ironically, successful stepmothers, too, had this experience, though on the opposite, positive end of the scale. Recalled Dusty, "One morning I just realized how much I was looking forward to having my stepson spend the weekend with us. As I shopped and planned for the weekend, I remember thinking, 'This is really cozy.' It didn't dawn on me until later that I was now looking at him as part of my family. After seven terrible years, we'd made it!"

Alana remembers, "In the space of one week, two of my friends asked me how things were going with my stepdaughter. I'd always had a terribly difficult time with her, and they were used to hearing me complain constantly. But apparently my complaints had ceased. When they brought it to my attention, I realized the two of us were actually getting along quite well."

Three Essential Ingredients for Success

This book is based on what we learned from stepmoms, together with our own personal experiences. Not surprisingly, the stepmoms who were successful shared three common characteristics. The reverse was also true—those who did not have these three ingredients did not succeed. Those who had two had only a fifty–fifty chance; those who had one, less chance still. This became more and more obvious, to the point that it was predictable—we could actually recognize a stepmom who would not make it.

1. The United Front
The first, which we have discussed in several different contexts because it is so crucial, is the united front, a.k.a. unconditional support, spousal unity. It is the foundation of your marriage and the basis of your success as a stepmom. If the couple relationship is not solid, if problems with the united front continue, you'll experience even more difficulties as time goes on. On the other hand, together you can work wonders if each of you provides the other with this unconditional support.

As we've discussed, most difficulties you experience as a stepmom are couple issues, not issues with your stepkids. If your stepson is rude, it's an issue with your mate, not the child. A child has to be taught to show his stepmother respect, with guidance from both of you. If this is not happening, it's a problem between spouses. You need to work *together* for the good of your marriage, the children, the whole stepfamily. If you cannot consider family matters as a couple reaching a joint position, you will almost certainly not succeed as a couple operating independently of each other.

2. Agreement about Finances

It's essential that you be in full agreement over financial issues. This is not to say it's essential to have enough money to go around—these days few people are in this position. But you and your mate must agree on the allocation of whatever money you do have. Money management is a day-by-day process. You cannot run the risk of disagreements cropping up on a daily basis, because strong emotions often accompany financial discussions, leading to further problems.

3. Outside Support

The third essential for you, as the stepmom, is some outside support, a nucleus of people who value you as a friend, beyond your role as a stepmother, who can encourage and comfort you, with whom you can share your successes and failures. It doesn't matter where you find these folks—from among your family and friends, groups you are part of, or professionals—your role is simply too heavy a load to carry without support.

Advantages of Life in a Stepfamily

The stepmom who feels she has conquered the troubled times, and is now moving on toward the good life with her stepfamily, needs to remember that the process of forming a stepfamily is continuous. You can never say, "It's finished"; only recognize that the worst is over and you're here to stay, continuing to build. Among the personal advantages you can enjoy as you move forward are these:

• You have become a stronger, wiser, more mature woman. You will have grown in ways you might not yet recognize.

• As you've worked together with your mate to resolve the difficulties you experienced, your marital relationship will have deepened and strengthened.

• You will feel a sense of accomplishment, achievement, personal satisfaction for a job you are doing well.

• You will enjoy being part of a unique group of people— your stepfamily—giving and receiving strength and support.

• You have acquired access to an extended family, different lifestyles, new ideas.

Several professionals have noted the advantages children in stepfamilies gain—advantages not often found in biological families. Some experts believe that children from stepfamilies, having experienced the breakup of their family of origin and the remarriage of at least one parent, are better equipped for life in our current society than children from an intact original family, who have been sheltered from what is fast becoming a common life experience. At a relatively early age, children in a stepfamily, even if only part-time members, acquire skills to cope with disruption, see sincere efforts at problem solving, perhaps for the first time in their lives. As long as they are given the necessary support, and provided they understand that it is the grown-ups in their lives who have the problems, these experiences will form models of behavior for their adult lives.

Stepfamily members also share the skills and talents of an additional adult woman along with those of her family, including stepsiblings, additional grandparents, aunts, uncles, and cousins. A stepmom can offer access to a multitude of new people with whom to make lifelong friends, to share new, exciting, different experiences and points of view.

If children come from a divorced family, they now have

the opportunity to observe a loving, successful marital relationship on which they can someday base their own. A girl has
access to another positive role model—an independent, accomplished woman who is ready and willing to offer support and
advice. A boy, too, can gain a confidant and a lifelong friend,
as well as learn how to make his future spouse a priority in
his life.

When children from a stepfamily become adults, raise families of their own, or perhaps join or form a stepfamily themselves, they will bring with them personal experience of living
in a successful stepfamily. The knowledge that this can be a
happy place in which to grow will be transferred to their own
children and stepchildren; finally, the skills they learned to
accomplish their success will be passed down to another
generation.

The Work behind Success

Stepmoms we spoke with during their first few years in a
stepfamily often used the word "work" to describe the actual
toil and labors of stepmotherhood: "It's just such hard work,"
"All I do is work," "It's more work than I imagined," etc. But
interestingly, when we asked the veteran stepmoms who felt
they had achieved success what had largely contributed to it
(other than the three essentials listed above), the term "work"
cropped up again, this time used in Webster's more positive
sense: "Physical or mental effort exerted to do or make something" (in this case a stepfamily); "purposeful activity."

Successful stepmoms, those with a commitment to make
stepfamilies a pleasant place to be, were willing to work in a
positive way to achieve their expected success. Further, they
didn't mind how hard the work was, as long as they saw
progress being made and signs that a well-functioning stepfamily was on the horizon.

According to Marta, part-time stepmom to five and mother
of two: "I'm known as the 'crisis management expert' in my
family. If anyone arrives at the airport without their ticket, it's

'Call Marta—she'll know what to do.' Lock ourselves out of the car—Marta will know how to open it. Break up with a girlfriend—Marta will be a good listener. My stepkids have called me at all hours for help and advice about life's little messes, and I'm building on that trust."

When Erica's thirteen-year-old stepdaughter weighed in at fifty pounds over the recommended healthy range for her age and height, it was her stepmom who became her partner toward a healthier lifestyle, while her siblings were calling her "Miss Piggy" and her mother denigrated her fitness goals. "We worked out a menu plan for both of us and scheduled long, fast walks together," recalled Erica. "It took time and work, but we both shaped up and, even better, became good friends."

Defining Success for Yourself

According to veteran stepmothers, you'll know it when it happens. "Something just clicks, and you know you've turned the corner." It is the rare stepfamily that would use the word "success" in connection with gaining wealth, fame, or rank, the context in which it is often used. But Webster's *New World Dictionary* provides an appropriate definition in terms of the stepfamily: "a favorable or satisfactory outcome or result"; "coming about, taking place, or turning out to be as was hoped for."

What do you, as one special stepmother, hope for?

When asked if they thought they were doing a good job, most stepmothers interviewed said they thought they were doing "the best they could." All were valiantly trying to do right by their family, often, unfortunately (and unnecessarily), at considerable cost to themselves. Rating their own performance on a scale of one to ten, few were in the three-to-seven range. They either were disappointed in their performance as a stepmom and rated themselves one or two or were reasonably happy with their achievements and gave themselves an eight-to-ten rating.

When questioned about the ingredients of success for

them, stepmothers came up with many different responses, but the most popular one was "just to feel comfortable."

Others are . . .

- to be happy

- not to spend all my time pleasing others

- to know when to step back

- to know how to balance all the relationships involved

- to allow independence in others

- to have a supportive partner

- to be a positive adult influence or figure

- to have maturity, patience, confidence, and self-esteem and to be flexible

- to have encouraged mutual respect among all members of the family.

Success is different for every stepmom, but it is important to know what you're aiming for. While it would be reassuring and a great morale booster if others were able to describe you as a "successful stepmother," the way you see yourself and the way you feel about yourself as a stepmother are of far greater importance.

One of our classes came up with the following "success" statement: If we could truly say we had "created a peaceful atmosphere in our home in which both full- and part-time stepfamily members felt welcome and comfortable and were able to fulfill their potential with the support and help of other members," we'd feel very pleased with ourselves.

That is an all-encompassing definition that we worked on for an entire session. When asked during interviews for their personal experiences of success, stepmothers volunteered these criteria:

- The year Donna's stepson returned from the Peace Corps in Africa on November 22 so he wouldn't miss her "Turkey Day" was when she knew she was a success.

- Sharon felt if her stepchildren remembered her birthday with a card, she would feel successful.

- For Elaine, each graduation in her large family of three children and four stepchildren, from kindergarten through graduate school, was an indication to her that she was a successful stepmom. The higher the number of children's achievements in any one year, the greater success she felt. She would attend each ceremony, decked out in slightly inappropriate splendor and bask in reflected glory. Another graduation, another feather in her cap, another success for her.

- Amy said, "I'd settle for simple acceptance, just so I didn't feel like an outsider all the time." For other women, an occasional "thank you" would suffice and would indicate some kind of minimal success.

- Kiki felt success was knowing "when to acknowledge that this is probably as good as it gets and not to try for the unattainable." This from a thirty-nine-year-old, battle-scarred stepmother who had almost given up but was now enjoying a period of relative peace. She explained that her stepkids seemed to accept her and her own children, when previously the house was ruled by tension and fighting.

Trust yourself. When your feel you are doing a good job contributing in your own way to the lives of your stepfamily, consider yourself successful.

Take Pride in Your Accomplishments

Overwhelmingly, stepmoms seemed unable to give themselves credit for what they were contributing to their family. We heard only a handful verbally pat themselves on the back.

Donna Smith remarks on this in her book *Stepmothering* (Harvester Wheatsheaf, 1990): "Stepmothers, in all their permutations, play a huge role in providing this [referring to a supportive environment, a sense of belonging and of being accepted which children want and need], and they should be valued for it. They need to have a more positive attitude toward themselves and the job they do as stepmothers, and this is linked, obviously, to social attitudes. I have found that, even when a stepmother can point to success in her stepfamily, her stepmother status is not a matter of personal pride. The ideal of the nuclear family is too deeply ingrained."

Action Box

- Review your balance sheet from chapter 19. If you don't already do so, remind yourself frequently of the items you listed in column 1, those gifts you bring your stepfamily.

- Remind yourself of the improvements you've seen within your family over the months or years you've been a stepmom, for which you have been responsible or have contributed toward.

- You're a pretty remarkable woman to have created all these positive issues! Tell yourself often—minimumly each morning when you awaken and before you go to sleep at night—that without you your family would be very much worse off, even though they might not know it. Congratulate yourself; reward yourself. Feel good about yourself for all your achievements!

Afterword

W e've met some extraordinary women, shared their thoughts and feelings, hurts and happiness, listened to their experiences, and learned a great deal from them.

Our commitment to these women and to you was to present with honesty the role of the stepmother and her particular, unique issues. We hope this book will contribute to the long-overdue dismantling of unacceptable myths, prejudices, and stereotypes of stepmotherhood, expose the role to scrutiny, and open a dialogue in support of the women who will inhabit this role after us. What a stepmom needs from our culture is an understanding of her role— impossible to achieve unless we, the stepmoms of today, start to make ourselves visible and articulate in our quest for support.

Raising a child to become a vital, self-supporting, independent, responsible adult is a glorious achievement. Helping to raise someone else's child might well be an even greater, more selfless accomplishment! We met stepmoms who were exhilarated by the love and appreciation they received from their stepfamilies. Many women told of the strong bonds of love and trust they had developed with their stepchildren. We know it's possible.

A Dilemma

But we faced a dilemma in concluding this book. we would love to have been able to tell you that life would be wonderful if only you did this, this, and that. We wanted to leave you with the confident feeling that once you know the secret, it would be easy.

Unfortunately, this isn't the case. We determined at the outset to reveal the intimate, day-to-day experiences of step-moms—often poignant, sometimes painful—complete with all the warts. By now you will realize what a complicated job stepmotherhood is. Stepfamily life is not simple, least of all negotiating what is arguably the most difficult of all human relationships—that of stepmother and stepchild.

What we firmly believe, however, is that like the rest of life, stepmotherhood is what you make of it. Successful step-moms have built each day on the previous day's successes, learning from the mistakes they made, trying different things different ways until they worked.

These women have earned the right to be proud of them-selves and their achievements, proud of their husbands, their own children and stepchildren, continuing to grow and move toward more success.

Our Hope for the Future

The future of our country, our personal future and legacy, lies with our children. Stepmothers—a silent constituency in America, perhaps throughout the world—play a huge part in the future of those children. and, although unacknowledged, are doing an amazing job. Our advice throughout has been to be proactive—if we don't look out for ourselves, nobody else will.

To that end, here's what we need:

We—our society at large and the stepmom herself—need to regard stepmotherhood with an entirely new attitude. There are four "branches" of motherhood—step, foster, adoptive, and biological. Some women become more than one type of mother—it is possible, though unusual, to fulfill all four simul-taneously, given the space, money, and wish to do so. Since the four types of motherhood entail performing nurturing and guiding of the children in her care, why the disparity of recognition? Why does one branch—stepmotherhood—receive very little positive acknowledgment, while the other three branches are applauded?

Equally crucial, a stepmother needs to value herself, her own worth, something she often finds hard to do in the climate that surrounds stepmotherhood. Having met so many stepmoms, we assure you, you are an impressive group of women. Recognize this, and be proud!

We need to lobby for step maternity leave. While a stepmom who will be taking on responsibilities for small children does not need time to recover physically from childbirth, as biological moms do, she certainly needs time to ease into her role emotionally and practically. New mothers usually have their house in order, the new baby's bedroom ready to welcome him, his necessities, from baby lotion to receiving blanket, ready and waiting. A stepmom, who might have stepkids arriving the first weekend after moving to a new location, can be required to share responsibility for several small children whom she may hardly know all at one time.

We need to persuade society to examine the role of the biological mother as she affects our stepfamilies. From the perspective of many stepmoms, the behavior of some mothers is an aberration of nature—doing untold harm to their own offspring, putting their own anger and desire for revenge above the needs and well-being of their children, while society looks away because she is "mother." Can we continue to accept this damage as being "normal"?

Finally, we must insist upon a new title for ourselves. Continuing to use the word "stepmother" means we are continually put in the burdensome position of having to "overcome" deeply held misperceptions and prejudices.

Not only does "stepmother" have ugly connotations, but it also causes confusion, tension and divided loyalties—as might any term that includes "mother"—in our minds, our stepchildren's minds and in the minds of mothers. Without the word "mother" in our title we'd feel emotionally freer to create this role in our own way and we'd seem less of a threat to our stepchildren's mom, enabling each of us to support the other for the benefit of children in stepfamilies.

Finding a brand new name for this role—one that accurately and positively describes who we are, how we see ourselves, and what we do in relation to our husband and his children will undoubtedly help everyone look at the role in a more enlightened way. Wouldn't it be wonderful to take on a new title that could evoke the same valued, life-affirming feelings in children and adults as "Fairy Godmother" or "Guardian Angel"? Let's put our collective heads together and do it.

We *must* start speaking up on these issues. We cannot expect others to understand our experiences unless we talk about them honestly.

Stepmoms of Tomorrow

As our daughters and stepdaughters grow up to become stepmothers themselves—as is increasingly the case—we cannot expect them to do so under the same cloud of prejudice as current stepmoms. No one would wish the experiences we heard to be revisited on another generation of stepmoms. There are ways we can and must respect and support the role, or young women will not be willing to take it on.

Please let us have your comments on what you liked and didn't like about this book. Let us have your suggestions as to what you felt was missing—anything you would like to have known but we didn't provide. And tell us about the sources of help you did receive and why you found them valuable.

Stepmoms, you are wonderful, life-affirming women. As author and writer, we are bursting with pride to be among you. Reach out and support one another!

Appendix 1

Research

The questionnaire reproduced here forms the basis of the ninety-five personal interviews carried out for this book over a period of five years across the United States, Canada, and the United Kingdom. The women were white, generally from a middle-income bracket, their ages ranging from twenty-five to seventy-two.

Following the structured (questionnaire) section of the interview, time was allowed for an unstructured portion during which the stepmom was prompted to talk about issues specific to her and her circumstances—some of which I could never have anticipated.

Each approach elicited different information, providing details over and above what was initiated by the questions or what was expected. The stepmom offered a supportive listener her thoughts, feelings, ideas, fears, and concerns on the subject.

This unstructured section was not given a time limit other than how long the stepmom and interviewer had available—which frequently became four or five hours, sometimes as long as six hours, in addition to the time taken for the structured portion.

Some follow-up interviews were conducted either in person or by telephone to learn the outcome of particular ongoing events taking place in the lives at the time of the original interview—for example, those expecting a baby or considering divorce.

The subject of stepmotherhood was also discussed on a more specific basis with approximately seventy other stepmoms, about-to-be stepmoms, and those considering stepmotherhood who attended support groups, focus groups, and classes. Information learned from these women is included.

Since anonymity was guaranteed, names, locations and sometimes the number and ages of children and stepchildren have been changed.

Given the many variables of any one stepmother who took part in this research—number and personalities of family members and extended-family members, varying outside influences, personal-background details, economic situation, health, custody arrangements, divorce climate where one is considered—I did not attempt to develop statistical information.

Stepmother Research

STATUS:

Is this your first marriage?

If not, were you divorced or widowed?

Do you have biological children?

Sex and ages?

Was your husband divorced or widowed?

Sexes and ages of husband's children?

PRIOR TO MARRIAGE:

1. Did you take the fact that your husband had children into consideration when deciding to marry him?

   Before marriage, as you anticipated becoming a stepmother, what were your feelings and frame of mind?

   With the benefit of hindsight, what would you have done differently either before your marriage or in the early stages?

   Did you do anything you now consider a mistake?

   Was your attitude, in retrospect, approximately correct?

2. Did you, your husband, or any member of your new family seek professional counseling (a) before or (b) during the marriage?
   If so, what prompted this?
   What type of counseling was used?
   Was it beneficial? If so, in what way?

3. How do you feel about the financial arrangements within your new family? (I'm looking not for dollar details but for your feelings.)
   Are you working?
   Do you contribute to the family expenses?
   Are you comfortable with the arrangements that exist should your husband predecease you?
   Are you and your biological children adequately taken care of in such an event?
   Are your stepchildren taken care of?
   Is there any conflict here between the way your biological children and stepchildren will be protected if your husband should die first?
   Are you satisfied with the way financial matters would be handled if you should predecease your husband?

4. Is your husband paying alimony or child support?
   How do you feel about this?
   Does this expense affect the financial stability of your new family?
   Describe your overall feelings about the fairness of these arrangements.

5. Do you consider you have a good relationship with your husband?
   Can you discuss all problems with him concerning his children and your own fairly easily?
   Does he understand your feelings, both positive and negative, about his children?
   Did you together work out guidelines for the smooth running of the household?
   Is he totally supportive of you when the children are present?

Describe any conflicts you may have in this area.
What have you learned that helps you resolve these conflicts?

6. How do you believe your stepchildren see you?
   Is this view of you realistic, in your opinion?
   If there are any negative aspects, do they bother you?
   If not, why? If they do, why?

7. How do you feel about yourself and the way you are working with your new family?
   Are you proud of yourself? Do you think you are doing a good job?
   Rate your performance on a scale of 1–10.

8. Describe your stepchildren, one by one.
   Do you like them? Love them?
   Do you believe you have contributed positively toward their upbringing?
   If so, describe. If not, why?

9. Have you at any time felt overwhelmed and unable to cope with the complexities you have encountered? Explain.
   Do you ever feel you are to blame (or are blamed by others) for problems and conflicts that arise? Explain.
   Are there more/different complexities than those you anticipated? Explain.

10. What is it in your past that has had the greatest bearing on the way you have handled your stepfamily circumstances?
    Is there any "personal baggage" you would like to have lost that would have made becoming a stepmother easier for you?
    If you have not had a biological child of your own, do you regret this?
    Was it hard for you to accept? What have you done to make it easier for yourself?

What is the single most difficult aspect of stepmothering for you?

Do you have any words of wisdom for other women in your position?

Any advice you'd like to offer?

Would you marry this same man again?

Perdita Kirkness Norwood
Author

APPENDIX 2

Recommended Reading List

New titles on parenting, stepparenting, and family life appear on an almost daily basis. The following are among those we found helpful when preparing this book, but they represent the tip of an enormous iceberg. We strongly suggest that stepmoms forage around in their local libraries and discount-chain bookstores for titles that appeal to them. Skim what looks interesting and helpful—you cannot buy every book that seems useful—then check to see if a particular title you'd like to reread is in your library. Nothing will make your life simpler than to continue to learn and research in the area of remarriage, stepfamilies, and related subjects. The more you learn, the less complex your role will become. Remember that most stepmoms told us, "If only I had known. . . ." Read, read, read, to make sure you are not among those who didn't know!

Titles preceded by an asterisk can be obtained (along with many others) from the Stepfamily Association of America: 1–800–735–0329.

Anton, Linda Hunt. *Never to Be a Mother: A Guide for All Women Who Didn't—or Couldn't—Have Children.* New York: HarperCollins, 1992. Ten steps to healing the heartache and leading a rich, childfree life. For stepmoms who question whether they wish to have a baby or whose husband does not want one.

*Artlip, Mary Ann, James A. Artlip, and Earl S. Saltzman. *The New American Family: Tools for Strengthening Step-Families*. Lancaster, Pennsylvania: Starburst, 1993. Provides results of a ten-page questionnaire filled out by more than 500 stepparents from forty-seven states.

Baldridge, Letitia. *Letitia Baldrige's More than Manners: Raising Today's Kids to Have Kind Manners and Good Hearts*. New York: Simon & Schuster–Rawson, 1997. Excellent section advising on the behavior of children in stepfamilies.

Beauvais-Godwin, Laura, and Raymond Godwin. *The Complete Adoption Book*. Holbrook, Massachusetts: Adams Media, 1997.

*Berman, Claire. *Making It as a Stepparent: New Roles/New Rules*. New York: Doubleday-Perennial, 1986. Provides a compassionate exploration of the dynamics of stepfamilies.

*Bernstein, Anne C. *Yours, Mine, and Ours: How Families Change When Remarried Parents Have a Child Together*. New York: Scribner, 1989. Explores changing family dynamics brought about when a divorced, widowed, or single parent chooses to have a child with a new spouse.

*Blau, Melinda. *Families Apart: Ten Keys to Successful Co-Parenting*. New York: Putnam, 1994. Divorce ends a marriage, but not a family. Provides a new approach to co-parenting with ten solid principles for maintaining communication, caring, and strong relationships.

Bloomfield, Harold H., with Robert B. Kory. *Making Peace in Your Stepfamily: Surviving and Thriving as Parents and Stepparents*. New York: Hyperion, 1993.

Breathnach, Sarah Ban. *Simple Abundance: A Daybook of Comfort and Joy*. New York: Warner, 1995. A "downshifting lifestyle book" for stepmoms who want to lead a happier, more fulfilling, and contented way of life. A perfect gift for a struggling stepmom to give herself.

Brothers, Joyce. *Widowed*. New York: Ballantine, 1992.

Brown, Beth E. *When You're Mom No. Two: A Word of Hope for Stepmothers*. Los Angeles: Servant-Vine Books, 1991.

*Burns, Cherie. *Stepmotherhood: How to Survive without Feeling Frustrated, Left Out, or Wicked*. New York: Times Books,

1985. A must-read for every stepmother and stepmother-to-be. Based on interviews with forty stepmothers, explores the unique role of the stepmom.

Caine, Lynn. *Being a Widow.* New York: Arbor House, 1988. A self-help book full of practical advice and wisdom for potential stepmoms who are not quite sure if they're ready to move on yet.

Chopra, Deepak. *The Seven Spiritual Laws of Success: A Practical Guide to the Fulfillment of Your Dreams.* San Rafael, California: Amber-Allen/New World Library, 1994. For stepmoms wishing to take the spiritual route, this can provide a different approach to resolving difficult issues.

Clark, Don. *Loving Someone Gay.* Berkeley, California: Celestial, 1987. A gay therapist offers sensitive, intelligent guidance to gay people and those who care about them. Revised and updated.

Doherty, William J. *The Intentional Family: How to Build Family Ties in our Modern World.* Reading, Massachusetts: Addison-Wesley, 1997. Including stepfamilies in his discussion, the author provides a manual for building a modern family, from daily routines to special events.

Edelman, Hope. *Motherless Daughters: The Legacy of Loss.* New York: Addison-Wesley, 1994. Helpful for stepmoms married to a widower with daughter(s).

*Einstein, Elizabeth, and Linda Albert. *Strengthening Your Stepfamily.* Circle Pines, Minnesota: American Guidance Service, 1986. Written by stepparents, for stepparents, about stepparenting. The authors separate myth from reality in addressing tough stepfamily issues.

*Engel, Margorie. *Weddings for Complicated Families: The New Etiquette.* Boston: Mount Ivy Press, 1993. Covers most issues a stepmom-to-be faces when making wedding plans.

Faber, Adele, and Elaine Mazlish. *Siblings without Rivalry: How to Help Your Children Live Together So You Can Live Too.* New York: Avon, 1987. Not specific to stepfamilies, but some very helpful suggestions.

Follett, Barbara Lee. *Checklist for a Perfect Wedding: The Indispensable Guide for Every Wedding, First or Second.* New

York: Doubleday, 1986. First-rate section, "Here Comes the Bride—Again; or, Always a Bride, Never a Bridesmaid."

Gates, Philomene. *Suddenly Alone: A Woman's Guide to Widowhood.* New York: Harper & Row, 1990. Written by an attorney, offers shared experience and clear, down-to-earth advice on how to cope with a new lifestyle and handle the practical problems.

Getzoff, Ann, and Carolyn McClenahan. *Stepkids: A Survival Guide for Teenagers in Stepfamilies and for Stepparents Doubtful of Their Own Survival.* New York: Walker, 1985. Contains an excellent, positive chapter, "What Is So Great about Stepfamilies?" Show to your stepkids!

Gottman, John, with Nan Silver. *Why Marriages Succeed or Fail.* New York: Simon & Schuster, 1994. A great resource for couples trying to improve their relationship.

Gray, John. *Men Are from Mars, Women Are from Venus: A Practical Guide for Improving Communication and Getting What You Want in Your Relationships.* New York: Harper Collins, 1992. A guide for improving communication and understanding your mate.

Jones, Merry Bloch, and Jo Ann Schiller. *Stepmothers: Keeping It Together with Your Husband and His Kids.* New York: Carol Publishing Group, 1992. Interesting case studies pointing out the complexity of the stepmother's role.

*Keenan, Barbara Mullen. *When You Marry a Man with Children: How to Put Your Marriage First and Stay in Love.* New York: Pocket Books, 1992. Provides help in resolving typical stepfamily problems.

Kelley, Patricia. *Developing Healthy Stepfamilies: Twenty Families Tell Their Stories.* Binghamton, New York: Harrington, 1995. A close look at twenty well-functioning stepfamilies—positive and upbeat—showing it can be done!

Lafayette, Leslie. *Why Don't You Have Kids?: Living a Full Life without Parenthood.* New York: Kensington, 1995.

Leman, Kevin. *Living in a Stepfamily without Getting Stepped On: Helping Your Children Survive the Birth Order Blender.* Nashville: Thomas Nelson, 1994. Focuses on how birth order affects stepfamily relationships.

*Maglin, Nan Bauer, and Nancy Schniedewind, eds. *Women and Stepfamilies: Voices of Anger and Love*. Philadelphia: Temple University Press, 1989. Women in stepfamilies describe their experiences from their perspective as mothers, stepmothers, stepdaughters, stepsisters, and stepgrandmothers. Excellent chapter, "There for Each Other: A Stepmothers' Support Group," for those interested in forming or participating in such a group.

Meryman, Richard. *Hope: A Loss Survived*. Boston: Little, Brown, 1984. For your mate, if you question that he is ready to move on yet.

Morris, Desmond. *Babywatching*. New York: Crown, 1991. For those who know little or nothing about babies. Some basic facts on the first year of life.

Newman, Margaret. *Stepfamily Realities: How to Overcome Difficulties and Have a Happy Family*. Oakland, California: New Harbinger, 1994.

Noble, June, and Willian Noble. *How to Live with Other People's Children*. New York: Hawthorn, 1977. Creating honest relationships within the stepfamily.

Papernow, Patricia L. *Becoming a Stepfamily: Patterns of Development in Remarried Families*. San Francisco: Jossey-Bass, 1993. Based on interviews with more than one hundred stepfamily members, describes stages of forming a cohesive group of people. (Papernow originally identified the stages of stepfamily development.)

Pickhardt, Carl E. *Keys to Successful Step-Fathering*. New York: Barron's, 1997. Guide to stepdads easing into their role. Nice gift for your mate if you have biological children.

Pipher, Mary. *Reviving Ophelia: Saving the Selves of Adolescent Girls*. New York: Ballantine, 1994. Helpful in understanding teenage stepdaughters.

————*The Shelter of Each Other: Rebuilding Our Families*. New York: Ballantine, 1996. Chapters 6 and 7 helpful for those considering psychotherapy. Not specific to stepfamilies.

Pogrebin, Letty Cottin. *Family Politics: Love and Power on an Intimate Frontier*. New York: McGraw-Hill, 1983. Chapter 5, "Power Struggles on the Home Front," and in particular pages 113–25, on the stepfamily, worthwhile for the stepmom.

Post, Elizabeth L. *Emily Post on Second Weddings.* New York: Harper-Perennial, 1991.

Roosevelt, Ruth, and Jeannette Lofas. *Living in Step: A Remarriage Manual for Parents and Children.* New York: McGraw Hill: TAB Books, 1977.

Rosin, Mark Bruce. *Stepfathering: Stepfathers' Advice on Creating a New Family.* New York: Simon & Schuster, 1987. Perfect for your mate if he is stepdad to your kids. Based on stories from fifty stepdads.

Rowlands, Peter. *Love Me, Love My Kids: A Guide for the New Partner.* New York: Continuum, 1983. Offers helpful advice for both potential stepmom and stepdad.

Rubin, Jeffrey, and Carol Rubin. *When Families Fight: How to Handle Conflict with Those You Love.* New York: William Morrow, 1989. Covers most issues a family might disagree over, "from the physical to the long smoldering to the petty." Not specifically step, but relevant to anyone and everyone, following the entire life cycle of a family.

Salk, Lee. *Familyhood: Nurturing the Values That Matter.* New York: Simon & Schuster, 1992.

Scarf, Maggie. *Intimate Partners: Patterns in Love and Marriage.* New York: Ballantine, 1987. Discusses causes of and cures for martial incompatibility. Can help in building your united front.

————*Unfinished Business: Pressure Points in the Lives of Women.* New York: Ballantine, 1986. Covers six decades of a woman's life and the physical and psychological pressure points that characterize each.

Schaffer, Judith, and Christina Lindstorm. *How to Raise an Adopted Child: A Guide to Help Your Child Flourish from Infancy through Adolescence.* New York: Crown-Copestone Press, 1989. Written by cofounders of Center for Adoptive Families, in Manhattan. Not step specific.

Secunda, Victoria. *Women and Their Fathers: The Sexual and Romantic Impact of the First Man in Your Life.* New York: Doubleday-Dell, 1993.

Sheey, Gail. *Passages*. New York: Bantam, 1984. Insights into the predictable adult crises most people experience while continuing to grow and reach their potential.

Simpson, Eileen. *Late Love: A Celebration of Marriage after Fifty*. New York: Houghton Mifflin, 1994.

Smith, Donna. *Stepmothering*. New York: Harvester Wheatsheaf, 1990.

Spock, Benjamin M. *A Better World for Our Children: Rebuilding American Family Values*. Bethesda, Maryland: National Press, 1994.

*Stepfamily Association of America, Inc. *Stepfamilies Stepping Ahead: An Eight-Step Program for Successful Family Living*. Lincoln, Nebraska: Stepfamilies Press, 1989. Developed by the founders of the Stepfamily Association of America, Emily and John Visher, following ten years of the group's experience. Free with S.A.A. membership.

Stoddard, Alexandra *Daring to Be Yourself*. New York: Avon, 1990. Take time for yourself! Ideas on creating beauty, harmony, and individuality in your life by developing your unique personal style.

Thomas, Shirley. *Parents Are Forever: A Step-by-Step Guide to Becoming Successful Co-Parents after Divorce*. Colorado: Springboard Publications, 1995. A commonsense, practical guide in dealing with the trauma following divorce.

Viscott, David. *I Love You, Let's Work It Out*. New York: Simon & Schuster, 1987. An aid to learning to live and love together.

*Visher, Emily B. and John S. Visher. *How to Win as a Stepfamily*. New York: Dembner Books, 1982. An optimistic, practical, success-oriented guide.

Wadia-Ells, Susan, ed. *The Adoption Reader: Birth Mothers, Adoptive Mothers and Adopted Daughters Tell Their Stories*. Seattle: Seal Press, 1995. More than thirty women explore the adoption experience through personal essays and stories that illustrate its complexity.

Walker, Glynnis. *Second Wife, Second Best?: Managing Your Marriage as a Second Wife*. New York: Doubleday, 1984. A must for every stepmother, as inevitably she is a second wife. Discusses different issues that need to be handled simultaneously with those of a stepmom.

Wallerstein, Judith S., and Sandra Blakeslee. *The Good Marriage: How and Why Love Lasts,* New York: Houghton Mifflin, 1995. An inside look at fifty American couples. Part 6 looks at remarriage; and chapter 25, "Coping with children."

Wegscheider-Cruse, Sharon. *Life after Divorce: Create a New Beginning.* Deerfield Beach, Florida: Health Communications, 1994. An affirmative book that shows how the trauma of divorce can give way to growth and the promise of a new life.

Zagone, Frank, and Mary Randolph. *How to Adopt Your Stepchild in California.* Berkeley, California: Nolo Press, 1994. Sound advice on this touchy decision. While written specifically for California's requirements, information on adoption process is useful in all adoptions.

INDEX